JURISPRUDENCE: THEORY AND CONTEXT

Blackburn
College

Library
01254 292120

AUSTRALIA

Law Book Company
Sydney

CANADA AND USA

Carswell
Toronto

NEW ZEALAND

Brookers
Auckland

SINGAPORE AND MALAYSIA

Sweet & Maxwell Asia
Singapore and Kuala Lumpur

JURISPRUDENCE:
THEORY AND CONTEXT

Third Edition

BRIAN BIX

London
Sweet & Maxwell
2003

Published by
Sweet & Maxwell Limited of
100 Avenue Road,
Swiss Cottage, London NW3 3PF
Typeset by Servis Filmsetting Ltd, Manchester, England
Printed and bound in Wales by Creative Print and Design Group

A CIP catalogue record for this book
is available from the British Library

ISBN 0421 830107

For Joseph Raz

Preface to the Third Edition

This book derives from past efforts to teach jurisprudence: in particular,
the struggle to explain some of the more difficult ideas in the area in a
way that could be understood by those new to the field, without at the
same time simplifying the ideas to the point of distortion. This text is
grounded in a combination of frustrations: the frustration I sometimes
felt as a teacher, when I was unable to get across the beauty and subtlety
of the great writers in legal theory[1]; and the frustration my students sometimes felt, when they were unable to understand me, due to my inability
to explain the material in terms they could comprehend.

I do not underestimate the difficulty of the task I have set myself, and
I am sure that this text does not always achieve all that it sets out to do.
At the least, I hope that I do not appear to he hiding my failures behind
legal or philosophical jargon. H.L.A. Hart once wrote the following in the
course of discussing an assertion made by the American judge and theorist Oliver Wendell Holmes, Jr.:

"To make this discovery with Holmes is to he with a guide whose words may leave
you unconvinced, sometimes even repelled, but never mystified. Like our own
[John] Austin . . . Holmes was sometimes clearly wrong; but again like Austin he
was always wrong clearly."[2]

I do not purport to be able to offer the powerful insights or the elegant
prose of Holmes and Hart, but I do strive to emulate them in the more
modest, but still difficult task, of expressing ideas in a sufficiently straightforward manner such that when I am wrong, I am "wrong clearly".

This book is part introductory text and part commentary. In the
preface to his classic text, *The Concept of Law*, Hart stated his hope that his
book would "discourage the belief that a book on legal theory is primarily a book from which one learns what other books contain."[3] My aims

---

[1] Unlike some writers, *e.g.* William Twining, "Academic Law and Legal Philosophy: The
Significance of Herbert Hart", (1979) 95 *Law Quarterly Review* 557, at pp. 565–580, I do
not distinguish between "Jurisprudence", "legal theory", and "legal philosophy", and I
will use those terms interchangeably.

[2] H.L.A. Hart, "Positivism and the Separation of Law and Morals", 71 *Harvard Law Review*
593 (1958).

[3] H.L.A. Hart, *The Concept of Law* (2nd ed., Clarendon Press, Oxford, 1994), p. vi.

are less ambitious: the present text *is* a book meant to inform readers what other books contain—the idea being that the primary texts are not always as accessible as they might be. However, this book is distinctly *not* meant as a substitute for reading those primary texts: the hope and the assumption is that readers will go to the primary texts first, and will return to them again after obtaining whatever guidance is to be offered in these pages. Additionally, there are a number of places in the text where I go beyond a mere reporting of the debate, and try to add my own views to the discussion. This is especially true of Chs 2 and 11, but in a number of other places throughout the book as well.

WHY JURISPRUDENCE?

Why study jurisprudence?

For many students, the question has a simple answer: for them, it is a required course which they must pass in order to graduate. For students in this situation, the questions about any jurisprudence book will be whether it can help them to learn enough of the material to get them where they need to be: passing the course (or doing sufficiently well in the course that their overall class standing is not adversely affected). However, even students who have such a minimal-survival attitude towards the subject might want to know what further advantage they might obtain from whatever knowledge of the subject they happen to pick up.

At the practical level, reading and participating in jurisprudential discussions develops the ability to analyze and to think critically and creatively about the law. Such skills are always useful in legal practice, particularly when facing novel questions within the law or when trying to formulate and advocate novel approaches to legal problems. So even those who need a "bottom line" justification for whatever they do should be able to find reason to read legal theory.

There is also a sense that philosophy, even where it does not have direct applications to grades or to practice, has many indirect benefits. Philosophy trains one to think sharply and logically; one learns how to find the weaknesses in other people's arguments, and in one's own; and one learns how to evaluate and defend, as well as attack, claims and positions. Philosophy could thus be seen as a kind of mental exercise program, on a par with chess or bridge (or theology). Giving the centrality of analytical skills to what both lawyers and law students do, one should not quickly dismiss any activity that can help one improve those skills.

At a professional level, jurisprudence is the way lawyers and judges reflect on what they do and what their role is within society. This truth is reflected by the way jurisprudence is taught as part of a *university* education in the law, where law is considered not merely as a trade to be learned (like carpentry or fixing automobiles) hut as an intellectual pursuit. For those who believe that only the reflective life is worth living, and who also spend most of their waking hours working within (or around) the legal system, there are strong reasons to want to think deeply about the nature and function of law, the legal system, and the legal profession.

Finally, for some (whether the blessed or the cursed one cannot say), jurisprudence is interesting and enjoyable on its own, whatever its other uses and benefits. There will always be some for whom learning is interesting and valuable in itself, even if it does not lead to greater wealth, greater self-awareness, or greater social progress.

THE SELECTION OF TOPICS

One can find entire books on many of the topics discussed in the present volume in short chapters (or parts of chapters). I have done my best to offer overviews that do not sacrifice the difficulty of the subjects, but I fear that some mis-reading is inevitable in any summary. In part to compensate for the necessarily abbreviated nature of what is offered, a list of "Suggested Further Readings" is offered at the end of each chapter (and there are footnote citations to the primary texts in the course of the chapters) for those who wish to locate longer and fuller discussions of certain topics.

A related problem is that in the limited space available, I could not include all the topics that are associated with jurisprudence (a course whose content varies greatly from university to university). The variety of topics included in one source or another under the category of jurisprudence is vast, so inevitably there always seems to be more missing from than present in any text. Through my silence (or brevity), I do not mean to imply that the topics not covered are not interesting, not important, or not properly part of jurisprudence.

It is inevitable that those using this book will find some chapters more useful for their purposes than others, even (or especially) if they are students using this book to accompany a general jurisprudence course. The topics in the first part of the book are usually not covered in university courses, though I believe that thinking through some of the questions raised there might help one gain a deeper or more coherent view of jurisprudence as a whole.

One caveat I must offer is that references to legal practice offered in this book will be primarily to the practices in the American and English[4] legal systems, as these are the systems with which I am most familiar. It is

---

[4] I am following the usual convention of using the term "English legal system" to refer to the legal system that extends over both England and Wales.

likely (though far from certain) that any comments based on those two legal systems would be roughly generalizable to cover all common law systems. The extent to which my lack of familiarity with civil law systems biases my views about legal theory and about the nature of law I must leave to others to judge.

In the preparation of the third edition of this book, many of the chapters have been expanded, and discussions of the most recent scholarship has been added throughout (along with the expected correction of small typographical errors from the prior edition).

Work on this book often overlapped work I was doing for other smaller projects: sometimes work done for the book was borrowed for other projects, and sometimes I found that work done for other projects could he usefully incorporated in the hook. An earlier version of parts of Chapter 2 appeared in "Conceptual Questions and Jurisprudence", 1 *Legal Theory* 415 (1995); earlier versions of parts of Chapters 5, 6, and 7 appeared in "Natural Law Theory", in *A Companion to the Philosophy of Law and Legal Theory* (D. Patterson, ed., Blackwell, Oxford, 1996), pp. 223–240; an earlier version of brief sections of Chapters 1 and 7 appeared in "Questions in Legal Interpretation", in *Law and Interpretation* (A. Marmor, ed., Clarendon Press, Oxford, 1995), pp. 137–154; and an earlier version of parts of Chapters 1, 2, and 14 appeared in "Questions in Legal Interpretation", 18 *Tel Aviv Law Review* 463 (1994) (translated into Hebrew). I am grateful to the publishers of these texts for allowing me permission to use material from those articles.

I would like to thank the following for their helpful comments and suggestions: Mark Addis, Larry Alexander, Jack Balkin, Lisa Bernstein, Scott Brewer, Keith Burgess-Jackson, Kenneth Campbell, Tom Campbell, Richard Delgado, Anthony M. Dillof, Neil Duxbury, Neal Feigenson, John Finnis, Stephen Gilles, Martin P. Golding, Aristides N. Hatzis, Alex M. Johnson, Jr., Sanford N. Katz, Matthew H. Kramer, Kenneth J. Kress, Brian Leiter, Andrei Marmor, Jerry Mashaw, Linda R. Meyer, Martha Minow, Thomas Morawetz, Martha C. Nussbaum, Frances Olsen, Dennis Patterson, Stanley L. Paulson, Margaret Jane Radin, Frederick Schauer, Scott Shapiro, A.J.B. Sirks, M.B.E. Smith, Larry Solum, Scott Sturgeon, Brian Tamanaha, Adam Tomkins, Lloyd L. Weinreb, Tony Weir, James Boyd White, Kenneth Winston, and Mauro Zamboni. I am also grateful for the research assistance of Galen Lemei and Erin Steitz.

Contents

PART A

Legal Theory: Problems and Possibilities

It is surprising how often one can go through entire jurisprudence books or entire jurisprudence courses without the most basic questions ever being raised, let alone resolved. The purpose of the opening chapters is to at least touch on some of these basic questions:

(1) In what sense is a general theory of law possible?

(2) What is the point of conceptual claims, and how can one evaluate them?

(3) In which senses can one speak of the relative merits of different legal theorists or of different approaches to law?

Some of these questions, and the answers suggested for them, will be applicable primarily to the second part of this book, which covers a number of individual theories about the law. Other questions will have resonance that extends throughout all the book's topics.

Chapter One

Overview, Purpose and Methodology

QUESTIONS AND ANSWERS IN JURISPRUDENCE

Part of the purpose in writing this book was to counter a tendency to treat jurisprudence as just another exercise in rote memorization. it is often tempting for jurisprudence students, especially those whose background is primarily in law rather than philosophy, to treat the major writers in the area as just a variation on black-letter, doctrinal law: that is, as points, positions and arguments to he memorized, in order that they can later be repeated on the final examination.

A second problem in the way in which legal theory is presented and studied is the tendency to see different legal theorists as offering competing answers to simple questions. Thus, H.L.A. Hart and Lon Fuller are thought to be debating certain easily stateable propositions in their 1958 exchange in the *Harvard Law Review*.[1] The only thing allegedly left for the student is to figure out which theorist was right and which one was wrong.

Legal theory would be more clearly (and more deeply) understood if its issues and the writings of its theorists were approached through a focus on questions rather than answers. Once one sees that different theorists are answering different questions and responding to different concerns, one can see how these theorists are often describing disparate aspects of the same phenomenon rather than as disagreeing about certain simple claims about law. This text will focus on the questions being answered (the problems to which the theories try to respond), and will frequently point out the extent to which apparently contradictory legal theories can be shown to be compatible.

When reading a particular claim by a legal theorist, it is important to ask a series of questions: Why is this theorist making this claim? Who might disagree, and why? While many theorists can be criticized for not

---

[1] H.L.A. Hart, "Positivism and the Separation of Law and Morals" 71 *Harvard Law Review* 593 (1958); Lon L. Fuller, "Positivism and Fidelity to Law: A Reply to Professor Hart", 71 *Harvard Law Review* 630 (1958).

making the *significance* of their claims clear, "charity" in interpretation is still advisable: one should assume that there is something of importance, or at least something controversial, in the theories. In the end, after a long struggle to find what is worthy, significant, or controversial about a theory, one might conclude that it is in fact trivial, poorly done, and a waste of the reader's time. However, that should never be one's starting assumption.

DESCRIPTIVE THEORY

The approach discussed above, emphasizing the extent to which different (and apparently competing) theorists might be seen as answering different questions, both derives from and helps to explain the under-discussed matter of how we can have descriptive theories of an ongoing social phenomenon such as law. Legal systems, and people's experiences of them, are extremely complex. Inevitably, a theory about law can capture only a portion of the relevant facts (this claim is not new to legal theory; the claim and its implications are discussed insightfully and in detail by H.L.A. Hart and John Finnis,[2] among others). Once one accepts the importance of selection in constructing social theories, the focus then turns to the basis on which selection occurs.

It is not surprising that theorists might have had varying criteria for selection, which correspond to the different issues which were troubling them or to the differing topics that were their particular interests. It may be open to someone to claim that there is only one proper viewpoint for theory, or that one set of issues or values is clearly more significant than all alternatives, but I have not found such arguments convincing, so this text will go forward on another basis.

The possibility that claims in legal theory may sometimes be relative to a particular purpose or a particular viewpoint does not empty legal theory of all significance or interest. I think the opposite may be true. However, it does mean that arguments within a theory or about a theory must be more subtly and more carefully made.[3] It is important to emphasize, though, that not all arguments in legal theory can be so cleanly and peacefully resolved.

In this text I will attempt to offer perspectives which may allow students to understand the significance of various ideas in jurisprudence. I hope

---

[2] Hart, *The Concept of Law*, pp. 82–91; John Finnis, *Natural Law and Natural Rights* (Clarendon Press, Oxford, 1980), pp. 1–11.

[3] Though the approach I advocate has some similarities with the more sophisticated versions of relativism, it is also compatible with a more traditional approach to truth. We need not say that there are many truths, only that the truth about a complex social or moral phenomenon is unlikely to be captured completely by any single theory alone.

to offer this assistance without harming the power or the complexity of the theories I am discussing, but in the end there can never be any adequate substitute for reading the theorists in their own words.

Another theme that will arise regularly throughout these discussions is the difficulty inherent in the project of legal theory. Partly this is the difficulty of any type of social theory a topic already touched upon. There are also problems in legal theory that come from the fact that many theorists appear to make "conceptual" claims, claims that purport to go to the nature of a concept *(e.g.* "law" or "rights") rather than to the working of a social process or institution. It is then important to know how to judge the success of such a project, and, even more basic, to deter- mine why such projects are worth attempting. Many of these general questions will he explored in the next chapter, but the same themes will be reflected in the later discussions of specific theorists and issues.

For those who have done some reading in jurisprudence, there is the strange phenomenon of some ideas that seem simultaneously familiar yet mysterious: one may know of Lon Fuller's idea of the internal morality of law, Kelsen's concept of the Basic Norm, the law and economics notion of wealth maximization, and the like, but not know why anyone would put forward arguments that unusual or that counter-intuitive. In this book, I hope to identify sufficiently the context—the problems being considered, as well as the philosophical tradition in which the theorist was writing—in which such ideas arise, that a reader might gain a better understanding of why such arguments might be needed (and why they might be persuasive).

TRANSFORMING THE QUESTION

In the first chapter of *The Concept of Law,* H.L.A. Hart considered the standard question of legal theory: "What is Law?"[4] Past theorists had given various answers to this question, from the mundane but unsatisfactory to the bizarre (among the responses are "what officials do about disputes", and "the prophecies of what the courts will do"[5]). What may be most remarkable about Hart's discussion is that he never directly answered the

---

[4] Hart, *The Concept of Law*, pp. 1–6.
[5] *ibid.* at p. 1. The first quotation is from Karl Llewellyn. See Karl N. Llewellyn, *The Bramble Bush: On Our Law and Its Study* (Oceana, New York, 1930), p. 3: "This doing of something about disputes, this doing of it reasonably is the business of law. And the people who have the doing in charge, whether they be judges or sheriffs or clerks or jailers or lawyers, are officials of the law. *What these* officials do about *disputes is, to my mind, the law itself.*" (footnote omitted). The second quotation is from Oliver Wendell Holmes, "The Path of the Law", 10 *Harvard Law Review* 457 at 461 (1897): "The prophecies of what the courts will do in fact, and nothing more pretentious, are what I mean by the law". The Holmes quotation, and the attitude towards law both quotations represent, will be discussed in greater detail in Ch. 17 ("American Legal Realism").

question he was considering. Instead, Hart's discussion achieved something far more subtle. The question is not so much answered (or avoided or circumvented) as transformed. Hart's argument is that when one question is asked, we are actually seeking the solution to an entirely different question or set of questions, and it is because we have been asking the wrong question(s) that the answers given have been so unsatisfactory.

Hart proposed that the question "What is Law?" is usually best seen as an attempt to consider one of three issues: "How does law differ from and how is it related to orders backed by threats? How does legal obligation differ from, and how is it related to moral obligation? What are rules and to what extent is law an affair of rules?"[6] Whether one agrees with Hart's analysis or not, one can see how he has succeeded in diverting attention from definitional obsessions to more mundane and manageable (though still far from simple) questions. Hart's response to the question, "What is Law?" was basically to counter, "why do you ask?" This is an attempt to simplify, or dissolve, a seemingly difficult or metaphysical question by trying to convert it or reduce it to questions relating to the proper descriptions of our practices. As Ludwig Wittgenstein described philosophy in general,[7] legal philosophy under a Hartian approach sees its primary purpose as a kind of therapy: a way of overcoming the temptation to ask metaphysical questions ("what is Law?" or "do norms exist"), and a method of transforming such questions into (re-)descriptions of the way we actually act.[8]

The way Ronald Dworkin dissolved the "debate" about whether the Nazi regime had law or not could be seen as a variation of this type of analysis. He wrote that when we look at matters closely, we may see that there is no real disagreement between those who say that the Nazis did have "law" and those who say that they did not. On one hand, we understand what people mean when they say that the Nazis *did* have law: that the Nazi institutions resemble our own and share the same history and original purposes. On the other hand, we also understand what people are trying to say when they insist that the Nazi regime did not have law: that what went on was so evil and procedurally flawed that the rules of that regime did not create moral obligations to obey them, in the way such rules do in just regimes.[9] The two claims are both reasonable, and they are also compatible. Seen in this way, the "debate" disappears, and we can turn our attention to other, perhaps more substantial, disputes.

One should not expect all debates to dissolve, clarify, or become less

---

[6] Hart, *The Concept of Law*, p. 13.
[7] See, *e.g.* Ludwig Wittgenstein, *Philosophical Investigations* (3rd ed. Macmillan, New York, 1968), paras 133, 255.
[8] *ibid.* at §109; Brian Bix, "Questions in Legal Interpretation" in *Law and Interpretation* (A. Marmor ed., Clarendon Press, Oxford, 1995), at pp. 137–141.
[9] Ronald Dworkin, "Legal Theory and the Problem of Sense", in *Issues in Contemporary Legal Philosophy* (R. Gavison ed., Clarendon Press, Oxford, 1987), at pp. 15–17.

heated by being "transformed"—re-characterized or seen from a new perspective. Many debates in jurisprudence, as elsewhere, reflect basic moral or political controversies, and no amount of transformation will relieve us of the obligations to make choices in these areas.[10] The trick is to separate true problems and true questions from muddles into which we have been enticed by our own somewhat confused and confusing ways of thinking and speaking. Unfortunately, there is no easy or foolproof method of effecting this separation; one can only offer analyses and await affirmation or rebuttal by one's peers.

Finally, there is another way in which one can "transform the question" in jurisprudence. One can move the focus back from the claims the theorists are making, and consider those theories in the contexts of the type of questions that the theorist was trying to answer and the type of problems that he or she was trying to solve. As Raymond Aron noted in another context, the interest of a theory depends largely on whether the theorist has asked, and attempted to answer, interesting questions.[11] The basis for this type of transformation, and how it might affect our thinking about jurisprudential claims, is discussed in greater detail in the next chapter.

TO WHAT EXTENT IS IT *LEGAL* THEORY?

To what extent is there or should there be *legal* theory? The question is not quite as strange as it sounds. In many of the discussions that go on in the name of jurisprudence, what is being considered is nothing more than the application to law of some more general theory from another area *(e.g.* moral theory, political theory, social theory). For example, traditional natural law theory (the topic of Ch. 5) is the application of a general ethical theory to law; legal positivism (Chs 3 and 4) is arguably the application of general principles of social theory to law; feminist legal theory critical race theory and critical legal studies (Ch. 19) are the application of particular critical social theories to law; and questions about justice, punishment, and the moral obligation to obey the law (Chs 8, 9 and 16) are the application of general moral theories to legal issues.[12]

Occasionally, there *are* arguments about what is or should be *distinctive*

---

[10] Elsewhere I have criticized theories that appear to be trying to elide difficult political and moral decisions by offering complicated theories of meaning or ontology. See Brian Bix, *Law, Language, and Legal Determinacy* (Clarendon Press, Oxford, 1993), pp. 45–49, 153–154, 176–177.

[11] Raymond Aron, *Main Currents in Sociological Thought* (R. Howard and H. Weaver, trans., Anchor Books, New York, 1970), Vol. 2, p. 232.

[12] For a useful analysis placing theories of adjudication squarely within general questions of social theory, see William Lucy, *Understanding and Explaining Adjudication* (Oxford University Press, Oxford, 1999), pp. 17–41.

about law. Lon Fuller's discussion of the "internal morality of law" (Ch. 6) arguably fits that category. The fact that issues within legal theory are often mere instantiations of more general problems and debates can help to keep jurisprudential arguments in perspective. Also, this hints at a way of testing the answers offered by participants in the jurisprudential debates: look at comparable responses in related areas of investigation. For example, in considering hermeneutic theories of law, we might consider the success or failure of hermeneutic theories in anthropology and sociology; and in evaluating the usefulness of applying economic analysis to legal questions, one might want to look at its track record in other areas of non-market behaviour.

Suggested Further Readings

Brian Bix, "Questions in Legal Interpretation", in *Law and Interpretation* (A. Marmor ed., Clarendon Press, Oxford, 1995), pp. 137–154.
H.L.A. Hart, *The Concept of Law* (Clarendon Press, Oxford, 1961), pp. 1–17.
—, "Definition and Theory in Jurisprudence", 70 *Law Quarterly Review* 37–60 (1954), reprinted in *Essays in Jurisprudence and Philosophy* (Clarendon Press, Oxford, 1983), pp. 21–48.
Thomas Morawetz, *The Philosophy of Law: An Introduction* (Macmillan, New York, 1980), pp. 1–52.

Chapter Two

Conceptual Questions and Jurisprudence

Conceptual analysis is an integral part of jurisprudence,[1] but the nature and purpose of such inquiries are often not clearly stated. This chapter attempts to elaborate some of the differing reasons underlying attempts at conceptual analysis, and what consequences may follow from choosing one objective rather than another. Once one sees that divergent purposes are often present in competing analyses of the same concept, one can understand why some "debates" in the jurisprudential literature are best understood as theorists talking past one another. While the chapter will be discussing problems that are inherent to many types of conceptual analysis, the primary focus will be on conceptual analysis within jurisprudence.[2] Along similar lines, since a significant portion of the conceptual claims made within jurisprudence come from those offering general theories of law, the analysis will begin by considering some of the hidden problems within such projects. Later sections of this chapter will consider how conceptual theories differ from other types of theories; indicate some connections between the problem of conceptual theories and other, better-known problems in philosophy; outline alternative ways of approaching the problem of conceptual theory; and discuss briefly the argument that conceptual analysis in jurisprudence should be replaced by naturalist analysis.[3]

---

[1] For example, arguably the most important and influential book in the area in the last half of the 20th century is Hart, *The Concept of Law*, which presents itself as a work of conceptual analysis. The work arguably most important to political theory during this same period, John Rawls, *A Theory of Justice* (Harvard University Press, Cambridge, Mass., 1972), might also be characterized as being devoted largely to conceptual theory. However, as Rawls was dealing with a political-moral concept, justice, his analysis was always going to have more of a prescriptive cast to it.

[2] For a provocative, parallel analysis of the problem of conceptual analysis in jurisprudence, approached from the direction of the social sciences, see Brian Tamanaha, *Realistic Socio-Legal Theory: Pragmatism and a Social Theory of Law* (Clarendon Press, Oxford, 1997), pp. 91–128.

[3] For an interesting critique of an earlier version of this chapter, which agrees with the material in part but also offers some criticisms and some suggested refinements, see Andrew Halpin, "Concepts, Terms, and Fields of Enquiry", 4 *Legal Theory* 187 (1998).

THE POSSIBILITY OF GENERAL JURISPRUDENCE

Most theoretical discussions about the nature of law begin with a confidence which belies the problems lurking at the foundations of any such inquiry: on what basis can we speak of a general theory of "law" at all? One could, after all, have a theory which tried to analyse and explain only one's own legal system.[4] However, most legal theorists are making a broader claim: one about law "in general".

To begin at the beginning, "law" is an English term which refers to a particular collection of institutions and practices.[5] Those institutions and practices will vary from country to country, and in each country over time. It is even more complicated when one goes to other countries where English is not the primary language: those countries may have institutions which are similar to those we call "law", and there may be a term in the native language which seems to correspond roughly to our term "law" (though even in the example of Germany, the word *"Recht"* has connotations quite different from those of its English equivalent, "law"[6]).

The problems obviously increase when we consider countries or societies which do not have institutions and procedures even roughly similar to our own[7]; this makes it all the more difficult to find a term in that culture's language which we could, with confidence, translate as "law". These may be societies where there appear to be no legal rules legislated and imposed by the state, apart from what we would call the conventional morality of the society, or where social pressure and mediation fulfill the functions that adjudication takes in our society. On what basis do we keep such social systems in—or out of—our definition of "law"?

The question is one of inclusion and exclusion. Which societies or systems does a theory about "law" purport to cover? If someone objects that a theory presented is not true for international law, or for French Law, or for the rules used by an aboriginal tribe in Australia, when can the theorist legitimately respond that the objection is irrelevant, since the counter-examples are "not really law"? This, in turn, leads to the inquiry

---

[4] To a limited extent, this is in fact what the theorist Ronald Dworkin does. However, as will be explained in Ch. 7, his theories of particular legal systems are examples of a general (interpretive) approach to all social practices. There is thus at least that one general claim: that this interpretive approach is appropriate for understanding *all legal systems.*

[5] Even to make the few simple comments I make in this and the following paragraphs, I have limited the word "law" to its application to state law and institutional law. I have put to one side the use of the term to apply to international law, religious law, scientific law, the regulations of games and societies, and other uses of the term.

[6] See Stanley L. Paulson, "Lon L. Fuller, Gustav Radbruch, and the 'Positivist' Theses", 13 *Law and Philosophy* 313 (1994), at 329–330.

[7] See generally Laura Nader, "The Anthropological Study of Law", 67 *American Anthropologist* 3 (1965).

as to how the theorist comes by his or her conclusions regarding which systems are and are not legal.

The theorist discussing "the nature of law" will probably have some initial notion of which institutions and processes fit into the category that he or she is trying to examine. However, one can wonder whether there are any reasons for dividing up the social world in this manner, placing the "law"/"non-law" border one place rather than another.[8] Looking at the same question in another way, one might wonder whether it makes sense to speak of "law" as a self-defined or unitary group at all. Perhaps there are only a large number of vaguely similar social institutions and practices, and there is no more sense to theorizing about them as a group as there would be for creating a theory about the similarities of all countries whose name began with the letter "C". One could also make the point in a slightly different way: that perhaps law is in some sense a "class", but not one about which anything of (philosophical) interest can be said.[9]

As noted above, most legal theorists do not explore these foundational questions at all; those who have considered the question have come to different responses. For example, Michael Moore, who devoted an entire article to the problem,[10] denied that different legal systems share the same nature in terms of sharing the same structure, institutions or processes. However, he thought that there was an existing category of social systems for study: all the systems *which served the same function* within their communities or countries (for example, we might define "law" in terms of dispute resolution or in terms of setting, interpreting and applying norms of behaviour).

Ronald Dworkin rejected the value of (though not the possibility of) a general theory of law, on the basis that any such theory (in his terms, any such "interpretation") that was valid for all the systems we would like it to cover would be at such a high level of generality that it would not tell us anything interesting.[11] His alternative was to offer a theory (interpretation) that applies only to a single legal system.

A third alternative,[12] one that I favour, combines elements of the above approaches. Under this alternative, legal theory is both a discussion of law in general and focused on a particular legal system. We look at a group of social systems, but as a means of understanding better our own legal

---

[8] Establishing a dividing line between "law" and "not law" has its purposes even within a legal theory, as will he discussed in the section, "Boundary Lines in Law", later in this chapter.

[9] See Frederick Schauer, "Critical Notice", 24 *Canadian Journal of Philosophy* 495 (1994) at 508.

[10] Michael S. Moore, "Law as a Functional Kind", *Natural Law Theory: Contemporary Essays* (R. George ed. Oxford University Press, Oxford, 1992), pp. 188–242.

[11] See Dworkin, "Legal Theory and the Problem of Sense", p. 16.

[12] It is based on comments made by Joseph Raz in informal conversations.

system. We therefore have an obvious, non-arbitrary basis for justifying discussing some countries' and communities' social systems whilst ignoring those of others: we choose the social systems which appear to us to be like our own legal system in significant ways. This approach does not require any prior claims about "law" or "legal systems" constituting a unitary, self-defined group. By losing the ambition to say something "necessarily true" about all legal systems, existing, historical or imaginary, one also loses the need to enter the murky world of metaphysical and social abstractions.

The above set of questions leads to a related line of inquiry: what is the status of the claims made within theories of law? Are these claims of sociology, anthropology or psychology discussing how people naturally or inevitably act in large groups? Are they metaphysical claims, about the "essence" or "nature" of Law?[13] Or are they (merely) claims about the way we use language (for example, the way we use the terms "law" or "legal")?

The short answer to the above is that different theories seem to he responding to different types of inquiries and are making different kinds of claims. As will be discussed in the remainder of this chapter, it is common and perhaps inevitable that conceptual theories, of which most general theories of law are examples, will "talk past one another".

HOW CONCEPTUAL THEORIES DIFFER

Conceptual claims, conceptual theories and conceptual questions are assertions or inquiries about labels (labels which often also serve as categories): for example, "law", "art" and "democracy". The point of conceptual questions is often obscure to students, and there are times when even the theorists involved in the exercise seem to lack a clear notion of their objectives.[14] Students sometimes react to long debates about "what is law?" or about "the nature of rights", by asking "who cares?" and "why does this matter?", while professionals often assume that such questions are purely matters of definition and are therefore uninteresting. While one by no means wants to encourage a dismissive or cynical approach to legal theory, the sceptical questions—"what is the point?", etc.—should always be kept in mind, and it is only by keeping such questions in mind that the issues (and the theorists) can be understood clearly and in depth.

Conceptual questions should be seen in contrast to other questions

---

[13] See, e.g. Ernest J. Weinrib, *The Idea of Private Law* (Harvard University Press, Cambridge, Mass., 1995), discussing the essence or nature of (private) law.

[14] This is by no means universal. Among the more articulate discussions of purpose are those in Hart, *The Concept of Law*, Ch. 1; Jules L. Coleman, "Negative and Positive Positivism", 11 *Journal of Legal Studies* 139 (1982), reprinted in Coleman, *Market, Morals and the Law* (Cambridge University Press, Cambridge, 1988), pp. 3–27; and Joseph Raz, *Ethics in the Public Domain* (Clarendon Press, Oxford, 1994), pp. 179–193.

theorists ask. Theories in the natural and social sciences usually attempt
to describe the world in such a way that we can better understand why past
events occurred or predict how future events will unfold.[15] How is light distorted by travel through water? How do animals react to changes in
amounts of daylight? What effect did Protestant thought have on the rise
of Capitalism?,[16] and so on. These are questions of cause and effect which
are in principle testable, through controlled experiments, careful observation, or the analysis of past events. These theories are useful, and, perhaps
equally important, they are falsifiable (if "falsifiable" is too strong for some
tastes, one might be able to use "rebuttable" as a substitute). If the data
we collect in the future does not fit the predictions made according to the
theory we should at least begin to suspect that the theory might be wrong.

Purely conceptual theories can be contrasted with two different kinds
of theories: (non-conceptual) theories in the natural sciences, and non-
conceptual theories in the social sciences. Theories in the natural sciences:

"consider[ ] the general characteristics of phenomena and establish[ ] regular or
necessary relations between them. This elaboration tends toward the construction
of a system of laws or relations that are increasingly general and, insofar as possible, of a mathematical nature."[17]

Non-conceptual theories in the social sciences also tend toward conclusions
about causation and causal regularities, but (in contrast to non-conceptual
theories in the natural sciences) the selection of relevant data tends to turn
at least in part on complicated, and contested, value judgments.[18]

Matters are necessarily different with questions and theories whose only
purpose appears to be to offer definitions or to delimit categories: for
example, "what is law?" and "what is art?" consider, by way of example,
all the different reasons someone might give for a claim that some artifact
fails to be "art": it does not have sufficient quality, it was not created with
the requisite intention, it is too functional or practical, or it is tied closely
into daily life or religious belief.[19] If I believe that certain works by Man

---

[15] One should also distinguish philosophical explanations that try to respond to problems
of the form "how is X possible, given Y and Z?" For example, "How is it possible that
we know anything, given the facts the skeptic enumerates? [and] How is it possible that
motion occurs, given Zeno's arguments?" Robert Nozick, *Philosophical Explanations*
(Harvard University Press, Cambridge, Mass., 1981), p. 8.
[16] See Max Weber, *The Protestant Ethic and the Spirit of Capitalism* (T. Parsons, trans., Scribner,
New York, 1976).
[17] Aron, *Main Currents in Sociological Thought*, Vol. 2, pp. 230–231.
[18] *ibid.* at pp. 231–238.
[19] As to the latter, see *e.g.* Patricia Nelson Limerick, "More than just Beads and Feathers",
New York Times Book Review, January 8, 1995 (in the context of reviewing two books about
Native American artifacts, discussing the argument that Native American culture, unlike
"Western" culture, does not "quarantine" aesthetic experience).

Ray are "not really Art" while you disagree, or if I think that the old Apartheid legal system in South Africa deserved to be called "law" and you do not, what is the nature of our disagreement?[20] What are we disagreeing about, and is it important? And how can we determine who is right?

A conceptual claim, as opposed to a claim that is meant to be predictive or explanatory, is not falsifiable (rebuttable).[21] However, as will be explained, I do not mean to imply that purely conceptual theories are immune to criticism. As will be argued, one can criticize conceptual theories for having greater or lesser success relative to their stated (or implied) purposes, and one can also criticize the theory's purpose (*e.g.* on the basis that it is not ambitious enough). It is important to clarify here: when I say that conceptual claims are not falsifiable, I am referring to theories which *divide up* the world into categories: this is "law" and this is not; or this is "art" and this is not. Of course, once a division is accepted, and a claim is made *about* a category (*e.g.* "all art is morally uplifting" or "all legal rules give moral reasons for action"), *that* claim will usually be falsifiable.[22]

Conceptual theories define terms by necessary and sufficient conditions. Such definitions cannot be directly verified or rebutted by empirical observation, though such definitions and theories are not entirely cut off from the empirical world. Consider the differences between the conceptual claim "swans are white" and the empirical claim "all swans are white". The latter assumes that we have already defined the category "swan" to our satisfaction, and it is a matter of discovering whether all members of that category are coloured white. A conceptual claim about swans, by contrast, could survive a discovery of a swan-like creature that was not white. That creature would simply, by definition, not be a swan. As Jay Rosenberg states (when discussing the contrast between philosophy and other forms of inquiry), the results of conceptual theory are not, immediately or primarily, about discovering new facts, "but rather a new clarity about what are and what aren't the old facts."[23]

The contrast is with scientific (and social scientific) theories that posit an empirical, causal connection between events. The contrast is also with historical theories that speak in terms of causation (*e.g.* "the development

---

[20] Colin McGinn once argued that it did not make sense to speak of people disagreeing about concepts; they could only be characterized as talking about different concepts. Colin McGinn, *Wittgenstein on Meaning* (Basil Blackwell, Oxford, 1984), pp. 146–147.

[21] I recognize that, at least in the opinion of some historians and theorists who take a hermeneutic approach to social theory, the reference to falsifiability may seem blunt or perhaps naïve. However, the term does work as a useful shorthand in summarizing the differing criteria of success for conceptual theories as contrasted with other types of theories in the social sciences.

[22] See Alan R. White, "Conceptual Analysis", *The Owl of Minerva* (C.J. Bontmepo and S.J. Odell eds, McGraw-Hill, New York, 1975), pp. 108–109, 113.

[23] Jay Rosenberg, *The Practice of Philosophy* (2nd ed., Prentice-Hall, Englewood Cliffs, N.J., 1984), p. 8.

of religious toleration leads to democracy"). However, within scientific and historical theories, there may be elements of the theory which assume or tacitly make a conceptual claim. (For example, one might ask: when someone says "the development of religious toleration leads to democracy", how are "religious toleration" and "democracy" being defined?)

The merit of a conceptual claim can only be evaluated once it is clear what the purpose of the claim is. The thesis defended in this chapter is that (descriptively or historically speaking) different conceptual claims have different purposes. Further, theorists often do not clearly state what purpose underlies their particular conceptual claims, which is what makes it difficult to evaluate the merit of such claims, or to compare two different claims.

It may he helpful to begin by placing the problem of conceptual theories in context. Most conceptual theories in law are odd not only for not being predictive or falsifiable, but also for being descriptive. There is something basically paradoxical about putting forward a descriptive theory about a social institution or a social phenomenon. Social practices change, and therefore it is often inappropriate (or at least premature) to use the regularities of the past to justify grand theoretical claims about a practice.[24]

For example, a theorist might, after careful observation of past practices within a given society or even within a number of societies, conclude that all legislation begins with a statement of purpose. The declaration is then made, that "all legislation contains a statement of purpose" or "a statement of purpose is one of the essential or defining elements of legislation". However, when the next enactment does not carry a statement of purpose, how can one argue against a person who states that the enactment nonetheless still warrants the label "legislation"? Is this the same or different from generalities in the natural sciences (as the discovery of a creature that seemed clearly to be a swan but was black rebutted the contention "all swans are white")?

This inquiry appears to be much like the old philosophical inquiry regarding which properties of some object or class are accidental and which are essential; similar questions are also raised in the modern philosophical topic of natural kinds theory.[25] Does the fact that legislation always seems to have a statement of purpose make that statement of purpose part of what makes a declaration "legislation", an aspect of how we can tell "legislation" from other types of documents? The problem is that talk about "essences" and the "nature" of items does not fit as

---

[24] I discuss in greater detail the problem of description in social sciences generally and in law in particular in Brian Bix, "On Description and Legal Reasoning", in *Rules and Reasoning* (L.R. Meyer ed., Hart Publishing, Oxford, 1999), pp. 7–28.

[25] See, *e.g.* Hilary Putnam, "The Meaning of 'Meaning'", in *Mind, Language and Reality* (Cambridge University Press, New York, 1975), pp. 215–271.

comfortably with human artifacts and social institutions as it does (say) with biological species or chemical elements.[26] The difference is in the way that categories that refer to human artifacts and social institutions do not figure in what is sometimes called "lawful explanations"; that is, we neither expect nor find evidence of necessary (universal, causal) relationships among those categories or between those categories and other phenomena. With human artifacts and social institutions, the categories themselves can be difficult to delimit; the basic fluidity and contestedness of conceptual definitions can be seen to derive from the fact that the boundaries of concepts like "art", "law" or "rights" are far from self-evident. This fluidity and contestedness of boundaries is central to understanding the problems and possibilities of conceptual analysis, and the theme will come up again later in this chapter.

If the problem regarding conceptual theories appears to have some similarities with the notion of accidental versus essential properties, it also seems related to the more modern rubric of "rule following": how can we tell the difference between a variation within a practice and a change to a different practice?[27] For example, can one change one of the rules of chess and still be playing "chess", or is it a different game that is only related to chess? Similarly, is it still "legislation" without a statement of purpose, and is it still "law" if it does not serve the common good? As practices change, and the label some conceptual/descriptive theory placed on the practice no longer fits the practice, are we to say that the original label was "wrong" (whatever that might mean here), or that the old practice is gone and a new practice has begun?

Legal theorists have come, rather late in the day perhaps, to explore seriously the methodology they use and the nature of the claims they offer. Joseph Raz, especially in his most recent work,[28] has entered this "meta-discussion," and offered some of the most insightful and provocative ideas in the growing literature. Two key—and related—questions are whether conceptual analysis is appropriate and whether one can speak of "necessary" truths in jurisprudence. Raz's answer to both questions is "yes". However, it is key to understanding this claim that Raz's idea of "necessity" is distinctly different from what one finds elsewhere in philosophy: sharply different from logical necessity, and almost as distant from the type of necessity discussed in the context of Platonic philosophy and "natural kinds" theories. Raz does not believe that the concept of law is

---

[26] See, e.g. John Dupré, "Natural Kinds and Biological Taxa", 90 *Philosophical Review* 66 (1981); Bix, *Law, Language and Legal Determinacy*, pp.162–171.

[27] See, e.g. Wittgenstein, *Philosophical Investigations*, §§ 143–242.

[28] Joseph Raz, "On the Nature of Law" (Kobe Lectures of 1994), 82 *Archiv für Rechts und Sozialphilosophie* 1 (1996); Joseph Raz, "Legal Theory", in *Blackwell Guide to Philosophy of Law and Legal Theory* (forthcoming, M. P. Golding and W. A. Edmundson eds, Blackwell, Oxford, 2004).

some eternal Platonist Idea, which would be the same for all people or for all times. For Raz, the concept of law we investigate is "our concept", "the product of a specific culture"—our own. And since what counts as "law" (under our concept) is independent of that concept, there were likely earlier cultures or alien cultures that did not or do not "share" or "have" our concept, yet still had law. While the concept of law has changed over time—not some unchanging Idea we are "discovering"—Raz treats the/our concept of law as something unique, a matter about which we can be right or wrong in our descriptions, and which we cannot simply re-invent for our own purposes (though he does note that since concepts of law are in flux, our theories of law, even mistaken theories, could influence the concept of law future generations have). Similarly, Raz rejects the notion that we (as theorists) can choose a concept of law based, say, on its fruitfulness in further research,[29] or even according to its simplicity or elegance; rather, it is a concept already present, already part of our self-understanding. Raz refers repeatedly to "*the* concept of law" which "exists independently" of the legal philosophy which attempts to explain it,[30] and "*the* nature of law" which general theories of law must strive to elucidate.[31]

As noted at the beginning of the chapter, one basic reaction to all of these kinds of inquiries is to wonder why or under what circumstances these types of questions are even worth asking. Why does it matter if we call the slightly changed game "chess" or not, or call the unjust system of dispute resolution "law" or not? This chapter is about articulating the possible reasons for such debates.

One ground-level reason for conceptual inquiries is to maintain a structure within which meaningful discussion can occur. The question of identity is important, in this sense, for we want to know whether two people who appear to be discussing the same subject are in fact doing so. The idea is that without some agreed subject underlying our disagreements about "justice", "democracy", "law" and so on, the great debates on these subjects would collapse into an uninteresting exchange of parties talking past one another.[32] To disagree is to disagree *about* something.

The common category grounding the discussion may be delimited by a proffered definition. For example, "when I talk about 'legal systems', I

---

[29] Joseph Raz, "Authority, Law and Morality", in *Ethics in the Public Domain* (Clarendon Press, Oxford, 1994), pp. 194–221, at p. 221.
[30] Joseph Raz, "Two Views of the Nature of the Theory of Law: A Partial Comparison", 4 *Legal Theory* 249, 280–281 (1998).
[31] See Raz, "On the Nature of Law", pp. 1–7; Raz, "Legal Theory". Jules Coleman seems to be advocating a similar analysis, of conceptual analysis in jurisprudence focusing on "our" concept of law. See Jules Coleman, "Incorporationism, Conventionality, and the Practical Difference Thesis", 4 *Legal Theory* 381 at 393 n. 59 (1998).
[32] See, *e.g.* Susan Hurley, *Natural Reasons* (Oxford University Press, Oxford, 1989), pp. 30–32.

mean the following: x, y, and z; and for all systems that fit that description, I believe the following is true: . . .". The question then becomes on what basis one selects one proffered definition over an alternative. I will return to that question later in this chapter.

An alternative approach is sometimes helpful in understanding conceptual claims. Many of the misunderstandings regarding conceptual debates arise because while conceptual claims purport (by their form if not by some more express statement) to be merely descriptive, they almost always have evaluative or prescriptive elements. Some of the disagreements present within conceptual "debates" might be better understood as disagreements regarding the best answer to a particular question or problem. For example, the various theories of "justice" could be seen as competing answers to the question, "what are the morally best set of rules, criteria or procedures for the distribution of goods in society?"

However, while seeing some disagreements about concepts as really being disagreements about the best answer to set (moral) questions may work in a few cases, it is unlikely to succeed as a general method of understanding conceptual theories. For example, we are still left with the problem of how to explain disagreements about terms like "law" and "democracy". Those who disagree about whether a particular governmental system was "democratic" or not might still agree about any normative question put to them, for example, whether that governmental system was the best one for the country which used it.

In summary, conceptual theories and claims set the boundaries of categories. The drawing of such boundaries can be helpful in establishing a common ground for investigation and discussion, but the placement of the boundaries is often contested. The question remains, on what basis can it be asserted that one conceptual theory is better than another? That question will be the focus of the next section.

ALTERNATIVE PURPOSES

If most conceptual debates are not straightforward descriptions and they are not alternative answers to simple normative questions, can these debates be understood in a way that does not dismiss them as nonsensical? They can be, if one starts by trying to understand the (various) purposes of conceptual definitions. One possible "purpose", broadly understood, is what one might consider as the default option: definition as stipulation.

Though some might say that arbitrary stipulations are theories "without purpose", or perhaps "no theory at all", for the present analysis it is convenient to consider them as an alternative to the other, "purpose-driven" approaches. Additionally, one should not overstate the extent to which stipulations are arbitrary: even where there is no strong purpose pointing towards one possible definition over alternatives, some stipulations will seem better than others, in the way that they track linguistic usage or help to clarify certain issues.[33] Wesley Hohfeld's proposed categories relating to rights and related normative concepts (which will be discussed in Ch. 10) is probably a good example of this approach: a stipulation meant to make our analysis of familiar matters clearer and more precise.

Some might argue that conceptual definitions can *only* be arbitrary, because there cannot be any one right way to divide up social reality. For example, one might argue that regarding questions like whether we describe the rules of wicked governments as "law", or whether we consider international law as really being "law", any answer is as true or as legitimate as any other. Under this analysis, there cannot be a "right" or "wrong" to conceptual definitions, only a "more or less convenient", and all that we can ask is that theorists be as clear as possible on the reasons behind their boundary lines, if there are any such reasons, and that they be consistent in their application of the boundaries.

Under this approach, a disagreement between two definitions of "law" or "democracy" would not be important; it would just be evidence of contrasting conventions. There would be no particular reason why you should not adopt my convention, or I yours, for the purposes of discussing some issue of mutual interest. However, if most conceptual definitions were merely arbitrary, it would be hard to explain the often-vigorous disagreements over which definition of "law" or "democracy" or the like was to be adopted; surely, these arguments are driven by more than pride that one's own arbitrary suggestion be accepted rather than another person's. On the other hand, if the definitions are not arbitrary stipulations, there needs to be some basis for claiming that one definition is better than another, and this is where one needs reference to the purpose of the definition.[34]

In conceptual debates, theorists rarely claim simply that their definitions of "law" or "democracy" "are true" or "better describe reality" compared to the alternatives, for too many questions would be begged by such a claim.[35] What could it mean, for example, to say that one's

---

[33] See the discussion of "virtuous stipulation" in Halpin, "Concepts, Terms, and Fields of Enquiry" at 195–198.

[34] As discussed earlier, even with "arbitrary" stipulations, it is open to theorists to say that one stipulation is "better" because it is more useful or more convenient for a particular purpose.

[35] This is reminiscent of Lon Fuller's criticism of (pre-H.L.A. Hart) legal positivism:
"[W]e encounter a series of definitional fiats. A rule of law is—that is to say, it really and simply and always is—the command of a sovereign, a rule laid down by a judge, a prediction of the future incidence of state force, a pattern of official behavior, etc. When we ask what purpose these definitions serve, we receive the answer, 'Why, no purpose, except to describe accurately the social reality that corresponds to the word "law."' When we reply, 'But it doesn't look like that to me,' the answer comes hack, 'Well, it does to me.' There the matter has to rest."
Fuller, "Positivism and Fidelity to Law" at 631.

conceptual analysis was "true"? Social reality simply does not come so cleanly marked off.

Once past the default option of stipulation, conceptual definitions usually have broadly one of three objectives: (1) they can be an attempt to track and explain linguistic usage; (2) they can be an attempt to discover the "significance" of a concept, hidden in our practices and intuitions regarding usage; or (3) they can impose moral or qualitative criteria which must be met before the label should be applied (perhaps on the basis that such criteria are deeply embedded in our usage).

The distinction between the second and the third category may be artificial or unnecessary, and I do not think anything turns on how many categories one constructs. That said, I think that there is some basis for distinguishing the second category, evaluations of "significance" that at least purport to be morally neutral (as with Hart's discussion of the significance of legal rights discussed below), and the third category, definitions which openly use and encourage moral judgments (as in the works of natural law theorists, also discussed below).

One possible basis for claiming that one conceptual theory was superior to another would be that the definition proffered better reflects the way we actually use the term. Occasionally one comes across a conceptual theory whose ambition is no greater than to track usage,[36] but this is unusual. Conceptual analysis is often tied to usage, but the tie is usually a loose one. This tie sometimes encourages the confusion that discussions about "what is law" or "what are rights" and similar questions are merely linguistic investigations.[37] However, conceptual discussions are rarely only about proper dictionary entries. Theorists who pay attention to usage usually do so because they believe that usage reflects some deeper, more interesting truth. At other times, to be sure, linguistic usage will not reflect any underlying conceptual connection, and is simply the product of accidents of style or philology.[38]

This leads us to consider the second justification for conceptual definitions: that a particular way of dividing up a subject matter is justified on the basis that this way better displays certain interesting or important aspects of the practice, aspects which may be hinted at by our linguistic usage.[39]

One example of this second approach can be seen in H.L.A. Hart's position in the debate about the best (conceptual) understanding of legal rights (which will be discussed in Ch. 10). Hart defended his "claim

---

[36] See Raz, *Ethics in the Public Domain*, pp. 179–82 (discussing linguistic approaches to the nature of law).

[37] See, *e.g.* Ronald Dworkin, *Law's Empire* (Harvard University Press, Cambridge. Mass., 1986), pp. 31–44 (arguing against "semantic theories" of law).

[38] See White, "Conceptual Analysis", pp. 110–111.

[39] See, e.g. Finnis, *Natural Law and Natural Rights*, pp. 3–11; Raz, *Ethics in the Public Domain*, pp. 216–218.

theory" of legal rights, even against an alternative definition that Hart conceded better fit the way we use the relevant legal terms, on the basis that his definition captured an important aspect of the way people perceive and experience legal rights.[40] The "claim theory" asserts that what is most significant or most interesting about legal rights is the role played by the right-holder's power and ability to choose. For most rights, the holder can waive the corresponding duty, or if the duty is breached, waive enforcement, or waive compensation for the breach, if it comes to that.

The alternative position is the "interest" or "benefit" theory of rights, often represented by Jeremy Bentham or Neil MacCormick.[41] Advocates of this position point out that there are a number of situations where we speak of rights where the putative right holder has no such power: on one end, inalienable rights, and on the other end, rights ascribed to children, legally incompetent adults, and animals. Therefore, it is better to define rights in terms of a certain kind of legally protected interest. There are some skirmishes on the boundaries: for instance, whether the example of third-party beneficiaries to contracts (who in some jurisdictions, have no power to enforce the contract) offers "evidence" for either side. However, mostly there is agreement about the overall situation: that "interest theories" of legal rights can better track usage, but at the cost of a somewhat awkward definition and no grand conclusion; by contrast, "claim/will theories" make an interesting assertion, but at the cost of a less than optimal fit with how we use the term. If conceptual claims are about disclosing what is "important" or "significant" about a concept, then Hart's theory of rights is tenable, despite its less than perfect fit with usage.

The problem with this second approach, conceptual definitions as being about what is "interesting" or "important" regarding some practice or attitude, is that these underlying judgments may be insufficiently objective ("objective" here meaning sufficiently independent of individual interests and perspectives that there would likely be a consensus on the matter in question). Importance may be best seen as a statement of utility—an appropriate answer to the question "why is X important" is "because it helps to obtain Y"—however, we might then be left without any consensus about proper ends (whether "Y" is worth pursuing, and, even if so, whether "Z" might not be the more important objective here). If we disagree about the purposes of a practice, we are also likely to disagree about which aspects of the practice are "important" or "significant" and why they are so. The result is a certain kind of theoretical stalemate. For example, it would be difficult for a theorist, basing his

---

[40] See H.L.A. Hart, "Legal Rights" in *Essays on Bentham* (Clarendon Press, Oxford, 1982), pp. 162–193.

[41] See Hart, *Essays on Bentham*, pp. 164–170 (summarizing Bentham's "benefit theory of rights"); Neil MacCormick, "Rights in Legislation" in *Law, Morality and Society* (P.M.S. Hacker and J. Raz eds, Clarendon Press, Oxford, 1977), pp. 189–209.

concept of "law" on a particular view of which ends law does or should pursue, to persuade a second theorist, with a different view about law's objectives and (thus) a different theory, that the first theory was superior to the second. (Arguably, this kind of unresolvable disagreement is part of what is going on in the debates between legal positivism and its critics.[42])

The third non-stipulative approach to conceptual questions is to set standards: a test the object or activity must pass before the relevant label has been earned. For example, one might believe that something should only be called "literature" if it has "passed the test of time", that is, if its high critical standing has not been significantly diminished over many years. Similarly, some might believe that a created object should only be called "art" if it reaches a certain quality or significance.

One may wonder what sense there is to giving normative tests for concepts in the social sciences. It is one thing to say that "literature" is very good fiction, where here the label becomes a short-hand for an evaluative judgment ("her books are fiction, to be sure, but I would hardly call them 'literature'"). However, when the term in question is one of general use, like "law", one could argue that it only invites confusion to use a term of general description as also implying a statement of worth.[43]

Although the justification for this approach to conceptual definitions is often not articulated, one possible argument for it often hinted at is as follows: terms like "art", "democracy", and "law", though they have a strong descriptive element, are rarely simply descriptive. There is a residual (positive) normative element that philosophers seeking analytical clarity cannot simply wish away.[44] In many circles, it would be considered insulting to be told that one's society did not really have "law" or that its government was not really "democratic". When we say, "we would not call what Nazi Germany had 'law'", or "we would not speak of 'a right' to be pun-

---

[42] See, e.g. H.L.A. Hart, "Postscript", in *The Concept of Law* (2nd ed., Clarendon Press, Oxford, 1994), pp. 248–249, contrasting his view that the primary purpose of law is to guide human behaviour with Ronald Dworkin's view that the primary purpose of law is to offer a moral justification for state coercion.

[43] See Hart, *The Concept of Law*, pp. 207–212. There are ethical concepts, described in the literature as "thick concepts", in which description and evaluation (or, to put the same point another way, description and reasons for action) are inextricably entwined: e.g. "rude". "cowardly", "brutal". See, e.g. Bernard Williams, *Ethics and the Limits of Philosophy* (Harvard University Press, Cambridge, Mass., 1985), pp. 140–152; Philippa Foot, "Moral Arguments", 67 *Mind* 502 (1958) at 507–509.

[44] Kenneth Winston, in summarizing the ideas of Morris Cohen and Lon Fuller, described a comparable notion in different terms. As I understand Winston's summary, a (teleological) "ideal element" is required for the intelligibility of all social institutions, including law (the ideal being the "principle of order, a limiting conception", which creates the conceptual structure within which actual subjects are perceived), and therefore any definition which does not incorporate such an element would be defective. Kenneth Winston, "The Ideal Element in a Definition of Law", 5 *Law and Philosophy* 89 (1986) at 98, 105–106.

ished for something we had done", the theorist is trading on our linguistic intuitions—when we think a label is appropriate and when inappropriate— and these intuitions sometimes contain judgmental elements. It is as if the intuitions reflect some truth about social phenomena, some truth we understand at the intuitive level but not yet, or not yet clearly, at an articulate level.

It may he helpful at this point to consider an example from the jurisprudential literature that cuts across different approaches to conceptual definitions. Simon Roberts criticized H.L.A. Hart's analysis of legal systems,[45] arguing that under Hart's analysis many communities (in particular, small tribes and so-called "primitive" societies) would be held not to have "law", as many such communities do not have the centralized legislative and adjudicative bodies Roberts believed to be assumed by Hart's model.[46] However, it is not clear why Hart could not simply reply to this challenge, that for his own purposes he has chosen an analysis and definition of law and of legal systems that only covers certain Western societies. He could have said: definitions are arbitrary; if other theorists want a wider definition, they are welcome to set one. (I do not claim that this was in fact Hart's position, only that a position of this sort is possible.)

It appears that there are two unstated premises in Roberts' criticism: first, that the conceptual definition of "law" is not (or should not be) an arbitrary matter; second, that all (or almost all) societies should be held to have legal systems. As regards the second point, the argument might be that saying that a community has a legal system is implicitly to state that this community is advanced, mature, and sophisticated, and that to say that a community does not have one is to say that it is "primitive" and unimportant. This type of argument fits into my third category, discussed earlier. However, the point remains that until a theorist offers grounds for judging conceptual definitions and the reasons for adopting one over another, arguments about the "truth" or "correctness" of a conceptual definition are ungrounded, and thus pointless.

Given all of the considerations discussed during the course of this chapter, it is not surprising that the different participants in the conceptual "debates" in legal theory—debates about how the concepts are best defined—are often best understood as talking past one another. One example may be the famous jurisprudential "debate" between H.L.A. Hart and Lon Fuller.[47] This is not the place to argue the matter in detail,[48] but briefly the summary would be as follows: Hart offered an analysis of law with the purpose of maximizing clarity in discussing law in general and particularly in the moral evaluation of legal rules; while Fuller

---

[45] From Hart, *The Concept of Law.*
[46] Simon Roberts, *Order and Dispute* (Penguin, Middlesex, England, 1979), pp. 23–25.
[47] Hart, "Positivism and the Separation of Law and Morals"; Fuller, "Positivism and Fidelity to Law".
[48] There will he much more on Hart in Ch. 3 and on Fuller in Ch. 6.

offered a moral test for applying the term "law", based partly on usage and partly on viewing law as a form of social ordering to be contrasted with other forms of social ordering.[49] The two positions are incompatible in the sense that a particular legal system might fail to be "law" under Fuller's analysis while it would be "law" under Hart's analysis. However, the two analyses are not inconsistent, in the sense that one can argue, without contradiction, that both are valuable and useful.

There is one further practical question to consider. I have argued that conceptual theories and claims can only be evaluated in light of their underlying purposes, but I have also noted that many, and perhaps most, such theories and claims fail to articulate their purposes. How then can any evaluation be done, if the reader must provide the standard against which the text will be tested?

I suggest that the best approach is the following. Where a theorist has not articulated a purpose for her claim, one should seek a purpose against which the theory would have some claim to success, without making the theory trivial.[50] Thus, to interpret a theory as merely tracking linguistic usage may make the theory largely successful, but (in the area of jurisprudence anyway) this is a relatively unambitious purpose, and a reader should see if the theory might also succeed at some more substantial purpose.

CONCEPTUAL ANALYSIS AND NATURALISM

Some writers have begun to question how much of traditional jurisprudence *has been* conceptual analysis, and, a related matter, how much of jurisprudence *should be* conceptual analysis.

For example, in an article on American legal realism, Brian Leiter argues that this school of thought has been misunderstood because commentators have assumed wrongly that the realists, like most legal theorists in the 20th century, were offering conceptual analyses.[51] Leiter argues

---

[49] Frederick Schauer has argued that Hart and Fuller could be seen to have had a common purpose, in that both were trying to put forward theories which would make it more likely that officials and citizens would resist unjust laws. See, *e.g.* Frederick Schauer. "Fuller's Internal Point of View", 13 *Law and Philosophy* 285 (1994) at 289–294; see also Philip Soper, "Choosing a Legal Theory on Moral Grounds", in *Philosophy and Law* (J. Coleman and E. F Paul eds, Blackwell, Oxford, 1987), pp. 31–48.

[50] This type of analysis is related to Donald Davidson's discussion of "charity" in interpretation. See Donald Davidson, *Inquiries into Truth and Interpretation* (Clarendon Press, Oxford, 1984), pp. 196–197, 200–201.

[51] Brian Leiter, "Legal Realism", in *A Companion to the Philosophy of Law and Legal Theory* (D. Patterson ed., Blackwell, Oxford, 1996), pp 262–265; see also Brian Leiter, "Rethinking Legal Realism: Toward a Naturalized Jurisprudence", 76 *Texas Law Review* 267 (1997). American legal realism will he discussed in Ch. 17.

that the American legal realists, at least in their theorizing about judicial decision- making, were in fact philosophical naturalists.[52]

"Naturalism" is the belief that there is no area of philosophical inquiry to which the sciences, broadly understood, are not applicable; in Leiter's terms, it is the belief that "philosophical theorizing ought to be continuous with and dependent upon empirical inquiry in the natural and social sciences."[53] Examples of such "naturalist" approaches are certain modern approaches to epistemology, which hold that considerations of how people actually arrive at their beliefs are relevant to the inquiry of how we ought to arrive at our beliefs.[54]

Leiter's observations about American legal realism are almost certainly right, and a helpful corrective to the way those theorists are often perceived. However, Leiter also seems to hint at a more general, and more controversial, claim about legal theory, when he comments at one point that jurisprudence in general is decades behind other areas of philosophy in abandoning pure conceptual analysis for naturalist analysis.[55]

An initial response is that it may be unwise to evaluate as a group all conceptual theories, even all conceptual theories in jurisprudence. One might argue that epistemology and judicial reasoning are to be distinguished from the type of conceptual questions that are often raised in jurisprudence. When considering how we know things or how judges can/should decide legal questions, there is an immediate attraction to the position that how people in fact do these activities should play an integral part in the analysis of how they *should* do them.

However, questions like "what is law" (or "what is art") and "the nature of 'rights' are of a different type altogether, for it is less clear how empirical claims *could* enter the analysis. It is not that empirical facts—what people actually do, or what there actually is—have no place at all in the analysis; as noted earlier, many theorists see a role for actual linguistic usage in constructing a conceptual theory. Rather, the problem is that the scope of the category ("law", "rights", "art") is as contested as the best

---

[52] Leiter, "Legal Realism", p. 263. Leiter does not claim that naturalist methodology completely supplanted conceptual analysis for the legal realists. He argues that in conceptual matters, the legal realists are best understood as having been "tacit legal positivists". *Ibid.* at 264.

[53] *ibid.* For the consequences this approach has for a wide variety of different philosophical inquiries, see David Papineau, *Philosophical Naturalism* (Basil Blackwell, Oxford, 1993).

[54] See, *e.g.* the papers collected in Hilary Kornblith, *Naturalizing Epistemology* (2nd ed., MIT Press, Cambridge, Mass., 1994).

[55] Leiter, "Legal Realism" at 262–264. Leiter expanded on some of these claims in later articles. See Brian Leiter, "Naturalism and Naturalized Jurisprudence", in *Analyzing Law: New Essays in Legal Theory* (Brian Bix ed., Clarendon Press, Oxford, 1998), pp. 79–104; Brian Leiter, "Realism, Hard Positivism, and Conceptual Analysis", 4 *Legal Theory* 533 (1998); "Naturalism in Legal Philosophy", in E. N. Zalta, ed., *Stanford Encyclopedia of Philosophy*, http://plato. stanford.edu/ (2002). For a response to the first of these articles, see Jules L. Coleman, "Second Thoughts and Other First Impressions", in *Analyzing Law*, pp. 278–285; Jules L. Coleman, *The Practice of Principle* (Oxford University Press, Oxford, 2001), pp. 210–217.

way of understanding the items that fit within the category.[56] Empirical observation is not likely to settle these contests, as the role of empirical facts *(e.g.* how important linguistic usage should be in constructing or evaluating the theories) is itself highly contested.

For all the reasons that make conceptual analysis in legal and political philosophy muddled, confused and confusing—the lack of articulation of underlying purposes, the varying and contrary purposes, and the contested nature of conceptual boundaries—I doubt that these discussions will (or should) soon be conquered by naturalism.[57]

BOUNDARY LINES IN LAW

One type of dispute within jurisprudence which can be understood as a consequence of conceptual debates are the arguments about boundary lines within law.

One such argument surrounds whether the collections of rules and related institutions in a society should warrant the label "law" if the society (and its legal system) is evil. A similar argument is sometimes raised regarding an unjust rule within a particular legal system. This set of issues will come up, in various guises, in the discussions about legal positivism (see Ch. 3), and natural law theory (see Ch. 5). One gets a sense in those discussions that the question of whether a particular rule or a particular rule system is given the title "law" or "legal" is not of great intrinsic importance. After all, it is only a name, albeit one that can carry significant moral or psychological reverberations. It is more that the label theorists give or withhold in these situations reflects (is a symptom of) their general approach to law— *e.g.* natural law theorists using law as an intermediate step in questions about how to act, as contrasted with legal positivists' quasi-scientific approach to law as a social phenomenon to be studied dispassionately.

A very different kind of argument appears to be going on when theorists wonder about which standards among those judges are obligated to apply, or among those judges in fact do apply, should carry the label "law" or "legal".[58] Such debates often arise in the context of a larger line-

---

[56] While one might argue that the scope of categories central to other disputes, *e.g.* the category of "warranted assertion" in epistemology, is also sometimes contested, I would argue that for such categories the disputes, if they exist at all, are very much at the margins, as contrasted with conceptual disputes in legal and political theory: where the disputes are pervasive and central.

[57] For a response to an earlier version of this section, see Leiter, "Naturalism and Naturalized Jurisprudence", pp. 92–100 and n.75.

[58] The debate between Joseph Raz and Ronald Dworkin on this point appears in Raz, "Legal Principles and the Limits of Law", in *Ronald Dworkin and Contemporary Jurisprudence* (M. Cohen ed., Duckworth, London, 1984), pp. 73–87; Ronald Dworkin, "A Reply by Ronald Dworkin", *ibid.* at pp. 260–263; and Raz, *Ethics in the Public Domain*, pp. 179–193.

drawing question, raised by larger-scale jurisprudential theories. When a theorist claims that a common law judge should always only declare the law that is already present rather than legislate new law, that there is no necessary connection between legal validity and moral value, or that one can always determine the content of a law without recourse to moral evaluation—in the context of such assertions much can turn on how (and where) one distinguishes law from non-law, legal standards from non-legal standards, and the like.

As was mentioned earlier in this chapter, drawing boundaries can be a game where all the rules and underlying purposes are hidden or at best vaguely stated. When a theory turns on the relation between two fluid, contested concepts (for example, whether the content of "legal rules" can always be determined without reference to "moral evaluation"), there will always be doubts regarding whether neutral criteria can be found to arbitrate the result, or whether every theory can simply define the terms in the way which supports its own claims.

Sometimes boundary lines are placed in the service of significant political decisions. This may be best exemplified in discussions about the continuity of legal systems—determining when one legal system ends and another one begins. This apparently abstract discussion has been used as the basis for determining under what circumstances legal rules and legal institutions from a former regime were still valid after that regime had been overthrown.[59] These are difficult political and moral decisions, and the judges may be excused if they search for an abstract and apparently neutral basis for their decisions. (One might even argue that this kind of search is often central to the legal process, and is not a product only of this particular controversy.) However, a judge's strong reliance on abstract analytical concepts and categories to decide these questions is inappropriate—and the simplest of reasons for that conclusion is that the abstract analytical concepts in question were not created with these moral/political problems in mind.[60] One should be hesitant to base decisions that may cost individuals their freedom or property on a theorist's toying with boundary lines.

On one hand, one is skeptical when purely analytic discussions are appropriated as the grounds to solve political and moral issues for which

---

[59] See, e.g. Madzimbamuto (Stella) v Lardner-Burke N.O. 1968 (2) S.A.L.R. 284; Uganda v Commissioner of Prisons, Ex p. Matovu [1966] East Afr. L.R. 514; see generally John M Finnis, "Revolutions and Continuity of Law", in Oxford Essays in Jurisprudence, Second Series (A.W.B. Simpson ed., Oxford University Press, Oxford, 1973), pp. 44–76; J.M. Eekelaar, "Principles of Revolutionary Legality", ibid. at pp. 22–43.

[60] Another reason for caution is how poorly equipped the judges often are to understand the concepts they are borrowing. Some of the "post-revolution" decisions turn on a badly misunderstood version of Hans Kelsen's remarks on "Change in the Basic Norm". For example, compare Madzimbamuto, at 314–321, with Hans Kelsen, General Theory of Law and State (Russell & Russell, New York, 1945), pp. 117–118, 220–221.

the original discussions are not well-suited. It almost seems unfair to the original theorists; perhaps they should have been put on notice that their writings might be used as the justifications for actions on particular moral problems, and the theorists could have reconsidered their positions with that thought in mind. As it is, some theorists can come off seeming like defenders of tyranny and injustice when that was neither their intentions nor their nature.[61]

CONCLUSION

In summary, conceptual debates in jurisprudence (and elsewhere) are often confusing because a central element in the discussion is left unstated. In proposing a conceptual claim, or in evaluating such a claim, it is critical to determine the purpose with which the claim is put forward. When the purpose is not articulated, there is the danger, at the least, that the participants in conceptual debates will misunderstand one another, and offer arguments that do not meet.

In this chapter, I have offered four alternatives for conceptual claims: (1) they are arbitrary stipulations; (2) they track linguistic usage; (3) they try to explain what is "important" or "interesting" about some matter; and (4) they establish an evaluative test for the label. My impression is that most conceptual claims in legal theory belong to the third or fourth categories.

Under the approach suggested in this chapter, one might not be able to say that a particular conceptual analysis was "right" or "true", at least not in the sense that there would be only one unique "right" or "true" theory for all conceptual questions, but I do not see this as a significant loss. It should be sufficient that one can affirm (or deny) that an analysis is good, or better than an alternative, for a particular purpose.

Suggested Further Readings

PHILOSOPHY AND CONCEPTUAL ANALYSIS GENERALLY

Isaiah Berlin, "The Purpose of Philosophy", in *Concepts and Categories* (Penguin, New York, 1981), pp. 1–11.
L. Jonathan Cohen, *The Dialogue of Reason* (Clarendon Press, Oxford, 1986).
Gilbert Harman, "Doubts About Conceptual Analysis", in *Philosophy in Mind: The Place of Philosophy in the Study of Mind* (M. Michael and J. O'Leary-Hawthorne ed., Kluwer, Dordrecht, 1994), pp. 43–48.

---

[61] One thinks of the long-standing argument about whether legal positivist theories helped to encourage the growth, or at least the acceptance, of National Socialism in 1930s Germany. See, *e.g.* Paulson, "Lon L. Fuller, Gustav Radbruch, and the 'Positivist' Theses".

Jay Rosenberg, *The Practice of Philosophy* (2nd ed., Prentice-Hall, Englewood Cliffs, N.J., 1984), pp. 5–11.
Alan R. White, "Conceptual Analysis" in *The Owl of Minerva: Philosophers in Philosophy* (C.J. Bontmepo and S.J. Odell ed., McGraw-Hill, New York, 1975), pp. 103–117.

CONCEPTUAL ANALYSIS IN JURISPRUDENCE

Jules L. Coleman, "Methodology", in *The Oxford Handbook of Jurisprudence and Philosophy of Law* (J. L. Coleman & S. Shapiro eds, K. E. Himma assoc. ed., Oxford University Press, Oxford, 2002), pp. 311–351.
Brian Leiter, "Naturalism in Legal Philosophy", in E. N. Zalta ed., *Stanford Encyclopedia of Philosophy*, http://plato.stanford.edu/ (2002).
Thomas Morawetz, "Law and Conceptual Analysis" in *The Philosophy of Law: An Introduction* (Macmillan, New York, 1980), pp. 11–16.
Joseph Raz, "Legal Theory", in *Blackwell Guide to Philosophy of Law and Legal Theory* (forthcoming, M. P. Golding & W. A. Edmundson ed., Blackwell, Oxford, 2004).
Philip Soper, "Legal Theory and the Problem of Definition" (book review), 50 *University of Chicago Law Review* 1170 (1983).
Brian Z. Tamanaha, *Realistic Socio-Legal Theory: Pragmatism and A Social Theory of Law* (Clarendon Press, Oxford, 1997), Ch. 4.
Kenneth Winston, "The Ideal Element in a Definition of Law", 5 *Law and Philosophy* 89 (1986).

PART B

Individual Theories About the Nature of Law

The heart of many jurisprudence courses is the discussion of the approaches to law of various well-known individual theorists. The following chapters offer an overview of five of the most highly-regarded legal theorists, locating some of the issues to which their theories were responses, and placing the theories within the context of larger movements in jurisprudence.

Each of the five offers a distinct, coherent, and comprehensive vision, not only of the nature of law but also of the nature of legal theory.

Chapter Three

H.L.A. Hart and Legal Positivism

AN OVERVIEW OF LEGAL POSITIVISM

Legal positivism is based on the simple assertion that the proper description of law is a worthy objective, and a task that need be kept separate from moral judgments (regarding the value of the present law, and regarding how the law should be developed or changed). In the more precise terms of theorizing about law, it is the view that a descriptive, or at least morally neutral, theory of law is both possible and valuable. Early advocates of legal positivism included Jeremy Bentham (1748–1832) and John Austin (1790–1859). One could also dig deeper, and place the roots of modern legal positivism with the philosophers and political theorists Thomas Hobbes (1588–1679) and David Hume (1711–1776).[1]

In simple terms, legal positivism is built around the belief, the assumption, the dogma, that the question of what is the law is separate from, and must be kept separate from, the question of what the law should be. The position can be summarized in the words of John Austin:

"The existence of law is one thing; its merit or demerit is another. Whether it be or be not is one enquiry; whether it be or be not conformable to an assumed standard, is a different enquiry. A law, which actually exists, is a law, though we happen to dislike it, or though it vary from the text, by which we regulate our approbation and disapprobation."[2]

---

[1] As the editors do in George Christie and Patrick Martin (ed.), *Jurisprudence: Text and Readings on the Philosophy of Law* (2nd ed., St Paul; West Publishing, 1995), Ch. 5. John Finnis goes a few steps further, and states that the groundwork for legal positivism (the establishment of human-posited law as a separate subject-matter) was laid by medieval writers, in particular by Thomas Aquinas. John Finnis, "The Truth in Legal Positivism", in *The Autonomy of Law* (R. George ed., Clarendon Press, Oxford, 1996), pp. 195–214. I discuss the connections and differences between Aquinas' view and modern legal positivism in Ch. 5.

[2] John Austin, *The Province of Jurisprudence Determined*, Lecture V (W.E. Rumble ed., Cambridge University Press, Cambridge, 1995) (first published in 1832), p. 157.

Legal positivism seeks from the study of law nothing more and nothing less than what is considered the foundation of modern social theory: that social institutions can be studied in an objective fashion, free from bias or ideology.[3] Such separation does not deny—in fact, theorists advocating legal positivism usually strenuously assert—that something identified as "a valid law" or "a valid legal system" may sometimes be sufficiently evil or unjust that it should not be obeyed.[4]

The notion that the description of a practice or an institution should be prior to and separate from its evaluation seems to modern audiences too obvious to need declaration, let alone justification.[5] However, the controversial nature of legal positivism becomes clearer when we keep in mind both the history of writing about law and the type of institution law is.

As to the first point: historically, much of the writing about law in general (as contrasted with writing about specific legal systems, which discuss which rules are in force or should be in force) involved moral and political inquiries regarding under what conditions government was legitimate and (the apparently related question) under what conditions citizens have a moral obligation to obey the law. To some, *the point* of a morally neutral description of law was unclear, especially if one thought that one had a moral or religious basis for criticism and prescription.[6]

As to the second point, law is a practice so infused with moral-sounding claims *(e.g.* that citizens "ought to do X", where "X" is some action required by the legal rules) and moral-sounding terminology *(e.g.* legal "rights" and "obligations")* that a strictly descriptive theory of law seems either difficult or inappropriate, for the same reason that a "descriptive theory of morality" or a "descriptive theory of justice" sound strange, though one *can* find descriptive theories of both types.

The attempt to place the study of law on a "scientific" foundation— objective and pure[7] of bias—led many of the early legal positivists to try

---

[3] This approach to social theory has been challenged in various ways, not least by those who believe that social practices cars only be understood in a "hermeneutic" way. On the connection between legal positivism, hermeneutic theory, and the possibility of neutral social and legal theory, see Stephen R. Perry, "Interpretation and Methodology in Legal Theory", in *Law and Interpretation* 97–135 (A. Marmor ed., Clarendon Press, Oxford, 1995); Brian Bix, "H.L.A. Hart and the Hermeneutic Turn in Legal Theory", 52 *SMU Law Review* 167 (1999).

[4] See, *e.g.* Hart, "Positivism and the Separation of Law and Morals", pp. 615–61.

[5] This is also the reason why I discuss legal positivism prior to natural law theory in this book. Though the latter has a longer history, to many people's way of thinking, legal positivism, separating description and evaluation, would seem the usual or default view, while natural law theory would seem the unusual position that needs to be explained or justified. As recently as the 19th century, exactly the opposite was the case.

[6] See, *e.g.* Richard Dien Winfield, *Law in Civil Society* (University of Kansas Press, Lawrence, Kansas, 1995), pp. 1–3.

[7] Hans Kelsen referred to his theory as *"reine Rechtslehre"*, the "pure theory of law". His view is discussed in Ch. 4.

to create a strictly empirical way of understanding legal actions and legal concepts, thus understanding them as functions of past, current or future facts. This search in legal theory can be seen as deriving from the broader search for a "scientific" approach to the social sciences that could match the approach used in the "hard sciences" (*e.g.* physics and chemistry) whereby theories would be based only on "objective" observations of events that could he easily reproduced or confirmed by other theorists (in somewhat more technical language, the "normative" in law was reduced to the "empirical").[8] Thus, legal rules were analyzed in terms of past tendencies to obey, the use by legislators of particular kinds of language, the future likelihood of the imposition of sanctions, predictions of what judges were likely to do, and so on.

H.L.A. Hart's significance comes in part from the way he moved legal positivism in a different direction. While he continued to insist on the importance of the conceptual separation of law from morality (the separation of describing what law is from advocating how law should be), he criticized attempts to analyze law in strictly empirical terms. In this, he was following a growing and influential view, that the social sciences require an approach distinctly different from that used in the hard sciences, an approach based on understanding not merely the actions that occur, but also the meaning those actions have to the participants in the practices or institutions being studied.[9]

SUMMARY OF HART'S POSITION

At the time that H.L.A. Hart (1907–1992) began forming his legal theory, an influential view within the legal theory literature was that law was best understood as the command of a sovereign to its subjects.[10] Hart's

---

[8] This sort of "science envy" was also exemplified in the rise of "formalism" in legal education, in particular in the influential ideas of Harvard Law School Dean Christopher Columbus Langdell. See, *e.g.* Anthony T. Kronman, *The Last Lawyer* (Harvard University Press, Cambridge, Mass., 1993), pp. 170–174. I discuss Langdell and legal formalism briefly at the beginning of Ch. 17.

[9] The foundational work advocating a hermeneutic approach to social theory is probably Max Weber, see Max Weber, *Economy and Society* (G. Roth and C. Wittich eds, Bedminster Press, New York, 1968), vol. 1, pp. 4–24; Max Weber, "Objectivity' in Social Science and Social Policy", in *The Methodology of the Social Sciences* (E. Shils and H. Finch ed., Free Press, New York, 1949), pp. 50–112. Hart's immediate influence (and a source almost as important as Weber on this topic) was Winch, *The Idea of a Social Science* (Routledge, London, 1958); see Hart, *The Concept of Law*, pp. 289, 297.

[10] This position is ascribed by Hart, and by many others, to John Austin. See, *e.g.* Hart, *The Concept of Law*, pp. 18–25. Some have argued that this misstates Austin's position, or at least that it misses many of the subtleties of his argument. See, *e.g.* W.L. Morison, *John Austin* (Edward Arnold, London, 1982), pp 178–205; Roger Cotterrell, *The Politics of Jurisprudence* (Butterworths, London, 1989), pp. 64–65, 74.

approach to legal theory can be seen as a reaction to the command theory, and he presented his theory in that way on a number of occasions, as will become evident in the course of the following summary.[11]

The "command theory" (identified primarily with Austin, though Bentham also put forward a version[12]) offered a picture of law as a matter of commands (orders hacked by threats) by a sovereign (one who is habitually obeyed by others, but who does not habitually obey anyone else) to citizens. Hart found weaknesses at almost every point. First, it was hard to speak of there being a sovereign—a person or entity that is habitually obeyed, but has no habit of obedience to any other person or entity—in most modern governments, where even the highest governmental roles and institutions are subject to legal restraints. Secondly, the concept of a sovereign creates difficulty in explaining the continuity of law: for when someone new takes over, that person has no history of being habitually obeyed. Thirdly, there is much that is significant within legal systems that is lost if one looks only to the commands backed by threats, or if one treats all aspects of the law as variations of commands backed by threats.

In summary, from Hart's perspective, the problem with Austin's approach to law, and indeed with most empirical approaches, was that they are unable to distinguish pure power from institutions and rules accepted by the community, unable to distinguish the orders of terrorists from a legal system.[13]

Hart's alternative view of law is grounded on his views of rules, in particular on a view of the difference between rules and habits. To an outside observer, there may be no way to distinguish someone acting in a particular way out of habit from her acting the same way in compliance with a rule. I may go to the movies every Saturday, but that is not because I think that there is some legal, moral or social/conventional rule that states that I should. According to Hart, the difference between these two kinds of regularities of behaviour can be seen through the participants' attitudes. With habits, the statement of the behaviour is nothing more than a description: I go to the movies every Saturday. With a rule, however, the statement can take on additional roles: as an explanation, a justification, and a basis for criticizing deviation. The statement

---

[11] Hart, "The Separation of Law and Morality", pp. 600–606; Hart, *The Concept of Law*, pp. 18–123.

[12] Some legal commentators consider Bentham's legal theory superior to Austin's, but Austin's is better known because Bentham's theory was most fully elaborated in a text that did not appear in its full form until over a century after the author's death. See Jeremy Bentham, *Of Laws in General* (Athlone, London, 1970); H.L.A. Hart, *Essays on Bentham* (Clarendon Press, Oxford, 1982), pp. 105–126.

[13] "Law surely is not the gunmen situation writ large." Hart, "The Separation of Law and Morality", p. 603.

has a normative role.[14] Many people are not merely "in the habit" of obeying the authorities; they have internalized the rules as reasons for acting in certain ways and for criticizing others when they do not act as required.

Hart's theory, here as elsewhere, is responding to the idea that when analyzing social institutions or social practices, a theory which takes into account, or helps to explain, the way participants understand those institutions or practices is, by that fact alone, significantly better than one which does not do so. Hart described his own work as "an essay in descriptive sociology"[15], in that he often relied on distinctions between concepts that were rooted in linguistic practice, linguistic practice which was in turn based on differences in behaviour and attitude.

As for seeing law as being orders backed by threats, this view seems to invite the confusion mentioned earlier, between imposed force and accepted norms. A legal system is something different from, and presumably something better than, the rule over a frightened populace by gangsters. Hart captured the core of this distinction in his discussion of the difference between feeling obliged and having an obligation.[16] We feel obliged to act in the way ordered by a gunman, because we fear the consequences if we do not act in that way. However, the moment the fear of possible consequences is removed, we would see no reason to act as demanded. Having an obligation under some valid normative system (whether the rules of a game we are playing, the canons of one's religion, or society's legal rules) is psychologically more complex. One acts because one believes that one ought to do so, not because, or not merely because, one fears the consequences of acting in a contrary way.[17]

Against a view that reduced all legal rules to variations on some single type, as (one reading of) Austin's theory seemed to reduce all legal rules to commands, Hart emphasized the multiplicity of law. He contrasted rules that imposed duties with those that conferred powers (whether power conferred on officials within the legal system, or the delegation of certain legal

---

[14] Hart, *The Concept of Law*, pp. 9–10, 55–58. For a recent provocative rethinking of the nature of rules, with a discussion of implications for legal theory, see Scott J. Shapiro, "The Difference That Rules Make", in *Analyzing Law* (Brian Bix ed., Clarendon Press, Oxford, 1998), pp. 33–62.

[15] Hart, *The Concept of Law*, p. v.

[16] As Randy Barnett has pointed out, Randy E. Barnett, *The Structure of Liberty: Justice and the Rule of Law* (Clarendon Press, Oxford, 1998), p. 19, John Locke emphasized a similar distinction, though in the context of discussing the connection between natural law and positive law: "Certainly, positive civil laws are not binding by their own nature or force or in any other way than in virtue of the law of nature, which orders obedience to superiors and in keeping of public peace. Thus, without this law, the rules can perhaps by force and with the aid of arms compel the multitude to obedience, but put them under an obligation they cannot." John Locke, *Essays on the Law of Nature* (W. von Leyden ed., Clarendon Press, Oxford, 1954), p. 119. Natural law will be discussed in Ch. 5.

[17] Hart, *The Concept of Law*, pp. 82–86.

powers to citizens, as can be said to occur through the operation of rules for contracts, wills, trusts, and so on), and he contrasted rules that applied directly to citizens ("primary rules") and rules that governed the operation of the rule-system itself ("secondary rules"). The secondary rules include rules of change, rules of adjudication, and the rule of recognition.[18] Rules of change are the rules which empower people to create new primary rules. This includes not only the authorization of legislative bodies, but also the empowerment of individuals to create new rights and duties through contracts, wills, trusts, and the like.[19] Rules of adjudication "empower[ ] individuals to make authoritative determinations of the question whether, on a particular occasion, a primary rule has been broken."[20] The nature and significance of "rule(s) of recognition" will be discussed in the next section.[21] Hart argued that there were two necessary and sufficient conditions for the existence of a legal system: (1) that the valid rules of the system "must be generally obeyed"; and (2) that the criteria set forth in the system's rule of recognition "must be effectively accepted as common public standards of official behaviour by its officials."[22]

There is no room here to discuss all aspects of Hart's legal theory in detail[23]; instead, I will offer brief discussions of four of the more telling topics in Hart's work: the rule of recognition, the internal aspect of rules, the "open texture" of rules, and the "minimum content of natural law". Hart's views will also come up, by way of contrast, in the discussions of Hans Kelsen (Ch. 4), John Finnis (Ch. 5), Lon Fuller (Ch. 6), and Ronald Dworkin (Ch. 7).

THE RULE OF RECOGNITION

Central to Hart's theory is the concept of a rule of recognition: a set of criteria by which the officials determine which rules are, and which rules

---

[18] *ibid.* at pp. 91–99.
[19] *ibid.* at pp. 95–96.
[20] *ibid.* at p. 97.
[21] Later commentators have pointed out that Hart was probably mistaken in his further implication that the distinction between primary and secondary rules matches that between duty-conferring and power-imposing rules; additionally, there are questions regarding whether the rule of recognition is best understood as a duty-imposing or power-conferring rule (or neither). See, *e.g.* Joseph Raz, *The Concept of a Legal System* (2nd ed., Clarendon Press, Oxford, 1979), p. 199. However, for present purposes these are matters of detail as against the general point that there is a variety of types of law, and that our understanding of this type of social system would be distorted by any attempt to analyze all of the law in terms of a single type of rule.
[22] Hart, *The Concept of Law*, p. 116.
[23] The two best sources for such an extended discussion are probably Neil MacCormick, *H.L.A. Hart* (Stanford University Press, Stanford, 1981); and Michael Bayles, *Hart's Legal Philosophy: An Examination* (Kluwer Academic Publishers, Dordrecht, 1992).

are not, part of the legal system. The standards applied are referred to as justifications for the actions of the officials, though to some extent the standards are also created by those actions. To explain: sometimes the standards applied are written down in an official text (*e.g.* a written constitution) or at the least are clearly expressed in criteria that the officials state that they are following (*e.g.* "to become valid law, proposed legislation must be passed by a majority of each House of the Congress and then signed by the President"). At other times, the standards the officials are following can only be determined after the fact by reference to the decisions they have made.

A number of issues have been raised by later commentators regarding the rule of recognition: *e.g.* whether it is best understood as a duty-imposing or power-conferring rule; and whether there can be more than one rule of recognition within a given legal system.[24] However, one should focus primarily on what the concept of a rule of recognition indicates, *i.e.* what it stands for. The rule of recognition expresses, or symbolizes, the basic tenet of legal positivism: that there are conventional criteria, agreed upon by officials, for determining which rules are and which are not part of the legal system; this in turn points to the separation of the identification of the law from its moral evaluation, and the separation of statements about what the law is from statements about what it should be. (The similarities and differences between Hart's rule of recognition and Kelsen's "Basic Norm" are discussed in Ch. 4.)

THE INTERNAL ASPECT OF RULES (AND OF LAW)

The "internal aspect" of rules[25] is central to Hart's approach to law. It can best be understood within the context of (and it has repercussions for) certain general problems of constructing social theories—a subject touched upon in earlier chapters, and in an earlier section of this chapter. There are two related problems to consider: how must social theories be different from theories in other areas, and to what extent can a social theory be "scientific".[26]

One problem that comes from trying to construct a theory of a social process like law, a problem that does not trouble theories about atomic composition, chemical interaction, photosynthesis and the like, is that law is a human creation, meant to serve human purposes, and requiring human participation. Because of these aspects, understanding any social

---

[24] Joseph Raz, *The Authority of Law* (Clarendon Press, Oxford, 1979), pp. 95–96.
[25] See Hart, *The Concept of Law*, pp. 55–58, 82–91.
[26] Some of the themes in this section are explored at greater length in Bix, "H.L.A. Hart and the Hermeneutic Turn in Legal Theory"; see also Thomas Morawetz, "Law as Experience: Theory and the Internal Aspect of Law", 52 *SMU Law Review* 27 (1999).

process, including law, will be different in kind from understanding processes which are purely physical, chemical or biological.

This is the context for analysing Hart's concept of the internal aspect of rules. The idea is that one cannot understand a social system unless one understands how the people who created the system or who participate in the system perceive it. This "hermeneutic" approach—that is, giving priority to trying to understand how other people perceive their situation is always in tension with those who want social theory to be more scientific.[27]

The "scientific" approach to social theory would rely only on data that was "objective", data on which different observers would always agree. The "scientific" approach to legal theory might he exemplified in various theorists' writings: for example, Christopher Columbus Langdell's view of legal theory as the search for the system of basic principles within the law,[28] and the American legal realists (to some extent reacting against Langdell's view[29]) emphasizing what judges "actually do" as contrasted with what they are saying that they are doing. Hart also specifically mentioned the work of the Scandinavian Legal Realist Alf Ross, who (according to Hart) "claimed that the only method of representation of the law fit to figure in a modern rational science of law was one which shared the structure and logic of statements of empirical science."[30]

Hart's argument is that whatever advantage a "scientific" approach might have, it simply is not adequate for a full understanding of law.[31] Law is a social institution set up to achieve certain human purposes, and also to give guidance to citizens. One can only understand purposive behavior and normative (rule-following) behaviour if one leaves one's spectator's perspective and tries to understand the perceptions of the participants in the system, that is, the perceptions of the people who are following the rules, and who perceive themselves as doing so. In Hart's terms, to understand "any form of normative social structure", "the methodology of the empirical sciences is useless; what is needed is a 'hermeneutic' method which involves portraying rule-governed behaviour as it appears to its participants".[32]

The attack on a purely scientific approach can be seen in Hart's distinction between habitual behaviour and rule-following, mentioned

---

[27] As earlier noted, Hart's hermeneutic approach derived primarily from the works of Max Weber and Peter Winch.

[28] See William Twining, *Karl Llewellyn and the Realist Movement* (University of Oklahoma Press, Norman, Oklahoma, 1985). pp. 10–11.

[29] See the discussion of American legal realism in Ch. 17.

[30] Hart, *Essays in Jurisprudence and Philosophy*, p. 13.

[31] For an excellent discussion of the problems of methodology in jurisprudence, with particular attention to Hart's work, see Perry, "Interpretation and Methodology in Legal Theory".

[32] Hart, *Essays in Jurisprudence and Philosophy*, p. 13.

earlier.[33] As noted, Hart emphasized the difference between rules and habits, a difference that resided primarily in the participants' perceptions of what they were doing, and in their reactions to and attitudes towards the actions about them. When an action was done "as a rule", rather than "as a habit", the rule is given as a justification of the action, and the rule is also the basis for any criticisms (including self-criticism) for any divergence from the prescribed actions.[34] By contrast, we tend to have no justifications at hand (and sometimes we are lacking for explanations of any kind) for our habits, and we certainly do not criticize or expect criticisms when there are deviations from those habits. Because a scientific, purely "external", approach to law would conflate habitual actions and rule-following, according to Hart it would inevitably miss some matters which are at the essence of law.

However, to say that one is going to take the perspective of a participant in the social practice is at best a first step. After all, most social practices have a large number of participants, all of whom do not share the same view of, or attitude towards, the practice. One prominent legal theorist, John Finnis (who is discussed at greater length in Ch. 5) argues that the perspective chosen should be that of a (hypothetical) practically reasonable person, who applies appropriate moral reasoning to conclude (if true) that the legal system creates binding (prima facie) moral obligations.[35] A second prominent legal theorist, Ronald Dworkin (the subject of Ch. 7), argues that one should theorize as if one were a participant in the social practice, offering an interpretation of that practice that makes it the (morally) best practice it can be.[36] Both of these perspectives are, from Hart's perspective, too extreme: he wants a legal theory that would be free from moral evaluations or moral commitments (unlike Finnis' approach), while remaining a descriptive theory of the practice rather than a participation in it (unlike Dworkin's approach).[37]

---

[33] Similarly, to a "scientific" observer, someone who obeyed the law merely out of fear of sanctions would look the same as someone who obeyed the law because he or she believed that the legal system was legitimate, though a legal positivist (with that position's dogmatic separation of description and moral evaluation) might be foreclosed from referring to that conflation as a basis for rejecting a purely external viewpoint.

[34] For the suggestion that one needs to distinguish the "emotional" and "volitional" aspects of the "internal point of view", see Neil MacCormick, *Legal Reasoning and Legal Theory* (Clarendon Press, Oxford, 1978), pp. 288–292; MacCormick, *H.L.A. Hart*, pp. 33–34.

[35] See Finnis, *Natural Law and Natural Rights*, pp. 3–18.

[36] See generally Dworkin, *Law's Empire*, pp. 45–113.

[37] See Hart, "Introduction", pp. 8–12; Hart, "Postscript", pp. 240–244; Hart, "Comment", in *Issues in Contemporary Legal Philosophy* (R. Gavison ed., Clarendon Press, Oxford, 1987), p. 39. As a matter of strict chronology, Hart's most important works were written prior to the works of Finnis and Dworkin; however, it is still accurate to say that Hart's position is a centrist position compared to the positions Hart rejected, but Finnis and Dworkin were later to defend.

Hart was trying to maintain a difficult middle position.[38] He argued that a legal theory should he constructed around the perspective of someone who accepted the legal system, but the theory itself (or, to put the matter differently, the theorist herself) need not, and should not, endorse the system (as one which is generally just or which creates binding moral obligations). In other words, the theory simultaneously: (1) attempts to take into account the participant's perspective, and (2) manages to choose among possible participants' perspectives without having to make moral judgments, while (3) keeping sufficient distance from the participants' perspective to allow for moral criticism of the whole system/enterprise. The danger is of Hart's position sliding towards an Austin-like external observer's theory on one side, and a position closer to Finnis' or Dworkin's on the other.

To put the matter a different way, the question is how to take seriously the need to accept the perspective of a participant in a practice while still maintaining a sufficient distance to be able to criticize the practice (and the participants). In social theory (or perhaps, more accurately "social sciences meta-theory"), this has led to an ongoing debate regarding whether an attempt to "explain each culture or society in its own terms . . . rules out an account which shows them up as wrong, confused or deluded."[39] Someone might argue: if you claim to understand the perspective of the believing participant of a particular practice, but you think the practice is irrational and cruel, then you have not really understood or properly incorporated the perspective of the believer, because that is not how it looks to her.[40] An additional complication, one whose implications are hard to tease out, is that in the social sciences one must consider the role of an internal point of view both in (1) the evaluation of data gathered, and in (2) the gathering of the data to be evaluated.[41] This additional point is unclear in its implications because it ties into the debate on what it would mean to "gather evidence" for a general theory of law, and what kind of evidence one would want, a debate alluded to earlier in this book (in Ch. 2).

One attempt at a defensible middle position between external points of view and fully committed internal points of view was articulated by Joseph Raz, in a position called "statements from a point of view" or

---

[38] An analysis similar to what follows, though in greater detail, was offered in H. Hamner Hill, "H.L.A. Hart's Hermeneutic Positivism: On Some Methodological Difficulties in *The Concept of Law*", 3 *Canadian Journal of Law and Jurisprudence* 113 (January 1990).

[39] Charles Taylor, *Philosophy and the Human Sciences* (Cambridge University Press, Cambridge, 1985), p. 123. Taylor defends the view that one can have an "interpretive" or *"verstehen"* approach while still retaining the ability to criticize that which is being explained.

[40] This position, derived from Peter Winch and Jürgen Habermas, is well summarized in Hill, "H.L.A. Hart's Hermeneutic Positivism", at 116–117.

[41] Hill, "H.L.A. Hart's Hermeneutic Positivism", at 123–125.

"detached normative statements".[42] These are statements which accept a particular normative position for the purpose of making a limited claim, but without endorsing that normative position. Thus, one can tell a vegetarian friend at a restaurant, "given your beliefs, you should not order that dish", even though the speaker is not a vegetarian. In a similar way, " [l]egal scholars—and this includes ordinary practising lawyers—can use normative language when describing the law and make legal statements without thereby endorsing the law's moral authority."[43] A lawyer can say to a client: if you accept the law as valid (as imposing moral obligations), then you should do X or should avoid doing Y. Whether Hart's analysis, with or without the help of Raz's addition, can maintain its precarious middle position is a difficult and important question.

A related problem for legal positivism (only partly connected with "internal aspects") is whether it is in fact possible to have a legal theory which is "purely descriptive"—and if "descriptive" is too strong a term, at least morally neutral. While legal positivism has always insisted that it aims to describe "law as it is" rather than "law as it ought to be", contemporary legal positivists have noted that the construction of theory inevitably involves elements of evaluation and selection, and is in that sense not purely "descriptive". However, legal positivists argue the forms of selection and evaluation involved go to judgments of "importance" and not to moral evaluation.[44] The alternative argument, associated with Stephen Perry and Ronald Dworkin, is that legal theory ineluctably involves moral evaluation, and the only question is whether the choices are made on the surface (and argued for) or are made tacitly (and without justification).[45]

OPEN TEXTURE

The problem of gaps in the law has been known for a long time. Aristotle wrote:

"When the law speaks universally, then, and a case arises on it which is not covered by the universal statement, then it is right, when the legislator fails us and has erred by over simplicity, to correct the omission—to say what the legislator himself would have said had he been present, and would have put into his law if he had known."[46]

---

[42] See Raz, *The Authority of Law*, pp. 153–157; see also Hart, "Introduction", pp. 14–15.
[43] Raz, *The Authority of Law*, p. 156.
[44] See, *e.g.* Julie Dickson, *Evaluation and Legal Theory* (Hart Publishing, Oxford, 2001).
[45] See, *e.g.* Stephen R. Perry, "Interpretation and Methodology in Legal Theory", in *Law and Interpretation* (A. Marmor ed., Clarendon Press, Oxford, 1995), pp. 97–135. Ronald Dworkin's work is discussed at length in Ch. 7.
[46] Aristotle, *Nicomachean Ethics*, Book V, 10: 1137b, in *The Complete Works of Aristotle*, Vol. 2 (J. Barnes ed., Princeton University Press, Princeton, 1984), p. 1796.

There are a number of different ways in which legal rules might fail to cover (unusual) factual situations that arise. Hart introduced the idea of "open texture" to discuss one such way.[47] If the legislators introduce a rule to deal with a particular set of circumstances, how is a judge to apply the rule to an entirely different type of situation? Hart's example is the rule, "No vehicles in the park", introduced to remove automobiles from the area, but then asking whether that rule should apply to motorcycles or roller skates or other objects which may or may not be "vehicles". Hart argued that with all general rules, there will be a "core of certainty"—central cases where the application is clear—and a "penumbra of doubt", where the application of the rule is uncertain.[48]

Part of the argument is that legislative purpose is incomplete or imprecise: the legislators have not considered all possible situations, so that legislative intent, even if clearly known, will not answer all possible problems in applying rules. Another part of the argument is that language is imprecise: there will he many occasions when it will be uncertain whether a general term (e.g. "vehicle") applies to the particular object in question (e.g. roller skates).

From these premises, Hart concluded that judges inevitably must use their discretion to make new law, on occasions where the legal rules have "open texture". He also noted that judicial lawmaking at the margins was a good thing, giving needed flexibility to the application of legal rules.[49]

Upon reflection, it is not a surprising conclusion that language is generally clear, but there are occasions when it is not. How to obey or comply with an order or request is usually obvious, but there are times when circumstances make the matter uncertain. A directive that may seem straightforward in one set of circumstances may seem confused or absurd when applied after a significant change of circumstances. There are aspects of the "open texture" debate that derive from the nature of language, aspects that derive from the nature of rules and rule-following, and aspects that derive from suggestions about the best way to construct a system for applying rules.[50]

---

[47] Hart, *The Concept of Law*, pp. 123–136. Hart's concept was related to and derived from an idea in Friedrich Waismann's philosophy of language. I discuss the connections and differences in greater detail in Bix, *Law, Language, and Legal Determinacy*, pp. 7–25.

[48] Hart, *The Concept of Law*, p. 123. The idea and image of a core of certainty surrounded by a penumbra of doubt might trace back either to the American judge and legal commentator Oliver Wendell Holmes, Jr., see, *e.g.* Oliver Wendell Holmes, Jr., *The Common Law* (M. D. Howe ed., Little Brown, Boston, 1963), p. 101 (originally published in 1881); Thomas C. Grey, "Molecular Motions: The Holmesian Judge in Theory and Practice", 37 *William & Mary Law Review* 19 at 34 and n.54 (1995); or to the British philosopher Bertrand Russell, see Bertrand Russell, "Vagueness", in *Collected Papers of Bertrand Russell*, Vol. 9 (J. Slated ed., Unwin Hyman, London, 1988), pp. 147–154.

[49] Hart, *The Concept of Law*, pp. 129–131.

[50] See Bix, *Law, Language and Legal Determinacy*, pp. 22–25.

Hart's discussion derives from concerns about the ability of rules to guide behaviour, and also about the need for, and advantages of, judicial lawmaking at the margins. The same set of considerations raises other problems that Hart did not consider in comparable length: for example, problems about the nature of legislative intention and how it can be discovered or derived, and problems about when it is legitimate for a judge to interpret a rule contrary to the rule's clear meaning or contrary to legislative intentions. For a variety of reasons, English jurisprudence (at least at the time Hart was writing) was not as focused on the legitimacy of judicial action as American jurisprudence has been in recent decades.[51]

In many ways, Hart's discussion of "open texture" was preliminary: there is much work that still must be done in disentangling arguments based on the nature of language and arguments based on the nature of rules, and Hart is probably too quick to conclude immediately from the existence of "open texture" that judges do (or should) have discretion in deciding hard cases.[52] However, Hart's primary purpose in putting forward the notion of "open texture" was to counter arguments from two directions. First, Hart was responding to the American legal realists,[53] some of whom had argued that judicial legislation showed that legal rules never or rarely determined the outcome in legal cases, and that rules were of no importance in understanding the law. Secondly Hart was responding to the natural law theorists[54], who argued that the way judges decided difficult questions showed that there was, contrary to the legal positivists, no conceptual separation between law and morality.[55]

To the point that rules by themselves do not always determine the results of cases, Hart's response was that this is true (and is caused by "open texture"), but that this occurs in only a relatively small number of cases. To the argument that judicial legislation shows the conceptual connection between law and morality, Hart responded that this way of seeing the matter tended to cloud, not clarify, our understanding of law—judges' interstitial legislation may be based in part on moral standards, but it does not follow that those standards are then best seen as having been "in the legal rules" all along.[56] Additionally, much judicial legislation

---

[51] Among the factors that create this more intense focus in the U.S. is the ability and willingness of American courts to invalidate legislation (under federal and state constitutional provisions), the controversial nature of some of those decisions, and the tension between such decisions and the strong democratic ethos in American political thought.

[52] These matters are discussed in greater detail in Bix, *Law, Language and Legal Determinacy,* pp. 7–10, 17–35.

[53] See Hart, *The Concept of Law,* pp. 136–147. American legal realism is discussed in Ch. 17.

[54] Traditional natural law theory is discussed in Ch. 5; on Fuller's natural law theory, more relevant to the critique of Hart's legal positivism, is discussed in Chap. 6.

[55] See, *e.g.* Hart, "Positivism and the Separation of Law and Morals", pp. 606–615; Anthony J. Sebok, "Finding Wittgenstein at the Core of the Rule of Recognition", 52 *SMU Law Review* 75, 84–90 (1999).

[56] See Hart, "Positivism and the Separation of Law and Morals", pp. 614–615.

is based on forwarding the purposes of legislation: purposes which can as easily be morally neutral or evil as virtuous.

THE MINIMUM CONTENT OF NATURAL LAW

Some commentators have made a great deal of Hart's discussion of "the minimum content of natural law",[57] seeing it as a great concession that undermines all that Hart had tried to claim earlier regarding the separation of law and morality. This view, I would argue, is a clear misunderstanding of Hart's discussion, though it may be that a certain lack of clarity in the text invites the mis-reading.

The text occurs in the context of a general discussion of the ways that law and morality can be said to overlap (for example, the way that conventional moral beliefs obviously affect the way that the law develops and the fact that ideas about how law and society ought to be affect how statutes—in particular, ambiguous statutes—are interpreted[58]), in order to show what is *not* claimed by the assertion that there is no necessary connection between law and morality (or, to put the point a different way, what is not excluded by the claim). The "minimum content of natural law" is just one more exploration along this borderline, a border that Hart believes separates legal positivism from natural law theory.

The particular argument is that there are certain contingent facts of the human situation in this century (and all past centuries): that we are all mortal and vulnerable, that resources are limited, and that we are all dependent to some extent on other people. These facts are contingent, in that it is not impossible (however unlikely it may be) that future scientific developments might change these facts (for example, some series of discoveries might make us physically invulnerable). However, given these facts, certain consequences are likely to follow. Among these, Hart speculated, is that any legal or moral[59] system that did not offer certain minimal protections (against murder, serious assault and theft) to at least a significant minority of the population would not—could not—survive for very long.

This is not a conceptual point, merely a prediction, and a reasonable one. Even if one were to take it as a concession to the natural law theorists, it is a trivial one, for two reasons. First, we are not likely ever to come across such a society; and if we did find a society which flouted these minimal requirements and survived, the correct response would be to

---

[57] Hart, *The Concept of Law*, pp. 195–200.
[58] *ibid.* at pp. 203–212.
[59] Here, Hart meant "moral" in the sense of the conventional morality which is accepted within a society (or a sub-culture), restrains the actions of its members, and is enforced by social sanctions of various kinds.

change Hart's series of criteria, not to conclude that either legal positivism or natural law theory had been proven wrong. Secondly this "minimum content" test does not reflect the usual lines of disagreement between legal positivists and natural law theorists. Advocates of natural law theory argue for a moral test for legal validity that sets far higher standards, not just the Hobbesian moral minimum that Hart discussed.[60] Most natural law theorists would want the right to declare as "not law" legal systems, or certain rules of legal systems, that would otherwise easily pass the minimal standards of Hart's discussion.

INCLUSIVE VERSUS EXCLUSIVE LEGAL POSITIVISM

In contemporary English-language legal positivism, much recent discussion has been on an internal debate between "inclusive legal positivism" (also sometimes called "soft" or "incorporationist" legal positivism) and "exclusive legal positivism" (also known as "hard" legal positivism). The debate between the two camps involves a difference in interpreting or elaborating one central point of legal positivism: that there is no *necessary* or "conceptual" connection between law and morality.

Exclusive legal positivism interprets or elaborates this assertion to mean that moral criteria can be neither sufficient nor necessary conditions for the legal status of a norm. In different terms: exclusive legal positivism states that "the existence and content of every law is fully determined by social sources."[61] Inclusive legal positivism, which has a number of prominent advocates,[62] interprets the separation of law and morality differently, arguing that while there is no *necessary* moral content to a legal rule (or a legal system), a particular legal system may, by conventional rule, make moral criteria necessary or sufficient for validity *in that system*.

The strongest argument for inclusive legal positivism seems to be its fit with the way both legal officials and legal texts talk about the law. Morality seems to be a *sufficient* grounds for the legal status of a norm in

---

[60] Hart, "The Separation of Law and Morality", p. 623.
[61] Raz, *The Authority of Law*, p. 46.
[62] Early advocates of inclusive legal positivism include Philip Soper, "Legal Theory and the Obligation of a Judge: The Hart/Dworkin Dispute", 75 *Michigan Law Review* 473 (1977); Jules L. Coleman, "Negative and Positive Positivism", 11 *Journal of Legal Studies* 139 (1982), reprinted in Coleman, *Market, Morals and the Law* (Cambridge University Press, Cambridge. 1988), pp 3–27; David Lyons, *Ethics and the Rule of Law* (Cambridge University Press, Cambridge, 1984); MacCormick, *Legal Reasoning and Legal Theory*. Hart later seemed to adopt or affirm inclusive legal positivism as the best reading of his own position. See Hart, "Postscript", pp. 250–254. Important later works include W.J. Waluchow, *Inclusive Legal Positivism* (Clarendon Press, Oxford, 1994); and Jules L. Coleman, *The Practice of Principle* (Oxford University Press, Oxford, 2001).

many common law cases (and decisions in which legal principles play a large role[63]), where a legal norm is justified only or primarily on the basis that morality requires it.[64] The more familiar example for inclusive legal positivism is not about *sufficient* grounds for legal validity, but *necessary* grounds: when constitution-based judicial review of legislation (*e.g.* in the United States) requires or authorizes the invalidation of legislation that runs afoul of moral standards codified in the constitution (*e.g.* regarding equality, due process, or humane punishment), this appears to make moral merit a necessary, but not sufficient, basis for legal validity.

Additionally, the inclusive view allows theorists to accept many of Dworkin's criticisms of legal positivism (see Ch. 7) without abandoning what these same theorists consider the core tenets of legal positivism (law's grounding in social facts and conventions). Inclusive legal positivism accepts that moral terms can be part of the necessary or sufficient criteria for legal validity in a legal system, but insist that the use of moral criteria is *contingent*—and derived from the choices or actions of particular legal officials—rather than part of the nature of law (and thus present in *all* legal systems).

The most prominent argument for exclusive legal positivism is offered by Joseph Raz, and is based on an asserted relationship between law and authority. Raz's approach to law is not easily summarized in a few sentences (or even a few dozen pages), but a short outline will be attempted. First, Raz offers the "social thesis" as the core of legal positivism: that what is law and what is not are matters of social fact (Raz favours a strong version of the social thesis that he dubs the "sources thesis"—that the existence and content of every law are fully determined by social sources).[65] This restatement of the legal positivist's separation between law and morality is tied to, and supported by, a distinction between deliberating as part of the process of coming to a decision, and the execution of the decision once made.[66] When judges are merely applying decisions already reached (by the legislature or by prior court decisions), they are applying existing law (determining what the law *is*); when judges consider moral

---

[63] *Compare* Ronald Dworkin, *Taking Rights Seriously* (Harvard University Press, Cambridge, Mass., 1977), pp. 14–45.

[64] See also Tony Honoré, "The Necessary Connection Between Law and Morality", 22 *Oxford Journal of Legal Studies* 489 at 494 (2002) ("'[T]he positive law of societies with legal systems . . . makes arguments addressed to critical morality admissible in the interpretation and application of law.").

[65] See Raz, *The Authority of Law*, pp. 37–52.

[66] See Raz, *Ethics in the Public Domain*, pp. 190–192. While some commentators have interpreted the "sources thesis" and similar views as being about certainty and predictability in the content of law, Raz himself insists: "The pursuit of certainty is no part of the sources thesis. Finality is." Joseph Raz, "Postema on Law's Autonomy and Public Practical Reasons: A Critical Comment", 4 *Legal Theory* 1 at 13 (1998). And by "finality", Raz did not mean "nonrevisability", but only that law should be seen as having settled (at least for the moment) issues on which it speaks. *Ibid.* at pp. 13–14 and n. 30.

factors in the creating a new rule, or in considering possible changes to an existing rule, that is determining what the law *should be*. This view takes no position on whether it is a good thing or a bad thing that judges legislate, or whether they should do so more often or less often than they currently do.[67] The point rather is that it is both analytically clearer, and in line with the way we usually think and talk about the law, to maintain a distinction between applying the law and making new law, between execution and deliberation. This approach allows Raz to say that moral reasoning has no part in stating "what the law is", but it often does (and probably should) have a part in saying how judges should decide cases "according to law".[68]

Secondly, it is in the nature of law (of a legal system) that it has or claims legitimate authority,[69] This means that legal rules purport to be "exclusionary reasons": "reasons to exclude a consideration from being the ground for a[ ] decision".[70] Raz's analysis ties together law, authority and practical reasoning. For Raz, the connection between authority and practical reasoning is a general one: authorities and authoritative reasons affect our moral deliberations; where there is an authority (which we recognise as such), our decision is based at least in part on what the authority (whether that authority is the law, a sacred text, a religious leader, an army commander, etc.) states we should do; we incorporate the authority's weighing of the relevant factors rather than simply weighing all the relevant considerations for ourselves. In Raz's terms:

"The authority's directives become our reasons. While the acceptance of the authority is based on belief that its directives are well-founded in reason, they are understood to yield the benefits they are meant to bring only if we do rely on them rather than on our own independent judgment of the merits of each case to which they apply."[71]

---

[67] For the position that Raz's strong separation thesis should be adopted, not as a philosophical analysis of the nature of law, of the way law always is, but rather as a prescription for how judicial decisions specifically and governments more generally *ought* to operate, see Tom D. Campbell, *The Legal Theory of Ethical Positivism* (Aldershot, Dartmouth, 1996).

[68] See Raz, "Postema on Law's Autonomy and Public Practical Reasons", pp. 4–6. Raz points out, by way of example, that judges have recourse to moral reasoning when they decide, often tacitly, that an existing legal rule is not so unjust that it should be overturned. Obviously, when judges decide, expressly, that the legal rule is so unjust that it should be overturned, the role of morality in reaching this legal decision is clearer. See *ibid.* at p. 4.

[69] See Raz, *Ethics in the Public Domain*, pp. 194–221.

[70] Joseph Raz, "Facing Up", 62 *Southern California Law Review* 1153 at 1158 (1989).

[71] Joseph Raz, *Practical Reason and Norms* (2nd ed., Princeton University Press, Princeton, 1990), p. 193. The phrase "the benefits they are meant to bring" refers to the argument that one treats a source as authoritative if in following the directives of that source one is more likely to get things right than if one deliberated and decided for oneself. See *ibid.*

Raz's view of authority is controversial; for criticisms, see, *e.g.* Stephen Lukes, "Perspectives on Authority", in *Authority* (J. Raz ed., New York University Press, New York, 1990), pp. 203–217; Ronald Dworkin, "Thirty Years On" (book review), 114 *Harvard Law Review* 1655 at 1671–1676 (2002).

For Raz, those subject to an authority "can benefit by its decisions only if they can establish their existence and content in ways which do not depend on raising the very same issues which the authority is there to settle."[72] In the context of law, this means that with legal rules, which are meant to make authoritative decisions on matters on which citizens would otherwise be subject to various moral (and prudential) reasons for action, we must be able to ascertain their content without recourse to further moral evaluation. Following this analysis, inclusive legal positivism must fail, it is argued, because it is inconsistent with a core aspect of law, the legal system's purporting to be a justified practical authority.[73]

The debate between inclusive and exclusive legal positivism remains hotly disputed, as does the argument over whether either offers a position fully defensible against contemporary critics of legal positivism.[74]

NON-NORMATIVE APPROACHES

In his book *Norm and Nature*,[75] Roger Shiner argued that legal positivism inevitably develops, as it becomes more sophisticated and responds to criticisms, towards positions close to those of natural law theory (he also argued that, in turn, natural law theory in its more sophisticated forms, develops in the direction of legal positivism). The basis of that argument can be seen in outline from issues discussed above. For example, an empirically-based theory of law like John Austin's (in Shiner's terminology, an example of "simple positivism") has a number of obvious defects, which appear to be remedied in H.L.A. Hart's theory (in Shiner's terms, an example of "sophisticated positivism"), with its use of an "internal point of view". However, as discussed earlier in this section, we are already approaching natural law theory, in that the line seems quite thin between viewing law through the perspective of citizens who accept the law as creating (prima facie moral) obligations (Hart's proposed "internal point

---

[72] Raz, *Ethics in the Public Domain*, p. 219.

[73] Another argument that has been offered for exclusive legal positivism derives from a claim about the nature of rules. Scott Shapiro has emphasized that it is in the nature of rules, including legal rules, that they make a difference in our practical reasoning, and that inclusive rules of recognition would fail to make a difference in this way, as they would merely point us towards moral evaluations already applicable to our choices. Scott J. Shapiro, "On Hart's Way Out", 4 *Legal Theory* 469 (1998).

[74] For a detailed discussion of the debates within legal positivism, and methodological issues, see Jules Coleman ed., *Hart's Postscript* (Oxford University Press, Oxford, 2001); see also, Dworkin, "Thirty Years On" (raising sharp criticisms of both inclusive and exclusive legal positivism). In Brian Bix, "Patrolling the Boundaries: Inclusive Legal Positivism and the Nature of Jurisprudential Debate", 12 *Canadian Journal of Law & Jurisprudence* 17 (1999), I give a moderately skeptical overview of some of these debates within legal positivism.

[75] Roger Shiner, *Norm and Nature* (Clarendon Press, Oxford, 1992).

of view"), and constructing one's theory around the conditions when law *in fact* imposes valid (prima facie) moral obligations.

In a review of *Norm and Nature*,[76] Frederick Schauer agreed with Shiner's basic analysis, but held that Shiner's view of "sophisticated legal positivism" was not the inevitable path that this approach to law need take. Schauer offered as an alternative an empirical, non-hermeneutic version of legal positivism, arguing that in relation to the Hartian version of legal positivism discussed above, his alternative was as tenable, but without the dangers of sliding into natural law theory In other words, Schauer was offering a kind of "return to Austin".[77]

Schauer's basic argument is that one can construct a version of the "internal point of view", where citizens' actions in conformity with the law, and officials' enforcement of the law, are all explained adequately on prudential terms (for example, the citizens fearing legal sanctions, and the officials fearing reprimand or removal from office, and hoping for appointment to a higher office.)[78] The point of this transformed "internal point of view" is that the aspect of "normativity" (the fact that citizens or officials accept the law as creating moral obligations, as offering (additional) reasons to act in compliance with what the law prescribes) is removed, and that it is that aspect of sophisticated legal positivism that sends it sliding towards natural law theory.[79]

We are then returned to Hart (and his many and various followers) to discover why a theory based on such a "bad man's view of the law"[80] is considered inadequate. Hart's answer would appear to be: because it fails to take into account the perspective of people who accept the law, those who follow its prescriptions for non-prudential reasons.[81] One argument is that this is the "central" or "focal" sense of law, which any theory should try to explain, while obeying the law for fear or favour is a "lesser" or "attenuated" sense of law.[82] Schauer's response is that focusing one's theory on citizens or officials who believe that law imposes moral obligations is dubious when theorists themselves are far from united on law's moral

---

[76] Frederick Schauer, "Critical Notice" (reviewing R. Shiner, *Norm and Nature* (1992)), 24 *Canadian Journal of Philosophy* 495 (1994).
[77] See Frederick Schauer, "Positivism Through Thick and Thin", in *Analyzing Law* (B. Bix ed., Clarendon Press, Oxford, 1988).
[78] Schauer, "Critical Notice", pp. 500–501.
[79] *ibid.* at pp. 498–501.
[80] See Holmes, "The Path of the Law", pp. 460–461.
[81] Hart was not entirely clear on whether prudential interests could be a sufficient basis for an "internal point of view". See Hart, *The Concept of Law*, p. 203 (including within an internal view those who accept the law because of "calculations of long-term interest").
[82] See Finnis, *Natural Law and Natural Rights*, pp. 6–18. One could also argue that those who accept the law (on non-prudential grounds) constitute a majority (or at least a significant minority) of the population. This, however, is an empirical claim, with little evidence available either in support or in opposition. See Schauer, "Critical Notice", p. 502.

status, with a number of legal positivists like Joseph Raz arguing strongly against the proposition that law creates prima facie moral obligations (see Ch. 16). The better approach, Schauer argues, is to leave the question completely open at the definitional level, and argue the issue out in the open.[83]

As against the conventional view that Hart's use of a (quasi-)hermeneutic approach in legal theory constituted a significant advance in legal positivism in particular and legal theory in general, Schauer's analysis may provide a radical challenge.

Suggested Further Readings

AUSTIN

John Austin, *Lectures on Jurisprudence, or The Philosophy of the Positive Law* (4th ed., R. Campbell ed., John Murray, London, 1879) (Thoemme Press reprint, Bristol, 2002).
—, *The Province of Jurisprudence Determined* (W. E. Rumble ed., Cambridge University Press, Cambridge, 1995).
Brian Bix, "John Austin", in E. N. Zalta ed., *Stanford Encyclopedia of Philosophy*, http://plato.stanford.edu (2001).
W.L. Morison, *John Austin* (Stanford University Press, Stanford, 1982).

HART

Michael Bayles, *Hart's Legal Philosophy: An Examination* (Kluwer Academic Publishers, Dordrecht, 1992).
P.M.S. Hacker and Joseph Raz ed., *Law, Morality, and Society: Essays in Honour of H.L.A. Hart* (Clarendon Press, Oxford, 1977).
H.L.A. Hart, *The Concept of Law* (2nd ed., P.A. Bulloch and J. Raz eds, Clarendon Press, Oxford, 1994) (the second edition includes a "Postscript", which is primarily a reply to Ronald Dworkin).
—, *Essays in Jurisprudence and Philosophy* (Clarendon Press, Oxford, 1983).
—, "Positivism and the Separation of Law and Morals", 71 *Harvard Law Review* 593 (1958).
Neil MacCormick, *H.L.A. Hart* (Stanford University Press, Stanford, 1981).

LEGAL POSITIVISM

Brian Bix, "Legal Positivism" in *Blackwell Guide to Philosophy of Law and Legal Theory* (forthcoming, M. P. Golding and W. A. Edmundson eds, Blackwell, Oxford, 2004).

---

[83] Schauer, "Critical Notice", p. 503; Schauer, "Positivism Through Thick and Thin", pp. 73–78.

Jules L. Coleman and Brian Leiter, "Legal Positivism", in *A Companion to the Philosophy of Law and Legal Theory* (D. Patterson ed., Blackwell, Oxford, 1996), pp. 241–260.

Robert P. George ed., *The Autonomy of Law: Essays on Legal Positivism* (Clarendon Press, Oxford, 1996) (includes essays by Joseph Raz, Neil MacCormick, John Finnis, Frederick Schauer, Jules Coleman, and Philip Soper).

Leslie Green, "Legal Positivism", in E. N. Zalta ed., *Stanford Encyclopedia of Philosophy*, http://plato.stanford.edu (2003).

Matthew Kramer, *In Defense of Legal Positivism: Law Without Trimmings* (Oxford University Press, Oxford, 1999).

David Lyons, *Moral Aspects of Legal Theory* (Cambridge University Press, Cambridge, 1993).

Joseph Raz, *The Authority of Law* (Clarendon Press, Oxford, 1979).

—, *Ethics in the Public Domain* (Clarendon Press, Oxford, 1994).

INCLUSIVE VERSUS EXCLUSIVE LEGAL POSITIVISM

Jules Coleman ed., *Hart's Postscript: Essays on the Postscript to the Concept of Law* (Oxford University Press, Oxford, 2001) (contributors include Joseph Raz, Jules Coleman, Stephen Perry and Jeremy Waldron).

Kenneth Einar Himma, "Inclusive Legal Positivism", in *The Oxford Handbook of Jurisprudence and Philosophy of Law* (J. Coleman and S. Shapiro eds, K. E. Himma. assoc. ed., Oxford University Press, Oxford, 2002), pp. 125–165.

Andrei Marmor, "Exclusive Legal Positivism," in *The Oxford Handbook of Jurisprudence and Philosophy of Law* (J. Coleman and S. Shapiro eds, K. E. Himma. assoc. ed., Oxford University Press, Oxford, 2002), pp. 104–124.

Chapter Four

Hans Kelsen's Pure Theory of Law

Hans Kelsen (1881–1973) was a prolific and influential Austrian legal theorist, who spent the last decades of a long, productive life in the United
States, having escaped Europe at the time of Hitler's rise to power. Kelsen's
work was important in international law as well as jurisprudence, and he
was a central figure in the drafting of the Austrian constitution after the
First World War.

Over the course of four decades of jurisprudential writing, Kelsen
published dozens of books and articles,[1] with his position on various
matters changing in subtle but important ways.[2] This presents a difficulty
for any attempted summary of Kelsen's view, a task already complicated
by the sophistication of Kelsen's theory and the unfamiliarity (to
American and English audiences at least) of the philosophical traditions
within which Kelsen was working, in particular, neo-Kantianism, a school
of thought that attempted to apply Immanuel Kant's ideas more broadly
to questions of social and ethical theory.[3]

---

[1] "Dozens" is actually a bit of an understatement. By one count, Kelsen published 387 separate works (approximately 100 of which dealt exclusively with legal theory). Of those 387
works, 18 books and 121 articles are available in English. Michael Hartney, "Appendix:
Bibliography of Kelsen's Publications in English", in Hans Kelsen, *General Theory of Norms*
(M. Hartney, trans. and ed., Clarendon Press, Oxford, 1991), pp. 440–454.

[2] Especially if one takes into account Kelsen's very last writings, which were unpublished
during his lifetime, some of his changes in ideas and attitude were actually quite dra-
matic, at times appearing to support just the set of views he had most vigorously opposed
60 years earlier. See Stanley L. Paulson, "Kelsen's Legal Theory: The Final Round", 12
Oxford Journal of Legal Studies 265 at 265–266 (1992). On the different "phases" of Kelsen's
work, see Hartney, "Introduction", in Kelsen, *General Theory of Norms*, pp. xx–liii; Stanley
L. Paulson, "Towards a Periodization of the Pure Theory of Law", in *Hans Kelsen's Legal
Theory* (L. Gianformaggio ed., G. Giappichelli, Torino, 1990), pp. 11–47.

[3] Because Kelsen wrote much of his important work in German (and until recently was
poorly served by his English translators) and because he wrote out of a different philosophical tradition (a continental tradition strongly influenced by Kant), his work has not
been as central to the development of English-language legal theory as might have been
warranted (in many countries, Kelsen is far better known and far more influential than
Hart). For the above reasons, I used Hart rather than Kelsen to introduce the topic of
modern legal positivism, even though most of Kelsen's works were published prior to the
publication of Hart's most important works.

The picture of Kelsen's theory presented will attempt to contain the general themes that continued throughout most of his writings, while there will be little attention paid to the ways in which Kelsen's view changed. Inevitably, the portrayal will be a simplification relative both to the full complexity of Kelsen's theory and to its transformations over time.

THE PURE THEORY OF LAW

Kelsen referred to his theory as "*reine Rechtslehre*", a "pure theory of law". In Kelsen's words, the theory was "pure" "because it only describes the law and attempts to eliminate from the object of this description everything that is not strictly 'law'".[4] Moral judgments, political biases, and sociological conclusions were all to be pushed aside as improper for a "scientific" description of the social institution of law.[5]

Chapter 3 noted the importance of the normative aspect of law for H.L.A. Hart's legal theory (it is central to the "internal aspect of rules", which in turn is central to Hart's theory and how it differs from empirical theories like that of John Austin). Within Kelsen's theory, the normativity of law is, if anything, an even more central and dominating factor. One could even say, with only slight exaggeration, that explaining the normative nature of law is the *sole* purpose of Kelsen's theory (as contrasted, say, with Hart, who is also interested in the difference between primary and secondary rules, the difference between duty-imposing and power-conferring rules, the open texture of rules, and so on). Most of what is puzzling to readers of Kelsen's legal theory can be better understood if one keeps in mind the theory's focus on normativity.

There are two basic starting points for understanding Kelsen's approach to legal theory. First, normative claims—arguments for how one ought to act or for how things ought to be—can be grounded only on (justified by) other normative claims.[6] This is the argument, usually attributed to David Hume, that one cannot derive a normative conclusion from purely factual premises: "one cannot derive an 'ought' from an 'is'". In other words, a purely factual description of a situation will never be sufficient, by itself, to justify a conclusion that something ought (morally) to be

---

[4] Hans Kelsen, *The Pure Theory of Law* (M. Knight, trans., University of California Press, California, 1967), p. 1.
[5] One should not over-read Kelsen's talks about a "science" of law. Here, "science" is the translation of the German *Wissenschaft*, whose meaning and application generally is broader than the English "science". For example, it is usual and uncontroversial to use the term *Wissenschaft* even when referring to literary theory.
[6] See Kelsen, *The Pure Theory of Law*, pp. 4–10.

done. One can only justify such a conclusion by first accepting or inserting a moral premise.[7]

Secondly, such lines of justification must necessarily come to an end at some point.[8] In day-to-day discussions each (normative) argument put forward is based on (justified by) some more general or more basic argument. We tend to forget that if we look closely enough at the chain of arguments in favour of a particular position, we will eventually come to an argument that is not justified by some other argument, and the validity of this final argument can only be based on its being tacitly or explicitly accepted (accepted "on faith", as it were).

Consider the following example. A religious person tells you that it is wrong to commit adultery. When you ask her why, she says, "because that is what is said in the Bible. "Being in an obstinate mood, you say "so what?", to which her response is that the Bible is the word of God. To a second "so what?", her patient response would be that we should all do as God tells us to do. However, if at this point, you ask why that is so, you are likely to get no more than a puzzled look. This line of argument has come to an end; either one accepts that one ought to do what God says or one does not.[9] And there is a sense in which the foundational argument, "we ought to do what God says", is entailed by or implied by the religious person's initial assertion that "one should not commit adultery". (This is not to say that one could not reach the same normative conclusion using other starting points, but only that for this particular person, *this* conclusion derives from or implies *that* starting point.)

Kelsen's argument was that there is a foundational argument implied ("presupposed") by legal statements just as there is a foundational argument implied by religious statements. In more technical language, Kelsen applied a "neo-Kantian" approach to legal theory, an approach based on aspects of Kant's theory of knowledge, in particular Kant's Transcendental Argument.[10]

---

[7] Which is not to say that the moral premise will not be "obvious" or something "everyone agrees with".

There are some philosophers who contest the general view that one cannot derive an "ought" proposition from an 'is' proposition. That is a complicated debate; for present purposes, one need note only that Kelsen's approach to law is grounded on the more conventional view that such a derivation is not possible.

[8] See Kelsen, *The Pure Theory of Law*, pp. 193–195.

[9] That the argument could be stretched a step or two further does not alter the basic analysis. For example, the religious person could say, "one ought to do what God says because He created humanity and all the world" with the implied claim that one ought to obey whoever (whatever) created us. However, there is no particular reason why everyone must accept that normative position.

[10] See, *e.g.* Kelsen, *The Pure Theory of Law*, pp. 201–205; Stanley L. Paulson, "The Neo-Kantian Dimension of Kelsen's Pure Theory of Law", 12 *Oxford Journal of Legal Studies* 311 (1992).

The best way to understand Kelsen's project may be to think of him as asking: "what follows from the fact that someone treats legal rules as valid norms?"[11] Like many important philosophers, Kelsen tried to show us what is interesting or paradoxical about matters which seem to us ordinary and unremarkable. For Kelsen, the ordinary and unremarkable fact to be considered is that while looking at a simple collection of actions, we sometimes see those actions as normative. Whenever one looks at people putting slips of paper into a box, and sees "voting"; or looks at a group of people raising and lowering their hands in various sequences, and sees "the passage of valid legislation", this translates empirical actions into normative meanings.[12] The translation is clearer on the occasions when someone says that since those certain actions have been done (the group of people raising and lowering their hands), one now "ought" to do something (*e.g.* pay a certain tax). The border between "is" and "ought" has been crossed, and the question is: what can be derived from that?

Here we need to return to the idea of the normative chain of justification. One starts with some simple legal-normative statement: for example, "one cannot park here (it is illegal to do so)". If the person making this statement was asked why it was so, she would probably note that this regulation was validly promulgated by some city council, judge, or administrator. If the questioner pushes further, the chain could be followed back: *e.g.* that the administrator was authorized to act in this area by an act of the legislature, and the act of the legislature was passed according to the procedures set down in the constitution.[13] Things get slightly trickier when one gets to the constitution itself. The document might itself have been a modification of an earlier basic law, or it might have been drawn up under the authorization of an earlier basic law. However, again, we will eventually come to a point either so foundational or so early in the society's legal history that one cannot go any further back, and no further justification can be offered.

Following the whole chain through then leads to the following implication: to assert the (normative) validity of the individual legal rule ("one cannot park on this street") is implicitly to affirm the validity of the foun-

---

[11] See Paulson, "The Neo-Kantian Dimension of Kelsen's Pure Theory of Law", p. 324.

[12] See, *e.g.* Hans Kelsen, *Introduction to the Problems of Legal Theory* (B.L. Paulson and S.L. Paulson, trans., Clarendon Press, Oxford, 1992), pp. 6–12. The notion that things are not "normative in themselves", but have normative meanings imposed upon them, can have radical implications. Compare the parallel comment by the philosopher Friedrich Nietzsche: "There are no moral phenomena at all, but only a moral interpretation of phenomena." Friedrich Nietzsche, *Beyond Good and Evil* (W. Kaufmann, trans., Vintage Books, New York, 1966), ("Epigrams and Interludes", No. 108), p. 85.

[13] There are complications for Kelsen's argument when an official acts within her area of authorization, but acts in an unauthorized (illegal) way. See, *e.g.* Stanley L. Paulson, "Material and Formal Authorisation in Kelsen's Pure Theory", 39 *Cambridge Law Journal* 172 (1980).

dational link of the chain (*e.g.* "one ought to do whatever Parliament orders"), for the same reason that affirming an individual religious belief implicitly affirms the foundational norm of the religion ("one ought to do whatever God commands"). To put the matter differently, the affirmation of the foundational norm is "presupposed" by any express or implied affirmation of individual legal rules. This affirmation of the foundational norm of a legal system ("one ought to do whatever is authorized by the historically first constitution"), is what Kelsen calls the "*Grundnorm*" or "Basic Norm".[14]

REDUCTION AND LEGAL THEORY

Hans Kelsen believed that all legal norms could and should be understood in terms of an authorization to an official to impose sanctions: if A (citizen) does X (wrong action), then B (an official) is authorized to impose Y (a sanction).[15]

Thus, Kelsen would want us to translate "you shall not murder", into the following instruction to an official: if any citizen murders, you (the official) have the authority to impose a sanction upon that person. As the instruction to the official is only an authorization, one might wonder how Kelsen can explain the fact that officials are *bound* to impose sanctions— it is not usually just a matter within their discretion. Kelsen would say that where officials have an obligation to act, this only means that there is another norm, instructing a higher official to the effect: "if the lower official does not impose a sanction in this situation, you are authorized to impose a sanction on that official"—and so it would go up the hierarchy.

This is a slightly awkward formalization of criminal laws as it stands, but its awkwardness becomes far greater when we try to put civil laws, in particular laws which confer powers, into the same form. For example, a statute authorizing the formation of wills might read: if A creates a valid will (by following certain procedural and substantive requirements), and then dies, and A's executor refuses to follow the instructions of the will, then B (an official) has the authority to impose a sanction on A's executor.[16]

Reduction is the natural tendency whenever one posits a theory or a model of behaviour. In some ways, it is the essence of the activity. To the

---

[14] See, e.g. Kelsen, *Introduction to the Problems of Legal Theory*, pp. 56–60.

[15] Kelsen's actual terminology is that the official "ought" to impose the sanction. but Kelsen uses the word "ought" broadly in a sense which is best summarized as "authorized to" rather than "should perform". See Hans Kelsen, "On the Basis of Legal Validity", 26 *American Journal of Jurisprudence* 178 at 178–179 n. b (1981) (S. L. Paulson, trans.) (translator's note on Kelsen's use of "bestimmen" and "sollen").

[16] See, e.g. Kelsen, *Pure Theory of Law*, pp. 114–130.

extent that one can discuss a complex social phenomenon, like law, in terms of one or two concepts, the process of theorizing seems to be a success. There is no point in a theory merely replicating the complexity of the phenomena about us. That gives us nothing. An explanation is necessarily a sifting of the important from the unimportant, the essential from the accidental.

There is something satisfying about being able to say something like "law is basically or essentially __" (where the blank might be filled in by "orders backed by threats" or "authorizations to officials to impose sanctions"). To understand the essence of something has always been considered a component of wisdom, so we tend to welcome the opportunity, when a theorist tells us that she has "discovered" what the essence is of law (or government or community or marriage).

On the other hand, simplification is often distortion. The more one tries to re-characterize the variety of experience as though it was homogenous, the more awkward and inaccurate the description will be. All social theorists (economists and anthropologists as well as legal and political theorists) must consider the proper balance between descriptive accuracy and explanatory power. (It is a problem that is particularly significant in understanding the limitations of the law and economics movement, which will be discussed in Ch. 18.) Kelsen's theory lies towards an extreme in reduction: an attempt to reduce all laws to a particular form.[17] However, as H.L.A. Hart pointed out when discussing John Austin's approach to law,[18] while such reductions seem to have the benefit of simplicity, this benefit is largely a surface matter, as the likely consequences of trying to force the various legal norms into a single structure are awkwardness, poor fit, and a risk of misleading the reader.

HART V KELSEN

Perhaps because of the limited dialogue between (or overlap in) H.L.A. Hart scholars and Hans Kelsen scholars, the differences between Hart and Kelsen are often poorly understood. Often, Kelsen is seen an imperfect stopping point between Austin's mistaken views and Hart's solutions (a position that does not stand up long under close examination). One text stated that Hart is merely Kelsen in clearer prose.[19] Even if this is meant

---

[17] Kelsen is neither the first nor the last theorist to make such an attempt. More recently J.W. Harris has attempted to analyze all laws in terms of duties. J.W Harris, *Law and Legal Science* (Clarendon Press, Oxford, 1979).

[18] Hart, *The Concept of Law*, pp. 27–42.

[19] Jeffrie G. Murphy and Jules L. Coleman, *Philosophy of Law* (revised ed., Westview Press, 1990), p. 27.

to be complimentary to Kelsen, it does a disservice to both theorists.[20] This section will briefly discuss some of the things which join and separate the two writers.

There is one question that theorists who focus on the normativity of law—and Hart as well as Kelsen would fit into this category—could be said to be trying to answer: how is a legal system to be distinguished from the orders of gangsters?[21] For Hart, this question led to an investigation of the differences in action and attitude between how we act when we are following a rule and how we act when we are being compelled to do the same action. This in turn led to Hart's discussion of the "internal aspect" of rules and of law, which is basic to his approach to legal theory.

Kelsen's response to the gangster/law question would be simple: those who see the actions of the people in power in a normative way, and thus presuppose the Basic Norm in dealing with official promulgations, see the people in power as legitimate authorities; those who do not see the actions this way will see the people in power as gangsters or their equivalent. In a sense, Kelsen's response is comparable to Hart's: the difference between the commands of valid law and the orders of gangsters is determined by, indeed is constituted by, the attitudes of the citizens or subjects.

Here, we also see how legal positivism links Hart and Kelsen: both analyze the difference between gangsters and legitimate government by focusing on the more or less "neutral" question of citizens' reaction. Hart and Kelsen's positions avoid making moral judgments. They pass by the more obvious answer to the gangster/law question, which would be quickly given by a natural law theorist: that the difference between legitimate leaders and gangsters is that the former act justly and for the common good, and the latter do not.

The differences between Hart and Kelsen are equally interesting and significant. While both Hart and Kelsen emphasized the normative aspect of law in response to and criticism of more reductive/empirical approaches, their notion of the "normative" differed.[22] Hart's view of the normative reduced to certain types of social facts, while Kelsen resisted any reduction of "normative" to facts.[23] While Hart's theory tried to track and explain actual social practices (with labeling of the work as "descriptive sociology", and the careful distinctions—*e.g.* feeling obliged v having an obligation, acting out of habit v following a rule, and the different kinds of rules), Kelsen's theory tended to be more

---

[20] One can find Hart's comments on Kelsen in Hart, *Essays in Jurisprudence and Philosophy*, pp. 286–342. However, one often gets the impression that Hart did not entirely understand Kelsen's work, in part because Kelsen's starting point was so different from the Anglo-American tradition within which Hart wrote.

[21] See Hart, *The Concept of Law*, pp. 6–7, 20–25, 82–83.

[22] Stanley L. Paulson, "Continental Normativism and Its British Counterpart: How Different Are They?", 6 *Ratio Juris* 227 (1993).

[23] *ibid.* at p. 236.

abstract—appropriate for what purported to be a "pure theory" and a neo-Kantian analysis.

The most obvious differences may he ones of methodology, which have been hinted at in passing over the course of this chapter and the previous one. Hart's analysis builds on close attention to actual practices (and how they are perceived by their participants) and linguistic usage. On the other side, Kelsen is offering a kind of logical analysis of law and of normative thinking in general.

There are interesting similarities and differences between Kelsen's Basic Norm and Hart's rule of recognition. Both the rule of recognition and the Basic Norm rest on the idea of chains of normative validity: a particular legal norm is only valid because it has been authorized by a more general or more basic legal norm. This chain of validity must end somewhere, with a foundational norm that carries no further justification, other than its "acceptance"[24] or its having been "presupposed".[25] It is again important to note the difference of approach and methodology here: Hart's theory is meant as an analytical description of actual practices, while Kelsen sought a theory purified even of sociological observation, and is best understood as a neo-Kantian transcendental deduction from the fact that we treat certain rules as legal norms.[26]

Both the idea of a (single) rule of recognition and a (single) Basic Norm derive from assumptions that societies' legal regulations occur or are viewed as occurring in a systematic way—all the norms fitting within a consistent, hierarchical structure of justification. If one does not think that legal systems must be systematic in this way, then one could conclude that there could be more than one rule of recognition or more than one Basic Norm.[27]

ON THE NATURE OF NORMS

Especially in his later works, Kelsen became caught up in questions regarding the nature of norms. Analysis in (metaphorical) terms of one norm "justifying" or "generating" another, and inquiries regarding whether a legal system can contain norms with contradictory contents, seemed to create a confusion in Kelsen, "between a norm as a kind of sentence or

---

[24] Hart, *The Concept of Law*, pp. 100–110.
[25] See Kelsen, *Introduction to the Problems of Legal Theory*, p. 59.
[26] See, *e.g.* Stanley L. Paulson, "The Neo-Kantian Dimension of Kelsen's Pure Theory of Law".
[27] See Joseph Raz, *The Authority of Law* (Clarendon Press, Oxford, 1979), pp. 122–145; Joseph Raz, *The Concept of a Legal System* (2nd ed., Clarendon Press, Oxford, 1980), pp. 197–200.

sentence-meaning and as a contingent entity created and repealed by certain social events."[28] Arguably, this line of inquiry was what was behind many of the changes in his theory over time, as well as some of the stranger notions of the later work (which have not been discussed in this chapter).[29]

At times, some members associated with "Scandinavian legal realism"[30] appear to make the converse mistake. The Scandinavian legal realists were opposed to anything in legal theory that had the flavor of metaphysics. When they looked for some object to correspond with legal concepts like "norm" and "right", they rejected any explanation that seemed to posit unworldly entities.[31] Instead, these theorists offered psychological and anthropological explanations to fill the vacuum. Consider the following discussion by Karl Olivecrona about rights:

"[T]he word 'right', as used in jurisprudence as well as common discourse, lacks semantic reference.

. . .

We have, however, the illusion that the word 'right' signifies a power over [an] object, though a power that we can never grasp. The illusion stems from the emotional background. Under certain circumstances, especially in situations of conflict, the idea of possessing a right gives rise to a feeling of strength. When I am convinced of having a right, I am in some way more powerful than my opponent, even if he be actually stronger."[32]

Both the assumption that abstract concepts represent "real entities" whose nature can and must be studied, and the contrary impulse, that abstract concepts must be immediately rejected as "metaphysical nonsense", are likely to lead theorists astray. One can avoid such problems by reacting to apparently abstract terms, like "norm" and "right", by asking merely for the rules that govern the use of those terms within the legal system in question, and treating the meaning of the terms as being no more than those rules of proper usage.[33]

---

[28] Hartney, "Introduction", pp. xlii–xliii.
[29] For an overview of those notions and changes, see, e.g. Hartney, "Introduction", pp. xlii–liii.
[30] See, e.g. M.D.A. Freeman, Lloyd's Introduction to Jurisprudence (7th ed. Sweet & Maxwell, London, 2001), pp. 855–901 ("The Scandinavian Realists"); Howard Davies and David Holdcroft, Jurisprudence: Texts and Commentary (Butterworths London, 1991), pp. 422–445 ("Scandinavian Legal Realism").
[31] For a brief and interesting example of this sort of anti-metaphysical analysis applied to legal concepts, see Alf Ross, "Tu-Tu", 70 Harvard Law Review 812 (1957); see also A. Vilhelm Lundstedt, Legal Thinking Revised: My Views on Law (Almqvist & Wiksell, Stockholm, 1956), pp. 93–100 ("Realities behind the false idea of legal rights") .
[32] Karl Olivecrona, Law as Fact (Stevens & Sons, London, 1971), p. 184.
[33] This type of metaphysics-avoiding analysis has roots in the writings of both H.L.A. Hart and Ludwig Wittgenstein. I discussed the approach in greater detail in Bix, "Questions in Legal Interpretation", pp. 137–141.

This is not to deny that important philosophical work can be done on an analytical theory of norms.[34] For the moment, it is sufficient to note that most legal theorists are not well equipped to do this sort of work, such inquiries tend to lead legal theorists far astray, and asking these sorts of questions is almost always irrelevant to what the legal theorists wish to know.[35]

Suggested Further Readings

Hans Kelsen, *General Theory of Norms* (M. Hartney, trans., Clarendon Press, Oxford, 1991).

—, *Introduction to the Problems of Legal Theory* (B.L. Paulson and S.L. Paulson, trans., Clarendon Press, Oxford, 1992).

—, *Pure Theory of Law* (M. Knight, trans., University of California Press, California, 1967).

Andrei Marmor, "The Pure Theory of Law", in E.N. Zalta ed., *Stanford Encyclopedia of Philosophy*, http://plato.stanford.edu (2002).

Stanley L. Paulson, "Continental Normativism and Its British Counterpart: How Different Are They?", 6 *Ratio Juris* 227 (1993).

—, "The Neo-Kantian Dimension of Kelsen's Pure Theory of Law", 12 *Oxford Journal of Legal Studies* 311 (1992).

Stanley L. Paulson and Bonnie Litschewski Paulson ed., *Normativity and Norms: Critical Perspectives on Kelsenian Themes* (Clarendon Press, Oxford, 1998) (includes contributions by H.L.A. Hart, Alf Ross, Carlos S. Nino, Joseph Raz, Neil MacCormick, and Georg Henrik von Wright).

Richard Tur and William Twining eds, *Essays on Kelsen* (Clarendon Press, Oxford, 1986) (includes contributions by Joseph Raz, Ota Weinberger, J.W. Harris, and Stanley L. Paulson).

---

[34] See, *e.g.* Georg Henrik von Wright, *Norm and Action* (Routledge & Kegan Paul, London, 1963).

[35] See Bix, "Questions in Legal Interpretation", pp. 137–141.

Chapter Five

Natural Law Theory and John Finnis

We take it for granted that the laws and legal system under which we live can be criticized on moral grounds, that there are standards against which legal norms can be compared and sometimes found wanting. The standards against which law is judged have sometimes been described as "a (the) higher law".[1] For some, this is meant literally: that there are law-like standards that have been stated in or can be derived from divine revelation, religious texts, a careful study of human nature, or consideration of nature. For others, the reference to "higher law" is meant metaphorically, in which case it at least reflects our mixed intuitions about the moral status of law: on one hand, that not everything properly enacted as law is binding morally; on the other hand, that the law, as law, does have moral weight—it should not be simply ignored in determining what is the right thing to do. (To clarify this last point: if the law had no intrinsic moral weight, we would feel no need to point to a "higher law" as a justification for ignoring the requirements of our society's laws.)

TRADITIONAL NATURAL LAW THEORY

The approach traditionally associated with the title "natural law" usually focused on arguments for the existence of a "higher law", elaborations of its content, and analyses of what should follow from the existence of a "higher law" (in particular, what response citizens should have to situations where the positive law—the law enacted within particular societies—conflicts with the "higher law").[2]

While one can locate a number of passages in the classical Greek

---

[1] See Franz Wieacker, *A History of Private Law in Europe* (T. Weir, trans., Clarendon Press, Oxford, 1995), p. 205.

[2] Some of the modern writers who are sometimes associated with natural law, like Lon Fuller and Ronald Dworkin, have approaches far outside the tradition described in this chapter. Both Fuller (Ch. 6) and Dworkin (Ch. 7) are discussed in greater detail later.

writers that express what appear to be natural law positions,[3] the best
known ancient formulation of a natural law position was offered by the
Roman orator Cicero (106 B.C.–43 B.C.).

Cicero was strongly influenced (as were many Roman writers on law)
by the works of the Greek Stoic philosophers (some would go so far as to
say that Cicero merely offered an elegant restatement of already established Stoic views). In a brief paragraph from Cicero, one comes across
most of the themes traditionally associated with natural law theory:

"True law is right reason in agreement with nature; it is of universal application,
unchanging and everlasting; it summons to duty by its commands, and averts from
wrongdoing by its prohibitions. And it does not lay its commands or prohibitions
upon good men in vain, though neither have any effect on the wicked. It is a sin
to try to alter this law, nor is it allowable to attempt to repeal any part of it, and
it is impossible to abolish it entirely. We cannot be freed from its obligations by
senate or people, and we need not look outside ourselves for an expounder or
interpreter of it. And there will not be different laws at Rome and at Athens, or
different laws now and in the future, but one eternal and unchangeable law will
be valid for all nations and all times, and there will be one master and ruler, that
is, God, over us all, for he is the author of this law, its promulgator, and its enforcing judge. Whoever is disobedient is fleeing from himself and denying his human
nature, and by reason of this very fact he will suffer the worst penalties, even if he
escapes what is commonly considered punishment."[4]

As noted, most of the themes of traditional natural law are already
present in Cicero (though, as might be expected in the first major treatment of a subject, some of the analysis is not always as systematic or as
precise as one might want): natural law is unchanging over time and does
not differ in different societies; every person has access to the standards
of this higher law by use of reason; and (as Cicero stated elsewhere) only
just laws "really deserve [the] name" law, and "in the very definition of
the term 'law' there inheres the idea and principle of choosing what is just
and true."[5]

Within Cicero's work, and the related remarks of earlier Greek and
Roman writers, there was often a certain ambiguity regarding the refer-

---

[3] These include passages in Plato, "Laws", Book IV, 715b, in *Plato: The Collected Dialogues*
(E. Hamilton and H. Cairns, ed., Princeton University Press, Princeton, 1961), p. 1306
("enactments, so far as they are not for the common interest of the whole community, are
no true laws"); and Aristotle, "Nicomachean Ethics", Book V, 7:1134b18–1135a5, in *The
Complete Works of Aristotle*, Vol. 2, p. 1790–1791; as well as Sophocles, "Antigone", in *The
Oedipus Plays of Sophocles* (P. Roche, trans., New York: Mentor, 1958), p. 210: "I never
thought your mortal edicts had such force [that] they nullified the laws of heaven, which
unwritten, not proclaimed, can boast a currency that everlastingly is valid".
[4] Cicero, *Republic* III.xxii.33, in *De Re Publica; De Legibus* (C.W. Keyes, trans., Harvard
University Press, Cambridge, Mass., 1928), p. 211.
[5] Cicero, *Law* II.v.11–12, in *De Re Publica; De Legibus*, pp. 383, 385.

ence of "natural" in "natural law": it was not always clear whether the standards were "natural" because they derived from "human nature" (our "essence" or "purpose"), because they were accessible by our natural faculties (that is, by human reason or the human conscience), because they derived from or were expressed in nature, that is, in the physical world about us, or some combination of all three.

As one moves from the classical writers on natural law to the early Church writers, aspects of the theory necessarily change and therefore raise different issues within this approach to morality and law. For example, with classical writers, the source of the higher standards is said to be (or implied as being) inherent in the nature of things. With the early Church writers, there is a divine being who actively intervenes in human affairs and lays down express commands for all mankind—though this contrast overstates matters somewhat, as the classical writers referred to a (relatively passive) God, and the early Church writers would sometimes refer to the rules of nature as expressing divine will. To the extent that the natural law theorists of the early Church continued to speak of higher standards inherent in human nature or in the nature of things, they also had to face the question of the connection between these standards and divine commands: for example, whether God can change natural law or order something which is contrary to it, a question considered by Ambrose and Augustine (among others) in the time of the early Church and by Francisco Suárez and Hugo Grotius hundreds of years later.

The most influential writer within the traditional approach to natural law is undoubtedly Thomas Aquinas (1224–1274). However, the context of Aquinas' approach to law, its occurrence within a larger theological project that offered a systematic moral system, should be kept in mind when comparing his work with more recent theorists.

Aquinas identified four different kinds of law: eternal law, natural law, divine law, and human (positive) law.[6] For present purposes, the important categories are natural law and positive law.

According to Aquinas, positive law is derived from natural law. This derivation has different aspects. Sometimes the natural law dictates what the positive law should be: for example, natural law requires that there be a prohibition on murder. At other times, the natural law leaves room for human choice (based on local customs or policy choices)[7]: thus while natural law would probably require regulation of automobile traffic for the safety of others, the choice of whether driving should be on the left or the right side of the road, and whether the speed limit should be set at 55 miles per hour or 65, are probably matters for which either choice

---

[6] Thomas Aquinas, *Summa Theologiae*, Question 91, in *The Treatise on Law*, (R.J. Henle, trans. and ed., University of Notre Dame Press, Notre Dame, 1993), pp. 148–184.
[7] Aquinas, *Summa Theologiae*, Question 95, Art. 2, corpus, in *The Treatise on Law*, p. 288.

would be compatible with the requirements of natural law. The first form of derivation is like logical deduction; the second Aquinas refers to as the "determination" of general principles.[8]

As for citizens, the question is what their obligations are regarding just laws and regarding unjust laws. According to Aquinas, positive laws which are just "have the power of binding in conscience".[9] A just law is one which is consistent with the requirements of natural law—that is, it is "ordered to the common good", the lawgiver has not exceeded its authority, and the law's burdens are imposed on citizens fairly. Failure with respect to any of those three criteria, Aquinas asserts, makes a law unjust[10]; but what is the citizen's obligation in regard to an unjust law? The short answer is that there is no obligation to obey that law. However, a longer answer is warranted, given the amount of attention this question usually gets in discussions of natural law theory in general, and Aquinas in particular.

The phrase lex iniusta non est lex ("an unjust law is not law") is often ascribed to Aquinas, and is given as a summation of his position and the natural law position in general.[11] This view is at least somewhat misleading on several counts. Aquinas never used the exact phrase above, though one can find similar expressions: "every human positive law has the nature of law to the extent that it is derived from the Natural Law. If, however, in some point it conflicts with the law of nature it will no longer be law but rather a perversion of law"[12]; and "[unjust laws] are acts of violence rather than laws; as Augustine says, 'A law that is unjust seems not to be a law'".[13] (One also finds similar statements by Plato, Aristotle, Cicero, and Augustine—though, with the exception of Cicero's, these statements are not part of a systematic discussion of the nature of law.)

Another question goes to the significance of the phrase. What does it mean to say that an apparently valid law is "not law", "a perversion of law" or "an act of violence rather than a law"? Statements of this form have been offered and interpreted in one of two ways. First, it might mean that an immoral law is not valid law at all. The nineteenth century English jurist John Austin interpreted statements by the English commentator Sir William Blackstone (e.g. "no human laws are of any validity, if contrary

---

[8] ibid. A similar distinction is drawn in Aristotle, "Nicomachean Ethics", Book V, 7:1134b18–1135a5, in The Complete Works of Aristotle, Vol. 2, p. 1790–1791.
[9] Aquinas, Summa Theologiae, Question 96, Art. 4, corpus, in The Treatise on Law, pp. 324.
[10] ibid. at pp. 325–326.
[11] A good discussion of "Lex Iniusta Non Est Lex", its meaning in general and its significance in Aquinas' work, can be found in Norman Kretzmann, "Lex Iniusta Non Est Lex: Laws on Trial in Aquinas' Court of Conscience", 33 American Journal of Jurisprudence 99 (1988).
[12] Aquinas, Summa Theologiae, Question 95, Art. 2, corpus, in The Treatise on Law, p. 288.
[13] ibid. at Question 96, Art. 4, corpus, in The Treatise on Law, p. 327.

to [the law of nature]"[14]) in this manner, and pointed out that such analyses of validity are of little value. Austin wrote: "Suppose an act innocuous, or positively beneficial, be prohibited by the sovereign under the penalty of death; if I commit this act, I shall be tried and condemned, and if I object to the sentence, that it is contrary to the law of God . . . the Court of Justice will demonstrate the inconclusiveness of my reasoning by hanging me up, in pursuance of the law of which I have impugned the validity."[15] Though one must add that we should not conflate questions of power with questions of validity—for a corrupt legal system might punish someone even if shown that the putative law was invalid under the system's own procedural requirements—we understand the distinction between validity under the system's rules and the moral worth of the enactment in question.

A more reasonable interpretation of statements like "an unjust law is no law at all" is that unjust laws are not laws "in the fullest sense".[16] As we might say of some professional, who had the necessary degrees and credentials, but seemed nonetheless to lack the necessary ability or judgment: "she's no lawyer" or "he's no doctor". This only indicates that we do not think that the title in this case carries with it all the laudatory implications it usually does. It may well be that for our purposes, knowing that this doctor is not competent is the most important fact; however, the fact that he does have the required certification is not thereby negated or made entirely irrelevant. Similarly, to say that unjust laws are "not really laws" may only be to point out that they do not carry the same moral force or offer the same reasons for action that come from laws consistent with "higher law". This is almost certainly the sense in which Aquinas made his remarks,[17] and the probable interpretation for nearly all proponents of the position.

To say that an unjust law is not law in the fullest sense is usually intended not as a simple declaration, but as the first step of a further argument. For example: "this law is unjust; it is not law in the fullest sense, and therefore citizens can in good conscience act as if it was never enacted; that is, they should feel free to disobey it." This is a common

---

[14] William Blackstone, *Commentaries on the Laws of England* (Clarendon Press, Oxford, 1765–1769), I.41.

[15] Austin, *The Province of Jurisprudence Determined*, Lecture V, p. 158, quoted in Hart, "Positivism and the Separation of Law and Morals", p. 616.

[16] Finnis traces the notion to Aristotle's idea of "focal meaning" and Max Weber's concept of "ideal types". See Weber. *The Methodology of the Social Sciences*, pp. 90–106; Aristotle, "Nicomachean Ethics", Book VIII, 4:1157a (different kinds of friendship): "Eudemian Ethics", Book VII, 2:11236a (different kinds of friendship); "Politics", Book III, 1:1275a–1276b (different kinds of citizen), in *The Complete Works of Aristotle*, Vol. 2, pp. 1829, 1958, 2023–2024.

[17] Elsewhere, Aquinas wrote: "But even an unjust law retains some semblance of the nature of law, since it was made by one in power and in this respect it is derived from the Eternal Law". Aquinas, *Summa Theologiae*, Question 93, Art. 3, reply 2, in *The Treatise on Law*, p. 212.

understanding of the idea that an unjust law is no law at all, but it expresses a conclusion that is controversial.

There are often moral reasons for obeying even an unjust law: for example, if the law is part of a generally just legal system, and public disobedience of the law might undermine the system, there is a moral reason for at least minimal public compliance with the unjust law. There is a hint of this position in Aquinas (he stated that a citizen is not bound to obey "a law which imposes an unjust burden on its subjects" if the law "can be resisted without scandal or greater harm"[18]), and it has been articulated at greater length by later natural law theorists, most recently by John Finnis,[19] as discussed below.

Aquinas' theory is in some ways more the structure of an ethical system rather than the full ethical system itself. For most of us, little practical guidance for difficult moral questions can be found from the advice, "good should be done and sought and evil is to be avoided"[20]; however, Aquinas offers few prescriptions on specific moral issues more precise than that. The assumption may have been that the teachings of the church and the holy books, combined with the reflections of a wise person,[21] would be sufficient to fill in the content of the moral system.

MEDIEVAL AND RENAISSANCE THEORISTS

In later centuries, discussions about natural law were tied in with other issues: assertions about natural law were often the basis of or part of the argument for individual rights and limitations on government; and such discussions were also often the groundwork offered for principles of international law.

Francisco Suárez (1548–1617) is regarded as the greatest scholastic thinker other than Aquinas, though Suárez's work on natural law theory breaks with Aquinas on at least two important matters. Suárez emphasizes "will" when analyzing natural (moral) law, while Aquinas had emphasized "reason"[22] (the extent to which moral standards are best

---

[18] *ibid.* at Question 96, Art. 4, reply 3, in *The Treatise on Law*, p. 323. *Ibid.* at Question 96, Art. 4, corpus, in *The Treatise on Law*, p. 327, Aquinas refers to obedience to unjust laws where this is necessary "to avoid scandal or disturbances." In John M. Finnis, *Aquinas: Moral, Political, and Legal Theory* (Oxford University Press, Oxford, 1998), p. 273 and n. 112, Finnis suggests that the Latin word Aquinas used, *turbationem*, which is commonly translated as "disorders" (and in the Henle translation I am using, "disturbances") might also be translated as "demoralization".

[19] Finnis, *Natural Law and Natural Rights*, pp. 359–362.

[20] Aquinas, *Summa Theologiae*, Question 94, Art. 2, corpus, in *The Treatise on Law*, p. 247.

[21] Cf. *ibid.* at pp. 245–246, where Aquinas distinguishes propositions which are self-evident to all and those that are self-evident only to the wise.

[22] I discuss the issues of "will" versus "reason" in Ch. 11.

understood as equivalent to the will of a lawmaker, here God, or the extent to which moral standards are best understood as derived from foundational axioms of reason); and Suárez's understanding of the "nature" in "natural law" was that knowledge of the good derived from knowledge of human nature, in contrast to Aquinas, who had advocated the converse position (that what is "natural" for human beings is what is reasonable, *i.e.* what is consistent with their nature as *reasonable creatures*).[23]

Suárez's writings strongly influenced Hugo Grotius (1583–1645), whose work on natural law theory established the foundations of modern international law, though Grotius did not share Suárez's focus on "will". Grotius wrote of the rules based on Reason that constrain what governments can legitimately do, and how nations can legitimately act towards one another.[24] As based on Reason, this was a natural law, as Grotius himself wrote, that would exist and bind us even if there were no God. By speaking of constraints on government based on individual rights, and by offering the possibility of a secular natural law theory, Grotius opened the path for the later liberal natural rights theories of, *e.g.* John Locke (1632–1704) and Jean-Jacques Rousseau (1712–1778).[25]

The eventual repercussions of natural law and natural rights thinking in political theory were far-reaching. To choose one well-known example, the American Declaration of Independence (1776) claims authority from "the Laws of Nature" and refers to the "unalienable rights" of "Life, Liberty, and the pursuit of Happiness"—itself a pleasantly hedonistic revision of John Locke's list of natural rights as life, liberty, and property.[26]

To return to natural law theory and to summarize: it is normally a mistake to try to evaluate the discussions of writers from distant times with the perspective of modern analytical jurisprudence. Cicero, Aquinas, and Suárez were not concerned with a social-scientific-style analysis of law, as the modern advocates of legal positivism could be said to be. The early natural law theorists were concerned with what legislators and citizens and governments ought to do, or could do in good conscience. It is not that these writers (and their followers) never asked

---

[23] See, *e.g.* Finnis, *Natural Law and Natural Rights*, pp. 45–46; Robert P. George, "Natural Law Ethics", in *A Companion to Philosophy of Religion* (P.L. Quinn and C. Taliaferro ed., Blackwell, Oxford, 1997), p. 462.

[24] See, *e.g.* Wieacker, *A History of Private Law in Europe*, pp. 227–238; J.M. Kelly, *A Short History of Western Legal Theory* (Clarendon Press, Oxford, 1992), pp. 224–227, 241–243.

[25] This is of course a simplification, and a lot of intellectual history to condense into a single short paragraph. At a minimum, one should also note the early social contract theory of Thomas Hobbes, and the great systematizer of natural law, Samuel Pufendorf (1632–1694). See, *e.g.* Wieacker, *A History of Private Law in Europe*, pp. 239–248.

[26] On Locke, see his "Second Treatise on Government", s. 6, in John Locke, *Two Treatises on Government* (P Laslett ed., 2nd ed., Cambridge University Press, Cambridge, 1967), pp. 288–289 (first published in 1690). On the transformation of Locke's ideas and language into the language of the American Declaration, see Pauline Maier, *American Scripture: Making the Declaration of Independence* (Knopf, New York, 1997), pp. 123–143, 160–170.

questions like "what is law?" However, they were asking the questions as a starting point for an ethical inquiry, and therefore one should not be too quick in comparing their answers with those in similar-sounding discussions by recent writers, who see themselves as participating in a conceptual or sociological task.

JOHN FINNIS

John Finnis' work is an explication and application of Aquinas' views[27]: an application to ethical questions, but with special attention to the problems of social theory in general and analytical jurisprudence in particular.

For Finnis, the basic questions are the ethical one, "how should one live?", and the meta-ethical one, "how (by what procedure or analysis) can we discover the answer to ethical questions?" These ethical and meta-ethical questions are primary; legal theory for Finnis is best understood as a small if integral part of the larger project.[28]

Finnis' response to these basic questions involves, among other things, the claim that there are a number of separate but equally valuable intrinsic goods (that is, things one values for their own sake), which he called "basic goods". In *Natural Law and Natural Rights*, Finnis lists the following as basic goods: life (and health), knowledge, play, aesthetic experience, sociability (friendship), practical reasonableness, and religion. These are "intrinsic" goods in the following sense: one can value, *e.g.* health for its own sake, but medicine only as a means to health. If someone stated that she was buying medicine, not because she or someone she knew was sick or might become sick, and not because it was part of some study or some business, but simply because she liked having a lot of medicine around, one might rightly begin to question her sanity

At this level, we can only distinguish the intelligible from the unintelligible. We *understand* the person who is materialistic and greedy however much we disapprove of that approach to life. The greedy person is seeking the same basic goods we are. Much of what is conventionally considered

---

[27] Finnis largely follows the interpretation of Aquinas and the approach to natural law theory proposed by Germain Grisez. One of Grisez's foundational works in this area is Germain C. Grisez, "The First Principle of Practical Reason: A Commentary on the *Summa theologiae*, 1–2 , Question 94, Article 2" , 10 *Natural Law Forum* 168 (1965). There are other commentators who put forward distinctly different interpretations and approaches. See, *e.g.* Russell Hittinger, *A Critique of the New Natural Law Theory* (University of Notre Dame Press, Notre Dame, 1987) (offering a critique of the "Grisez-Finnis" view of Aquinas and natural law theory). A detailed explication of Finnis's view of Aquinas can be found in Finnis, *Aquinas*.

[28] For a clear overview of natural law that could serve as a concise restatement of Finnis's theory, see Robert P. George, "Natural Law and Positive Law", in *The Autonomy of Law: Essays on Legal Positivism* (R.P. George ed., Clarendon Press, Oxford, 1996), pp. 321–334.

morality occurs in Finnis' theory at the second level of discussion: the principles for how we should deal with and combine the quest for various intrinsic goods.

Finnis describes the list of basic goods, and other aspects of his moral theory, as "self-evident", but he does not mean this in the sense that the truth of these propositions would be immediately obvious to all competent thinkers. Part of what makes a proposition self-evident is that it cannot be derived from some more foundational proposition; thus, self evident is here the opposite of provable.[29] However, while self-evident propositions cannot be proven, they can be supported by consistent observational data and by dialectical arguments. Also, it is not the case that everyone will be equally adept at reaching these "self-evident" conclusions. Those of substantial experience, and who are able and willing to inquire deeply may be better able to discover the self-evident truths than would others. (Aquinas, similarly, at one point wrote of propositions which are only self-evident to the wise.[30])

Because there are a variety of basic goods, with no hierarchy or priority among them, there must be principles for how to choose when the available options promote different goods. This is one basis for contrasting Finnis' position with utilitarian moral theories, under which all goods can be compared according to their value in a single unit, *e.g.* promoting happiness. On a simple level, we face such choices when we consider whether to spend the afternoon playing basketball (the value of play) or studying history (the value of knowledge). The choice is presented in a sharper form when we must choose whether to lie (choosing against the value of knowledge), in a situation where we believe that lying would lead to some significant benefit or avoid a greater evil. Morality offers a basis for rejecting certain available choices, but there will often remain more than one equally legitimate choice (again there is a contrast with utilitarian theories, under which there would always be a "best" choice).

For Finnis, the move from the basic goods to moral choices occurs through a serious of intermediate principles, which Finnis calls "the basic requirements of practical reasonableness". Among the most significant, and most controversial, is the prescription that one may never act directly against a basic good (as lying is an action against knowledge or torture an action against life (and health)), regardless of the benefit one believes will come from taking that path.[31] In other words, the ends never justify the

---

[29] See Robert P. George, "Recent Criticism of Natural Law Theory" (book review), 55 *University of Chicago Law Review* 1371 at 1386–1393 (1988) (explaining and defending this aspect of Finnis' argument).

[30] Aquinas, *Summa Theologiae*, Question 94, Art. 2, corpus, in *The Treatise on Law*, p. 246.

[31] Predictably, within this approach, much turns on characterization of an action. Harming another person in self-defense would likely be justified on the ground that the purpose of the action is to defend one's own life (the basic good of "life/health"); the harm to one's attacker would be characterized as only a side-effect, even if one that is foreseeable or inevitable.

means where the chosen means entail a harming of a basic good. Other intermediate principles listed in *Natural Law and Natural Rights* include that one should form a rational plan of life; have no arbitrary preferences among persons; foster the common good of the community; and have no arbitrary preferences among the basic goods.[32]

Law enters the picture as a way of effecting some goods—social goods which require the co-ordination of many people—that could not be effected, easily or at all, without it, and as a way of making it easier to obtain other goods.[33] Thus, the suggestions Finnis makes about law and about legal theory are in a sense derivative of his primary concern with ethics. As to questions regarding the obligation to obey the law, Finnis follows Aquinas: one has an obligation to obey just laws; laws which are unjust are not "law" in the fullest sense of the term and one has an obligation to comply with their requirements only to the extent that this is necessary to uphold otherwise just institutions.[34]

NATURAL LAW THEORY VERSUS LEGAL POSITIVISM

Given that Finnis' starting point is so different from that of the legal positivists, it is surprising to discover some similarities in their theories.[35] These similarities occur because even though Finnis' theory might he seen as primarily a prescriptive account—a theory of how we should live our lives—certain descriptive elements are necessarily assumed.[36] First, if one is going to ask what implications morality has for law, one must first understand what "law" is. Secondly it is part of Finnis' project to consider which proposals within various aspects of legal regulation are foreclosed and which allowed by a general ethical theory.[37] Further, Finnis believes that a proper ethical theory is necessary for doing descriptive theory well, as valuation is a necessary and integral part of theory construction.[38]

Like Hart, Finnis emphasized the need to use an "internal point of view" in analyzing a legal system[39], and like Joseph Raz, Finnis believes

---

[32] Finnis, *Natural Law and Natural Rights*, pp. 100–127.

[33] *ibid.* at pp. 260–264.

[34] *ibid.* at pp. 354–362.

[35] Finnis elsewhere discussed the ways in which a natural law theorist can affirm, more or less on the terms offered, nearly every "dogma" associated with modern legal positivism. See Finnis, "The Truth in Legal Positivism", pp. 203–205.

[36] One could also offer historical reasons for the similarities. Finnis was H.L.A. Hart's student at Oxford, and Joseph Raz was first a classmate and has more recently been a colleague of many years.

[37] See, *e.g.* Finnis, *Natural Law and Natural Rights*, pp. 169–173 (property law), pp. 188–192 (bankruptcy).

[38] *ibid.* at pp. 6–18.

[39] *ibid.* at pp. 3–13.

that our understanding of legal systems should centre on the fact that law affects our reasons for action.[40] As noted earlier (in Ch. 3) regarding the "internal point of view", Finnis makes an important amendment to Hart's approach. He argues that in doing legal theory, one should not take the perspective of those who merely accept the law as valid (Hart appears to include even those who accept the law as valid for prudential reasons); the theory should assume the perspective of those who accept the law as binding *because* they—correctly—believe that valid legal rules create (prima facie) moral obligations. The difference may seem minor, but it means crossing a theoretically significant dividing line: between the legal positivist's insistence on doing theory in a morally neutral way and the natural law theorist's assertion that moral evaluation is an integral part of proper description and analysis. Finnis' approach to descriptive theory, unlike Hart's, requires that the theorist judge the moral merits of the legal system(s) being described, and it is just the propriety or necessity of such moral evaluations in the process of descriptive theory which has been the dividing line in recent times between legal positivism and natural law theory.

A similar difference or change can be seen be in comparing Raz's practical reasoning approach to law and Finnis' approach. For Raz, what is central is that law *purports to* create moral reasons for action[41]; for Finnis, what is central is that under certain conditions law *does* create moral reasons for action. The difference may seem slight, but it is also significant.

In the context of Finnis' approach to natural law theory, one can locate two related differences between natural law theory and legal positivism. First, natural law theory asserts that a morally neutral theory of law is not possible, or, at least, not valuable.[42] Second, natural law theory focuses on how, whether, and when positive law adds to our set of moral obligations (roughly—it does so only when the rules enacted are consistent with moral principles and promulgated by a party acting within its authority)[43]; this is a question that legal positivism, by its basic principles, avoids trying to answer. The contrast between natural law theory and legal

---

[40] *ibid.* at pp. 12–13. Also like Raz, Finnis believes that values (and value choices) are incommensurable, and that this has important consequences for legal theory and moral theory. See Joseph Raz, *The Morality of Freedom* (Clarendon Press, Oxford, 1986), pp. 321–366; John M. Finnis, "On Reason and Authority in *Law's Empire*", 6 *Law and Philosophy* 357 at 370–376 (1987); John M. Finnis, "Natural Law and Legal Reasoning", 38 *Cleveland State Law Review* 1 at 7–9 (1990); John Finnis, "Concluding Reflections", 38 *Cleveland State Law Review* 231 at 234–241 (1990).

[41] See Raz, *Ethics in the Public Domain*, p. 199.

[42] See Brian Bix, "On the Dividing Line Between Natural Law Theory and Legal Positivism", 75 *Notre Dame Law Review* 1613 (2000).

[43] See, *e.g.* John Finnis, "On the Incoherence of Legal Positivism", 75 *Notre Dame Law Review* 1597 at 1607–08 (2000).

positivism may be characterized in another way: that natural law theory sees law primarily as a kind of reason for action (potentially adding to our moral reasons for action), and therefore argues that law cannot be understood except in the context of what would make for a *good* (moral) reason for action. One obviously could not, or should not, approach law, understood in this manner, in a morally neutral way. Legal positivism, instead, focuses on the law as a type of social institution, and within that focus a morally neutral theory seems both possible and valuable. Whether there is any theory that can persuasively portray both the practical reasoning aspect of law and the social practice/institution aspect of law remains to be seen.

OTHER DIRECTIONS

There are a wide variety of other modern theories which are self-described, or described by others, as being "natural law theories". Robert George has produced a series of works which have explained, developed, and applied the Aquinas/Grisez/Finnis approach to natural law.[44] Deryck Beyleveld and Roger Brownsword offer a natural law theory based on Alan Gewirth's argument that moral principles are presupposed by practical reason.[45] Lloyd Weinreb has constructed a natural law theory which he connects with the ancient Greek view of such issues: the existence of a normative natural order, and the role of legal and moral norms as mediating questions of free will and responsibility.[46] Randy Barnett offers an instrumental and political variation of natural law: given the goal of promoting happiness while living together in society, and given certain facts about human nature, society should follow certain principles of justice (which for Barnett turn out to be those of classical liberalism/libertarianism).[47] And Michael Moore has constructed a natural law theory based on a metaphysically realist (Platonist) theory of morality and meaning.[48]

---

[44] See, *e.g.* Robert P. George, *In Defense of Natural Law* (Clarendon Press, Oxford, 1999).
[45] See, *e.g.* Deryck Beyleveld and Roger Brownsword, *Law as a Moral Judgment* (Sweet & Maxwell, London, 1986); Alan Gewirth, *Reason and Morality* (University of Chicago Press, Chicago, 1978).
[46] See, *e.g.* Lloyd L. Weinreb, *Natural Law and Justice* (Harvard University Press, Cambridge, Mass., 1987); Lloyd L. Weinreb, *Oedipus at Fenway Park: What Rights Are and Why There Are Any* (Harvard University Press, Cambridge, Mass., 1994).
[47] See Barnett, *The Structure of Liberty*.
[48] See, *e.g.* Michael S. Moore, "A Natural Law Theory of Interpretation", 58 *Southern California Law Review* 277 (1985); Michael S. Moore, "Moral Reality Revisited", 90 *Michigan Law Review* 2424 (1992); Michael S. Moore, *Educating Oneself in Public: Critical Essays in Jurisprudence* (Oxford University Press, Oxford, 2000).

Suggested Further Readings

JOHN FINNIS

John M. Finnis, *Aquinas: Moral, Political, and Legal Theory* (Oxford University Press, Oxford, 1998).
—, *Fundamentals of Ethics* (Georgetown University Press, Washington, D.C., 1983).
—, *Moral Absolutes: Tradition, Revision, and Truth* (Catholic University of America Press, Washington, D.C., 1991).
—, *Natural Law and Legal Reasoning*, in *Natural Law Theory: Contemporary Essays* (R.P. George ed., Clarendon Press, Oxford, 1992), pp. 134–157.
—, *Natural Law and Natural Rights* (Clarendon Press, Oxford, 1980).
—, "Natural Law Theory: The Classical Tradition", in *The Oxford Handbook of Jurisprudence and Philosophy of Law* (J. Coleman and S. Shapiro, eds, K. E. Himma, assoc. ed., Oxford, Oxford University Press, 2002), pp. 1–60.
"Propter Honoris Respectum: John Finnis", 75 *Notre Dame Law Review* 1597–1892 (2000)
Robert P. George, "Recent Criticism of Natural Law Theory" (book review), 55 *University of Chicago Law Review* 1271 (1988) (contains a summary, explanation and defense of Finnis's theory).

NATURAL LAW THEORY

Thomas Aquinas, *The Treatise on Law* (R.J. Henle ed., University of Notre Dame Press, Notre Dame, 1993) (*Summa Theologiae*, Questions 90–97).
Brian Bix, "Natural Law Theory", in *A Companion to Philosophy of Law and Legal Theory* (D. Patterson ed., Blackwell, Oxford, 1996), pp. 223–240.
—, "Natural Law Theory: The Modern Tradition", in *The Oxford Handbook of Jurisprudence and Philosophy of Law* (J. Coleman and S. Shapiro, eds, K. E. Himma, assoc. ed., Oxford, Oxford University Press, 2002), pp. 61–103.
—, "On the Dividing Line Between Natural Law Theory and Legal Positivism", 75 *Notre Dame Law Review* 1613 (2000).
John Finnis, ed., *Natural Law*, 2 Volumes (Dartmouth Pub. Co., London; New York University Press, New York, 1991) (a wide-ranging collection of law review articles on natural law theory).
Robert P. George, *In Defense of Natural Law* (Clarendon Press, Oxford, 1999).
Robert P George, ed., *Natural Law Theory: Contemporary Essays* (Clarendon Press, Oxford, 1992) (a collection of recent articles on natural law theory).
Mark C. Murphy, "The Natural Law Tradition in Ethics", in E. N. Zalta ed., *Stanford Encyclopedia of Philosophy*, http://plato.stanford.edu (2002).
Lloyd L. Weinreb, *Natural Law and Justice* (Harvard University Press, Cambridge, Mass., 1987).

Chapter Six

Understanding Lon Fuller

A SECOND KIND OF NATURAL LAW THEORY

The beginning of the last chapter offered an overview of natural law theory. To be more exact, it offered an overview of *one type* of natural law theory, which was described as "traditional natural law theory". One could divide most of the theorists who have been labeled—or who have labeled themselves—as "natural law theorists" into two groups. The first group would include the theorists discussed in Ch. 5: Cicero, Aquinas, Suárez, and Finnis, among many others. The second group reflects debates of a different kind and a more recent origin; its approach focuses more narrowly on the proper understanding of law as a social institution or a social practice. (The two types of approaches are by no means contradictory or inconsistent, but they reflect sets of theoretical concerns sufficiently different that it is rare to find writers contributing to both.)

The second (or "modern") set of approaches to natural law arose as responses to legal positivism, and the way legal positivists portrayed (and sometimes caricatured) traditional natural law positions. While attacks on the merits of natural law theory can be found in the works of John Austin, Oliver Wendell Holmes, Jr., and Hans Kelsen, most recent discussions of "natural law theory" derive from the 1958 "Hart-Fuller Debate" in the *Harvard Law Review*.[1] In this exchange, H.L.A. Hart set the groundwork for a restatement of legal positivism. Part of his defence and restatement involved demarcating legal positivism from natural law theory, and the demarcation point offered was the conceptual separation of law and morality. Lon Luvois Fuller (1902–1978) argued against a sharp separation of law and morality, but the position he defended under the rubric of "natural law theory" was quite different from the traditional natural law

---

[1] H.L.A. Hart, "Positivism and the Separation of Law and Morals", 71 *Harvard Law Review* 593 (1958); Lon Fuller, "Positivism and Fidelity to Law—A Response to Professor Hart", 71 *Harvard Law Review* 630 (1958).

theories of Cicero, Suárez, and Aquinas (as will be discussed in detail below).

In part because of responses to legal positivists like Hart, a category of "natural law theories" has arisen which is best understood by its contrast to legal positivism, rather than by its connection with the traditional natural law theories of Cicero, Suárez, and Aquinas. While the traditional theories were generally taking a particular position on the status of morality (that true moral beliefs are based in or derived from human nature or the natural world, that they are not relative, that they are accessible to human reason, and so on), a position which then had some implications for how legislators, judges, and citizens should act, as well as for all other aspects of living a good life; this second category of "natural law theories" includes theories specifically about law, theories which hold that moral evaluation of some sort is required in describing law in general or particular legal systems, or in determining the legal validity of individual laws.

The two most prominent members of this second group are Lon Fuller, who referred to his approach as a "Natural Law" approach, and who is the subject of the present chapter; and Ronald Dworkin, who only occasionally and with some reluctance takes on that title, and who is the subject of the next chapter.

FULLER'S APPROACH

Fuller rejected what he saw as legal positivism's distorted view of law as a "one-way projection of authority": the sovereign gives orders and the citizens obey. Fuller believed that this approach missed the need for cooperation and reciprocal obligations[2] between officials and citizens for a legal system to work.

Additionally, Fuller criticized legal positivists for misunderstanding the centrality of the ideal of law (which he alternatively described as "order", "good order" and "justice") in any understanding of law itself. To exclude the ideal from a theory of law on the basis of a "separation of description and evaluation" is to miss the point entirely: the social practice and social institution of law is by its nature a striving towards such ideals.[3]

Fuller characterized law as "the enterprise of subjecting human

---

[2] See, e.g. Lon L. Fuller, *The Morality of Law* (revised ed., Yale University Press, London, 1969), p. 39 ("There is a kind of reciprocity between government and the citizen with respect to the observance of rules").

[3] See Winston, "The Ideal Element in a Definition of Law", pp. 98, 103–104, 109; see also Lon L. Fuller, "Human Purpose and Natural Law", 53 *Journal of Philosophy* 697 (1956), reprinted at 3 *Natural Law Forum* 68 (1958); Lon L. Fuller, "A Rejoinder to Professor Nagel", 3 *Natural Law Forum* 83 (1958).

conduct to the governance of rules".[4] Law is a way of governing people, to be contrasted with other forms of governance, for example, managerial direction.[5] Law is a particular means to an end, a particular kind of tool, if you will.[6] With that in mind, one can better understand the claim that rules must meet certain criteria relating to that means, to that function, if they are to warrant the title "law". If we defined "knife" as something that cuts, something which failed to cut would not warrant the label, however much it might superficially resemble true knives. Similarly, if we define law as a particular way of guiding and coordinating human behaviour, if a system's rules are so badly constructed that they cannot succeed in effectively guiding behaviour, then we are justified in withholding the label "law" from them.[7]

Another way to view the same analysis is to point out that those in authority are not entirely free when they create law. They must respond to and adapt to the external order, to factors beyond their control: aspects of human nature (in particular how people interact, and how they react to various forms of guidance), the nature of society (which institutional structures work and which do not), and the resources available.[8]

Fuller offered, in place of legal positivism's analyses of law based on power, orders, and obedience, an analysis based on the "internal morality" of law. Like traditional natural law theorists, he wrote of there being a threshold that must be met (or, to change the metaphor, a test that must be passed) before something could be properly (or in the fullest sense) be called "law". Unlike traditional natural law theorists, however, the test Fuller applies is one of function and procedure rather than one primarily of moral content.

The internal morality of law consists of a series of requirements which Fuller asserted that a systems of rules must meet—or at least substantially meet—if that system was to be called "law". (At the same time, Fuller wrote of systems being "legal" to different extents, and he held that a

---

[4] Fuller, *The Morality of Law*, p. 96. Kenneth Winston argues that the quoted characterization "is meant to define not law in general but only the process of legislation." Winston, "Introduction", in Lon L. Fuller, *The Principles of Social Order*, p. 30, n.33 (Duke University Press, Durham, NC., 1981).

I declined to call Fuller's characterization a "definition" of law, as there is evidence that Fuller had little regard for the project of "defining law". See Winston, "The Ideal Element in a Definition of Law", p. 91 (quoting from a letter Fuller wrote in which he discussed this matter). However, I believe that Fuller's discussions are, like other "definitions of law", at least in part a conceptual claim about law. (On "conceptual claims", see Ch. 2.)

[5] Fuller, *The Morality of Law*, pp. 207–214.

[6] In many of the writings discussed, Fuller was speaking primarily, if not exclusively, of legislation. In other writings, Fuller focused on adjudication, mediation, contractual agreements, and managerial direction. See Fuller, *The Principles of Social Order*.

[7] Weinreb, *Natural Law and Justice*, pp. 102–103.

[8] See Winston, "Introduction", pp. 13–14.

system which partly but not fully met his requirements would be "partly legal" and could be said to have "displayed a greater respect for the principles of legality" than systems which did not meet the requirements at all.[9])

The eight requirements are: (1) laws should be general; (2) they should be promulgated, that citizens might know the standards to which they are being held; (3) retroactive rule-making and application should be minimized; (4) laws should be understandable; (5) laws should not be contradictory; (6) laws should not require conduct beyond the abilities of those affected; (7) they should remain relatively constant through time; and (8) there should be a congruence between the laws as announced and as applied.[10]

Fuller's approach is often contrasted with that of traditional natural law positions. Fuller at one point tried to show a connection, writing that "Aquinas in some measure recognized and dealt with all eight of the principles of legality". On the other hand, Fuller also realized that there were significant differences: he once referred to his theory as "a procedural, as distinguished from a substantive natural law". However, he chafed at the dismissal of his set of requirements as "merely procedural": an argument frequently made by critics that his "principles of legality" were amoral solutions to problems of efficiency, such that one could just as easily speak of "the internal morality of poisoning".[11] Such criticisms misunderstand the extent to which our perceptions of justice incorporate procedural elements. This is a matter Fuller himself brought up through an example from the (then) Soviet Union. In that country, there was once an attempt to increase the sentence for robbery, an increase also to be applied retroactively to those convicted of that crime in the past. Even in the Soviet legal system, not known for its adherence to the "Rule of Law", there was a strong reaction by lawyers against this attempt to increase sentences retroactively. It is a matter of procedure only, but still it seemed to them—and it would seem to us—a matter of justice.[12] Following the rules laid down (just as one example of procedural justice) is a good thing, and it is not stretching matters to characterize it as a moral matter and a matter of justice.

(Some commentators would contest the idea that procedural ideals, like "following the rules laid down" are a part of justice, or carry any sort of moral weight. Matthew Kramer takes a middle position, arguing that procedural ideals *are* a part of justice, but carry no intrinsic moral weight:

---

[9] Fuller, *The Morality of Law*, pp. 122–123.
[10] *ibid.* at pp. 33–91.
[11] *ibid.* at pp. 200–202.
[12] *ibid.* at pp. 202–204. Lloyd Weinreb analyzes our concept of justice as having two aspects, which are sometimes in tension: people getting what they deserve, and the following of the rules laid down. Weinreb, *Natural Law and Justice*, pp. 184–223.

that is, it is not even presumptively immoral to act contrary to the rules already laid down.[13])

There were times when Fuller overstated the importance of his "principles of legality". When critics argued that a regime could follow those principles and still enact wicked laws, Fuller stated that he could not believe that adherence to the internal requirements of law were as consistent with a bad legal system as they were with a good legal system.[14] There are various ways that this "faith" can be understood. One argument could be that a government which is just and good will likely be good on procedural matters as well. It is also worth noting that when proper procedures are followed (e.g. the requirement that reasons be publicly given for judicial decisions) some officials might be less willing to act in evil or corrupt ways.[15] The contrary claim, that governments which are evil will be likely to ignore the procedural requirements, also has some initial plausibility. There have been regimes so evil that they have not even bothered with any of the legal niceties, with establishing even the pretense of legality, and to some extent Nazi Germany is an example.[16] However, there have also been regimes, generally condemned as evil, which have at least at times been quite meticulous about legal procedures (South Africa before the fall of Apartheid or East Germany before the fall of Communism may be examples). Since the principles of legality can be understood as guidelines for making the legal system more effective in guiding citizen behaviour, wicked regimes would also have reasons to follow them.[17]

Thus, while following the principles of legality is itself a moral good, and whilst it may indicate a government committed to morally good actions, and may hinder base actions, it is probably claiming too much for those principles to say that following them would *guarantee* a substantively just system. However, one should not conclude, as some critics have, that the evaluation of Fuller's entire approach to law should turn on the empirical question of whether there have ever been (or ever could be) wicked governments which, for whatever reason, followed the rules of procedural justice. Like the question of whether there can ever be, over the long term, "honor among thieves", the ability to maintain procedural fairness amidst significant iniquities, is an interesting topic for speculation, but little more. The main points of Fuller's position—that a value judgment about the system described is part of the way we use the word "law"; and that there is analytic value to seeing law as a particular kind

---

[13] Matthew H. Kramer, *In Defense of Legal Positivism: Law Without Trimmings* (Oxford University Press, Oxford, 1999), pp. 23–32.

[14] See Fuller, "Positivism and Fidelity to Law", p. 636.

[15] *ibid.* at pp. 636, 652; Fuller, *The Morality of Law*, pp. 157–159.

[16] See, *e.g.* Ingo Müller, *Hitler's Justice: The Courts of the Third Reich* (D.L. Schneider, trans., Harvard University Press, Cambridge, Mass., 1991).

[17] For the argument that wicked governments would have prudential reasons to abide by Fuller's principles, see Kramer, *In Defense of Legal Positivism*, pp. 65–71.

of social guidance, which is to be contrasted with other forms of social guidance, and which can be more or less effective according to how well it meets certain guidelines—are not undermined by pointing out (if true) that some legal systems which are substantively unjust seem to do well on questions of procedural justice.[18]

Those who approach natural law through the Hart-Fuller debate sometimes over-emphasize the question of when a rule or a system of social guidance merits the label "law" or "legal". There is a danger in such a focus, in that debates about proper labeling (not just whether something is "law" or not, but also whether an object is "art" or not, whether a particular form of government is "democratic" or not, and so forth) often lose real moral, sociological, or conceptual arguments beneath line-drawing exercises. As mentioned earlier (in Ch. 2), it is always open to theorists to stipulate the meaning of the terms they use, even for the limited purpose of one discussion only. To say that it is important that the products of a wicked regime be called "law" or not indicates that there is something further at stake (for example, whether and when citizens have a moral obligation to obey the law), but the burden must be on the advocate to clarify what that further point is. It may often be preferable to bypass questions of labeling and line-drawing, to face directly whatever further substantive issues may be present.

FULLER AND LEGAL PROCESS

Lon Fuller was a significant influence on the "legal process" approach to law, an approach that was important in American legal thought in the 1950s and 1960s. Lon Fuller's work can be seen, in an indirect way, as being a response to American legal realism (the focus of Ch. 17): Fuller's internal morality of law as a kind of reaction against the cynicism and focus on power of the realists. By contrast, legal process was a more direct response to the challenge of the realists.

The legal process school conceded many of the American legal realists' criticisms of the "formalist" judging of that period—that legal materials were frequently indeterminate, and that some extralegal values or norms would be required to decide many legal disputes; however, the legal process theorists argued that there was nonetheless room for a distinctively *legal* response to disputes. Legal process saw the distinctive legal response as involving understanding the relative strengths and weaknesses of different institutions and decision-making processes ("institutional

---

[18] See Sebok, "Finding Wittgenstein at the Core of the Rule of Recognition", p. 79: "For Fuller, more traditional natural law theory had put the cart before the horse by asking what the law should achieve before fully understanding how the law was to achieve anything."

competence"), and thus being able to determine whether (for example) it would be best to use adjudication, arbitration, agency rule-making, or public legislation to resolve a particular dispute. Additionally, legal process offered a picture of adjudication in which courts *had* discretion, but this discretion was bounded by a proper understanding of the judicial role.

The legal process approach focused on the question of *how* and *by whom* decisions should be made: what is the best procedure for finding the answer to this sort of question?, and which institution would be best placed to resolve a problem of this sort?[19] "By emphasizing reason as well as fiat in law, by demonstrating the essential irrationality of non-purposive legal interpretation, by reinforcing the interconnection of reason and principle and, most importantly of all, by arguing that adjudication is an institutionally discrete, rationalistic, rights-oriented and hence principle based process of decision-making, Fuller contributed significantly to the construction of a distinctive post-realist 'process jurisprudence'."[20] The legal process approach combined Fuller's emphasis on the functions of law and added detailed attention to the relative institutional competences of various institutions within the law, and how these institutions interact.

Especially at times when there is pervasive doubt of achieving certainty or consensus in resolving basic social questions (as doubt in American legal thought earlier this century had been fuelled by the criticisms of formalism developed by the legal realists), it is proper to focus on the question of who should decide and how. There is a sense, however, that in the way the legal process approach developed, questions of process and institutional competence were over-emphasized, leading to an indifference to the justice of results reached and a mistaken and extreme version of judicial restraint.[21]

Legal process was an intermediate movement in recent American jurisprudential thought. As noted, it can be seen as a kind of mainstream response to the challenges raised by American legal realism.[22] In turn, critical legal studies, discussed in Ch. 19, developed in large part in reaction to legal process.[23]

---

[19] See Henry M. Hart, Jr, and Albert M. Sacks, *The Legal Process: Basic Problems in the Making and Application of Law* (W. Eskridge and P. Frickey ed, Foundation Press, New York, 1994). The influential basic text of the legal process school was completed in 1958, and widely circulated, but never formally published until 1994. For a detailed discussion of the context, development, and subsequent criticisms of "Legal Process" (both the book and the movement), see William N. Eskridge, Jr and Philip Frickey's "An Historical and Critical Introduction to *The Legal Process*", in *ibid.* at pp. li–cxxxvi.

[20] Neil Duxbury, *Patterns of American Jurisprudence* (Clarendon Press, Oxford, 1995), p. 232.

[21] *ibid.* at pp. 233–241.

[22] See, *e.g.* Morton Horwitz, *The Transformation of American Law 1870–1960* (Oxford University Press, Oxford, 1992), pp. 254–255.

[23] See, e.g. Mark Kelman, *A Guide to Critical Legal Studies* (Harvard University Press, Cambridge, Mass., 1987), pp. 186–212.

Suggested Further Reading

Symposium on Lon Fuller, 13 *Law and Philosophy* 253–418 (1994) (with articles by
Kenneth Winston, Jeremy Waldron, Frederick Schauer, Stanley L. Paulson,
and Gerald Postema).

Lou Fuller, "Positivism and Fidelity to Law—A Response to Professor Hart", 71
Harvard Law Review 630 (1958).

—, *The Morality of Law* (revised ed., Yale University Press, New Haven, 1969) (the
revised edition contains a helpful reply to critics).

—, *The Principles of Social Order* (K.I. Winston ed., Duke University Press, Durham,
N.C., 1981) (collected essays with a helpful introduction by Kenneth Winston).

Matthew H. Kramer, "Scrupulousness Without Scruples: A Critique of Lon
Fuller and His Defenders, 18 *Oxford Journal of Legal Studies* 235 (1998), reprinted
in modified form in *In Defense of Legal Positivism: Law Without Trimmings* (Oxford
University Press, Oxford, 1999), pp. 37–77.

Robert S. Summers, *Lon L. Fuller* (Stanford University Press, Stanford, California,
1984).

Chapter Seven

Ronald Dworkin's Interpretive Approach

Ronald Dworkin (1931–) is probably the most influential English-language legal theorist of this generation. Over the course of 30 years, he has developed a sophisticated alternative to legal positivism. Though his theory has little resemblance to the traditional natural law theories of Aquinas and his followers, Dworkin has occasionally referred to his approach as a natural law theory, and it is on the natural law side of the theoretical divide set by the Hart-Fuller debate. At the same time, it may sometimes be helpful to see Dworkin's work as establishing a third alternative to legal positivism and natural law theory: an interpretive theory of law.

EARLIER WRITINGS

In Dworkin's early writings,[1] he challenged a particular version of legal positivism, a view which saw law as being comprised entirely of rules, and judges as having discretion in their decision-making where the dispute before them was not covered by any existing rule. Dworkin offered an alternative vision of law, in which the resources for resolving disputes "according to law" were more numerous and varied, and the process of determining what the law required in a particular case more subtle.

Dworkin argued that along with rules, legal systems also contain principles. Legal principles are moral propositions that are stated in or implied by past official acts (*e.g.* statutes, judicial decisions, and constitutional provisions). While rules act in an "all or nothing" way (if a rule applies, it is conclusive, it decides the case), principles can apply to a case without being dispositive. Principles (*e.g.* "one should not be able to profit from one's own wrong" and "one is held to intend all the foreseeable consequences of one's actions") have "weight" favouring one result; there can be—and often are—principles favouring contrary results on a single legal question.

---

[1] Collected in Dworkin, *Taking Rights Seriously* Harvard University Press, Cambridge, Mass., (1977).

There is still a legal positivist-like separation of law and morality in this view of law, in that judges are told to decide cases based not on whatever principles (critical) morality might require, but rather based on a different and perhaps inconsistent set of principles: those relied upon, or implicit in, past official actions.

Dworkin argued for the existence of legal principles (principles which are part of the legal system, which judges are bound to consider where appropriate) by reference to legal practice (in the United States and England). Particularly telling for Dworkin's argument are those "landmark" judicial decisions where the outcome appears to be contrary to the relevant precedent, but the court still held that it was following the "real meaning" or "true spirit" of the law; and also more mundane cases where judges have cited principles as the justification for modifying, creating exceptions in, or overturning legal rules.

Because there are (numerous) principles as well as rules, there will be few if any occasions where the law "runs out" and judges must decide the case without legal guidance; but at first glance, legal determinacy might seem to be undermined by the abundance of sometimes-contrary material. However, Dworkin had a response to that problem. Under his approach, judges consider a variety of theories regarding what the law requires in the area in question, rejecting those which do not adequately "fit" past official actions. Among the theories that adequately "fit", the judge chooses the one which best combines "fit" and moral value, making the law the best it can be. Two tenets of Dworkin's early writings were thus indirectly related: that law contains principles as well as rules; and that for nearly all legal questions, there are unique right answers.

While there are reasons to conclude that Dworkin had overstated the differences between his view of the law and that of H.L.A. Hart, and also that he made out the line between rules and principles to be clearer than it (sometimes) is in practice,[2] what remains is the insight that a purely rule-based approach to the nature of law or the nature of judicial reasoning (whether such a view could ever fairly have been attributed to Hart or not) would be problematic. There is always the sense of moral standards qualifying the rules (e.g. that a rule should not apply as written if it would lead to an absurd result, or if one of the parties had acted inequitably, and so on) as somehow already having been present in the law, even before the standards are constructive interpretation articulated or decisions based upon them are announced.[3]

---

[2] See, e.g. Hart, 'Postscript", pp. 259–263; Raz, "Legal Principles and the Limits of Law".
[3] See N. E. Simmonds, *Central Issues in Jurisprudence* (Sweet & Maxwell, London, 1986), pp. 2–4.

CONSTRUCTIVE INTERPRETATION

In his later works, Dworkin offered what he called "an interpretive approach" to law.[4] (While Dworkin has said little about the relationship between his earlier writings and his later work, the later work is probably best seen as a reworking of earlier themes within a philosophically more sophisticated framework. (However, Jules Coleman has offered the interesting view that there are basic differences between Dworkin's earlier and later writings, grounded on the fact that the political philosophy of the earlier writings was "rights-based liberalism", while the political philosophy of the later writings was that of "liberal community".[5])

In *Law's Empire*, Dworkin argued that "legal claims are interpretive judgments and therefore combine backward- and forward-looking elements; they interpret contemporary legal practice as an unfolding narrative".[6] According to Dworkin, every time a judge is confronted with a legal problem, he or she should construct a theory of what the law is. That theory must adequately fit the relevant past governmental actions (legislative enactments and judicial decisions),[7] while making the law the best it can be.[8]

According to Dworkin, both law (as a practice) and legal theory, are best understood as processes of "constructive interpretation", interpretation that makes its object the best it can be (in Dworkin's words, an interpretation which makes it "the best possible example of the form or genre to which it is taken to belong"[9]). Constructive interpretation is both an imposition of form upon an object being interpreted (in the sense that the form is not immediately apparent in the object) and a derivation of form from it (in the sense that the interpreter is constrained by the object of interpretation, and not free to impose any form the interpreter might choose). One can think of constructive interpretation as being similar to the way people have looked at collections of stars and seen there pictures of mythic figures, or the way modern statistical methods can analyse points on a graph (representing data), and determine what line (representing a mathematical equation, and thus a correlation of some form between variables) best explains that data.

Dworkin believes that constructive interpretation is also the proper approach to artistic and literary interpretation, and his writings frequently compare the role of a judge with that of a literary critic. Both the applicability of constructive interpretation to artistic interpretation and

---

[4] Dworkin, *Law's Empire*, pp. 46–48.
[5] Jules L. Coleman, "Truth and Objectivity in Law", 1 *Legal Theory* 33 at 48–54 (1995).
[6] Dworkin, *Law's Empire*, p. 225.
[7] *ibid.* at pp. 227–228. 245–258.
[8] *ibid.* at pp. 52, 143.
[9] *ibid.* at p. 52.

the treatment of legal interpretation and artistic interpretation as analogous, are controversial claims.[10]

Constructive interpretation depends upon being able to assign a distinctive value or purpose to the object of interpretation, whether that object is a work of art or a social practice. It is that value or purpose which serves as the criterion for determining whether one interpretation of the object is better or worse than an alternative. For the constructive interpretation of law, Dworkin states that the purpose of law is to constrain or justify the exercise of government power.[11]

The past actions of officials, whether judges deciding cases and giving reasons for their decisions or legislators passing statutes, are the data to be interpreted constructively. In making the law, or an area of the law, the best it can be, the criteria Dworkin mentions most often are, as before, "fit" and moral value. For some legal questions, the answer may seem easy because only one theory shows adequate "fit". However, where the law is unsettled or inconsistent, or where the legal question is novel, there will be alternative theories with adequate "fit". Among these, some will do better on "fit", others better on moral value. In making comparisons among alternative theories, the relative weighting of "fit" and moral value will itself be an interpretive question, and will vary from one legal area to another (e.g. protecting expectations may be more important regarding estate or property law, while moral value may be more important for civil liberties questions).[12]

Dworkin also writes of "Integrity": the belief that judges should decide cases in a way which makes the law more coherent, preferring interpretations which make the law more like the product of a single moral vision. Dworkin wrote, "Judges who accept the interpretive ideal of integrity decide hard cases by trying to find, in some coherent set of principles about people's rights and duties, the best constructive interpretation of the political structure and legal doctrine of their community."[13] The interpretation of the law should, to the extent possible (given the relevant interpretive constraints) "express [] a coherent conception of justice and fairness."[14] In some ways, the development of an interpretive theory around the concept of "Integrity" can be seen as a somewhat grander, somewhat more sophisticated version of the spirit underlying common law reasoning: a form of decision-making based in part on consistency, though a consistency sensitive to principle, and in part on a belief that past decisions were rough approximations or intuitions about justice and fairness.[15]

---

[10] For contrary views, see, e.g. Andrei Marmor, *Interpretation and Legal Theory* (Clarendon Press, Oxford, 1992), pp. 35–60; Richard A. Posner, *Law and Literature: A Misunderstood Relation* (rev. ed., Harvard University Press, Cambridge, Mass., 1998), pp. 209–268.
[11] Dworkin, *Law's Empire*, pp. 93, 109, 127.
[12] *ibid.* at pp. 228–258.
[13] *ibid.* at p. 255.
[14] *ibid.* at p. 225.
[15] See Simmonds, *Central Issues in Jurisprudence*, p. 89. On common law reasoning, see Ch. 13.

Dworkin's writings (both earlier and later) can be seen as attempts to come to terms with aspects of legal practice that are not easily explained within the context of legal positivism. For example: (1) the fact that participants in the legal system argue over even the most basic aspects of the way the system works (for example, arguments over the correct way to interpret ambiguous statutes, and over how one should apply constitutional provisions to new legal questions), not just over peripheral matters or the application of rules to borderline cases; (2) even in the hardest of hard cases, the lawyers and judges in the case speak as if there were a unique correct answer which the judge has a duty to discover; and (3) in landmark cases, where the law seems on the surface to have changed radically, both the judges and commentators often speak of the new rule having "already been present" or the way law "works itself pure."[16]

A standard response to Dworkin's work (both to his early writings and to the later interpretive approach) is that judges and legal theorists should not look at law through "rose-coloured glasses", making it "the best it can be"; rather, they should describe law "as it is". The key to understanding Dworkin, in particular his later work, is to understand his response to this kind of comment: that there is no simple description of law "as it is"; or, more precisely, that describing what law "as it is" necessarily involves an interpretive process, which in turn requires determining what is the best interpretation of past official actions.[17] Law "as it is", law as objective or non-controversial, is only the collection of past official decisions by judges and legislators (which Dworkin refers to as the "pre-interpretive data", that which is subject to the process of constructive interpretation). However, even collectively, these individual decisions and actions cannot offer an answer to a current legal question until some order is imposed upon them. That order is the choice, the moral-political choice, between tenable interpretations of those past decisions and actions.

If asked, say, "what is the law regarding economy recovery for nervous distress", it is quite possible that the lawyer one asks will not be able to offer any authoritative source which speaks directly to the specific problem posed; that is, the question may be unsettled in the laws of that jurisdiction. It may be that the lawyer can point to certain statutes that have been passed that are relevant, and to certain decisions that have been made by courts at various levels on related matters, and perhaps even to the writings of commentators suggesting that future decisions on this question come out one way rather than another, but it may be that none of these items directly and conclusively answers the question posed. To get that answer, the lawyer must go through a certain kind of reasoning process, deriving an answer from the various materials. For Dworkin, this is an act of "interpretation".

---

[16] *Omychund v Barker* (1744) 26 ER. 15 at 23.
[17] The first three chapters of *Law's Empire* contain the arguments underlying this conclusion. See Dworkin, *Law's Empire*, pp. 1–113.

What of the situations where there do seem to be authoritative legal sources directly on point? For example, the lawyer might triumphantly announce that the appellate court had rendered a decision on the very issue just a few weeks earlier. Is that the end of the matter? Is there then no need for "interpretation"? Even putting aside possible questions of whether the appellate court decision might not be subject to a different interpretation (its language perhaps having been ambiguous), Dworkin might point out that a skilled advocate could still argue, looking at all the relevant past legal decisions, that the appellate court decision was mistaken and should be overturned, or that the decision was too broad and it will probably later be overturned or limited to a few situations.

The interpretive approach has the advantage of reflecting, and being able to account for the way that law (or at least certain areas of the law) is regularly subject to change and re-characterization. This strength may also be the approach's weakness: that it emphasizes the possibility of revision too much and the likelihood of settledness too little; and that it celebrates the notion of the great individual judge rethinking whole areas of law and thereby deflecting attention from the important roles of consensus and shared understandings.[18]

A related kind of challenge has been offered to Dworkin's approach to law: that it is legal theory for (or from the perspective of) judges, rather than the full theory of law it purports to be.[19] Making the best theory of law one can from the relevant past legal decisions may be the appropriate prescription if one is a judge within a legal system.[20] However, why would one take the same perspective if one were merely a citizen in the society?

For many citizens, the perspective wanted on the law is similar to that of Justice Holmes' "bad man"[21]: people want to know what they have to do to avoid legal sanctions, or, to put the matter differently, what they can get away with without facing sanctions. From the perspective of the ordinary citizen, there are a number of reasons to think of law in terms of a prediction of how judges (and police officers) will interpret the rules. Not only is there the desire to avoid legal sanctions, but if law is going to succeed in co-ordinating behaviour, then it is important that different citizens view what the law requires in roughly the same way (for example, if

---

[18] For a more detailed discussion of some of these themes, see Gerald Postema, "'Protestant' Interpretation and Social Practices", 6 *Law and Philosophy* 283 (1987) (Dworkin accepted the "Protestant" description in *Law's Empire*, p. 413; and "Thirty Years On", p. 1684); see also Bix, *Law, Language and Legal Determinacy*, pp. 111–116, 125–129.

[19] See, *e.g.* Raz, *Ethics in the Public Domain*, pp. 186–187; Bix, *Law, Language and Legal Determinacy*, pp. 118–120.

[20] Though Dworkin recommended that if the legal system is sufficiently wicked, the judge should not try to make the legal system "the best it can be"; he or she should just lie about what the law requires. Dworkin, "A Reply by Ronald Dworkin", p. 258.

[21] Holmes, "The Path of the Law", pp. 460–461; see generally William Twining, "The Bad Man Revisited", 58 *Cornell Law Review* 275 (1973).

they all have comparable ideas about what traffic laws or anti-pollution laws require). Arguably, this kind of consensus is unlikely to come about—or at least less likely to come about if citizens were to take up Dworkin's interpretive approach to the law.

What is distinctive to Dworkin's approach, and part of what makes it seem suspicious to many other theorists, is that the continuity between what would usually be thought to be jurisprudential questions (the nature in law in general or the basic nature of a particular legal system) and what would usually be considered practical or doctrinal legal questions (what the law in this jurisdiction requires on some issue). Constructive interpretation is Dworkin's response to both kinds of queries, and he has expressly offered that "no firm line divides jurisprudence from adjudication or any other aspect of legal practice."[22] Most theorists discussing the nature of law would be more hesitant to find implications of their general theories for more particular questions of legal doctrine, finding such implications, if at all, only on occasional, and usually highly unusual cases. By contrast, Dworkin argues that one's jurisprudential stance is implied in every legal dispute settled.[23]

RIGHT ANSWERS

For a long time, the idea most closely associated with Dworkin's work in legal theory was the "right answer thesis", the claim that all (or almost all) legal decisions have a unique right answer. It is interesting to note some of the ways that the presentation of this view, and attacks on it, have changed over time.

There are three themes that persist throughout Dworkin's many discussions of his "right answer thesis". The first is that this claim reflects our practice: that even in difficult decisions, judges and lawyers discussing, arguing, and deciding cases act as if, and talk as if, there were a right answer to be found. This reference to practice often elicits responses along the lines that judicial "right answer" rhetoric is just a matter of show or a matter of convention, and that judges in more reflective moments endorse a contrary position.[24]

A second theme, which has become more prominent in the Dworkin's later writings, is that there are right answers to legal questions for the simple reason that judges must reach a result in the questions placed before them, and some answers are better than others.[25] Every other

---

[22] Dworkin, "Legal Theory and the Problem of Sense", p. 14.
[23] Dworkin writes: "Jurisprudence is the general part of adjudication." *ibid.* at p. 15.
[24] See, *e.g.* Hart, "Postscript", pp. 273–275. For a response to this kind of argument, see Dworkin, "Legal Theory and the Problem of Sense", pp. 11–13.
[25] See, *e.g.* Dworkin, "A Reply by Ronald Dworkin", pp. 275–278.

argument Dworkin raises, and he raises quite a few, could be considered just a variation on this point.

While a theorist like Joseph Raz is concerned with distinguishing among judicial decisions, differentiating those that are based on legal standards and those that are based on extra-legal standards, and between those which apply prior decisions ("apply existing law") and those that make fresh decisions ('make new law"),[26] Ronald Dworkin finds such distinctions to be besides the point. He sees no reason not to view every standard a judge is required to apply as a "legal" standard.[27] Arguments about which aspects of judicial decisions are based on "legal" factors and which on "extra-legal" factors seem to him of little interest.

A third theme is that the best way—and perhaps the only way—to prove or disprove the existence of unique right answers in (all) legal cases is to consider individual, difficult cases, and construct an argument that a particular result is the unique, correct one, or to argue that in this case, no one answer is better than the alternatives.[28] There is unlikely to be a global argument establishing or refuting legal determinacy.

General challenges have been raised to the possibility of right answers under Dworkin's approach based on problems of incommensurability (whether one can meaningfully state that one theory is better than another when one alternative is better on one value, e.g. "fit", and the other alternative is better on a different value, e.g. "moral worth")[29] and demonstrability (that given Dworkin's other premises, he cannot conclude both that there are unique right answers to all legal questions and that these right answers will not be demonstrable at least in principle under optimal conditions).[30] These are interesting and difficult topics,[31] but there is not time to deal with them adequately in the present text.

Some of Dworkin's later interpretive discussions treated the issue of "right answers" only in passing or by implication. The most recent work seems to go even further, treating the issue as an irritating distraction:

"We should now set aside, as a waste of important energy and resource, grand debates about . . . whether there are right or best or true or soundest answers or

---

[26] See, e.g. Raz, *Ethics in the Public Domain*, 187–192.
[27] Dworkin, "A Reply by Ronald Dworkin", pp. 261–262.
[28] See, *e.g.* Ronald Dworkin, "Pragmatism, Right Answers, and True Banality", in *Pragmatism in Law and Society* (M. Brint and W. Weaver ed., Westview Press, Boulder, Colo., 1991), p. 365.
[29] The debate between Dworkin and various critics on the issue of incommensurability is summarized in Bix, *Law, Language and Legal Determinacy*, pp. 96–106.
[30] See Michael S. Moore, "Metaphysics, Epistemology and Legal Theory" (book review), 60 *Southern California Law Review* 453 at 480–483 (1987).
[31] On incommensurability generally, see Ruth Chang ed., *Incommensurability, Incomparability, and Practical Reason* (Harvard University Press, Cambridge, Mass., 1997); On the implications of incommensurability for law, see "Symposium: Law and Incommensurability", 146 *University of Pennsylvania Law Review* 1169–1731 (1998).

only useful or powerful or popular ones. We could then take up instead how the decisions that in any case will be made should be made, and which of the answers that will in any case be thought right or best or true or soundest really are."[32]

On the other hand, while the tone of this quotation is dismissive, it continues a theme mentioned earlier: there are at least "best answers" to legal questions, even if for some reason one hesitates about calling them "right answers".

Why might the discussion of the "right answer thesis" be worth the effort? One point is a psychological/sociological one directed at judges and advocates. If they believed that in difficult cases there was likely to be a unique correct answer, however difficult it might be to discover, and however much competent lawyers might disagree about which answer was the correct answer, the efforts and arguments would be directed at the legal materials: trying to construct an argument for one answer or another being the right one. On the other hand, if it were thought that because of the law running out, or incommensurability problems, or the indeterminacy of language, or whatever, that there were usually no unique right answers for the more difficult legal questions, then the attention of advocates and judges in such cases might turn too quickly (whatever "too quickly" might mean here) to legislative questions of which proposed legal rule would be best. Dworkin would argue that it is better (that it is the better interpretation of our own practices) that courts remain, to the extent possible, "forums of principle", attempting to discover the answer to legal disputes within the existing legal materials.

DWORKIN V HART

Dworkin's early work gained prominence for its attacks on legal positivism, in particular H.L.A. Hart's version of legal positivism. What little direct response there was from Hart tended to come late in his life, and a good portion of it was only published posthumously.[33]

The "debate" between Dworkin and Hart, like the "debate" between Hart and Fuller, may be best understood as not having been a debate at all, as the term is normally used. The differences between the two theorists are not so much contrary views on particular issues, but both more and less than that: Hart and Dworkin had differing ideas about which

---

[32] Dworkin, "Pragmatism, Right Answers, and True Banality", p. 360.
[33] I am thinking in particular of Hart, "Comment", published in 1987; and Hart, "Postscript", published posthumously in 1994. For completeness one should also note Hart, *Essays in Jurisprudence and Philosophy*, pp 137–141 (reproducing material first published in 1977), which discussed aspects of Dworkin's work, but more by way of reporting than critique.

questions and which concerns in legal theory are the most pressing.[34]
This is not to say that there are not some overlapping issues about which
one could accurately state that the theorists have contrary positions,
only that to focus on these direct disagreements would tend to underestimate the extent to which the theorists were actually talking past one
another.

In one of his responses to Dworkin, Hart began by contrasting theories about law in general versus theories about a particular legal system
(or, as he read Dworkin's theory, theories about how judges in a particular legal system should decide cases).[35] This claim brings up, among other
things, the question about the possibility of general jurisprudence (an
issue considered in Ch. 2) and the proper characterization of Dworkin's
theory.

Elsewhere in the same article, Hart offered a contrast among possible
types of legal theory, a contrast based on images. One type of theory is
to be used "within" the legal system: for example, in telling a judge how
to decide disputes. Another type of theory involves looking at the system
"from the outside". Basing the argument on the images, one would say
that a theory cannot be simultaneously part of the legal system and a
description of the system from the outside.[36] In some ways, this last argument is a strange one for Hart to have put forward, for one of the most
significant aspects of Hart's approach to law (as discussed in Ch. 3) was
that it demanded that we look at the perspectives of citizens within a legal
system, the "internal point of view", in constructing a theory of law.

The main question for this exchange between Dworkin and Hart is
how much we can rely on the images, on the metaphors, alone, in evaluating or creating arguments. It does sound strange to say that a theory is
simultaneously part of the system and the best explanation of the system.
However, arguments of this kind, with all their hints of circularity, are
actually relatively common in modern philosophy; examples include the
hermeneutic circle in literary theory, and John Rawls' use of reflective
equilibrium in moral and political theory.

To the extent that there is a true conflict between Dworkin and Hart,
it is at those times when Dworkin states or implies that there is no room
for a substantive, detailed and interesting descriptive theory of law (that
is not interpretive). This struggle can be seen not only in Hart's insistence
of the space for and need for a (non-interpretive) descriptive theory of law
in general, but also in his disagreement with any attempt to recast legal
positivism as being about justifying present/future coercion,[37] and his
claim that even if the "sense" of legal propositions in most or all legal

---

[34] This is a point Hart himself noted. See Hart, "Comment", pp. 36–40.
[35] *ibid.* at pp. 36–38.
[36] *ibid.* at p. 40.
[37] Hart, "Postscript", pp. 241–242.

systems is interpretive/evaluative, it does not follow that descriptive theory of such matters need similarly he interpretive/evaluative.[38]

DEBUNKING QUESTIONS

Commentators will sometimes query "the real reason" for or "the real motivation" behind some line of analysis. This type of challenge has its roots in American legal realism[39] and its most enthusiastic recent proponents are in the critical legal studies movement (topics to he discussed in Chs 17 and 19); the topic is raised here, because while the claim is rarely considered from the perspective of the theorist being "debunked", this is a perspective from which such claims may lose some of their force.

Critics sometimes claim that the terms used by practitioners or theorists are labels without content, which only serve to mislead. If we look at the actual practice, the argument goes, we would find only an attempt to rationalize particular results. Additionally (as conclusion if not as premise), these arguments usually hold that it is all but nonsensical to say that one theory is better than another at explaining law. All that is going on in descriptive legal theory, this approach states, is an attempt to legitimate particular judicial decisions or methods.

Such analyses can be provocative, though there are times when one is concerned with how easily they seem to be produced. There are many such arguments about: for example, the early American theorists, like Christopher Columbus Langdell, who tried to portray legal reasoning and the judicial process as scientific, were trying to defend unpopular conservative judicial decisions as "objective", as required by deductive reasoning that the judges could not legitimately side-step. The American legal realists who debunked this formalistic approach could themselves be debunked: their positive program legitimized legal reform and justified the use of policy arguments in the courts.[40] Similarly, H.L.A. Hart, with his arguments based on the "open texture" of language, could be seen as justifying limited judicial legislation in difficult cases. In the same line of analysis, Ronald Dworkin's approach, in terms first of the "right answer thesis" and later with the "interpretive approach", could be seen as offering a way of legitimizing the apparently political nature of the Warren Court's jurisprudence in the United States, at a time when the decisions of that court were attacked as "anti-democratic".[41]

The critics seem to be arguing that theories of interpretation merely

---

[38] *ibid.* at p 244.
[39] See, *e.g.* Felix Cohen, "Transcendental Nonsense and the Functional Response", 35 *Columbia Law Review* 809 (1935).
[40] See Horwitz, *The Transformation of American Law 1870–1960*, pp. 185–212.
[41] See Peter Gabel, Book Review, 91 *Harvard Law Review* 302 (1977).

decorate and legitimate the choices made by judges, while hiding the real reasons (motivations) for the decisions, and that few decisions are actually determined (or precluded) by the theoretical prescriptions (for example, "neutral principles",[42] "the Grand Style of Judging",[43] or "the judicial virtues"[44]) judges are told to follow.

Dworkin has responded to attempted "debunkings" of this type by claiming that they are irrelevant to his project. Why does it matter, he asks, that there might be historical, psychological or sociological explanations for why a particular theory was put forward or was well-received?[45] Even if it can be proven that a theory serves the interests of a certain class or group at the expense of others, or that the theory expresses the *Zeitgeist* of its era of origin, why should this matter? In the end, the question is whether the theory is right, or whether it is at least better than alternative theories. Historical, psychological and sociological explanations are marginal to investigations into a theory's correctness.

Debunking explanations may not be completely irrelevant, in that we can rightly be suspicious of philosophical positions—whether these be ethical theories, social theories, or legal theories—that match the theorist's self-interest or that theorist's particular prejudices regarding how the world should be. However, suspicion is not proof, and as long as argument about the merits of a theory can be conducted on neutral grounds (according to criteria accepted by the participants in the field regarding what makes for stronger and weaker arguments and for better and worse theories[46]), then the "debunking" arguments can work only to justify beginning a debate about the theory in question; the eventual judgment about its merits will be based on other grounds.

Suggested Further Readings

Marshall Cohen ed., *Ronald Dworkin and Contemporary Jurisprudence* (Duckworth, London, 1984) (contains critical essays and a long reply by Dworkin).
Ronald Dworkin, *Law's Empire* (Harvard University Press, Cambridge, Mass., 1986).
—, *A Matter of Principle* (Harvard University Press, Cambridge, Mass., 1985).
—, "My Reply to Stanley Fish (and Walter Benn Michaels): Please don't Talk about Objectivity Any More", in *The Politics of Interpretation* (W.J.T. Mitchell ed., University of Chicago Press, London, 1983), pp. 287–313.

---

[42] Herbert Wechsler, "Toward Neutral Principles in Constitutional Law", 73 *Harvard Law Review* 15 (1959).
[43] Karl Llewellyn, *The Common Law Tradition: Deciding Appeals* (Little, Brown & Co., Boston, 1960).
[44] Hart, *The Concept of Law*, pp. 204–205
[45] *See, e.g.,* Dworkin, *Law's Empire*, pp. 271–274 (discussing critical legal studies).
[46] Of course, the skeptic might argue that there are no "neutral grounds": all criteria already express the interests or the pre-conceptions of certain groups.

—, "On Gaps in the Law", in *Controversies about Law's Ontology* (P. Amselek and N. MacCormick eds, Edinburgh University Press, Edinburgh, 1991), pp. 84–90.

—, *Taking Rights Seriously* (revised ed., Duckworth, London, 1977) (the revised edition contains a "Reply to Critics").

—, "Thirty Years On" (book review), 115 *Harvard Law Review* 1655 (2002).

Stephen Guest, *Ronald Dworkin* (2nd ed., Edinburgh University Press, Edinburgh, 1997).

Jurisprudence Symposium, 11 *Georgia Law Review* 969–1424 (1977) (includes discussions of Dworkin's early work by H.L.A. Hart, Kent Greenawalt, Stephen Munzer, and David Richards, and a reply by Dworkin).

Andrei Marmor, *Interpretation and Legal Theory* (Clarendon Press, Oxford, 1992).

Nicos Stavropoulos, *Objectivity in Law* (Clarendon Press, Oxford, 1996).

Symposium on *Law's Empire*, 6 *Law and Philosophy* 281–438 (1987).

PART C

Themes and principles

There are issues in legal philosophy that are not comfortably constrained within the discussion of particular legal theorists or jurisprudential movements, and which seem to have repercussions simultaneously at different levels of concern. That is, issues like justice, punishment, and the obligation to obey the law can be understood and considered both at a level of practical concern about what should be done in certain circumstances, and as inextricably part of the larger puzzle about how to think about law. There are also themes, like "will v reason" and the problem of "finality v authority" that seem to recur, in various guises, in a variety of different jurisprudential debates. The following chapters explore such issues and themes.

Chapter Eight

Justice

"Justice" refers to the family of moral concepts connected particularly with law and politics—"politics" here being understood broadly in the sense of public decision-making regarding the distribution of goods. Justice is a subset of morality. Thus, one can sensibly speak of something being "right" or "wrong" on occasions where it seems inapt to speak of "justice".[1] Additionally, justice seems to refer to the relatively rigid application of rules and standards, where right action might sometimes require more nuanced treatment (either "equity" or "mercy"). Aristotle wrote: "when men are friends they have no need of justice".[2]

There are various ways of dividing up the domain of justice. The most famous distinction is probably Aristotle's, between "corrective justice" and "distributive justice".[3] Corrective justice involves rectification between two parties where one has taken from the other or harmed the other. Modern discussions of corrective justice often occur within the context of arguing about appropriate standards within tort law and contract law. Distributive justice involves the appropriate distribution of goods among a group ("giving each person his or her due"). Most of the better known modern discussions of justice, which usually treat justice primarily as about the proper structuring of government and society, are basically discussions of distributive justice.

The relationship between corrective and distributive justice is a matter of controversy. One question is whether there is a conceptual connection between the two. Aristotle argued that both forms of justice were matters of "proportion"[4]: that both when one person has harmed another, and

---

[1] For example, white one might sensibly say that it is wrong for someone to make no use of substantial natural talents, it would sound strange (to most people) to say that it is "unjust" of that person to waste those talents.

[2] Aristotle, *Nicomachean Ethics*, Book VIII, 1:1155a, in *The Complete Works of Aristotle*, Vol. 2, p. 1825. Some would also contrast justice—treatment according to what is due—with right (or at least expected and acceptable) action within a family where we accept and prefer "our own" regardless of their merit.

[3] *ibid.* at Book V, 3:1131a–4:1132h, in *The Complete Works of Aristotle*, Vol. 2, pp. 1785–1787.

[4] *ibid.* at Book V, 3:1131a–b, in *The Complete Works of Aristotle*, Vol. 2, pp. 1785–1786.

when there has been a mal-distribution of goods, matters are out of proper proportion. A quite different question is the connection between the two as a matter of moral evaluation. That is, how do the two interact? For example, if one lives in a society which is distributively unjust (some people have much more than others, without basis or warrant), does this in any way mitigate the demand for corrective justice *(e.g.* when the deserving take from the undeserving)?[5] Many people seem to feel this way often at an unreflective level, as when someone will claim that there is nothing wrong in deceiving a large insurance company or some other large corporation, the implicit premise being that these companies have themselves benefited from some wrongdoing, and therefore it would not be unjust to take from them.

Along with corrective justice and distributive justice, the term "justice" is also frequently used to refer to following the rules laid down.[6] This has obvious applications to law ("no retroactive punishments"), but is relevant also to other aspects of daily life ("not changing the rules in the middle of the game" and the like).[7] "Justice" is also often used to describe the appropriateness of punishments for crimes; the topic of punishment will be considered in the next chapter.

The remainder of this chapter will focus on some of the more influential recent theories of justice.

JOHN RAWLS AND SOCIAL CONTRACT THEORY

John Rawls' book, *A Theory of Justice*,[8] is probably the most influential

---

[5] See, *e.g.* Stephen R. Perry, "The Distributive Turn: Mischief, Misfortune and Tort Law", in *Analyzing Law: New Essays in Legal Theory* (B. Bix ed., Clarendon Press, Oxford, 1998) pp. 142–143; Coleman, "Second Thoughts and Other First Impressions", pp. 308–310.

[6] See, *e.g.* Aristotle, *Nicomachean Ethics*, Book V, 7:1134b in *The Complete Works of Aristotle*, Vol. 2, pp. 1790–1791: "Of political justice part is natural, part legal,—natural, that which everywhere has the same force and does not exist by people's thinking this or that; legal, that which is originally indifferent, but when it has been laid down is not indifferent . . ." This sort of "procedural" or "formal" justice was discussed in greater detail in the context of Lon Fuller's work, in Ch. 6.

[7] Lloyd Weinreb gives the example of the chariot race in the *Iliad*, which was part of the funeral commemoration for Patroclus. Achilles announced prizes for the race, including a mare for second place. Antilochus finishes second, but Achilles wanted to give the mare to Eumelos, the best charioteer of the group, who finished last only because of the meddling of the gods. Antilochus protests that Achilles may give Eumelos whatever Achilles wishes, but the mare, the prize for second place, is rightly his. See Homer, *The Iliad*, Book 23 (W.H.D. Rouse trans., Thomas Nelson and Sons, Edinburgh, 1938); Weinreb, *Natural Law and Justice*, p. 186.

[8] John Rawls, *A Theory of Justice* (Harvard University Press, Cambridge, Mass., 1972). For detailed discussions of Rawls's work, see *e.g.* Norman Daniels ed., *Reading Rawls: Critical Studies of A Theory of Justice* (Basic Books, New York, 1990); Robert Paul Wolff, *Understanding Rawls: A Reconstruction and Critique of A Theory of Justice* (Princeton University Press, Princeton, 1977).

book of political theory written in the twenthieth century.[9] For John Rawls (1921–2002) and many of the competing approaches, theories of justice are about the appropriate way to structure government and society—that is, political theory, writ large.[10]

To the question of why is a theory of justice needed, Rawls would probably respond: because publicly agreed terms of social co-operation are both necessary and possible.[11] For Rawls, justice is the structural rules of society, within which people who (inevitably) have different sets of values and goals in life, can co-exist, co-operate, and, to some extent, compete. Rules are necessary for people to co-operate to create social and individual goods within society. The question then becomes: *On what terms are people to co-operate, and how are the social goods to be distributed?* Theories of justice are answers to that question, or at least constraints on the answer.

How do we determine which principles to follow? If I write out some principles, and declare that they are fair, many will disagree with me. If I claim to prove that these principles derive from basic foundational axioms, some will contest my derivation, while others will argue that the axioms I have chosen are the wrong ones. However, if we were all to agree on principles, however they might be derived, then we would seemingly have no basis for arguing against the fairness of their application to us. Consider an analogy: there might be substantial room for disagreement if the question is whether two hundred dollars is a fair price for painting the fence around your house; the issue would be substantially changed if it was noted that I had *agreed* ahead of time, after negotiation, to paint the house for that amount. In that case, most people would likely presume that my being paid that (agreed) price was fair, even if they might have thought prior to the agreement that a different price was more appropriate.[12]

---

[9] One commentator recently stated: "two decades after the publication of John Rawls's *A Theory of Justice* (1971)[,] [o]ne cannot, at least in the English-speaking world, think about justice without taking one's position relative to that work." Ruth Anna Putnam, "Why Not a Feminist Theory of Justice?", in *Women, Culture, and Development: A Study of Human Capabilities* (M.C. Nussbaum and J. Glover ed., Clarendon Press, Oxford, 1995), p. 303.

[10] In this sense, there is a distant family relation between Rawls' theory of justice and Plato's. Plato viewed justice both for individuals and for societies as involving the elements of the whole being arranged appropriately to create overall harmony. Plato, *Republic*, Book II, pp. 357–367; Book IV, 441–445; Book IX, 588–592, in *Plato: The Collected Dialogues*, pp. 605–614, 683–688, 816–819.

[11] See Rawls, *A Theory of Justice*, pp. 3–6.

[12] The presumption that an agreed price can be fairly/justly imposed on the person who agreed to it is subject to inquiries regarding that person's mental capacity, whether that person had been subject to duress, whether there had been any fraudulent representations by the other party, and so on. There are also arguments that some agreements are so one-sided in their terms that the consent of the parties is insufficient to justify the agreement's enforcement.

The notion of agreement as the foundation of "just" or "legitimate" principles for governing society is the basis of the "social contract" tradition in political theory, which goes back at least to Thomas Hobbes' work in the seventeenth century, and continues in the recent, influential work of John Rawls and David Gauthier.[13] These political theorists were working from the starting point that a government can *legitimately* govern its citizens if those citizens expressly granted the government those powers.

Some of the early social contract theorists wrote of a historical express agreement among citizens to create a government and empower it to maintain order and protect citizens' rights. Of course, even if there had been such a historical agreement, the question remains why later generations, who had not been party to this social contract, should be bound by its terms.

John Locke offered the notion of "tacit consent": that while many of us have not offered any express agreement to be subject to the government and to be bound by its rules, we have done actions which have tacitly expressed our consent (or, at least, have put us in a position where consent could fairly be ascribed to us). Examples of actions which might be said to give tacit consent to the government would include voting in an election, accepting government benefits, or simply remaining in the country (and thereby benefiting from it) after one was of age, and had the legal right to leave.[14]

As will be discussed in greater detail later (in Ch. 11), modern social contract theorists, Rawls included, have transformed the inquiry from an investigation of what historical figures *actually* agreed, and how those agreements might still bind people today, to a discussion of what *reasonable people might* agree to, *were* they to try to reach agreement. As I note in that chapter, this is a more substantial change than it might at first appear, just as the inquiry about how much I should be paid for painting the fence changes if it turns out that I expressly agreed ahead of time to a particular price.[15] The question is whether actual choice is carrying the heavy moral weight, or whether the weight is being carried by an abstract notion of "reasonableness".

For Rawls, the focus is a "thought experiment": a hypothetical discussion among citizens within a community. Even though the discussion is entirely fictional, it does not mean that we would necessarily become any more optimistic about how quickly we could come to consensus. (A thought experiment will not lead to useful conclusions, it will not give a

[13] For a selection of social contract theory texts, including works by Thomas Hobbes, Samuel Pufendorf, John Locke, Jean-Jacques Rousseau, Immanuel Kant, John Rawls, and David Gauthier, see Michael Lessnoff ed., *Social Contract Theory* (New York University Press, New York, 1990).
[14] Many variations on the consent theory appear in the related context of whether there is an obligation to obey the law (see Ch. 16), and can be traced at least to Plato's *The Crito*, where Socrates argues for his own obligation to comply with the unjust death penalty verdict imposed upon him.
[15] See also Dworkin, *Taking Rights Seriously*, pp. 150–153.

basis for persuading other people about some point of ethics, if one does not use realistic assumptions.) The starting point for Rawls, and for other social contract theorists, is that there is no point in making arguments from foundational moral beliefs (or religious beliefs or political dogmas) for many people would not accept those starting points.

If one cannot derive the principles of government from foundational axioms on which all agree (because there *are* no foundational axioms on which all agree, or at least none of sufficient substance or specificity to be of use), perhaps we can at least reach agreement after open and free discussion. If we do come to principles in this way, there would seem to be no basis then for objecting to the principles thus agreed upon. However, we would likely never come to consensus after free discussion because, Rawls argues, our different positions in life create differing self-interest (and bias). And nothing short of consensus would do, for the dissenters from a majority vote would have a sound ground for objecting to having principles imposed upon them without their consent. Self interest will often bias people's thinking, to favour principles that make them better off, or at least create resistance to principles of justice, however fair, which would result in a decrease of their well-being. Therefore, Rawls suggests, imagine instead a discussion among people similarly situated—or similarly unsituated, similarly ignorant of their position in society.

Thus, as part of Rawls' thought experiment, we are to imagine negotiators who are magically shorn of all knowledge which might be the basis for self-interested bias: knowledge of their gender, wealth, race, ethnicity, abilities, and general social circumstances. They would also be ignorant of their own views on the good life (*e.g.* born-again Christian, hedonist, art-centred, or materialist), which would likely also bias their views on how to organize society.[16] Rawls calls this starting point, of imagined negotiators behind a "veil of ignorance",[17] "the original position".[18]

This is the first part of Rawls' argument: that the result of this thought experiment, this hypothetical negotiation, would be legitimate principles of justice (this is why Rawls refers to this theory as "justice as fairness"—justice as the result of agreement by persons under fair conditions). The second part of Rawls' work is an argument about what principles would in fact result. One can accept the first part and not the second (arguing that Rawls has improperly calculated what principles would result from the original position); one can also accept the second part and not the first (arguing that

---

[16] This also reflects Rawls' notion that "the right is prior to the good". See Rawls, *A Theory of Justice*, p. 31: principles of justice should be the structure in place *within which* citizens can follow their diverging views of the good.

[17] *ibid.* at pp. 12, 136–142.

[18] Rawls calls his approach "justice as fairness", which was also the name of the articles in which he first introduced his ideas about justice. See John Rawls, "Justice as Fairness", 54 *Journal of Philosophy* 653 (1957), in expanded form, 67 *Philosophical Review* 164 (1958).

the original position is not the right way to derive principles of justice, but that the principles Rawls comes up with nonetheless are the right ones).[19]

RAWLS' TWO PRINCIPLES

Rawls first considers whether negotiators in the original position would adopt utilitarianism.[20] He argues that this is not likely: for utilitarianism allows some to suffer if the suffering is outweighed by the benefits to others; and as negotiators would not know if they would be in the advantaged or the disadvantaged group, they would not want to take the risk that they might be in the suffering group. This exemplifies the cautious ("risk-averse") attitude that Rawls attributes to the negotiators,[21] which seems to produce many of the argument's conclusions.

The two principles of justice Rawls concludes that the negotiators would agree to are the following:

• First Principle: "Each person is to have an equal right to the most extensive system of equal basic liberties compatible with a similar system of liberty for all."

• Second Principle ("The Difference Principle"): "Social and economic inequalities are to be arranged so that they are both: (a) to the greatest benefit of the least advantaged, . . . and (b) attached to offices and positions open to all under conditions of fair equality and opportunity."[22]

---

[19] Rawls, *A Theory of Justice*, p. 15.

[20] *ibid.* at p. 14. Rawls defines as follows the utilitarianism with which he contrasts his own approach: "society is rightly ordered, and therefore just, when its major institutions are arranged so as to achieve the greatest net balance of satisfaction summed over all individuals belonging to it." *Ibid.* at p 22 (footnote omitted). Rawls sees utilitarianism as the predominant moral philosophy (at least as applied to political issues) in the English-speaking world, and therefore the primary alternative and competitor to consider when putting forward a theory of justice. See John Rawls, *Political Liberalism* (Columbia University Press, New York, 1993), pp. xvi–xvii.

[21] Rawls refers to the "maximin" principle: that people would want to maximize the worst-case scenario they could possibly face. Rawls, *A Theory of Justice*, pp. 152–155. Rawls argued that negotiators would be particularly inclined to be risk-averse because: (a) the likelihood of various options are far from clear and would be hard to ascertain; (b) there is a great deal to lose in the worst-case scenario; and (c) there is not that much to gain (advantages above the worst case are of relatively modest value; having a lot of money is better than having a modest amount; but the difference is not as great as that between having a modest amount and being in the underclass). *Ibid.* at pp. 155–156.

[22] *ibid.* at p. 302. In later works, the first principle is slightly altered: instead of speaking of each person having the "most extensive system of equal basic liberties compatible with a similar system of liberty for all", the principle refers to each person having an equal claim to "a fully adequate scheme of equal basic rights and liberties, which scheme is compatible with the same scheme for all." Rawls, *Political Liberalism*, p. 5. The change was made in response to a criticism by H.L.A. Hart. See *ibid.* at p. 5, n. 3.

For the first principle, "basic liberties" includes, among other things, political liberty, freedom of speech and assembly, freedom of conscience, the right to hold personal property, and the right to fair treatment under the law.[23]

The first principle is to have "lexical priority" over the second: that is, the equality of liberty is not to be sacrificed (traded off) for compensating benefits in wealth or equality of resources.[24] Rawls argues that it would be irrational for the negotiators to take chances with their liberty.[25]

As for the distribution of resources, the topic of Rawls' second principle, the beginning position the negotiators might consider is the equal sharing of social wealth. Again, the cautious negotiators would not want to create substantial inequalities on the chance that they might be at the bad end of the scale. The only reason someone might accept anything other than an equal share is if the inequalities that would be allowed would result in each and every person doing even better than they would have done in an equal-sharing system. This may occur because inequalities create competitive incentives that increase productivity, that in turn increase both individual and social wealth.[26]

Why not just let the free market system work as it will? Because, Rawls states, even putting aside concerns about social class perpetuating itself, natural liberty "permits the distribution of wealth and income to be determined by the natural distribution of abilities and talents. Within the limits allowed by the background arrangements, distributive shares are decided by the outcome of the natural lottery; and this outcome is arbitrary from a moral perspective."[27] The reference to "natural lottery" indicates the extent to which significant inequalities derive from chance, not merit. From the perspective of the Rawlsian negotiators, on the chance that they might be someone born unlucky in the natural lottery—with few natural talents, born to a poor family, in a benighted area, and so on— they want to make sure that they are not unjustly punished for that bad fortune.

Rawls includes a "just savings principle", as a means of ensuring justice between generations: "Each generation must not only preserve the gains of culture and civilization, and maintain intact those just institutions that have been established, but it must also put aside in each period of time a suitable amount of real capital accumulation." Rawls, *A Theory of Justice*, p. 285.

[23] *ibid.* at p. 61.

[24] *ibid.* at pp. 42–44, 61, 151–152.

[25] Contrast the argument that has been used at various times to defend government actions in Singapore, South Korea, Hong Kong, amid other countries, that the citizens in those countries had willingly and reasonably given up rights to liberty in exchange for greater material well-being

[26] *ibid.* at p. 151. Rawls states that it is an assumption that no one will make their negotiation decisions based on envy.

[27] *ibid.* at pp. 73–74.

RAWLS' LATER MODIFICATIONS

Rawls wrote a number of important articles which expanded or modified ideas in *A Theory of Justice*,[28] which later appeared, in modified form, as the book *Political Liberalism*.[29] The extent to which the later work diverged from either the content or the intention of the earlier work has been a matter of controversy. Rawls himself allows that there are differences, though he tends to hold them to be less comprehensive and less radical than other commentators have claimed. The (apparent or perceived) differences may be summed up in the title of one of the intermediate articles: "Justice as Fairness: Political not Metaphysical". Many readers read *A Theory of Justice* as making broad claims about the nature of justice, which were in turn based on claims about the basic nature of human beings.

The later work makes its claims clearly on a less ambitious scale: "justice" is presented as a set of institutions and practices to allow people with distinctly different ideas about the good life to co-exist and prosper. The claims of the theory are to be seen as "political, not metaphysical"; as a *modus vivendi* for co-existence by people within society who have quite different "theories of the good" (*e.g.* based on different religious or ethical belief systems).[30] The principles of justice attempt to reflect an "overlapping consensus"—values which people with a variety of theories of the good can nonetheless support because these values appear in the various theories of the good.[31] This re-interpretation of the theory as a political conception of justice was continued in the published (but unfinished) *Justice as Fairness: A Restatement*.[32]

ROBERT NOZICK AND LIBERTARIANISM

There have been a number of responses to Rawls' theory of justice. One of the most important and thought-provoking was from the libertarian theorist, Robert Nozick (1938–2002), in his book, *Anarchy, State and*

---

[28] See John Rawls, "Kantian Constructivism in Moral Theory", 77 *Journal of Philosophy* 515 (1980); "The Basic Liberties and Their Priority", in *The Tanner lectures on Human Values*, Vol. 3 (University of Utah Press, Salt Lake City, 1982), pp. 1–87; "Justice as Fairness: Political not Metaphysical", 14 *Philosophy & Public Affairs* 223 (1985); "The Idea of an Overlapping Consensus", 7 *Oxford Journal of Legal Studies* 1 (1987); and "The Priority of Right and Ideas of the Good", 17 *Philosophy & Public Affairs* 251 (1988).

[29] John Rawls, *Political Liberalism* (Columbia University Press, New York, 1993).

[30] See Rawls, *Political Liberalism*, pp. 4–22.

[31] *ibid.* at pp. 9–11, 58–66.

[32] John Rawls, *Justice as Fairness: A Restatement* (E. Kelly ed., Harvard University Press, Cambridge, Mass., 2001).

Utopia.[33] The main project of the book was to defend a minimalist state (a "night watchman state"), defending it on one side against anarchists who believe that state power over individuals can never be justified, and on the other side against theorists (like Rawls) who advocate an interventionist state that will redistribute wealth, help the poor, and the like.

In response to Rawls, Nozick's first question is: why are we talking about a just *distribution?* Rawls had written: "As a first step, suppose that the basic structure of society distributes certain primary goods, that is, things that every rational man is presumed to want."[34] Nozick points out that most of the goods which we own or want to own are *not* "distributed" in the sense of being divided among people at one given time by the government or "the basic structure of society" or any other centralized power. "What each person gets, he gets from others who give to him in exchange for something, or as a gift".[35] The issue for government will not be one of "distribution", but of "*re*distribution".

Secondly, Nozick points out that any sort of "*patterned*" distribution (*e.g.* justice requires that everyone to have an equal amount, or that the distribution of goods be according to need, merit, intelligence, ability, effort, etc.) will be vulnerable: it will likely be regularly and continually disrupted by the voluntary independent choices of individuals. Nozick uses the example of the star athlete, working after hours, who many people will pay to see from whatever wealth they have.[36] This type of transaction, along with gifts, bequests, and private contractual agreements, will all serve to undermine whatever "just" pattern has been set. (And how can anyone complain about the resulting distribution, which was caused by the voluntary actions of people dealing with their own resources as they saw fit?) Someone who believes that justice requires a patterned distribution will then be left with two equally unpleasant options: forbid all voluntary independent actions that affect people's holdings, or impose regular, intrusive redistributive taxes.[37]

Nozick's alternative approach is not so much "just (re)distribution" but "justice in holdings". According to Nozick, there are two ways in which one can justly own some thing: (1) one could have acquired the object consistently with the principles of just acquisition (the appropriation of unheld things: *e.g.* claiming and working unclaimed land); or (2) one could have obtained the thing, with accordance to the principles of just transfer, from someone else who was herself entitled to own the thing (*i.e.* a voluntary transaction, whether by exchange or gift, with no fraud, duress, or the like). No one is entitled to own a thing where the ownership cannot

[33] Robert Nozick, *Anarchy, State, and Utopia* (Basic Books, New York, 1974).
[34] Rawls, *A Theory of Justice*, p. 62.
[35] Nozick, *Anarchy, State, and Utopia*, p. 149.
[36] *ibid.* at pp. 160–164.
[37] *ibid.* at pp. 163–164.

be traced by the (perhaps repeated) application of one or both principles.[38] This Nozick refers to as an "historical" principle of justice, to be
contrasted with "end result" or "end state" principles.[39] What follows
from Nozick's analysis is that society/government has no right to redistribute goods, violating people's just claim to the objects they own, for
some general benefit. However, society does have the right—and probably the duty—to redistribute goods to correct some prior injustice in
holdings.[40]

Two significant objections can be raised to Nozick's approach. First,
even accepting the basic approach, how can or should society respond if
it is not some small percentage of property holdings which are unjust, but
the injustice rather reaches the vast majority of such holdings? For
example, one might argue that almost all American holdings can be
traced back to an unjust displacement of Native Americans; and, additionally, a significant portion of the holdings can be traced to unjust
enslavement of African-Americans. It is far from clear whether Nozick's
approach can be of significant use with a starting point like that.[41]

A second line of criticism inquires why property rights should have
such a high, indeed almost absolute, standing in our moral or political
thinking. Many would argue that others within our community, and the
community itself, have claims upon us and our resources which justify
infringements on our holdings, however otherwise beyond reproach those
holdings may be.[42]

MICHAEL SANDEL, COMMUNITARIANISM, AND CIVIC REPUBLICANISM

A distinctively different critique of Rawls came from Michael Sandel,
whose arguments have been associated with an approach to political and
moral theory called communitarianism.[43] Some communitarians have

---

[38] *ibid.* at pp. 150–153.

[39] *ibid.* at pp. 153–155.

[40] *ibid.* at pp. 152–155.

[41] Nozick at a couple of points, *ibid.* at pp. 152–153, 230–231, seems to realize some of the
problems with rectifying significant historical injustice, and even suggests, at p. 231, that
it may be best "to view some patterned principles of distributive justice as rough rules of
thumb meant to approximate the general results of applying the principle of rectification of injustice."

[42] See, *e.g.* James W. Harris, "Rights and Resources—Libertarians and the Right to Life",
15 *Ratio Juris* 109 (2002). For a collection of critical views of Nozick's position, see Jeffrey
Paul ed., *Reading Nozick: Essays on Anarchy, State, and Utopia* (Rowman and Littlefield,
Totowa, N.J., 1981).

[43] Sandel's critique appears in Michael J. Sandel, *Liberalism and the Limits of Justice*
(Cambridge University Press, Cambridge, 1982; 2nd ed., 1998). In a Preface to the
Second Edition, Sandel notes that the label "communitarian" does fit to some extent the

argued that the liberal view of justice[44] is valid only to the extent that the liberal view of individuals is correct: cut-off people who have no connections with one another, and who co-operate only to the extent that it is useful in achieving each individual's short-term or long-term goals. Communitarians contest this view of persons.

Liberals and libertarians ground their theories of justice on an analysis which treats people as essentially atomistic: in this view, an individual is, essentially, just a metaphysical will, an ability to choose any form of good, any set of values, etc., and an ability to step back from prior such choices, evaluate them, and perhaps decide to modify them.

Sandel argues that this does not reflect real life, at any level. We come into the world as part of a family, a community, an ethnic and religious group, etc. and this is an essential part of our identity at all stages of our lives. What follows from this? Sandel suggests that justice/ethics should centre on, or at least take into account, our connections: our responsibilities as members of our communities, citizens of a country, etc.

More specific to the current topic: Sandel is suspicious of the view of individuals that underlies Rawls' analysis, and is particularly clear in the "original position". For Rawls, we can speak of the choosing individual separate from his or her view of the good, and indeed separate from all of his or her attributes, beliefs, attachments and affiliations. This is a minimal self or simple will that makes choices, a view of human essentials that can he traced from Rawls at least back to Immanuel Kant.[45] For Sandel and other communitarians, it is unwise and likely distorting to view individuals separate from the families, communities and other attachments which shape individuals long before those individuals can make mature, informed and autonomous choices.

Communitarians do not all believe in the same things, and to the extent that their positions do converge, it tends to be on criticisms of the basic points of liberal individualism. The conventional view of society is that government is there to protect individual rights (for some, the focus would be on rights of liberty and conscience, for others, on rights of property

---

critique of Rawls and contemporary liberal political theory given in the book. However, he adds: "[t]he 'liberal-communitarian' debate that has raged among political philosophers in recent years describes a range of issues, and I do not always find myself on the communitarian side." Sandel, *Liberalism and the Limits of Justice*, 2nd ed., at p. ix. On communitarianism generally, see Daniel Bell, "Communitarianism", in E. N. Zalta ed., *Stanford Encyclopedia of Philosophy, http://plato.stanford.edu* (2001).

[44] In the context of the communitarianism-liberalism debate, and in a number of other settings in political theory, "liberalism" is to be understood broadly, as any approach which emphasizes individualism and individual rights against the state. In this sense, most ideological conservatives can be called "liberal", as can the vast majority of major politicians in the U.K. (whether Conservative, Liberal-Democrat, or Labour) and in the U.S. (whether Republican or Democrat).

[45] See Sandel, *Liberalism and the Limits of Justice* (2nd ed.), pp. 6–9.

and free contract) and to resolve disputes between individual claims. The public good is defined as either the protection of the basic rights and the framework within which they can be fully realized (*e.g.* the free market), or simply the summation of (conflicting) individual preferences. Communitarians tend to emphasise the importance of community, and the importance of (responsible) membership in a political community. The argument is that "membership of a political community is a good that liberalism neglects, ignores, or whose sense it cannot successfully capture by its own terms."[46] It is important to recognise, respect and protect the intermediate institutions that play such a large role in our identities and our lives. In considering principles and legal rules, the focus should be on communities, and on society: how adopting one principle or rule rather than another might help or hurt society, not just how it might affect the autonomy of atomistic individuals. For example, the advantage of free public education should be seen not primarily in how it equips individuals to succeed in the marketplace, but in how educated people will make better citizens.[47]

It is not just a different justification for the same rules. A focus on communities might lead to different policies: communitarians are less likely than liberals to defend pornography and less likely than conservatives to defend corporate rights, *e.g.* regarding the rights of corporations to move or shut down when this means the massive loss of employment and vitality to the local community.

Michael Walzer offers another communitarian critique of justice: that notions of justice arise *within* a community, a tradition, and a particular set of circumstances.[48] This is a challenge to a basic notion underlying conventional theories of justice (and, indeed, conventional theories of morality): that what is right is *universally* right—for all people, and for all times.[49] One should not overstate the disagreement here: Walzer is willing to speak of "a core morality differently elaborated in different cultures"[50]; however, for Walzer, critical debate occurs within the "thicker" culturally-based moral-

---

[46] David Archard, "Political and Social Philosophy", in *The Blackwell Companion to Philosophy* (N. Bunnin and E.P. Tsui-James ed., Blackwell, Oxford, 1996), p. 270 (discussing communitarianism).
[47] See Michael J. Sandel, "Morality and the Liberal Ideal", *The New Republic*, May 7, 1984, at pp. 15–17.
[48] See Michael Walzer, *Thick and Thin: Moral Argument at Home and Abroad* (University of Notre Dame Press, Notre Dame, 1994), pp. 2–11; Michael Walzer, *Spheres of Justice* (Basic Books, New York, 1983), pp. 4–6; Michael Walzer, *Interpretation and Social Criticism* (Harvard University Press, Cambridge, Mass., 1987), pp. 3–32.
[49] See, *e.g.* Aristotle, *Nicomachean Ethics*, Book V, 7:1134h, in *The Complete Works of Aristotle*, Vol. 2, pp. 1790–1791, where Aristotle distinguishes between that part of justice "which everywhere has the same force and does not exist by people's thinking this or that", and that part of justice which derives from compliance with conventional laws.
[50] See Walzer, *Thick and Thin*, p. 4 (footnote omitted).

ities. "The hope that minimalism, grounded and expanded, might serve the cause of a universal critique is a false hope."[51] For Walzer, questions of justice, and responses to those questions, will, and should, be debated within the context of a particular community and a particular tradition.

Communitarianism is a near relation to an approach to political theory known as "republicanism" or "civic republicanism" (not to be confused with the "Republican" political parties in the U.S. and elsewhere).[52] The connection may be only indirect, in the sense that one approach does not logically follow from the other, but both are responses to and reactions against the same views and attitudes; that is, both oppose or question the emphasis on individuals and individual interests at the heart of conventional theories of law and justice. Civic republicanism is the idea that *civic virtue*, the participation in public, political life, is an important value that should be emphasized. According to this approach, one of the tasks of government is to make the citizenry more virtuous and encourage participation in the public good.[53]

Civic republicanism has a robust theory of the public good, and our duties, as citizens or officials, to serve that public good, which places it as the diametrical opposite of public choice theory (which will be discussed in Ch. 18). Public choice theory argues, claims, or assumes that there is no such thing as the public good (or at least that the "public good" is rarely sought and even more rarely realised); rather, there is only, or mostly, the conflicting claims of different individuals and interest groups.

FEMINIST CRITIQUES

A number of interesting criticisms of conventional discussions of justice have been put forward by feminist theorists.[54] For example. Susan Moller Okin and Ruth Anna Putnam (among others) have argued that works about justice written by men tend to focus too narrowly on justice in

---

[51] *ibid.* at p. 11. Walzer adds: "The morality in which the moral minimum is embedded, and from which it can only temporarily be abstracted, is the only full-blooded morality we can ever have."

[52] On civic republicanism, see J.G.A. Pocock, *The Machiavellian Moment: Florentine Political Thought and the Atlantic Republican Tradition* (Princeton University Press, Princeton, 1975); Philip Pettit, "Republicanism", in E. N. Zalta ed., *Stanford Encyclopedia of Philosophy*, http://plato.stanford.edu (2003).
For the application of civic republicanism to law, see *e.g.* Frank I. Michelman. "The Supreme Court 1985 Term—Foreword: Traces of Self-Government", 100 *Harvard Law Review* (1986); Cass R. Sunstein, "Beyond the Republican Revival", 97 *Yale Law Journal* 1539 (1988).

[53] Philip Pettit offers a somewhat different perspective on civic republicanism, when he argues that the core of the view is a particular theory of freedom—that citizens should never be exposed to political domination—and that republican views about the proper structure of government and society follow from that. Pettit, "Republicanism".

[54] Feminist approaches to law and legal theory will be discussed in greater detail in Ch. 19.

116   JUSTICE

political life and the distribution of goods, not giving enough emphasis to
the implications of how the workplace is structured for family life, or
family life for the workplace.[55] Additionally, the argument is that most
theories of justice have tended to assume a traditional household, with its
gendered division of labour, and these theories assume that division to be
just, an assumption feminists contest.[56] The claim is not that it is unjust
for women to work in the home rather than seek wage work (if that is their
choice), but that it is unjust to have legal or social norms that state that
women can or should *only* work in the home.[57]

Martha Fineman has argued that liberal individualism is built around
a presumption of self-sufficiency, when the reality is that all of us are inevitably dependent for significant parts of our life (when we are very young)
and many others at other times due to age, sickness or disability.
Additionally there are also "derivative dependencies", as those who care
for the inevitably dependent (in many societies, the child-care tends to fall
predominantly on mothers) are often unable or less able to support themselves. Legal, political, or moral theories built around assumptions of self-
sufficiency, which have no place for inevitable and derivative dependencies,
will present a false picture of society and will usually fail to deal with the
challenges that come from these dependencies.[58]

A related line of feminist criticism comes from those who believe that
certain values often associated with women, involving caring and nurturing, are often excluded from (male) theories of justice, morality and moral
development.[59] I will return to this line of argument in Ch. 19, where I
discuss the role it plays within feminist legal theory.

Suggested Further Readings

Aristotle, *Nicomachean Ethics*, Book V.
Schlomo Avineri and Avner de-Shalit eds, *Communitarianism and Individualism*
(Oxford University Press, Oxford, 1992) (includes discussions by well-known
figures associated with communitarianism, including Charles Taylor, Alasdair
MacIntyre, Michael Walzer; Will Kymlicka and Michael Sandel).

---

[55] See Susan Moller Okin, *Justice, Gender, and the Family* (Basic Books, New York. 1989), pp.
89–97; Ruth Anna Putnam. "Why Not a Feminist Theory of Justice?" in *Women, Culture,
and Development: A Study of Human Capabilities* (Martha C. Nussbaum and Jonathan Glover
eds, Clarendon Press, Oxford, 1995), pp. 298–331.
[56] See Okin, *Justice, Gender, and the Family*, pp. 8–10, 90–97.
[57] See, *e.g. ibid.* at pp. 103–104.
[58] See Martha A. Fineman, *The Neutered Mother, the Sexual Family, and Other Twentieth Century
Tragedies* (Routledge, New York, 1995); Martha A. Fineman, "Contract, Marriage and
Background Rules," in *Analyzing Law: New Essays in Legal Theory* (B. Bix ed., Clarendon
Press, Oxford, 1998), pp. 183–195.
[59] See, *e.g.* Carol Gilligan, *In a Different Voice* (Harvard University Press, Cambridge, Mass., 1982,
rev. ed., 1993); Robin West, *Caring for Justice* (New York University Press, New York, 1997).

Robert Nozick, *Anarchy, State, and Utopia* (Basic Books, New York, 1974).
Susan Moller Okin, *Justice, Gender, and the Family* (Basic Books, New York, 1989).
Plato, *The Republic.*
John Rawls, *Justice as Fairness: A Restatement* (E. Kelly ed., Harvard University Press, Cambridge, Mass., 2001).
—, *Political Liberalism* (Columbia University Press, New York, 1993).
—, *A Theory of Justice* (Harvard University Press, Cambridge, Mass., 1971, rev. ed., 1999).
Alan Ryan ed., *Justice* (Oxford University Press, Oxford, 1993) (a collection of readings, including Plato, Aristotle, Cicero, David Hume, John Stuart Mill, Karl Marx, John Rawls and Robert Nozick).
Michael Sandel, *Liberalism and the Limits of Justice* (2nd ed., Cambridge University Press, Cambridge, 1998) (second edition adds a preface, which comments on communitarianism, and a chapter responding to Rawls' *Political Liberalism*).
Robert C. Solomon and Mark C. Murphy ed., *What Is Justice? Classic and Contemporary Readings* (Oxford University Press, New York, 1990).

Chapter Nine

Punishment

Was the punishment too harsh, or not harsh enough? It is difficult to answer the question of what would be a "fair" or "appropriate" punishment for a particular crime or a particular criminal until one has a clear sense of what one thinks the *purpose(s)* of punishment are.

Like other questions which fall under moral philosophy (broadly understood), the suggested purposes of punishment can be divided generally between approaches which see punishment as something of value in itself versus those that see punishment as a means to some other end.[1] The rest of this chapter will be devoted to summarizing the alternative approaches.[2]

RETRIBUTION

Those who see punishment as something of value in itself speak of the *justice* in punishing wrongdoers, and the need for *retribution* for the wrongful action. The idea of retribution seems to have ancient roots. Famously, the Bible states: "Wherever hurt is done, you shall give life for life, eye for eye, tooth for tooth, hand for hand, foot for foot, burn for burn, bruise for bruise, wound for wound."[3] This narrow and extreme conception of retribution, encouraging retaliation in kind (also known as "*lex talionis*"), has

---

[1] Ethical theories based on doing something because it is the right thing to do, or is one's duty, are known as "deontological", to be contrasted with "consequentialist" theories, which justify actions based on achieving some good state of affairs.

[2] It is useful to point out the extent to which the following discussion of punishment, like most such discussions, is artificially narrow. Philosophical discussions about the justice of punishment usually *start* with an assumption that the person convicted in fact did the crime: that there is no problem of enforcement error or problem of corruption and bias among those in power. Taking those issues into account would obviously complicate the moral analysis significantly. One writer who has focused on those issues is Randy Barnett. See Barnett, *The Structure of Liberty*, pp. 231–256.

[3] *Exodus* 21: 23–25, from *The New English Bible* (Oxford University Press, New York, 1971), p. 84.

few supporters[4], as matching "eye for eye" or "death for death" either has come to seem barbaric, or at least seems a concept difficult to apply universally (what is the "eye for eye" punishment for securities fraud?). However, the general notion of retribution, that the severity of the punishment should reflect the severity of the evil done, has many supporters.

A philosophical grounding for retribution was offered by Immanuel Kant (1724–1804), who argued that any approach to punishment *other than* retribution would be a deviation from the strict requirements of justice, and would also be immoral because it treated the subject of punishment disrespectfully, as a means to an end, rather than as an end in himself or herself.[5] Never one for half measures, Kant added: "Even if a civil society were to be dissolved by the consent of all its members . . . , the last murderer remaining in prison would first have to be executed, so that each has done to him what his deeds deserve and blood guilt does not cling to the people for not having insisted upon this punishment; for otherwise the people can be regarded as collaborators in this public violation of justice."[6]

Retribution theorists often speak in terms of "proportionality"[7]: that more serious crimes should receive more severe penalties. Obviously, determining the scale of relative culpability, or a formula for determining blameworthiness, is going to be a complicated process, which will leave ample room for controversy.[8] For example, how should one compare violent and non-violent crime? Should one focus on the action from the criminal's perspective or on the harm done?[9] Also, what role should there

---

[4] Once the concept is understood at a more general level *e.g.* that the punishment should somehow "fit" the crime, and perhaps reflect some of the same sorts of evil, it is easier to find supporters. See, *e.g.* Jeremy Waldron, *"Lex Talionis"*, 34 *Arizona Law Review* 25 (1992); Stephen P. Garvey, "Can Shaming Punishments Educate?", 65 *University of Chicago Law Review* 733 at 775–783 (1998).

[5] Immanuel Kant, *The Metaphysics of Morals* [AK 6:331–338] (M. Gregor, trans., Cambridge University Press, Cambridge, 1996), pp. 104–110 (first published, 1797) ("On the Right to Punish and Grant Clemency"). For a modern philosophical defense of retribution: see Michael S. Moore, "The Moral Worth of Retribution" in *Responsibility, Character and the Emotions* (F Schoeman ed., Cambridge University Press, Cambridge, 1987), pp. 179–219.

[6] Kant, *The Metaphysics of Morals* [6:333], p. 106. In recent years, some Kant scholars have raised questions whether he should be known as an "arch-retributivist"; these scholars have pointed to other passages in Kant's work which show his recognition of a deterrent function for punishment. See *e.g.* Thomas E. Hill, Jr., *Respect, Pluralism and Justice: Kantian Perspectives* (Oxford University Press, Oxford, 2000), pp. 173–199.

[7] See, *e.g.* H.L.A. Hart, *Punishment and Responsibility: Essays in the Philosophy of Law* (Oxford University Press, Oxford, 1968), pp. 233–234.

[8] For an excellent example of a theorist working through these (and other) issues, see Andrew Ashworth, *Sentencing and Criminal Justice* (Weidenfeld & Nicolson, London, 1992), pp. 55–170.

[9] For example, for three people driving with equal recklessness, the consequences might be quite different: one might return home safely, a second cause injury, and a third cause death. It is merely circumstances (what some call "moral luck") that equivalently wrongful behavior led to quite different levels of harm.

be for various sorts of exculpatory factors (everything from provocation to drunkenness to a deprived childhood)?[10]

"MAKING SOCIETY BETTER": CONSEQUENTIALISM/ UTILITARIANISM

"Consequentialism" is the belief that options should be evaluated by their consequences. "Utilitarianism" is a type (actually, a cluster of types) of consequentialism, whereby the consequences to be considered in the evaluation are the pleasure and pain of individuals, which are to be summed up; the option should be chosen which maximizes the sum of pleasure and pain for everyone (thus, the utilitarian maxim: "the greatest good for the greatest number"). Any evaluation of punishment which focuses on its future effects will be based on an express or implied foundation of consequentialism.

Many people think of punishment and limitations on punishment largely in terms of what the punishment can accomplish. Whether they support the death penalty may turn on whether they are convinced that this punishment deters other people, whether it reduces the total amount of future crime. This is to focus on a future state of affairs. The most common future-oriented, consequence-oriented, justification for punishment is "deterrence": the notion that the purpose of punishment is to prevent crime. The roots of deterrence theory are at least as old as those of retribution theory. This is from Plato:

"The purpose of the penalty is not to cancel the crime—what is once done can never be made undone—but to bring the criminal and all who witness his punishment in the future to complete renunciation of such criminality, or at least to recover in great part from that dreadful state."[11]

"Deterrence" can be separated into individual or "particular" deterrence (*the person punished* will not violate the law again) and "general" deterrence (the punishment of some will deter *others* from violating the law).

Other writers focus on "rehabilitation": that the exclusive or primary objective and justification of punishment is the effort to change the criminal into a responsible member of society, through whatever means work,

---

[10] Another factor most people would include is whether the criminal has done this, or similar, crimes before (this factor becomes an overwhelming factor in jurisdictions where multiple convictions authorize or mandate a large increase in the sentence imposed—the so-called "two strike" and "three strikes" laws). See, *e.g.* Ashworth, *Sentencing and Criminal Justice*, pp. 141–170. However, this factor seems to have less to do with "retribution", with giving punishment according to the "badness" of the act or the person, and more to do with "deterrence", which will he discussed in the next section.

[11] Plato, "Laws", Book XI, 934a-b, in *Plato: The Collected Dialogues*, p. 1486.

whether imprisonment or some alternative to imprisonment. This is also a consequentialist approach, as it focuses on the future and on the good of society, rather than on the evil or culpability of the criminal or the criminal act.

Most of those who favour a utilitarian (or other consequentialist) approach to punishment are quick to note that they do so only as regards the *extent* of punishment for offenders, *not* for determining *who* should he punished.[12] They would not authorize the punishment of an innocent person, even if it could be shown that by doing so society as a whole would be better off in the long run. Similarly, they would not want someone punished who was not responsible for his or her actions, whatever the long-run benefits to society.

OTHER OBJECTIVES

There are a variety of other objectives commentators sometimes offer for punishment which might not fit comfortably in the categories discussed above.

One is the expressive purpose of punishment: punishment as a way of expressing society's distaste for certain sorts of activities.[13] The notion is that prohibiting an action and punishing violators of the prohibition is worth doing, even if the punishment otherwise has no effect in deterring crime, if this serves to express society's moral beliefs. Sometimes commentators will distinguish "expressive" purposes of prohibition and punishment from "educative" purposes. In expression, the state or the majority is using the criminal law to state their opposition to certain practices (*e.g.* adultery), even if the law is unlikely to be widely enforced. In education, the state (or some interest group within the state) is trying to *change* people's attitude towards an activity: *e.g.* trying to persuade people that an activity once thought acceptable *(e.g.* sexual harassment) is not, or that an activity once thought a minor sin *(e.g.* driving while drunk) is in fact a major misdeed.

A purpose sometimes raised for the punishment of incarceration is the obvious one of incapacitation: whatever other effects imprisonment might have, it at least removes a criminal from the streets, therefore protecting the general public, at least for a while, from injury.

Finally, some commentators have argued that shaming the wrongdoer has been, and should be, both a type of punishment and a purpose of punishment. On the other side, those who believe that shame is an inap-

---

[12] See, *e.g.* Hart, *Punishment and Responsibility*, pp. 1–27, 193–209.
[13] See, *e.g.* Joel Feinberg, "The Expressive Function of Punishment", in *Doing and Deserving: Essays in the Theory of Responsibility* (Princeton University Press, Princeton, 1970), pp. 95–118.

propriate means or objective argue that this approach does not adequately respect the human dignity of the person being punished.[14]

Suggested Further Readings

Anthony Duff and David Garland eds, *A Reader on Punishment* (Oxford University Press, Oxford, 1994).

George P. Fletcher, "Punishment and Responsibility", in *A Companion to Philosophy of Law and Legal Theory* (D. Patterson ed., Blackwell, Oxford, 1996), pp. 514–523.

Martin P. Golding, *Philosophy of Law* (Prentice-Hall, Englewood Cliffs, N.J., 1975), Chs 4 and 5.

H.L.A. Hart, *Punishment and Responsibility: Essays in the Philosophy of Law* (Clarendon Press, Oxford, 1968).

Sanford H. Kadish and Stephen J. Schulhofer eds, *Criminal Law and its Processes* (7th ed., Aspen Publishing, New York, 2001), pp. 95–171 ("The Justification of Punishment").

Michael S. Moore, "The Moral Worth of Retribution", in *Responsibility, Character and the Emotions* (F. Schoeman ed., Cambridge University Press, Cambridge, 1987), pp. 179–219.

---

[14] For an overview of "shaming" in punishment, see, *e.g.* Toni M. Massaro, "Shame, Culture, and American Criminal Law", 89 *Michigan Law Review* 1880 (1991); Toni M. Massaro, "The Meanings of Shame: Implications for Legal Reform", 3 *Psychology, Public Policy and Law* 645 (1997). For an argument against the use of shaming, see *e.g.* James Q. Whitman, "What is Wrong with Inflicting Shame Sanctions?", 107 *Yale Law Journal* 1055 (1998).

Chapter Ten

Rights and Rights Talk

According to some commentators, ancient Roman Law and medieval legal systems had no concept that compared to the modern notion of "rights". The closest analogue, "*ius*" referred instead to "the right thing to do" or "what is due according to law".[1] Even those commentators who think that ancient and medieval law *did* have a concept of "rights" comparable to our own agree that it played a far lesser role in legal thought then, compared to modern legal thought.[2]

Rights and rights-talk are pervasive within modern discussions of law and government, a pervasiveness which sometimes leads to certain forms of confusion. The discussions of rights often exemplify a basic problem in conceptual analysis: the way abstract arguments can become entangled in particular policy views.

Rights come in at least two types: legal rights and moral rights, depending on whether the claim in question is grounded on the authoritative sources (*e.g.* statutes, judicial decisions, or constitutional provisions) of a particular legal system, or on a moral theory. Jeremy Bentham (1748–1832) famously argued that talk of moral rights (or "natural rights" or "human rights") was "simple nonsense . . . nonsense upon stilts."[3] The idea is that while legal rights have a clear correlate in the world, in legal texts and the willingness of legal officials to enforce them through various enforcement procedures, no such clear correlate exists for moral rights. However, this skeptical view of moral rights is not shared by many.

---

[1] See, *e.g.* Finnis, *Natural Law and Natural Rights*, pp. 205–220: David M. Walker, ed., *The Oxford Companion to Law* (Clarendon Press, Oxford, 1980), p. 1070 (entry on "Right"); Brian Tierney, *The Idea of Natural Rights: Studies on Natural Rights, Natural Law and Church Law 1150–1625* (Scholars Press, Atlanta, 1997).

[2] "It is an exaggeration to say, as [Sir Henry] Maine did, that [the Romans] constructed their system without the conception of a right, but they certainly did not attach anything like the same importance to it as do modern lawyers." H. F. Jolowicz, *Roman Foundations of Modern Law* (Oxford University Press, Oxford, 1957), pp. 66–67 (footnote omitted).

[3] Jeremy Bentham, "Anarchical Fallacies", reprinted in *Nonsense upon Stilts: Bentham, Burke and Marx on the Rights of Man* (J. Waldron ed., Methuen, London, 1987), pp. 46–69, at 53 (the text was written between 1791 and 1795, but not published for the first time until 1816).

One regular source of confusion in discussions about rights is the way that two different types of questions often go under the same label. First, conceptual questions about the nature of rights: like other conceptual questions, discussions about the (conceptual) nature of rights generally attempt either to offer a definition/delimitation for the purpose of clarity or to discover some element distinctive to the social phenomenon expressed in the way we use the term.[4] For example, one conceptual claim sometimes made is that one can only have rights to something beneficial.[5] This derives from, or at least is supported by our linguistic intuitions: that it makes sense to say "I have a right that you pay me five dollars", but not to say "I have a right that the state imprison me for five years as punishment for what I have done".[6] Additionally, there are often conceptual debates about whether certain classes of entities (*e.g.* future generations, animals, the environment, and foetuses) are capable of having rights.

In contrast to conceptual questions are policy questions: to what extent *should* this legal system—or all legal systems—protect a certain category of people, activities, places or things? It is easy when reading articles about rights to confuse the conceptual issues and arguments with the issues and arguments about policy matters.

A common confusion of this type occurs in discussions about abortion, as when someone responds to an argument in favour of legalizing abortion by saying "foetuses have rights". This mixes two levels of discussion, two different types of questions. It is compatible to say both: (1) (as a conceptual matter) I do not think it makes sense to speak of foetuses as having rights; and (2) (as a matter of policy or morality) I believe that abortion is wrong and immoral because it involves severely harming foetuses, which should not be allowed except in the most extreme circumstances. Of course, deciding that a certain type of entity (*e.g.* a foetus) *can* have (moral or legal) rights is different from saying that foetuses *do* have such rights. Finally, there can be circumstances where an entity has rights, but it is not protected because other parties have stronger countervailing rights. Thus, it is compatible to believe both: (1) foetuses are capable of having rights; and (2) abortion should be allowed

---

[4] See Ch. 2.
[5] See generally Hart, *Essays on Bentham*, pp. 174–188 (discussing Bentham's "Benefit Theory of Rights"); MacCormick, "Rights in Legislation", pp. 202–205. For more recent writings on this debate, see the texts cited in n. 12, below.
[6] Even this probably goes too far. Theorists who believe that being punished for one's crimes is a sign of being treated by society with dignity could (and sometimes do) speak of one's having a "right to punishment". See, *e.g.* Herbert Morris, "Persons and Punishment", 52 *Monist* 475 (1968). However, note that this does not undermine the general point, that it only makes sense to speak of one's right to X, when X is perceived as being, directly or indirectly, a positive thing. Here, these commentators see punishment as a kind of benefit (being treated with respect).

in most circumstances (because foetuses in fact do not have rights relevant to this situation, or whatever rights they have are overridden by the conflicting rights of the mother).

To put the matter another way, from the statement "Y is capable of having rights", it does not follow that Y has any rights, and it does not follow that whatever rights Y has will trump the conflicting legal interests in the matter under consideration.

The confusion in this area is encouraged by the use of rights rhetoric in political discourse (more prevalent in the United States than in most other countries). When people want to say that making sure that no one goes homeless is a worthy and important government objective, they often use the shorthand "human beings have a right to shelter", and when people want to express their belief that abortion should be prohibited, they sometimes choose the shorthand, "unborn babies have rights too!" Because talk of rights—legal rights, natural rights, human rights—is so entwined in political struggles, it is not surprising that many discussions of rights are muddled. The next section will discuss an important effort to try to clear up the confusions in talk about rights, proposed by Wesley Hohfeld earlier last century.

HOHFELD'S ANALYSIS

Wesley Hohfeld (1879–1918) wrote a pair of famous articles in which he tried to make "rights-talk" clearer.[7] First, he argued that the use of the word "right" in legal discourse was often loose, covering four different kinds of legal concepts:

(1) "rights", narrowly understood as claims correlative to other persons' duties;

(2) "liberties",[8] meaning at the least that the holder has no legal duty to refrain from the activity in question (the law may or may not expressly protect the ability to partake in the activity in question);

(3) "powers", the ability to change legal relationships *(e.g.* through contracts and wills); and

---

[7] Wesley Hohfeld, "Some Fundamental Legal Conceptions as Applied in Judicial Reasoning", 23 *Yale Law Journal* 16 (1913); Wesley Hohfeld, "Fundamental Legal Conceptions as Applied in Judicial Reasoning", 26 *Yale Law Journal* 710 (1917).

[8] In his articles, Hohfeld uses the word "privilege" for this concept, but in the current legal literature, the concept is usually labeled as "liberty"; "privilege" has a different set of connotations.

(4) "immunities", which correlate with disabilities of another (as constitutional rights correlate with disabilities of the government to act in certain ways).[9]

Hohfeld also offered two sets of connections among legal concepts through the visual image of squares:

(1) **(Claim-)Right   Duty**   (2) **Power   Liability**

   Liberty   No-Right   **Immunity   Disability**

Within each box, concepts which are across from each other are "correlates", and those which are at a diagonal are opposites. If I have a claim-right regarding some matter, then someone else has a duty. If I have a liberty regarding some matter, then I do *not* have a duty; and so on.

It is important to note that Hohfeld is *not* making an empirical claim when he states, for example, that claim-rights are correlated with duties. Hohfeld's definitions—along with the correlates included as part of the definitions—were stipulations. Thus, it makes no sense to criticize Hohfeld on the basis that his definitions are false. As stipulations, Hohfeld's definitions can be evaluated as helpful or confusing, but not as empirically true or false.[10] It would make no more sense to say that one had discovered a Hohfeldian claim-right without a corresponding duty, than it would to say that one had discovered a married bachelor. The question is only whether Hohfeld's proposed analytical clarifications are more helpful than confusing or misleading, and most commentators seem to think that they are.

Secondly, Hohfeld argued that all rights-statements ("rights" here understood either narrowly, in their first sense, as claims correlative to another party's duty, or broadly, as involving any of the four legal concepts named) should be reducible to a three-variable proposition: A has a right against B for X (where A and B are people or institutions, and X is an object or activity). For example, "Sarah has a right against John for five dollars" or "I have a right that Congress not interfere with my publishing this book".[11]

---

[9] Hohfeld, "Some Fundamental Legal Conceptions as Applied in Judicial Reasoning", pp. 28–58; see also Hohfeld, "Fundamental Legal Conceptions as Applied in Judicial Reasoning", p. 717; J.W. Harris, *Legal Philosophies* (2nd ed. Butterworths, London, 1997), pp. 83–93.

[10] See Matthew H. Kramer, "Rights Without Trimmings", in Matthew Kramer, N.E. Simmonds and Hillel Steiner, *A Debate Over Rights* (Clarendon Press, Oxford, 1998), pp. 22–24. For a discussion of stipulations in theory, see Ch. 2. For the claim that Hohfeld's analysis of the connections between these legal concepts expresses a necessary or conceptual truth about rights, see Sean Coyle, "Are There Necessary Truths About Rights?", 15 *Canadian Journal of Law and Jurisprudence* 21 (2002).

[11] Hohfeld, "Fundamental Legal Conceptions as Applied in Judicial Reasoning", pp. 742–766.

Among the problems that this kind of analysis avoids is when someone says "we have a right to education" or "we have a right to a job", but the speaker is unwilling to say (or thinks it unnecessary to say) whom this right is against. If someone claims that she has a right to a job, does she think that it is the government's obligation to give her a job, or perhaps the obligation of the largest employer in town, or perhaps the obligation of anyone with the means to offer employment? If the claimant is not willing to specify in such cases whom the right is against, one can suspect that the reference to rights is merely a form of rhetorical emphasis: "we have a right to a job" then becomes nothing more than a way of saying "we want a job very much" or "it would be a very good thing were someone to offer us jobs".

WILL THEORY VERSUS INTEREST THEORY

In the analytical tradition, there are two primary conceptual theories about the nature of rights.[12] The first is known as the "interest" or "beneficiary" theory of rights, and is associated with Jeremy Bentham (1748–1832) and Neil MacCormick (1941–). This view equates having a right with being the intended beneficiary of another party's duty.[13]

The second approach is the "will" or "choice" theory of rights, and is associated primarily with H.L.A. Hart (1907–1992). It equates rights with a party's "being given by the law exclusive control, more or less extensive, over another person's duty so that in the area of conduct covered by that duty the individual who has the right is a small-scale sovereign to whom the duty is owed."[14]

The relative advantage of the will theory is that it seems to point to something distinctive about rights in a way that the interest theory does not. The disadvantages of will theories of rights include that (1) they seem to exclude or to treat as lesser forms of rights inalienable rights (including some constitutional rights or "human rights"), or rights held by infants or other legally incompetent persons; and (2) they seem less clearly

---

[12] For a recent and detailed overview of the debates about the best conception of rights, see, e.g. Kramer, "Rights Without Trimmings", pp. 60–101; N.E. Simmonds, "Rights at the Cutting Edge", in Kramer, Simmonds and Steiner, *A Debate Over Rights*, pp. 134–152, 195–232; Hillel Steiner, "Working Rights", in *A Debate Over Rights*, pp. 233–301.

[13] See H.L.A. Hart, "Legal Rights", in *Essays on Bentham* (Clarendon Press, Oxford, 1982), pp. 162–193 at 174–181 (discussing Bentham's views); Neil MacCormick, "Rights in Legislation", in *Law, Morality and Society* (P.M.S. Hacker and J. Raz eds, Oxford: Clarendon Press, 1977), pp. 189–209. Joseph Raz's somewhat more general formulation of the view equates a party's having a right with "an aspect of [that party's] well-being (his interest) is a sufficient reason for holding some other person(s) to be under a duty." Joseph Raz, *The Morality of Freedom* (Clarendon Press, Oxford, 1986), p. 166.

[14] Hart, "Legal Rights", p. 183.

applicable when talking about *moral* rights, as contrasted with legal rights (and thus are not good candidates for conceptual theories of "rights generally").[15]

OTHER TOPICS

There are a number of topics within the area of rights that I do not have time to consider here. A sample will give a sense of how wide (and deep) the discussion of rights can go. First, to what extent can or should an analysis of legal rights be the basis of a general theory of rights (which would include moral as well as legal rights)?[16] Secondly, can a connection be drawn between rights, and the capability to have and claim rights, and the intrinsic dignity of human beings and the respect due all human beings?[17] Thirdly, Hohfeld's three-variable approach to legal rights to the contrary, does there remain a place and a need for a two-variable rights claim ("A has a right to X"), because there are exceptional cases of rights without correlative duties, because rights may he generative of duties in a case-by-case manner (a judge deciding in a particular case that *because* the plaintiff has a certain right, additional duties should be newly imposed on the defendants),[18] or because rights *in rem* are not properly analyzable in terms of rights *in personam*?[19] Fourthly, to what extent does the recognition of rights or an emphasis on rights help or hinder the search for progress and social justice?[20] Fifthly, why are some interests and demands perceived as rights and others are not?[21] Sixthly, do (moral) rights sometimes entail a (moral) right to do wrong?[22]

---

[15] Both will theories and interest theories can have trouble with third-party beneficiaries of transactions, depending on whether and when the legal system in question offers the right of enforcement to such beneficiaries. See, *e.g.* MacCormick, "Rights in Legislation", pp. 208–209.

[16] See Joseph Raz, "Legal Rights", 4 *Oxford Journal of Legal Studies* 1 (1984), reprinted in *Ethics in the Public Domain*, pp. 238–260.

[17] See Joel Feinberg, "The Nature and Value of Rights", 4 *Journal of Value Inquiry* 19, 28–29 (1970).

[18] See, *e.g.* MacCormick, "Rights in Legislation", pp. 199–202; Harris, *Legal Philosophies*, pp. 88–91; *cf.* Kramer, "Rights Without Trimmings", pp. 22–60, 101–111 (defending Hohfeld's analysis from a variety of attacks, and criticizing various misunderstandings of Hohfeld).

[19] See J.E. Penner, *The Idea of Property in Law* (Clarendon Press, Oxford, 1997), pp. 23–31.

[20] This topic will be discussed briefly in the section on critical legal studies in Ch. 19; see also Morton J. Horwitz, "Rights", 23 *Harvard Civil Rights–Civil Liberties Law Review* 393 (1988); Patricia J. Williams, "Alchemical Notes: Reconstructing Ideals From Deconstructed Rights", 22 *Harvard Civil Rights–Civil Liberties Law Review* 401 (1987).

[21] See, *e.g.* Alon Harel, "What Demands are Rights? An Investigation into the Relation between Rights and Reasons", 17 *Oxford Journal of Legal Studies* 101 (1997).

[22] See, *e.g.* Jeremy Waldron, *Liberal Rights: Collected Papers 1981–1991* (Cambridge University Press, Cambridge, 1993), pp. 63–87 ("A Right to Do Wrong").

Suggested Further Readings

Kenneth Campbell, "Legal Rights", in E. N. Zalta ed., *Stanford Encyclopedia of Philosophy*, http://plato.stanford.edu (2001).

H.L.A. Hart, "Legal Rights", in *Essays on Bentham* (Clarendon Press, Oxford, 1982), pp. 162–193.

Wesley Hohfeld, "Some Fundamental Legal Conceptions as Applied in Judicial Reasoning", 23 *Yale Law Journal* 16 (1913).

—, "Fundamental Legal Conceptions as Applied in Judicial Reasoning", 26 *Yale Law Journal* 710 (1917).

F. M. Kamm, "Rights", in *The Oxford Handbook of Jurisprudence and Philosophy of Law* (J. L. Coleman and S. Shapiro eds, K. E. Himma, assoc. ed., Oxford University Press, Oxford, 2002), pp. 476–513.

Matthew Kramer, Nigel Simmonds and Hillel Steiner, *A Debate Over Rights: Philosophical Enquiries* (Clarendon Press, Oxford, 1998).

David Lyons, *Rights* (Wadsworth, Belmont, Calif., 1979).

Neil MacCormick. "Rights in Legislation", in *Law, Morality and Society* (P.M.S. Hacker and J. Raz eds, Oxford: Clarendon Press, 1977), pp. 189–209.

Carlos Nino ed, *Rights* (New York University Press, New York, 1992) (contributors include Robert Alexy, Neil MacCormick, Joel Feinberg, H. L. A. Hart and John Rawls).

Joseph Raz, "Legal Rights", 4 *Oxford Journal of Legal Studies* 1 (1984) reprinted in *Ethics in the Public Domain* (Clarendon Press, Oxford, 1994), pp. 238–60.

Jeremy Waldron ed., *Nonsense upon Stilts: Bentham, Burke and Marx on the Rights of Man* (Methuen, London, 1987).

Chapter Eleven

Will and Reason

A theme that runs through discussions within law and about law is the contrast of will as against reason. "Will" represents answers which are the product of choice and decision, whether made by individuals, groups, or institutions. "Reason" represents answers which are the product of analysis: answers given because they are "right" rather than because they have been chosen by someone empowered to decide.

The English and American legal systems in practice show many elements of both will and reason. Statutory law and administrative law are primarily "will", the application of choices made by officials in authority. Contract law and estate law are also largely a matter of "will", enforcing the choices made by private parties. On the other side, common law reasoning (the subject of Ch. 13) is to a significant extent a matter of "reason", the elaboration and application of basic principles on a case by case basis. Some older cases even offer justifications of their conclusions in a natural law sort of way, referring to what (capital "R") "Reason" requires.

These general statements are hedged, and for good reason. For example, statutory interpretation in the courts often involves analysis that looks far more like analysis from general principles than it does like a search for the legislators' choices and intentions. Similarly, modern contract law often involves the legal (judicial) imposition of terms regardless of the parties' intentions, and the application of rules of interpretation that do not always defer to what the parties meant. On the other side, common law decisions sometimes have elements of "will": in that later decisions sometimes are said to turn on what an earlier court intended by a particular rule or declaration. Also, it was once argued for common law reasoning, as against the codification of legal rules in statutory form, that common law decisions reflect "the popular will", through custom.[1]

American constitutional law seems to be a continual battleground between "will" and "reason", in the ongoing debate regarding whether the general terms and broad prescriptions of the United States Constitution

---

[1] See Horwitz, *The Transformation of American Law 1870–1960*, pp. 117–121.

are to be interpreted according to the intentions and understandings of those who wrote and ratified the provisions or according to our present-day best understanding of the values and principles mentioned.[2]

Finally, one can see "reason" and "will" as representing the opposite aspects of law that any good legal theory must incorporate, although most theories tend to emphasize one while ignoring or minimizing the other. Lon Fuller referred to the poles as "reason" and "fiat"; Morris Cohen referred to them as (on the one side) the ideal to which all law aspires, and (on the other side) the hard facts that may only partly embody (or seem to defy) the ideal.[3]

LEGAL POSITIVISM AND NATURAL LAW THEORY

As one can divide aspects of law (or even individual legal decisions) according to whether they are matters (primarily) of "will" or of "reason", so can one divide legal theories.[4] Legal positivist theories work best with the "will" aspects of law. The phrase "positive law" is itself a reference to the setting down—by human rule-makers—of legal standards, as contrasted with the discovery of "natural" or "divine" legal standards through the operation of reason.

By way of example, H.L.A. Hart's "rule of recognition" analysis becomes far more complicated (and less persuasive) when one tries to apply it to law that arises from custom and common law reasoning, the aspects of modern legal systems that most clearly enter the "reason" category.[5] Legal positivism's analysis (whether one chooses the version of Austin, Hart, or Kelsen) works best when one can point to an official who creates the legal standard.

There are occasions, especially with customary law and (less often) with common law decisions, when an official purports only to "declare" law which already existed, whose existence was not due exclusively to a prior official's act of law-creation. Some theorists treat these kinds of declarations as "legal fictions" or rhetorical devices, stating that the officials in

---

[2] See, e.g. Paul Brest, "The Misconceived Quest for the Original Understanding", 60 *Boston University Law Review* 204 (1980); Richard Kay, "Adherence to the Original Intentions in Constitutional Adjudication: Three Objections and Responses", 82 *Northwestern University Law Review* 226 (1988).

[3] Winston, "The Ideal Element in a Definition of Law", p. 103, citing Morris Cohen, *Law and the Social Order* (Archon Books, New York, 1967) (originally published in 1933), p. 248 *et seq.*

[4] Roger Shiner's book, *Norm and Nature* (Clarendon Press, Oxford, 1992), is constructed along a similar axis: instead of will and reason, Shiner uses system ("norm") and value ("nature").

[5] See Hart, *The Concept of Law*, pp. 44–49, 100–103; Finnis, *Natural Law and Natural Rights*, pp. 238–245.

these situations are in fact only making new law. However, to the extent that one wants to take the officials' statements at face value, legal positivist analyses will be awkward (at best) in explaining what occurred, and an analysis based on "reason" will work better than one based on "will".

Natural law theory, by contrast, is best justified by, and is most easily applied to, the "reason" aspects of law.[6] As discussed in Ch. 5, traditional natural law theory (Aquinas' theory and similar) is about the (direct and indirect) derivation of standards from first principles, and using those standards to guide officials and criticize official actions and promulgations that fall short.

However, even within this tradition, there were significant debates (though the significance may be less clear to us than it was to the participants) about whether law was best understood in terms of "reason" or "will": in particular, whether the natural law was a product of divine will or divine reason. The debate, which may seem quite dry and "theological", had implications for how one viewed the universe and faith: the view on one side being that the universe was orderly, and thus accessible to human reason, and reason was compatible with faith (as Aquinas attempted to demonstrate); the opposing view tended towards contrary views about the accessibility of the universe to reason and the compatibility of faith and reason.[7] Echoes of these debates can be seen in the slightly less abstract debates in later centuries about the nature and legitimacy of the modern nation-state. Are the actions and enactments of officials to be followed because they represent the (express or delegated) will of the sovereign, or are these actions and enactments legitimate only to the extent that they are consistent with the natural rights of the people and the natural powers (and limits to power) of government?[8]

"Modern" natural law theory (e.g. the theories of Lon Fuller and Ronald Dworkin), involve the "reason" side of the "reason"/"will" dichotomy in a different way: for these theories hold that the law is not simply what legal officials have ordered/posited/enacted; rather, the application of (moral) reasoning is also required to determine what the law requires.

---

[6] Though there are will/reason tensions even within natural law theory. In particular, religion-grounded natural law theories, which see natural law and justice as emanations of God's goodness, but discoverable by the exercise of human reasoning or conscience, sometimes face the quandary of whether divine revelation is thus made superfluous (and whether God could change Natural Law or order something that was contrary to it). See, e.g. Kelly, *A Short History of Western Legal Theory*, pp. 102–104; Weinreb, *Natural Law and Justice*, pp. 64–66.

[7] See Weinreb, *Natural Law and Justice*, pp. 64–66; Francis Oakley, "Medieval Theories of Natural Law: William of Ockham and the Significance of the Voluntarist Tradition", 6 *Natural Law Forum* 65 (1961).

[8] See, e.g. Weinreb, *Natural Law and Justice*, pp. 67–90; Kelly, *A Short History of Western Legal Theory*, pp. 222–229, 258–271.

SOCIAL CONTRACTS AND ECONOMIC ANALYSIS

John Rawls' well-known method for deriving or justifying theories of justice, "the original position",[9] can he helpfully analyzed through the "will"/"reason" rubric.

For Rawls, principles of justice are whatever principles would be agreed upon in a thought experiment, by hypothetical persons who are ignorant of their strengths and weaknesses and their circumstances within society.[10] First, one can note that the plurality of decision-makers is superfluous: there is no reason to believe that any of the decision makers ignorant of their nature and circumstances would decide differently from the others, since they are but clones of one another.[11]

More importantly, what Rawls has constructed is an analysis from reason, dressed up as an analysis from will. There are no actual persons choosing, only a thought experiment about what a strange variant on a real person might choose. However, the grounds for respecting answers given by choice are quite different from the grounds for respecting answers given by reason.[12]

To some extent, the same claim can be made about many of the social contract approaches in political theory (as can be found, in quite different variations, in Hobbes, Locke, and Rousseau).[13] Such approaches portray a government's legitimacy as deriving from an agreement between citizens to establish that authority. The description of that agreement tends to be somewhat vague, and to the extent that it is claimed that there was some such agreement in the distant past, such claims are almost certainly false (in any event, it would be difficult to demonstrate why those now living should be bound by the terms of the ancient agreement[14]). The social contracts referred to in these theories are best understood as ways of discussing what powers reasonable persons *would* agree to delegate to a governing authority, and under what conditions. However, for

---

9 See Ch. 8.
10 Rawls, *A Theory of Justice*, pp. 11–22, 136–142; Rawls, *Political Liberalism*, pp. 22–28, 304–310.
11 A similar point is made in Walzer, *Interpretation and Social Criticism*, p. 11.
12 See, *e.g.* Dworkin, *Taking Rights Seriously*, pp. 150–154 (discussing Rawls' "original position").
13 This is not true for all writers on the social contract. Immanuel Kant, for example, expressly stated that talk of an original contract is not historical, but is merely "an idea of reason". See Weinrib, *The Idea of Private Law*, pp. 85–86 (summarizing and quoting from Kant).
14 Such arguments when made are usually in terms of our actions showing our "tacit consent" to the terms of the old agreement. There are many problems with arguments from "tacit consent" as are outlined below, in Ch. 16 ("The Obligation to Obey the Law").

our purposes, there is a great difference between the terms to which "reasonable" persons "would" agree and terms to which actual persons *have* agreed. The first is an argument of reason, the second an argument from will, and each brings a moral force or legitimacy of a different kind.

A similar disguising of "reason" arguments as "will" arguments can be found in the law and economics movement.[15] In early articles, Richard Posner sought to create a moral justification for his economic ("wealth maximization") approach to law. He argued that choosing more efficient (or more wealth-maximizing) institutions, standards and procedures over those that were less efficient is consistent with traditional notions of autonomy and consent. He conceded that people often did not consent expressly to the more efficient institutions, but that often there was no practical method of eliciting such express consent. In such situations, Posner asserted, it was sufficient, and consistent with "the principle of consent" that we ask the hypothetical question of whether the parties *would have* agreed to those institutions.[16]

The simple reply is that hypothetical consent is different in kind from actual consent. There are times when the two nearly converge, when an individual considers how she might have responded to a hypothetical situation in the recent past, or when someone tries to consider how a close friend would have decided some question.[17] However, once we are speaking about judges or commentators discussing how a group of unknown people would choose, any semblance of an exercise of personal, individual will is absent.

Posner offered an interesting response. He wrote: "If there is no reliable mechanism for eliciting express consent, it follows, not that we must abandon the principle of consent, but rather that we should be satisfied with implied (or more precisely, perhaps, hypothetical) consent where it exists."[18] There are two subtle problems with the response. First, while there may be a place to speak of implied or hypothetical consent, there is always the danger that there is a kind of misleading or misrepresentation

---

[15] See Ch. 18.

[16] Richard Posner, "The Ethical and Political Basis of the Efficiency Norm in Common Law Adjudication", 8 *Hofstra Law Review* 487 at 494 (1980). For criticisms of Posner's consent analysis, see *e.g.* Jules L. Coleman, "The Normative Basis of Economic Analysis: A Critical Review of Richard Posner's *The Economics of Justice*", 34 *Stanford Law Review* 1105 at 1117–1131 (1982); Ronald Dworkin, *A Matter of Principle* (Harvard University Press, Cambridge, Mass., 1985), pp. 275–280.

[17] The latter situation is raised in American law in medical decision-making, where the patient is temporarily or permanently incompetent to decide for herself. A close friend or relative may be asked to consider, taking into account everything known about the patient's values and attitudes, how that patient would have decided had she been competent. See, *e.g. Cruzan v Director, Missouri Health Dept.*, 497 U.S. 261 at 289–292 (1990) (O'Connor, J., concurring).

[18] Richard Posner, *The Economics of Justice* (Harvard University Press, Cambridge, Mass., 1983), p. 96.

going on: masking an argument that is largely one of reason to make it appear to be one of will, for readers who find will-based arguments more persuasive. Secondly, it is not clear why, when "consent" in its fullest form is not available, we *must* offer analysis or seek argument in terms of some hybrid or diluted variation of "consent". Sometimes consent-based (will-based) arguments will simply be out of place, and recourse must be had to arguments of an entirely different kind (most likely reason-based).

Suggested Further Readings

Brian Bix, "Will versus Reason: Truth in Natural Law, Positive Law, and Legal Theory", in *Truth* (forthcoming, K. Pritzl ed., Catholic University of America Press, Washington, D.C., 2004).

Vernon J. Bourke, *Will in Western Thought: An Historico-Critical Survey* (Sheed and Ward, New York, 1964).

Lon L. Fuller, "Reason and Fiat in Case Law", 59 *Harvard Law Review* 376 (1946).

Francis Oakley, "Medieval Theories of Natural Law: William of Ockham and the Significance of the Voluntarist Tradition", 6 *Natural Law Forum* 65 (1961).

Lloyd L. Weinreb, *Natural Law and Justice* (Harvard University Press, Cambridge. Mass., 1987), pp. 63–96.

Chapter Twelve

Authority, Finality and Mistake

The American judge and legal commentator Oliver Wendell Holmes, Jr. (1841–1935) once wrote, "The prophecies of what the courts will do in fact, and nothing more pretentious, are what I mean by law."[1] This comment trades on an ongoing tension in law (and, indeed, in all rule-based decision-making): should one focus on the rules which are purportedly the basis of decisions, or on the decisions themselves?

In the English case, *Davis v Johnson*,[2] the primary issue had been the proper interpretation of a statute protecting women from domestic violence, but there was a secondary issue regarding under what circumstances the English Court of Appeal had the authority to refuse to follow its previous decisions. In the Court of Appeal, Sir George Baker suggested that a new category be added to the limited list of exceptional circumstances in which the Court of Appeal was allowed to overrule its previous decisions[3]: where there is "a conflict between a statutory provision and a decision which has completely misinterpreted the recent statute and failed to understand its purpose".[4] He summarized his argument by saying: "The statute is the law—the final authority."[5]

On appeal, the House of Lords upheld the Court of Appeal's interpretation of the statute, but rejected that court's attempts to expand its authority to overrule its previous decisions. For present purposes, though, the most interesting comment in the Lords was given as an aside to the main debate. Lord Diplock was stating that his reading of the statute was contrary to that of his four colleagues, but, he added:

---

[1] Holmes "The Path of the Law", p. 461. This quotation is also discussed in Ch. 17, on American legal realism.
[2] [1979] A.C. 264.
[3] Among the accepted circumstances for the Court of Appeal to overrule its own prior decisions are when it must choose between prior conflicting decisions, its earlier decisions was expressly or implicitly overruled by the House of Lords, or the prior decision was made *per incuriam*. *Young v Bristol Aeroplane Co. Ltd* [1944] K.B. 718.
[4] *Davis v Johnson*, at 290.
[5] *ibid.*

"This cannot affect the disposition of the instant appeal nor will it affect the application of the Act in subsequent cases; for the section means what a majority of this House declares it means."[6]

The comments of Sir George Baker and Lord Diplock represent two contrary views about the nature of law, legal validity, and mistake, two views which are always in tension in the way we talk about law.

The first view emphasizes fidelity to the authoritative sources of law, treating the decisions of judges (and the actions of other officials who implement the law, including the police) as attempts to interpret those sources, attempts that can go wrong. This view also assumes a hierarchy of sources, where texts, primarily statutes and written constitutions always have priority over statements and actions which purport to be interpretations or applications of those texts.[7]

In a like spirit, Ronald Dworkin wrote (in the context of a discussion of civil disobedience): "A citizen's allegiance is to the law, not to any particular person's view of what the law is",[8] where it is clear from the context that "any particular person's view of the law" included decisions handed down by judges, even sometimes decisions by the highest court in the land.

The second view notes that the decisions of judges (and other officials) are often themselves sources of law, and, in effect if not in theory, can override the actions and choices of other officials (including the legislators who enacted the law being enforced). An American legal theorist, John Chipman Gray, writing early in the twentieth century, stated:

"The Law of the State or of any organized body of men is composed of the rules which the courts, that is, the judicial organs of that body, lay down for the determination of rights and duties."

He continued: "The difference in this matter between contending schools of Jurisprudence arises largely from not distinguishing between the Law

---

[6] *ibid.* at 323.

[7] The debate about the relative priority of texts and their interpretations also occurs in the context of the interpretation of the United States Constitution. Compare *Cooper v Aaron*, 358 U.S. at 1, 18 (1958) ("It follows that the interpretation of the Fourteenth Amendment enunciated by this Court . . . is the supreme law of the land") and Edwin Meese III, "The Law of the Constitution", 61 *Tulane Law Review* 979 at 989 (1987) ("Once again, we must understand that the Constitution is and must be understood to be superior to ordinary constitutional law"); see also Michael Stokes Paulsen, "The Most Dangerous Branch: Executive Power to Say What the Law Is", 83 *Georgetown Law Journal* 217 (1994) (arguing that all three branches of the U.S. government have equal authority to interpret the U.S. Constitution, and that the President is not bound by the Supreme Court's pronouncements regarding constitutional validity connected with the exercise of powers entrusted to the executive branch).

[8] Dworkin, *Taking Rights Seriously*, p. 214.

and the Sources of the Law."[9] The above quotation, along with Justice Holmes' earlier quotation, "The prophecies of what the courts will do in fact, and nothing more pretentious, are what I mean by law", have the attractions of both iconoclasm and worldliness, but they have well-known weaknesses as well.

The worldly and cynical approach will never suffice on its own, if one believes that judges sometimes act in good faith: that is, if one believes that not all judges merely disguise their own political biases in legal language; and that at least some judges perceive their actions as trying to decide "according to law", at least occasionally deciding a case one way even though they personally would rather it come out another, on the basis that they are bound by precedent or statutory wording.[10] This is not to say that Holmes or Gray thought that judges were always deciding cases according to their personal preferences. However, to explain the actions of judges acting in good faith, we must be able to understand talk of what the law requires which is at least partly independent of how the law is interpreted by judges.

We also need this (partial) conceptual independence to make sense of the idea of legal mistake. If an enactment means whatever a majority of the House of Lords (or the Supreme Court) says it means, how could we make sense of a later court decision overruling the earlier interpretation as mistaken?[11]

In *The Concept of Law*, in the course of a discussion about "formalism and rule-scepticism", Hart mentioned an imagined game called "Scorer's Discretion", under which "there was no rule for scoring save what the scorer in his discretion chose to apply."[12] The purpose of the reference was to make a point to those whose discussions about the law over-emphasized the fact that the decisions of officials in the system often were final, even when the decisions were mistaken. The decisions may be final, but the officials are acting under an obligation to make their decisions through the application of certain rules. Thus, it is both right and wrong to say "the law is what the officials say it is", just as it is both right and

---

[9] John Chipman Gray, *The Nature and Sources of the Law* (Columbia University Press, New York, 1909), p. 82.
[10] That judges, though attempting to decide "according to law", may be strongly affected by unconscious biases, raises a quite different, if still significant, set of problems.
[11] Examples of a country's highest court overruling its own prior decisions include *Board of Education v Barnette*, 319 U.S. (624 (1943); *Garcia v San Antonio Metropolitan Transit Authority*, 469 U.S. 528 (1985); *R. v Shivpuri* [1987] A.C. 1; and *Murphy Brentwood District Council* [1990] 3 W.L.R. 414. The first two cases listed are American cases involving the proper interpretation of constitutional texts; of the two English cases, *Murphy* involved the application of common law principles. Overruling on common law matters raises different conceptual questions than does overruling on an interpretation of an authoritative text, but these differences are beyond the scope of the present discussion.
[12] Hart, *The Concept of Law*, p. 142

wrong in the context of many games to say "a score occurs whenever the scorer says it does".[13] It is right, in the sense that the decision is final (or, in Hart's phrase, "unchallengeable"). It is wrong, in the sense that it disregards the fact that the most officials are, most of the time, attempting to apply and be bound by rules (and all officials at the least purport to be constrained in that manner).

The difference between real games and "Scorer's Discretion", and the difference between (most, and probably all) legal systems and systems where the law can be usefully equated with "what the judges say it is", is the tension between authority and correctness—a tension that one can see as well in games as one can in law. The cynical response that "whatever is done is right" or "whatever is authorized by the officials is right" is counterbalanced by the way that citizens and officials (even some biased officials) refer to the rules to justify their decisions, and will use the rules to warrant a modification of past (allegedly erroneous) decisions.

The tension between authority and correctness has a slightly different spin in language. It may be that according to the appointed and self-appointed experts (including the "authoritative" reference dictionaries) the way most people use certain words (e.g. "hopefully") is in error. However, over time, if enough people use those words in those ways, that meaning (the one now thought of as "mistaken") *will be* the meaning of those words. The attachment of meanings to words is arbitrary: one cannot sensibly talk, in the long run, of *everyone* being wrong about the meaning of a word. There is a corresponding situation in the law.

While it makes sense to say that some legal officials were mistaken in their interpretation or application of particular legal standards, if that "mistake" is reaffirmed often enough by enough important members of the legal hierarchy, that "mistake" now *is* the ("settled") law of that legal system. As with language, there is something at best quite strange about stating that *all* legal officials have been wrong *for a long time* about what the law is on a particular issue (and very close to absurdity to speak of a whole legal community being wrong about its own legal system[14]). The reason this claim is only strange, and not nonsensical (as it arguably would be in the case of language), is that in law there are authoritative texts, which can always in theory justify a change in even the most settled law.[15]

---

[13] *ibid.* at pp. 142–143. As pointed out to me by Neal Feigenson, the issues raised in this discussion can also be seen as trading on the tension between "will" and "reason", a theme discussed in the previous chapter.

[14] See Marmor, *Interpretation and Legal Theory*, pp. 96–97.

[15] One famous example being the use of the guarantee of equal protection in the United States Constitution to justify overturning the "settled" legal conclusion that racial segregation was constitutionally permitted. Compare *Plessy v Ferguson*, 163 U.S. 537 (1896) (affirming the constitutionality of racial segregation) with *Brown v Board of Education*, 347 U.S. 483 (1954) (holding racial segregation to be in violation of constitutional protections).

Suggested Further Readings

Larry Alexander and Frederick Schauer, "On Extrajudicial Constitutional Interpretation", 110 *Harvard Law Review* 1359 (1997).
Brian Bix, "A.D. Woozley and the Concept of Right Answers in Law", 5 *Ratio Juris* 58 (1992), reprinted in modified form in *Law, Language and Legal Determinacy* (Clarendon Press Oxford, 1993), pp. 79–88.
Jules L. Coleman, "Truth and Objectivity in Law", 1 *Legal Theory* 33 (1995).
H.L.A. Hart, *The Concept of Law* (2nd ed., Clarendon Press, Oxford, 1994), pp. 136–147 ("Varieties of Rule-Scepticism" and "Finality and Infallibility in Judicial Decision").

Chapter Thirteen

Common Law Reasoning and Precedent

At most English and American law schools, the first year is taken up primarily with teaching the concepts, rules, and modes of analysis from the traditional common law subjects (Contracts, Torts, Criminal Law, and Property), no matter how much the subjects in practice have become dominated by codified rules. The extent to which common law reasoning continues to be central or dominant in the practices of "common law legal systems" is a matter of debate,[1] but it still appears to be central to the way legal actors in common law countries *view* their own systems (as both exemplified by and reinforced by the place of common law reasoning in legal education).

In past centuries, judges and theorists described the English common law as rules in force by "long and immemorial usage."[2] This is not a position seriously maintained any more; it neither fits the facts of common law rules that have changed markedly over the course of centuries (and, sometimes, over the course of decades), nor does it offer a morally attractive vision. Some ancient customs and long-standing rules (*e.g.* slavery, subjugation of women) may not warrant our respect. As Justice Oliver Wendell Holmes, Jr., wrote: "It is revolting to have no better reason for a rule of law than that so it was laid down in the time of Henry IV."[3] In more recent discussions (though the view goes back many hundreds of years), common law decision-making is more likely to be thought of in terms of a form of common or collective reasoning, or a common or collective form of moral intuition.[4]

---

[1] One can argue that even where most cases turn on the interpretation of a statute, an administrative regulation, or a constitutional provision, the law is often developed (rightly or wrongly) by the judges in an incremental case-by-case method that is very similar to traditional common law reasoning.

[2] Sir Matthew Hale, *The History of the Common Law of England* 21 (6th ed., Henry Butterworth, London, 1820) (first published, 1713).

[3] Oliver Wendell Holmes, Jr., "The Path of the Law", 10 *Harvard Law Review* 457, 469 (1897).

[4] See the overview offered in Gerald J. Postema, "Philosophy of the Common Law", in *The Oxford Handbook of Jurisprudence and Philosophy of Law* (J. L. Coleman and S. Shapiro eds, K. E. Himma., assoc. ed., Oxford University Press, Oxford, 2002), pp. 588–622.

Common law reasoning involves the (1) incremental development of the law, (2) by judges, (3) through deciding particular cases, with (4) each decision being shown to be consistent with earlier decisions by a higher or co-equal[5] court. To put the matter a different way, common law reasoning is the uneasy but productive mixture of moral intuition, hierarchical discipline, and principled consistency.

The common law, in this sense of the term, contrasts with laws developed from statutes, administrative regulations, or constitutional provisions. Common law systems (such as Great Britain, the United States,[6] Canada, Australia and New Zealand), systems based historically on the English common law, can also be contrasted with civil law systems, which predominate on continental Europe and can be traced to ancient Roman Law.[7]

Though judges and some legal theorists characterize common law decisions as "discovering existing law" rather than making new law, in difficult cases the effect will usually be the same: a retroactive application of a standard to actions that occurred at a time when that standard had not been clearly promulgated. This led Jeremy Bentham (1748–1832), an ardent opponent of judicial legislation and common law decision-making, to comment:

"It is the judges . . . that make the common law. Do you know how they make it? Just as a man makes laws for his dog. When your dog does anything you want to break him of, you wait till he does it, and then beat him for it. This is the way you make laws for your dog: and this is the way judges make law for you and me."[8]

The fourth point given for common law reasoning above, the effort to show that current decisions are consistent with prior decisions (at least those made by a higher or comparable court) is the idea of precedent, of "*stare decisis*"—to abide by, or adhere to, decided cases. The central idea of precedent derives from a basic notion of justice: that like cases should

---

[5] Whether prior decisions by the same court are binding varies jurisdiction to jurisdiction, and even court by court within a jurisdiction. Within England and Wales, the Court of Appeal is generally bound by its earlier decisions, *Young v Bristol Aeroplane Co. Ltd* [1944] K.B. 718, while the House of Lords is not, *Practice Statement (Judicial Precedent)* [1966] 1 W.L.R. 1234.

[6] There is one state in the United States, Louisiana, which has a civil law system.

[7] "The characteristics of civil law systems are, normally, the existence of codes covering large areas of the law and setting down the rights and duties of persons in fairly general terms, the use of terminology and concepts and frequently of principles that can be traced back to the Roman law, a less strict regard for judicial precedents, and a greater reliance on the influence of academic lawyers to systematize, criticize, and develop the law in their books and writings." Walker, *The Oxford Companion to Law*, p. 223 (entry on "civil law systems").

[8] Jeremy Bentham, "Truth versus Ashhurst", in *The Works of Jeremy Bentham* (W. Tait, Edinburgh, 1843), vol. V, pp. 233–237, at p. 235.

be treated alike. However, this principle merely begins the analysis. One might say of legal cases what is said of snowflakes: that no two are exactly alike. In what sense, then, can any case determine how a later case should be resolved? The answer is, that though the second case (inevitably) is different from the first, the differences are not morally or legally significant. Perhaps the first case happened on a Wednesday, and the second on a Friday; or the first defendant had blond hair, and the second defendant has red hair: these are not the kind of differences which seem likely to *justify* treating the second defendant differently from the first. At least *some* differences seem clearly to be morally irrelevant. For a large percentage of differences, the moral significance, or lack thereof, will be a matter on which reasonable minds can disagree—and it is those sorts of disagreements which have generated hundreds of volumes of reported cases (and millions of hypotheticals in law school classroom discussions).

The notion of adherence to precedent, deciding in the same way as earlier cases, leads to one of the paradoxes of common law reasoning: that precedent is only of crucial importance when the prior case was *wrongly decided* (or at least could have been decided a different way with equal legitimacy). Here is why: if the one morally correct way to resolve a particular legal dispute is to hold the defendant liable, then that is how the court should decide, just as a matter of doing the right thing, regardless of how past cases came out. If a prior court deciding the same question came out the same way (holding the defendant liable), this gives *another* reason for holding the defendant liable the second time the case comes up, but it is a *superfluous* reason; morality or public policy already require that result. It is only if morality or public policy would have prescribed a verdict *in favour of* the defendant, or if morality and public policy would have been indifferent on the question, that a prior decision *against* the defendant would affect our "all things considered" judgment about who should win.[9]

It is like the parent of many children who has to figure out whether her young daughter is old enough to be given a bicycle of her own. The daughter may well be quick to point out that an older sibling had been given a bicycle at the same age. Precedent! It may be that the "all things considered" best decision *is* for the child to have the bike, even without taking into account past practices. However, past practices will only affect what we should otherwise do when the past practice was *not* clearly the right answer.

The above analysis might be modified or clarified in the following way. If we take the perspective not of a particular decision-maker figuring out

---

[9] As Justice Scalia states: "The whole function of the doctrine [of *stare decisis*] is to make us say that what is false under proper analysis must nonetheless be held to be true, all in the interest of stability." Antonin Scalia, "Response", in *A Matter of Interpretation* (A. Gutmann ed., Princeton University Press, Princeton, 1997), p. 139.

a particular decision, but rather the perspective of someone trying to set up an institutional process which will increase the chance of correct decisions being made, precedent is important even when the prior decision was correct, because precedent constrains fallible later decision-makers who might otherwise he tempted to incorrect decisions.[10]

Common law reasoning is far more than respect for precedent. It is also a belief that there is value to the incremental development of rules and principles, evolving, mostly cautiously, through the consideration of highly detailed factual situations. Part of the magic of common law reasoning, and part of the complexity of the role of precedent within such a system, is that cases are subject to re-characterization. The judge or panel of judges deciding the first case may believe that the basis for a result is one legal-moral principle, and that the crucial facts are A, B, and C. A later court, considering a similar case, may well revisit the first case *in light* of subsequent cases, and conclude that the principle displayed in the first case was different than the decision-maker(s) thought—either broader or narrower than claimed by the first court—and that the first court may also have been wrong about which facts were significant (*e.g.* stating that one of the facts mentioned by the first court was in fact irrelevant or superfluous, or that an additional fact *not* emphasized by the first court was also central to the case coming out the way it did). A later court is said to he bound *only* to the "holding" (or *"ratio decidendi"*) of the prior case—the principles *necessary* for the disposition; however, the later court has some freedom in interpreting what the holding was of the prior case.

It is common to hear it argued that what constitutes the *"ratio"* of a prior case, and what the *"obiter dictum"*[11] (in principle, the latter can be legitimately ignored), is indeterminate or entirely subject to manipulation; I will not consider the charge (or its possible responses) in detail here.[12] A comparable point for cynical comment is the ability of a later court to characterize a prior case in a way which means that it is no longer on point: "distinguishing" (rather than "following" or, where the court has the power, "overruling") the case. The cynical comment often made is that the ability to distinguish a case is unlimited, and thus a judge may give the appearance of respecting all the prior cases without having her decisions be in any way constrained by those cases.[13] As noted above,

---

[10] *cf.* Frederick Schauer, *Playing by the Rules*, (Clarendon Press, Oxford, 1991) pp. 158–162 (discussing the way that rules serve to allocate power).

[11] Latin for "a remark in passing".

[12] For two attempts to respond to this challenge, see Rupert Cross and J.W. Harris, *Precedent in English Law* (4th ed. Clarendon Press, Oxford, 1991), pp. 39–96, particularly pp. 52; and Neil MacCormick, "Why Cases Have *Rationes* and What These Are", in *Precedent in Law* (L. Goldstein ed., Clarendon Press, Oxford, 1987), pp. 155–182, particularly pp. 180–182.

[13] See the discussion in Frederick Schauer, *Playing by the Rules*, pp. 181–187.

there would appear to be at least some limits, however minimal, on the ways in which one can distinguish a prior case (assuming a judge who cares at least a little about not being overruled, and about maintaining the respect of his or her peers).

Given all the strange twists and turns of common law reasoning, one might be tempted to conclude that this seems an utterly bizarre way to run a legal system, were it not for the fact that common law reasoning seems to reflect at a more public level the way people develop their own moral principles and views on life. This sort of gradual development of principles and concepts, and the testing of intuitions against real and hypothetical fact situations, also is related to the way of thinking through moral questions John Rawls described in *A Theory of Justice*. Rawls' idea of "reflective equilibrium" involves the testing of particular judgments against broader theories, and vice versa, with adjustments being made when they are found to be inconsistent.[14]

In common law reasoning, as in individuals' moral reasoning, the statement of principles is likely to be tentative and subject to significant revision when first facing a novel set of questions.[15] After enough decisions have been made at a specific level, a more confident statement of principle at a higher level of generality might be assayed. In common law reasoning, such a broad restatement will usually be consistent with a long run of cases; occasionally, though, a judge will recharacterize the prior cases in a surprising way, but a way which persuades by the force of the judge's rhetorical power or the force of the moral vision underlying the re-characterization. Examples of such landmark decisions include Lord Atkin's speech in *Donoghue v Stevenson*[16] and Judge (later Justice) Cardozo's decision in *MacPherson v Buick Motor Co.*,[17] both of which established a general principle that allowed recovery in tort even in the absence of privity of contract between plaintiff and defendant.[18]

Suggested Further Readings

Larry Alexander, "Precedent", in *A Companion to Philosophy of Law and Legal Theory* (D. Patterson ed., Blackwell, Oxford, 1996), pp. 503–513.
Brian Bix, "Law as an Autonomous Discipline", in *The Oxford Handbook of Legal*

---

[14] See Rawls, *A Theory of Justice*, pp. 48–51.
[15] Consider some recent examples: the legality—and morality—of new reproductive technologies, surrogacy, and cloning; or the appropriate way to apply traditional rules of intellectual property to computer programs or scientifically transformed bacteria.
[16] [1932] A.C. 562.
[17] 217 N.Y. 382; 111 N.E. 1050 (1916).
[18] I discuss some of these themes, and their application to *R. v Brown* [1994] 1 A.C. 212, in Brian Bix, "Consent, Sado-Masochism and the English Common Law", 17 *Quinnipiac Law Review* 157 (1997).

150 COMMON LAW REASONING AND PRECEDENT

Studies (forthcoming, P. Cane and M. Tushnet eds, Oxford University Press, Oxford, 2003).

Benjamin N. Cardozo, *The Nature of the Judicial Process* (Yale University Press, New Haven, 1921).

Rupert Cross and J.W. Harris, *Precedent in English Law* (4th ed., Clarendon Press, Oxford, 1991).

Melvin Aron Eisenberg, *The Nature of the Common Law* (Harvard University Press, Cambridge, Mass., 1988).

Martin P. Golding, *Legal Reasoning* (Broadview Press, Ontario, 2001).

Laurence Goldstein ed., *Precedent in Law* (Clarendon Press, Oxford, 1987) (includes contributions by Gerald Postema, Neil MacCormick, and Michael Moore).

Edward H. Levi, *An Introduction to Legal Reasoning* (University of Chicago Press, Chicago, 1949).

Stephen R. Perry, "Judicial Obligation, Precedent, and the Common Law", 7 *Oxford Journal of Legal Studies* 215 (1987).

Gerald J. Postema, "Philosophy of the Common Law", in *The Oxford Handbook of Jurisprudence and Philosophy of Law* (J. L. Coleman and S. Shapiro eds, K. E. Himma, assoc. ed., Oxford University Press, Oxford, 2002), pp. 588–622.

Frederick Schauer, "Is the Common Law Law?" (book review), 77 *California Law Review* 455 (1989).

A.W.B. Simpson, "English Common Law" in *The New Palgrave Dictionary of Economics and the Law*, Vol. 2 (P. Newman ed., Macmillan, London, 1998), pp. 57–70.

—, "The Ratio Decidendi of a Case and the Doctrine of Binding Precedent", in *Oxford Essays in Jurisprudence* (A.G. Guest ed., Oxford University Press, Oxford, 1961), pp. 148–175.

Chapter Fourteen

Statutory Interpretation and Legislative Intentions

Questions of statutory interpretation turn on the relationship between courts and legislatures (keeping in mind that there is no necessary reason that rules be made and applied by separate institutions, though there are many practical advantages to this separation), and between government and citizens. For example: Should judges fill in gaps in legislation? In applying rules, what importance should be given to the intentions of the rule-makers and what importance to the expectations of the public?

These and similar controversies are basically political questions, which may be informed by different theories about institutional competence and institutional behaviour, but it is unlikely that many such questions will be resolved by reference to statements about the nature of law or about the nature of language. This observation may seem obvious, but it is surprising how often it is ignored in the writings of legal theorists.[1]

Given that issues of statutory interpretation are primarily matters of convention to be decided within each legal system, there is not much that can or should be said at the level of general jurisprudential theory. However, there are a few claims that have been made by legal theorists that are worth noting, as well as some clarifications of terms and concepts that may facilitate discussion in this area.

LEGISLATIVE INTENTION

As a number of commentators have pointed out, there are many subtleties, complications and paradoxes involved when discussing legislative intentions.[2] Some derive from the fact that "intentions" in the context of a group promulgating a rule simply cannot refer to the same things as the identical concept ("intention") means when referring to one individual conversing

---

[1] In Bix, *Law, Language and Legal Determinacy*, pp. 154–156, 176–177, I make a similar point in response to metaphysically-realist approaches to law and legal interpretation.

[2] See, *e.g.* Dworkin, *Law's Empire*, pp. 313–354. I discussed some of these issues in another context in Bix, "Questions in Legal Interpretation", pp. 142–146.

with another. To the extent that individual, conversational intention is partly a matter of what the speaker was actually thinking when she spoke, there is no readily available analogue in context of a group. (Does a group have thoughts and intentions separate from those of its individual members? And if we are to focus on the individual members, how are we to "sum up" those thoughts and intentions when they are conflicting?) Additionally, legislation usually involves an expectation that the rule promulgated will be used as guidance for the indefinite future by persons not known to the legislators— a purpose or set of expectations far different from what one finds most of the time in individual conversations. Legislation is also more likely to involve a variety of different types of intentions: for example, intentions about what a text means, intentions regarding how the text should be interpreted, and intentions regarding how it should be applied.[3] The authors of a standard requiring "reasonable" behaviour could believe that a particular type of action would be "unreasonable" under the standard, but might at the same time believe that judgments of reasonableness should be made by judges according to contemporary standards at the time of judging.

The question then is, what follows from the fact that there are these differences between legislation and individual communication? A variety of responses have been offered: for example, that legislative intentions should only be legally relevant under certain conditions (generally conditions that make those intentions seem more similar to intentions in a conversational context, *e.g.* when all the legislators shared the same intention and when that intention was relatively recent[4]); that legislative intention and legislative history should play no role in the interpretation of statutes[5]; and that legislative intention is best understood as having nothing to do with intention, but is just a shorthand for saying that certain types of facts should be taken into account when constructing the best interpretation of a statute.[6]

"PLAIN MEANING"

The English courts say that they are trying to discover Parliament's intention regarding a statute, but until quite recently[7] neither the judges nor

---

[3] See Marmor, *Interpretation and Legal Theory*, pp. 165–172; Larry Alexander, "All or Nothing at All? The Intentions of Authorities and the Authority of Intentions", in *Law and Interpretation* (A. Marmor ed., Clarendon Press, Oxford, 1995), pp. 357–404.

[4] See Marmor, *Interpretation and Legal Theory*, pp. 155–184.

[5] See, *e.g.* Antonin Scalia, *A Matter of Interpretation* (A. Gutmann ed., Princeton University Press, Princeton, 1997), pp. 16–37; Jeremy Waldron, "Legislators Intentions and Unintentional Legislation", in *Law and Interpretation* (A. Marmor ed., Clarendon Press, Oxford, 1995), pp. 329–356.

[6] See Dworkin, *Law's Empire*, pp. 313–354.

[7] See *Pepper v Hart* [1993] A.C. 593 (allowing reference to Parliamentary debates (*Hansard*) to aid the interpretation of statutes in certain limited circumstances).

the lawyers appearing before them were allowed even to refer to the record of Parliamentary debates. The focus instead was (and largely still is) on the "literal" or "plain" meaning of the statute. Lord Reid explained: "We are seeking the meaning of the words which Parliament used. We are seeking not what Parliament meant but the true meaning of what they said."[8] Though perhaps not optimally phrased, Lord Reid's point seems clear enough. Yet the eminent commentator Sir Rupert Cross wrote about this quotation: "This is not one of Lord Reid's most helpful remarks because if the true meaning of what someone says is not what he intended to say, it is difficult to know what it is."[9]

Sir Rupert seemed to have overlooked the obvious and familiar distinction between the meaning we wish to get across and the meaning our words in fact convey to the reader or listener,[10] a distinction justified by the frequency of misstatements, misunderstandings, cultural differences between speaker and listener, differing assumptions and expectations, and so on. At the least, Sir Rupert was asking a great deal of the phrase "the true meaning".

In *Davis v Johnson* (discussed in the previous chapter), Lord Justice Cumming-Bruce in the Court of Appeal supported emphatically the traditional approach to interpreting statutes by stating: "An Act means what the words and phrases selected by the parliamentary draftsmen actually mean, and not what individual members of the two Houses of Parliament may think they mean."[11]

Lord Justice Cumming-Bruce wanted to distinguish what individual legislators *thought about* a text from what the text *actually means*; but actual meanings do not announce themselves for all to hear. To be slightly cynical about matters: in actual practice, the choice becomes one between what the legislators thought the text means (as best this can he cobbled together from the legislative history) and what the judges think the text means. This is not to say that there are not good reasons for preferring the latter to the former, only that the judges are fooling themselves if they think that their access to meaning is different from and better than that of other people—as though one group had direct access to meanings, while other groups could only offer *interpretations* of meanings, interpretations which were particularly vulnerable to mistake.

---

[8] *Black-Clauson International Ltd v Papierwerke Waldhof-Aschaffenburg A.G.* [1975] 1 All E.R. 810 at 814. For comparable language from the United States Supreme Court, see *Schwegmann Bros. v Calvert Distillers Corp.*, 341 U.S. 384 at 397 (1951) (Jackson, J., concurring) (quoting O.W. Holmes, Jr.: "We do not inquire what the legislature meant; we ask only what the statute means.").

[9] Rupert Cross, *Statutory Interpretation* (Butterworths, London, 1976), pp. 39–40. (The quotation is not repeated in the third edition of that text, which came out in 1995.)

[10] A distinction which sometimes goes under the label of "speaker meaning" versus 'linguistic meaning". See, *e.g.* Robert Audi ed., *The Cambridge Dictionary of Philosophy* (Cambridge University Press, Cambridge, 1995), p. 758 (entry on "speech act theory").

[11] *Davis v Johnson* [1979] A.C. 316.

It seems relatively clear what justice Cumming-Bruce was getting at: a statute should be interpreted according to the plain or conventional meaning of its text; when there is a conflict, the conventional meaning of the text should take precedence over any more idiosyncratic meaning that the legislators might have attached to the text. There are, however, two unspoken assumptions in the argument. The first is that there is a conventional meaning to be found. One could argue regarding particular texts in particular circumstances (and some might offer a similar argument regarding all of language all of the time) that no consensus or near-consensus in meaning exists; all there is are the different readings of different groups.[12] The second assumption is that the judge will be able to interpret the text in line with its conventional meaning: one could argue (especially in England, where the judiciary has been, at least until recently, relatively homogenous in its background and personal characteristics and far from representative of the general population[13]), that judges are at least as likely to succumb to idiosyncratic interpretations as are legislators.

The American approach to statutory interpretation has, at least in the last century,[14] been far more receptive than the English courts (before *Pepper v Hart*) to arguments based on legislative history. In recent years, however, there has been a push, led by Supreme Court Justice Antonin Scalia,[15] to interpret statutes strictly in line with the literal meaning of their texts: with no reference to legislative history and, here apparently going even further than the traditional English approach,[16] no exceptions for when a literal interpretation leads to an absurd result.[17] The opposition to legislative history, and indeed to most other common law methods of determining legislative intentions, is presented with a strong "rule of law" justification:

[12] Claims along those lines, if perhaps not quite as radical, have been made by theorists identified with critical legal studies (Ch. 19) and postmodernism (Ch. 21).

[13] See John Griffith, *The Politics of the Judiciary* (Fontana, London, 1985).

[14] In the United States, judicial use of legislative history in interpreting statutes only became common in the early decades of the 20th century, growing with frequency throughout that century. See, *e.g.* Scalia, *A Matter of Interpretation*, pp. 30–31. There is evidence that the criticism of the use of legislative history, by Justice Scalia and by a variety of commentators, has led to a steady decline in the past decade in that practice among American judges.

[15] See Scalia, *A Matter of Interpretation*. For a thoughtful critique of Scalia's position, see William N. Eskridge Jr., "Textualism, The Unknown Ideal?" (book review), 96 *Michigan Law Review* 1509 (1998).

[16] For the "Golden Rule", allowing that where the ordinary meaning of statutory language would "produce an inconsistency, or an absurdity or inconvenience so great as to convince the Court that the intention could not have been to use them in their ordinary signification", a different reading of the language can and should be made. See, *e.g. River Wear Commissioners v Adamson* (1877) 2 App. Cas. 743 at 764–765 (*per* Lord Blackburn).

[17] Eskridge certainly assumes that there is no "absurdity" exception in Scalia's textualism: see Eskridge, "Textualism, the Unknown Ideal?", p. 1549, and there is support in the strong language Scalia uses in *A Matter of Interpretation*, though I have been unable to find a place where the "absurdity" exception is expressly rejected.

"[I]t is simply incompatible with democratic government, or indeed, even with fair government, to have the meaning of a law determined by what the lawgiver meant, rather than by what the lawgiver promulgated . . . It is the law that governs, not the intent of the lawgiver."[18]

The basic claim is that people should only be bound by publicly promulgated rules, and legislative history is often not easily accessible (even putting aside the argument that such history is often written by people other than the lawmakers themselves, and it usually not expressly assented to by anything like a majority of the legislators).[19]

The opposing position is that the basic institutional structure of the United States and Great Britain has a legislative body which has the authority to make decisions for the country, decisions which are to be carried out by other officials, including the courts. Thus, it is important for the courts to figure out what the lawmakers intended—to be a "faithful agent."[20] In this sort of debate, the "rule of law" values will frequently conflict with the "authority" values—a troubling conflict, as both values are likely central to evaluating the legitimacy of governmental action.

Whatever the approach to statutory interpretation adopted by a judiciary (and other officials with the duty to implement legislation) within a legal system, it is important that the rules of interpretation be relatively predictable, stable and determinate. This allows for more effective legislative drafting. For example, if the legislature knows that committee reports will be taken into account in interpreting a statute, then important clarifying information will likely be placed in such reports. On the other hand, if interpretation will be based only on "plain meaning", then little attention will be paid to committee reports, and more attention will likely be given to a clearer and/or more detailed statutory text. Certainly, it would be inviting mis-communication and mis-interpretation for statutes enacted under one set of interpretive conventions to be subject to a different set of conventions.[21]

---

[18] Scalia, *A Matter of Interpretation*, p. 17.
[19] See, *ibid.* at pp. 16–18, 23–25. Other arguments offered for a "plain meaning" approach to statutory interpretation that excluded recourse to legislative history include: that it saves time and expense (of attorneys and judges); it arguably constrains "willful" judges, who use, or would be tempted to use (ambiguous) legislative history to achieve the results they prefer; and that it would force legislatures to be more careful in their drafting. See *ibid.* at pp. 9–14, 16–37; Eskridge, "Textualism, The Unknown Ideal?", pp. 1511–1515, 1540–1542.
[20] See, *e.g.* Eskridge, "Textualism, The Unknown Ideal?", pp. 1548–1551; Posner, *Law and Literature*, pp. 237–258.
[21] See Eskridge, "Textualism, the Unknown Ideal?", p. 1541 and n. 115.

Suggested Further Readings

Rupert Cross; John Bell and George Engle, *Statutory Interpretation* (3rd ed., Butterworths, London, 1995).

Ronald Dworkin, *Law's Empire*, Ch. 9 (Harvard University Press, Cambridge, Mass., 1986) ("Statutes").

William N. Eskridge, Jr., "Textualism, The Unknown Ideal?" (book review), 96 *Michigan Law Review* 1509 (1998).

William N. Eskridge, Jr.; Philip P. Frickey and Elizabeth Garrett eds, *Cases and Materials on Legislation: Statutes and the Creation of Public Policy* (3rd ed., West Group, St. Paul, 2001).

Andrei Marmor, *Interpretation and Legal Theory*, Ch. 8 (Clarendon Press, Oxford, 1992) ("Legislative Intent and the Authority of Law").

Andrei Marmor ed., *Law and Interpretation* (Clarendon Press, Oxford, 1995) (includes articles on statutory interpretation by Michael Moore, Joseph Raz, Jeremy Waldron, Larry Alexander, Heidi Hurd and Meir Dan-Cohen).

Joseph Raz, "Intention in Interpretation", in *The Autonomy of Law* (R. George ed., Clarendon Press, Oxford, 1996), pp. 249–286.

Antonin Scalia, *A Matter of Interpretation: Federal Courts and the Law* (Amy Gutmann ed., Princeton University Press, Princeton, 1997) (an essay by Justice Scalia, with commentary by five academics, including Laurence Tribe and Ronald Dworkin, and a response by Justice Scalia).

Chapter Fifteen

Legal Enforcement of Morality

As many writers have pointed out, the phrase "legal enforcement of morality" is a misleading title for the issues that are usually raised under that label. No one seriously contends that the government should not establish any legal rules that are consistent with, and could be seen as enforcing, moral norms. There is, and has always been, a large overlap between legal and moral standards. If one were to disallow the legal enforcement of moral standards, most of what passes for criminal law (prohibiting murder, robbery, rape, etc.), tort law (requiring compensation for negligently or intentionally inflicted harms), contract law (enforcing promises), and much of the rest of the legal system, would thereby be considered improper. Those who are concerned about whether and how the law enforces morality are not considering such a wholesale overhaul of the legal system.

In the reference to "the legal enforcement of morality", a certain subset of moral standards is usually indicated, though there is no consensus for the dividing line advocates would draw between moral standards the law should enforce and those that the law should not enforce.

DIVIDING LINES

The dividing line most often mentioned in discussions of what moral standards the law should and should not enforce is that proposed by John Stuart Mill (1806–1873) in the pamphlet, "On Liberty": "The only purpose for which power can rightfully be exercised over any member of a civilised community against his will is to prevent harm to others."[1] The supporting arguments for this assertion are partly based on assertions about government (what it is well-placed to do and what it is poorly placed to do; or arguments about the limits that should be placed on its powers),

---

[1] John Stuart Mill, "On Liberty", Ch. 1, in *On Liberty and Utilitarianism* (Bantam, New York, 1993), p. 12 ("On Liberty" was originally published in 1859).

and partly based on assertions about individuals within society (the central place of liberty and autonomy in our lives; and the likelihood that society will be better off if a great variety of values and approaches to life are tolerated).[2]

The last point may be the one for which Mill is best known. Mill supported "ethical confrontation",[3] the idea that moral progress is more likely to occur when alternative views about morality, politics and how one should live are subject to open discussion, both in the literal sense and in the sense that ways of living based on these alternative values are tolerated and thereby remain open to public view.

The line drawn between actions that harm others and those that do not has strong intuitive appeal to many: "if my actions do not harm anyone else, then they are no one else's business, especially not the State's." However, in societies where insurance is pervasive (and in some circumstances required by law), where governments may either run the health service or provide health care of last resort, and where the government may provide social services to those left destitute, there may no longer be many actions which are purely self-regarding. For example, if my reckless behaviour leaves me severely injured, the state may end up paying for my medical bills or supporting my children. My action, which on the surface seemed only self-regarding, had effects on those around me, and repercussions to a wider group through increased taxes and insurance premiums.

Such facts, which of course vary from country to country, undermine some of the persuasive power of Mill's dividing line, but the line retains much of its substantial intuitive appeal.[4]

TOPICS

Discussions under the title "the legal enforcement of morality" often focus on matters relating to sexuality—e.g. homosexuality,[5] pornography,[6]

---

[2] The arguments are well elaborated in Mill, "On Liberty", and in H.L.A. Hart, *Law, Liberty and Morality* (Oxford University Press, Oxford, 1963).

[3] Here I am borrowing a term, and some analysis, from Waldron, *Liberal Rights*, pp. 120–121.

[4] For an interesting overview of the application of Mill's "Harm Principle" to tort law and government regulation, and some suggestions for how the principle should be limited, see Richard A. Epstein, "The Harm Principle—and How it Grew", 45 *University of Toronto Law Journal* 369 (1995).

[5] See, *e.g. Bowers v Hardwick*, 478 U.S. 186 (1986) (upholding the constitutionality of a criminal law on sodomy as applied to private homosexual conduct).

[6] See, *e.g. American Booksellers Assoc. Inc. v Hudnut*, 771 F.2d 323 (7th Cir. 1985), affirmed mem., 475 U.S. 1001 (1986) (invalidating as unconstitutional a feminist anti-pornography ordinance).

surrogate motherhood,[7] and sado-masochism[8]—reflecting the high level of interest and attention that such issues naturally attract. However, one should note that there are a number of issues in this area that are not connected with sexuality: *e.g.* requiring the wearing of helmets while riding a motorcycle or bicycle and the wearing of seat belts while driving or riding in a car; laws prohibiting suicide and assisted suicide; banning the use and sale of certain kinds of drugs (distinguishing the dangers the substances cause only to the user as against the dangers the user might cause others while "under the influence"); and other activities that are dangerous but attractive to some (for example, cliff diving). One should also consider the regulation of food, drugs, machinery, etc. Under a Millian approach, consumers should be given the facts they need to make an informed choice about use or consumption, but there would be no restraint on the production or consumption of dangerous items. Finally, there are also questions which seem to fall under the question, "the legal enforcement of morality", but which seem unconnected to Mill's proposed demarcation of self-regarding action. For example, should the state create and enforce a legal duty of one citizen to rescue another from danger, when that rescue cannot be accomplished without endangering the rescuer?[9]

As a number of the above examples might indicate, there is much room for argument, even if one accepts Mill's dividing line of "harm to others". For example, does this harm include "offence to others" (as religious believers would be deeply offended by blasphemous actions or statements, were such actions or statements to be publicized)—and should we distinguish between the offence one feels when confronted by the activity or comment and offence one might feel by the mere knowledge of what other people are doing in private? H.L.A. Hart, for example, while arguing for a position close to that of Mill, allowed for legal legislation to protect "public decency".[10] However, he refused to go further, to add protections against offence based on what others do in private? He wrote: "a right to be protected from the distress which is inseparable from the bare knowledge that others are acting in ways you think wrong, cannot be acknowledged by anyone who recognises individual liberty as a value."[11]

HART V DEVLIN

In many places, the discussion of the legal enforcement of morality is too strongly influenced by the exchange between H.L.A. Hart and Lord

---

[7] See, *e.g. Re Baby M.*, 537 A.2d 1227 (N.J. 1988) (finding a surrogacy contract invalid).
[8] See, *e.g. R. v Brown* [1994] 1 AC. 212 (upholding the application of criminal assault statutes to private, consensual sado-masochistic activity).
[9] See, *e.g.* Ernest J. Weinrib, "The Case for a Duty to Rescue", 90 *Yale Law Journal* 247 (1980).
[10] Hart, *Law, Liberty, and Morality*, pp. 38–48.
[11] *ibid.* at p. 46.

Patrick Devlin in the 1960s.[12] The exchange was unhelpful in some ways, in that it centred on Lord Devlin's somewhat idiosyncratic position (and his less than optimal arguments in its defence).

Before one can understand Lord Devlin's position, and why it is particularly weak, one must first understand the distinction between "critical" and "conventional" morality (the same distinction is sometimes offered using different terminology[13]; the terminology is obviously not important as long as the distinction is clearly understood and applied). A statement of critical morality is an attempt to state what is morally true, while a statement of conventional morality is an attempt to capture what most people *believe* to be morally true.

This is a type of distinction that one finds in areas other than morality: one could say, for example, that while the conventional belief is that Charles Dickens is the greatest English novelist of all time, the better view is that Jane Austen deserves that honour. On one side are statements about reality, about the way things really are; on the other side are statements about people's beliefs.[14] To determine the truth in critical morality, one might think long and hard about the arguments on either side of the debate; to determine the truth in conventional morality, one would be better advised to conduct an opinion poll.

This is not to say that there can be no connection between conventional and critical morality. For example, someone might believe that there is no such thing as (objective) moral truth; all there is are people's biases and preferences. This person might (but need not) add: the proper way to act is however most people think it is proper to act. For someone with this (extreme) view, it could be said that conventional morality and critical morality merge.

Most of Lord Devlin's writings on the legal enforcement of morality support the reading that he believes that law should enforce conventional morality (I hedge here, because Lord Devlin was not always as careful as he might have been to make sure that his arguments were always consistent). The argument seems to be as follows: society is held together by its shared morality; actions which undermine the shared morality undermine society; so society is justified in protecting itself through using the law to enforce society's conventional morality.[15]

---

[12] Patrick Devlin, *The Enforcement of Morals* (Oxford University Press. Oxford, 1965); Hart, *Law, Liberty, and Morality.*

[13] Hart refers to the same distinction under the terms "positive" and "critical" morality. See Hart, *Law, Liberty, and Morality*, pp. 17–24.

[14] Another way to consider the contrast is as follows: it makes perfect sense to say "most people in this society believe X ('that Dickens is the greatest novelist', 'that capital punishment is morally acceptable', or the like), but I do not believe it", while it is nonsensical to say "it is true (as a matter of critical morality) that adultery is wrong, but I do not believe it".

[15] Devlin, *The Enforcement of Morality*, pp. 9–10. Devlin's views on these matters are related to ideas first put forward by the social theorist Emile Durkheim. For a discussion of Durkheim's views and their relation to the Hart-Devlin debate, see W. John Thomas,

The problem is that beliefs about moral matters change. At any given time in a community, there may be a consensus on some moral questions, while on other questions there will be sharp divisions. Over time, an issue may go from being a matter of consensus to being a matter of controversy, and given enough time, an issue for which there was a consensus one way may eventually be a matter of consensus the other way (examples of this last phenomenon may include the issues of slavery and religious toleration).

How can we know that our laws are enforcing society's moral consensus rather than just protecting the last generation's prejudices against a consensus forming around another position? Devlin recognized change in conventional moral beliefs only in terms of greater or lesser "tolerance" on certain issues.[16] However, when we are respectful of religious minorities, we do not see ourselves as being "tolerant" regarding deviations from the old rules of persecuting such minorities; we see ourselves as following a new rule that such respect is correct. A similar analysis could be offered about Devlin's own example of homosexuality. Many of those who believe that homosexual acts should not be criminalized do not see themselves as being "lax" about the immorality of homosexuality; they simply do not think it is immoral at all.[17]

The assumption that changes in conventional moral thinking are only changes in our "laxness" about moral matters or in our "tolerance" of deviation, indicates the extent to which Lord Devlin confused or conflated conventional and critical morality. He assumed that there was some true moral thinking to which we would always return. At the least, this is just bad moral history and moral sociology. One would not have spoken of the American and English societies of the nineteenth century as having become more lax or tolerant regarding not returning slaves to their masters. The fact is that conventional moral opinion changes, and it can, over time, change radically (and sometimes for the better).

There would be many questions one would have to face if one were

---

"Social Solidarity and the Enforcement of Morality Revisited: Some Thoughts on H.L.A. Hart's Critique of Durkheim", 32 *American Criminal Law Review* 49 (1994).

[16] Devlin, *The Enforcement of Morality*, p. 18.

[17] This type of question arises in the philosophy of language under the rubric of "rule-following": how do we know that someone is deviating from a particular rule, rather than conforming to a different rule? See Saul Kripke, *Wittgenstein: On Rules and Private Language* (Harvard University Press, Cambridge, Mass., 1982). Similar questions arise in moral philosophy and in law. For example, a standard type of legal question is, when an insurance policy covers a variety of medical procedures but does not cover pregnancy, is that policy failing to follow (perhaps in a discriminatory way) a general rule ("all medical procedures are covered"), or is it (legitimately) following a different rule which excludes pregnancy from the class of procedures covered? See *Geduldig v Aiello*, 417 US. 484 (1974) (the exclusion of pregnancy from an otherwise comprehensive list of disabilities covered by state disability insurance did not violate constitutional guarantees of equal protection).

serious about wanting to enforce conventional, as opposed to critical, morality. The first would be: why was one doing so? Lord Devlin stated that a society is held together by its morality, and argued from this that society had an interest in preventing anything that would "undermine" the shared morality, for that would undermine society. Lord Devlin is here creating an argument from a metaphor. One could just as easily (and I would argue more accurately) say that anything which *changed* the shared morality would thereby change society. More to the point, matters tend also to work in the other direction: it is the society which shapes the (conventional) morality, and when society changes, the (conventional) morality changes with it.

As indicated earlier, if conventional morality of the moment is what matters, there is no reason to enforce the last generation's conventional morality at the cost of this generation's. What complicates matters further is that on many (if not most) moral matters, there is no consensus at all.

A NEW START

For all the reasons given above, Lord Devlin's position is probably not the most formidable opponent for someone advocating a Mill-like libertarian approach to the question of the legal enforcement of morality. More significant arguments have been presented for a position that some have labeled "perfectionism", which entails the view that the government has a legitimate interest in promoting certain views as to what the good life is. (Most of the modern theorists who support legislative enforcement of public morality have at the same time rejected the arguments and positions Devlin offered.[18])

Writing in response to Mill, James Fitzjames Stephen (1829–1894) argued in favour of legislation whose purpose was "to establish, to maintain, and to give power to that which the legislator regards as a good moral system or standard." After further argument, he offered the conclusion that "the object of promoting virtue and preventing vice must be admitted to be both a good one and one sufficiently intelligible for legislative purposes."[19] As against the argument that government was not well placed to reach final conclusions about what is morally worthy and what is not, Stephen writes: "How can the State or the public be competent to determine any question whatever if it is not competent to decide that gross vice is a bad thing?"[20]

As to liberty, Stephen had little patience with discussion in the

[18] *e.g.* Robert P George, *Making Men Moral* (Clarendon Press, Oxford, 1993), pp. x, 71–82.
[19] James Fitzjames Stephen, *Liberty, Equality, Fraternity* (S. Warner ed., Liberty Fund, Indianapolis, 1993), Ch. 4, pp. 96–97 (the book was originally published in 1873).
[20] *ibid.* at p. 84.

abstract.[21] The proper question, he argued, is liberty towards what end, allowing freedom from which restraints?[22] Liberty to live a worthless or evil life he could not see as a matter worthy of great defence or deference: "It is one thing however to tolerate vice so long as it is inoffensive, and quite another to give it a legal right not only to exist, but to assert itself in the face of the world as an 'experiment in living' as good as another, and entitled to the same protection from law."[23] For Stephen, the primary question was one of balance: could significant good be accomplished (by criminalizing vice, and thereby, one hopes, reducing its frequency) without being outweighed by the costs of compulsion, error, infringements on liberty and privacy, and so on?[24]

A similar, "perfectionist" defence of legal enforcement of morality has been more recently offered by Robert George. George's position was that no "norm of justice or political morality" was violated by legislation protecting public morality, though toleration of moral wrongdoing may sometimes be justified on prudential grounds.[25] Some communitarian theorists urge greater community (individual, institutional, and official) involvement in creating and maintaining a moral order, with legal coercion (and the role of law in expressing values, even when the rules in question are not enforced) a small but integral part of the process.[26]

One can be a perfectionist and still support a view similar to that of Mill. Joseph Raz has put forward[27] a connected set of views grounded on four principles:

---

[21] *cf.* Scalia, *A Matter of Interpretation*, p. 42: "All governments represent a balance between individual freedom and social order, and it is not always true that every alteration of that balance in the direction of greater individual freedom is necessarily good."

Stephen also points out that while Mill argues in general terms that society has no business using coercion or pressure against behaviour that does not directly harm others, he seems to accept social pressure against immoral behaviour: it is only the restraint and coercion of the criminal law that Mill seems to oppose. Stephen himself sees reasons for constraint in the use of the criminal law against immoral behaviour, but, he points out, this is quite different from Mill's earlier and broader claim that society has no legitimate interest in exerting pressure against immoral behaviour (that does not directly harm others). See Stephen, *Liberty, Equality, Fraternity*, pp. 87–92.

[22] Stephen, *Liberty, Equality, Fraternity*, pp. 115–116

[23] *ibid.* at p. 101. See also Joseph Raz, "Liberty and Trust", in *Natural Law, Liberalism and Morality: Contemporary Essays* (R. George ed., Clarendon Press, Oxford, 1996), p. 120 ("An autonomous life is valuable only to the extent that it is engaged in *valuable* activities and relationships.").

[24] Stephen, *Liberty, Equality, Fraternity*, pp. 91–92, 105–108.

[25] George, *Making Men Moral*, p. viii.

[26] See, *e.g.* Amitai Etzioni, *The Spirit of Community: Rights, Responsibilities, and the Communitarian Agenda* (Crown Publishers, New York, 1993). pp 23–53.

[27] See Raz, "Liberty and Trust"; see also Joseph Raz, "Autonomy, Toleration, and the Harm Principle", in *Issues in Contemporary Legal Philosophy* (R. Gavison ed., Clarendon Press, Oxford, 1987), pp. 313–333; Joseph Raz, *Ethics in the Public Domain*, pp. 3–109.

(1) "People's lives are successful and fulfilling to the extent that they are spent in whole-hearted and successful engagement in valuable activities and relationships";

(2) for most people today,[28] autonomy is an important component of living a good life; that is, it is important that a person's activities and relationships be chosen by the person himself or herself;

(3) moral pluralism: that there are a variety of moral goods, and a variety of ways of living a morally good life, but these goods and ways of life are, either in theory or in practice, inconsistent (e.g. one cannot be both a monk and a great general; and it is difficult to excel at ballet, chess, and poetry all at the same time); and

(4) governments have a duty to promote the well-being of people,[29] which entails, among other things, "mak[ing] sure that attractive options are available and that meaningless and worthless options are eliminated".[30]

The conclusion of these principles, for Raz, is that government has a place in shaping the options available to its citizens, but the importance of autonomy, and, a different, if related value,[31] the importance of liberty, combine to limit severely the circumstances in which coercive moral paternalism will be justified.

All of the above is to be distinguished from purely prudential arguments that the law should refrain from acting for certain kind of moral objectives because the law is not well suited to achieve such objectives (though these prudential arguments are taken into account, in one way or the other, by most of the theories mentioned). For example, one could argue that the American experiment of Prohibition, when the sale of alcohol was prohibited, was doomed to failure because people's desire for alcohol is too strong.

One can also put forward a different kind of argument about the incompatibility of law and moral objectives. The argument is that, by the nature of things, one cannot force someone to act morally through the threat of legal sanctions. Under this view, it is in the nature of moral action that one *voluntarily* make the proper choices. Choices coerced

---

[28] Raz notes that there are (traditional) communities in which a flourishing life can be had (and perhaps can *only* be had) in a life in which there is little autonomy. Raz, "Liberty and Trust", pp. 120–121.

[29] A government's duties to its citizens may well be greater than its duties to non-citizens; but most would argue that governments also have substantial moral duties to non-citizens (certainly those living within the country's borders, and probably also to inhabitants of other countries whose well-being is affected by the actions of the government in question).

[30] *ibid.* at p. 114.

[31] See *ibid.* at pp. 115–120.

through the fear of legal sanctions may lead to people conforming outwardly with the choices required by an ethical code, but will lack the crucial inner purpose or intention.[32] If someone avoids illegal drugs or pornography only because she fears being caught by the authorities, then, this view states, the person should no more get the credit for acting morally than if she were acting the way she was because of the orders of a gunman. Ronald Dworkin makes a somewhat different point: even if the threat of criminal sanctions coerced someone into giving up an immoral lifestyle, and he or she even came to endorse and appreciate the change, this person's life might still not be better: "We would not improve someone's life, even though he endorsed the change we brought about, if the mechanism we used to secure the change lessened his ability to consider the critical merits of the change in a reflective way."[33] Of course, both of the above arguments relate to the value of state coercion from *the perspective of the person coerced*, that is, along the lines of a paternalistic justification (the people coerced are better off). The arguments do not touch on a justification based on social good: that the coercion is justified, assuming it is effective, because the society is better in some way because it has fewer people who act in immoral ways.

Finally, there are many theorists who would support the government acting to declare certain activities or lifestyles as immoral, doing nothing to support those activities and lifestyles, and trying to protect children from such paths, but who believe that it would not be appropriate for the state to coerce adults regarding those options.[34]

Suggested Further Readings

Larry Alexander, "Harm, Offense, and Morality", 7 *Canadian Journal of Law and Jurisprudence* 199 (1994).
Patrick Devlin, *The Enforcement of Morals* (Oxford University Press, Oxford, 1965).
Gerald Dworkin, "Paternalism", in E. N. Zalta ed., *Stanford Encyclopedia of Philosophy*, http://plato.stanford.edu (2002).
Gerald Dworkin ed., *Morality, Harm and the Law* (Westview Press, Boulder, Colo., 1994).

---

[32] *cf.* John Finnis, "Liberalism and Natural Law Theory", 45 *Mercer Law Review* 687 at 697–698 (1994). As Finnis points out, this position is consistent with the view that the State, through its statements and its funding decisions, should favour virtuous choices over immoral choices.
[33] Ronald Dworkin, "Liberal Community", 77 *California Law Review* 479 at 486 (1989).
[34] See, *e.g.* John M. Finnis, "Is Natural Law Theory Compatible with Limited Government", in *Natural Law, Liberalism and Morality: Contemporary Essays* (R. George ed., Clarendon Press, Oxford, 1996), pp 7–9; *cf.* Aquinas, *Summa Theologiae*, Question 96, Art. 2, corpus, in *The Treatise on Law*, p. 316 (human law should not attempt to prohibit all vices, "but only the more serious ones from which it is possible for the majority to abstain and especially those which are harmful to others and which, if not prohibited, would make the preservation of human society impossible").

Joel Feinberg, *The Moral Limits of the Criminal Law* (Oxford University Press, Oxford, 1984–1988), four volumes.

Robert P. George, *Making Men Moral* (Clarendon Press, Oxford, 1993).

Robert P. George ed., *Natural Law, Liberalism, and Morality: Contemporary Essays* (Clarendon Press, Oxford, 1996) (including essays by John Finnis, Stephen Macedo, Michael Sandel, and Joseph Raz).

Kent Greenawalt, "Legal Enforcement of Morality", in *A Companion to the Philosophy of Law and Legal Theory* (D. Patterson ed., Blackwell, Oxford, 1996), pp. 475–487.

H.L.A. Hart, *Law, Liberty, and Morality* (Oxford University Press, Oxford, 1963).

John Stuart Mill, "On Liberty", in *On Liberty and Utilitarianism* (Bantam Books, New York, 1993), pp. 1–133.

James Fitzjames Stephen, *Liberty, Equality, Fraternity* (Liberty Fund, Indianapolis, 1993).

Jeremy Waldron, *Liberal Rights* (Cambridge University Press, Cambridge, 1993), Chs 1–8.

Chapter Sixteen

The Obligation to Obey the Law

The topic of the moral content of law has come up in a number of ways in earlier discussions in this book. Among the individual theorists: the natural law theorists, like John Finnis, whose analyses of law are tied directly to when and whether the law "binds in conscience" (Ch. 5); H.L.A. Hart defining and defending legal positivism on the basis that the description of law must be separated from its evaluation (Ch. 3); Lon Fuller writing of the "internal morality" of law (Ch. 6); and Ronald Dworkin's assertion that moral evaluation is integral to any proper description ("interpretation") of the law (Ch. 7). One can also find it in other topics: *e.g.* the question discussed in the previous chapter, of what relationship law should have to morality, in terms of which parts of morality should or should not be enforced through the legal system.

The current topic is the other side of the question. Instead of, "from the perspective of law, what is the place of morality?", this chapter will consider, "from the perspective of morality, what is the place of law?" In simpler terms, the question is whether there is a moral obligation to obey the law—a moral obligation that attaches to a rule simply because of its legal validity, its membership within a legal system. With exceptions, most of the writers who discuss a moral obligation to obey the law are considering quite modest claim:

(1) *not* that one must obey laws however unjust the legal system—the question usually assumes a generally just legal system; and

(2) *not* that one must obey the law whatever the circumstances—the obligation is at most a presumptive or "prima facie" obligation, which can be overridden if a stronger moral obligation requires a contrary action.[1]

---

[1] Just as one is justified in violating the moral obligation to keep a promise to meet a friend for lunch in order to keep a stronger moral obligation to tend to a sick parent, so one would be morally justified in violating a law if some more important matter is involved (*e.g.* violating the speed limit to get a seriously ill friend to the hospital).

One way to approach the problem of the obligation to obey the law is to consider what you would do, if you were driving at 3 am, and came upon a stop light at an intersection, and you could see that there were no pedestrians and no cars (in particular, no police cars) in sight. Would you stop?

Many people obey the law for prudential reasons: they fear imprisonment or a fine, or they worry that being caught doing something illegal would harm their reputations or their careers. Some people would stop at the stop light at 3 am just out of habit: it is easier for them simply to obey the law unreflectively, rather than to take the trouble on each occasion to calculate all the moral or prudential factors. Such concerns are not what the debate on the obligation to obey the law is all about. The question is whether the legal status of a command, authorization or prohibition, by itself, without more, adds any *moral* reasons for doing or not doing the action indicated.

Various types of arguments have been offered to try to justify the conclusion that there is an obligation to obey the law: arguments based on consent, gratitude, reciprocity, and consequences. These different concepts will be explained in greater detail presently. For the moment, it is worth noting that for all of these arguments, the type of situation like the one described above, coming to an intersection at 3 am, will always be the one that gives the most trouble. In this type of situation, disobedience does not seem to risk harming anyone or anything, and the disobedience looks like it would go undetected. This last point is important not only because sanctions for the violator will be avoided, but also because there would not be an argument that our disobedience sets a bad example, and would undermine other people's respect for the legal system.[2]

OBLIGATION AND CONSENT

One of the standard arguments for the obligation to obey the law is based on consent. The argument goes that by some action (or inaction), we have implicitly consented to obeying society's law. This action may be voting, accepting government benefits, or simply not leaving the country.[3] The first response is usually that it is not proper to understand these activities as constituting consent to the laws or to the state, either because the citizens do not perceive the action in that way, or because the citizens often do not have effective alternatives.

Another interesting response is that even if the action in question could

---

[2] As discussed in Ch. 5, some natural law theorists have argued that there is sometimes a moral obligation to act in compliance even with an unjust law if disobedience would undermine a generally just legal system.

[3] This last figures both in Plato's "Crito" and in Locke's discussion of implied consent to the government's authority.

be held to constitute consent, that does not end the question over whether the citizen's acting in this way then has an obligation to obey the society's laws. One must remember that the argument here has two steps, and that both steps must be proven for the argument to succeed. The two steps are: (1) a certain action (say, voting) constitutes "consent" to obeying the society's laws; and (2) anyone who consents in this way is morally obligated to obey the law. The second need not follow from the first.

The reason the second conclusion may fail to follow from the first is that, as a moral matter, acts of consent may have limited force. If I agree to paint your fence for $100, most people would conclude that my promise is a consent to undertake the obligation to paint the fence (for the payment named), an obligation I would not have except for my promise. However, the moral evaluation of the situation might change if what I agreed to was to paint your entire house for one dollar, or to kill your father, or to do anything you told me to do over the next month. The mere promise, even taking into consideration the (nominal) exchange payment, is not sufficient to maintain the large moral claim.

For this particular context, the claim is that the putative act of consent, voting or not leaving or whatever, is not sufficient to justify creating the broad obligation to obey *whatever* the government might enact from *that day onward*. As a moral matter, we might conclude that this is too much to place on a single promise, especially here where the "promise" is an action that has other purposes and meanings.

Arguing over what should be called "consent" too often masks the real moral questions: how do we create moral obligations for ourselves, and what are the limits of those obligations?

OTHER APPROACHES

A second approach for grounding a general moral obligation to obey the law is consequentialist: there is a general moral obligation to obey, because of the bad consequences to society if people did not have such an obligation. Thomas Hobbes presents the extreme version of this perspective: that the law is to be obeyed, even when it is unjust, because the alternative is the chaos of the state of nature, the war of all against all.[4] A more subtle consequentialist argument comes from A.M. Honoré.[5] He begins his discussion of the obligation to obey the law by trying to refute those who claim that not only is there no such obligation, but that we

---

[4] See, *e.g.* Thomas Hobbes, *Leviathan* (R. Tuck ed., Cambridge University Press, Cambridge, 1996), Ch. 20, pp. 144–145 (first published in 1651): "And though of so unlimited a [Sovereign] Power, men may fancy many evill consequences, yet the consequences of the want of it, which is the perpetuall warre of every man against his neighbour; are much worse."

[5] A.M. Honoré, *Making Law Bind* (Clarendon Press, Oxford, 1987), pp. 115–138.

should not be much worried by this fact. Honoré states that the most difficult moral questions, like the most difficult legal questions, are so closely
contested that they are likely to turn on where the burden of proof lies.
Regarding the obligation to obey the law, if the initial presumption is that
the law should be obeyed, then more often than not, the final moral judgment will be for obedience. However, if, following those theorists who
claim that there is no obligation, the initial presumption is that the law
need not be obeyed, then, Honoré argues, people will tend more often to
disregard the law, leading to an "attitude of disobedience" and the break-
down of the order and cooperation needed for society to function.

A third argument sometimes offered is one of benefit or gratitude: it is
immoral for those who have received substantial benefits from the state
(police protection, free education, social benefits of some kind, and so on)
not to respond with the small obligation that governments ask in return:
obedience to the law. The analogy is often made with the duty of gratitude children owe their parents.[6]

A fourth type of argument grounds the obligation on a straightforward
assertion of "a duty . . . to support and to further just institutions."[7] In a
way, this is simply the modern echo of the traditional natural law position: "Positive human laws are either just or unjust. If they are just, they
have the power of binding in conscience, a power which comes from the
Eternal Law from which they are derived".[8]

A fifth approach, a fairness or reciprocity argument for an obligation
to obey the law, differs in a basic way from other approaches in that it
speaks less of a duty owed to the state (based on consent or gratitude) or
owed abstractly (as one might conceive the duty to avoid bad consequences), and more of a duty to one's fellow citizens. H.L.A. Hart wrote:
"when a number of persons conduct any joint enterprise according to
rules and thus restrict their liberty those who have submitted to these
restrictions when required have a right to a similar submission from those
who have benefitted by their submission."[9]

THE ARGUMENT AGAINST A GENERAL MORAL OBLIGATION TO OBEY

In the course of the Hart-Fuller debate (discussed in Chs 3 and 6), Fuller
challenged the legal positivists on the following terms: if the validity of a

---

[6] An argument from gratitude, and an analogy to children's gratitude to parents, is offered
in Plato, "Crito", 50d–51d, in *Plato: The Collected Dialogues*, pp. 35–36.
[7] Rawls, *A Theory of Justice*, p. 334.
[8] Aquinas, *Summa Theologiae*, Question 96, Art. 4, corpus, in *The Treatise on Law*, p. 324.
[9] See H.L.A. Hart, "Are There Any Natural Rights?", 64 *Philosophical Review* 175 at 185
(1955). For a similar argument elaborated at greater length, see John Rawls, "Legal
Obligation and the Duty of Fair Play", in *Law and Philosophy* (S. Hook ed., New York
University Press, New York, 1964), pp. 3–18.

law is one thing, and its moral value something entirely separate, then how can the legal positivists speak of there being a "moral dilemma" about whether to obey a morally dubious law?[10] If law is just a label for something which may or may not be morally worthy, then there is no reason to believe that just because something is required or prohibited by law, that by itself is a *moral* reason for doing or not doing that action.

Fuller may have thought of his challenge as a knockdown argument, but a number of recent commentators, including some prominent legal positivists, have accepted, without shame or apology, that the legal status of a norm may give it no intrinsic moral weight.[11] These theorists do not argue that we should never obey the law, or even that there are never *moral* reasons for doing what the law tells us to, only that the moral reasons must go beyond the simple declaration, "because the law says so".

For Joseph Raz, we have a moral reason to do as the law states, if and when we believe that we are more likely to make the morally best choice by following the law than by making our own judgment of the situation. For example, if the question is whether to use a particular detergent or not, with the issue being that it might damage the environment, we might defer to the legislature's judgment, on the basis that they have acted to allow or prohibit the detergent only after hearing scientific testimony to which we do not have access.

For another kind of example, consider pure problems of co-ordination. These are problems where it does not matter much what is chosen, as long as everyone chooses the same way. A standard example is which side of the road cars drive on. For such choices, there are reasons for acting as the law states, for the government is sufficiently prominent to make such choices and expect them to be followed by other citizens.

There are also co-ordination situations where some choices might be better than others, but there is great value to everyone choosing the same way, even if it is not the optimal choice. An example might be fighting water pollution. As a pollution expert, you might know that the clean-up program the government has chosen is not the best plan, but you also know that the government's plan, enacted in legislation with sanctions for deviation, is the one most likely to be followed by most people, and that everyone cooperating in that scheme is more likely to achieve results than if different persons went off trying to effect different schemes. Under such a situation, you might have good reason to follow the government's plan, even when you know it is not the best.

Of course, the most common situation when one has a moral obligation

---

[10] Fuller, "Positivism and Fidelity to Law", p. 656: "It is like saying I have to choose between giving food to a starving man and being mimsy with the borogoves."

[11] See, *e.g.* Joseph Raz, "The Obligation to Obey: Revision and Tradition", 1 *Journal of Law, Ethics & Public Policy* 139 (1984); Raz, *The Morality of Freedom*, pp. 70–105; M.B.E. Smith, "Is There a Prima Facie Obligation to Obey the Law?", 82 *Yale Law Journal* 950 (1973).

to act as the law requires is when the action is the moral thing to do whatever the law might say. For most of us, we do not rob or murder because it would be wrong, not because the law tells us not to. However, in such situations, the fact that the law prohibits the action appears to add nothing to the moral calculation that the action ought not be done.

The skeptics respond to the arguments offered to support an obligation to obey (summarized above), by saying that such arguments are insufficient to ground an obligation, or at least insufficient to ground a *general* obligation. If ignoring the stop light at 3 am causes no harm and does not create a bad example, it is hard to see how the action would undermine a just institution or a joint enterprise. It is far from clear why any consent we have given, or any duty of fair play or gratitude we might have, should extend to all the government's laws, however trivial, or however harmless the disobedience.[12]

The types of arguments one comes across (in the literature as well as in classroom discussions) on the topic of the obligation to obey the law often reflect a constant changing of perspectives and questions. To arguments like Raz's, the objection goes: "how can you know that you have a better idea of what is morally right than the legislature has?", or "if everyone made their own choices about how to act, rather than deferring to the legislature, there would be anarchy".[13] There often is a certain "we"/"them" attitude when discussing the obligation to obey the law, with the unstated assumption being that "we" are looking for the correct attitude for "them" to have. It is probably better if the discussion remains on the level of "our" deciding how "we" ought to act (or how "we" ought to go about deciding how "we" ought to act). This is not to say that we should ignore the way self-interest will likely bias people's evaluation of their moral obligations, including our own biases; however, this is only one factor among many in our evaluations, and we should not always err on the side of submission to authority.[14]

In any event, one should not confuse:

(1) the ethical question, what should I do in this situation?

(2) the meta-ethical question, how do I determine what is the morally correct thing for me to do? and

(3) the political consideration: from a particular perspective, what is the set of beliefs and attitudes we want or need the public to hold?

This chapter deals only with the first two questions.

---

[12] See Smith, "Is There a Prima Facie Obligation to Obey the Law", at 953–964.
[13] This view is present, to some extent, in Honoré's approach, discussed above. For a sophisticated argument that seems to verge on that sort of argument without ever quite succumbing to it, see John M. Finnis, "Law as Co-ordination", 2 *Ratio Juris* 97 (1989).
[14] See Raz, "The Obligation to Obey", p. 151.

CONNECTIONS

While the obligation to obey the law is often treated as a separate topic (as it is in this text), in many ways the issue is ill-suited for such treatment. From any discussion of the questions raised by the issue, it becomes clear that one's answer to whether there is an obligation to obey the law will depend on one's conclusions regarding a series of more basic questions: both basic questions of moral theory *(e.g.* what can/does ground our moral duties: benefit? consent? co-operation? consequences? necessity and interdependence?); and basic questions of legal theory (how do we determine the existence or validity of a law or legal system?).

For example, if one's starting point is a traditional form of natural law theory, one's conclusion about whether something is "law" (or "law in its fullest sense") will already incorporate much of the answer about whether or to what extent one has an obligation to obey the law (one has such an obligation for just laws, "laws in their fullest sense"; for unjust laws, there may still be a minimal obligation of public compliance so as not to undermine a generally just legal system).[15] Legal positivism offers no comparable guidance. Its motto, that the validity of law is one thing, its merit another, indicates that legal positivists will have to find answers elsewhere, in whatever moral theory they bring to their deliberations.

Suggested Further Readings

William A. Edmundson ed., *The Duty to Obey the Law: Selected Philosophical Writings* (Rowman & Littlefield, Lanham, Maryland, 1999) (contributors include John Rawls, Robert Paul Wolff, M. B. E. Smith, A. John Simmons, Joseph Raz, and Philip Soper).
John Finnis, "The Authority of Law in the Predicament of Contemporary Social Theory", 1 *Notre Dame Journal of Law and Public Policy* 115 (1984).
—, "Law as Co-ordination", 2 *Ratio Juris* 97 (1989).
Ruth C. A. Higgins, "Obedience, Respect, and the Law" (forthcoming, Oxford University Press, Oxford, 2004).
A.M. Honoré, *Making Law Bind* (Clarendon Press, Oxford, 1987), pp. 115–138.
Joseph Raz, *The Authority of the Law* (1979), pp. 233–289.
A. John Simmons, *Moral Principles and Political Obligations* (Princeton University Press, Princeton, 1979).
M.B.E. Smith, "Is There a Prima Facie Obligation to Obey the Law?", 82 *Yale Law Journal* 950 (1973).
—, "The Duty to Obey the Law", in *A Companion to the Philosophy of Law and Legal Theory* (D. Patterson, ed. Blackwell, Oxford, 1996), pp. 465–474.

---

[15] This is a position of the natural law theorists Thomas Aquinas and John Finnis, as discussed in Ch. 5.

PART D

Modern Perspectives on Legal Theory

The last set of chapters discusses general approaches to law and legal education that have come to prominence in the twentieth century, with all but the first (American legal realism) grounded primarily in the last few decades.

If one thinks of theory as being divided between the "pure philosophy" tendency to ask questions simply to learn ("philosophy" is a Greek word meaning "love of knowledge" or "love of wisdom") and the belief that inquiry should always be focused on the ethical question of how we should live our lives, the approaches outlined in most of these chapters can be seen as pulling jurisprudence toward the latter attitude. These approaches are concerned primarily with doing justice rather than being concerned primarily with true understanding. The pull is not entirely in one direction only as those who point to economics or literature, or to racism or sexism, as being the key to understanding the legal system, are also trying to make a point about the nature of things, as well as about how things could be made better.

Chapter Seventeen

American Legal Realism

"Legal realism" is the label that was given to a group of American legal theorists in the 1920s, 1930s, and 1940s, who challenged the ideas about legal reasoning and adjudication dominant in judicial and legal academic writing at the time. Their influence on legal thinking, particularly in the United States, but elsewhere as well, can be summarized by the fact that the phrase, "we are all realists now", has become a kind of legal-academic cliché.[1]

Among those writers who described themselves (or who were described by others) as "realists", there was little by way of agreed views, values, subject-matter, or methodology. It has become commonplace to note that the differences among those writers were sufficiently significant that it approaches distortion even to refer to "the legal realists", as though it were a coherent movement (one commentator writing recently went so far as to refer to legal realism as a "feel" or "mood"[2]). With those disclaimers noted, the chapter will try to note the general outline of American legal realism.

Many of the themes (and much of the tone) of the legal realists can be found in the work of Oliver Wendell Holmes Jr (1841–1935) who (by most ways of delimiting the realist movement) wrote most of his influential work at an earlier period.[3] In *The Common Law*, published in 1881, Holmes wrote:

"The life of the law has not been logic: it has been experience. The felt necessities of the time, the prevalent moral and political theories, intuitions of public policy,

---

[1] See, *e.g.* Twining, *Karl Llewellyn and the Realist Movement*, p. 382.
[2] Duxbury, *Patterns of American Jurisprudence*, pp. 68–69.
[3] Roscoe Pound was another important precursor for American legal realism. See, *e.g.* Roscoe Pound, "The Scope and Purpose of Sociological Jurisprudence" (Pt I), 24 *Harvard Law Review* 591 (1911); (Pt II) 25 *Harvard Law Review* 140 (1912). The complication with Pound is that his later work was sometimes critical of legal realism, and was itself the subject of legal realist critiques. See Roscoe Pound, "The Call for a Realist Jurisprudence", 44 *Harvard Law Review* 697 (1931); Karl N. Llewellyn, "Some Realism about Realism: Responding to Dean Pound", 44 *Harvard Law Review* 1222 (1931).

American legal realism may also be traceable, at least in part, to Rudolf von Jhering, and other German theorists of the late 19th century. See James E. Herget and Stephen Wallace, "The German Free Law Movement as the Source of American Legal Realism", 73 *Virginia Law Review* 399 (1987).

avowed or unconscious, even the prejudices which judges share with their fellow-men, have had a good deal more to do than the syllogism in determining the rules by which men should be governed."[4]

In these few sentences one can find (or at least read in) most of the themes for which the American legal realist movement would be remembered.

The "realism" in "legal realism" is the use of that term in its colloquial meaning: "being realistic" as being worldly, perhaps somewhat cynical, looking beyond ideals and appearances for what is "really going on". This realism was made vivid in another image of Holmes': that we should cut through all the false moralistic language of the lawyers, judges, and legal commentators, by taking on the perspective of "the bad man", who wants to know only what the courts are "likely to do in fact".[5] The "bad man" is the client who wants to know which actions will land him in jail or cost him a fine, and which will not; everything else is superfluous and besides the point.[6]

In overview: first, the main focus of this "realism" was on judicial deci-sion-making—that a proper understanding of judicial decision-making would show that it was fact-centred; that judges' decisions were often based (consciously or unconsciously) on personal or political biases and constructed from hunches; and that public policy and social sciences should play a larger role.[7] Secondly, feeding into this central focus on adjudication was a critique of legal reasoning: that beneath a veneer of scientific and deductive reasoning, legal rules and concepts were in fact often indeterminate and rarely as neutral as they were presented as being. It was the indeterminacy of legal concepts and legal reasoning that led to the need to explain judicial decisions in other terms (hunches and biases) and the opportunity to encourage a different focus for advocacy and judi-cial reasoning: social sciences and "public policy". (These two themes are clearly interconnected, so there is a certain arbitrariness in where one starts in the discussion, and even in where one places various sub-issues—for example, the emphasis on the social sciences could be as easily dis-cussed under either of the two themes.) This chapter will discuss those two themes at greater length, after first summarizing legal formalism, for

---

[4] Holmes, *The Common Law*, p. 5.
[5] See Holmes, "The Path of the Law", at 460–461.
[6] *ibid.* at 459–462.
[7] Again here Holmes is an important early influence. See, *e.g.* Oliver Wendell Holmes, "Privilege, Malice, and Intent", 8 *Harvard Law Review* 1 (1894), where Holmes argued that decisions regarding privilege, which are often presented as having been the result of logical deductions from general premises, are in fact based on conscious or unconscious decisions of policy, which should be discussed more openly. Holmes stated:
"Perhaps one of the reasons why judges do not like to discuss questions of policy . . . is that the moment you leave the path of merely logical deduction you lose the illusion of certainty which makes legal reasoning seem like mathematics. But the certainty is only an illusion, nevertheless." *ibid.* at 7.

arguing against a formalism approach to law may be the only thing that all the legal realists had in common.

THE TARGET: FORMALISM

The form of legal analysis dominant at the time the realists were writing was criticized as "formalistic", by which it was meant that the argument was presented as if the conclusion followed simply and inexorably from undeniable premises. Once the proper label was found for an object or action ("contract", property", "trespass", and so on), the legal conclusion soon followed.[8] The notion that most judicial decisions should or could be deduced from general concepts or general rules, with no attention to real-world conditions or consequences, critics labeled "mechanical jurisprudence".[9] A famous example was the United States Supreme Court's decision in the "Sugar Trust Case", *United States v E. C. Knight Co.*[10] The United States Government had challenged a monopoly in the manufacture of sugar, but the challenge was rejected on the basis that regulating manufacturing was outside the Congress's power to regulate interstate *commerce*, however obvious it might seem that a company's controlling 98 per cent of the nation's sugar refining capacity might have implications for interstate commerce in that good. The case was decided on labels; real-world consequences were treated as irrelevant to (or subversive of) the proper legal analysis.[11]

An equally distinctive version of formalism was influential in American legal education. Christopher Columbus Langdell, Dean of the Harvard Law School and originator of the "Case Method" of teaching law,[12]

---

[8] In large part because of the American legal realists' critique, "formalism" has become primarily a pejorative term in legal commentary. There are, however, still some who treat the formal elements of law respectfully, or even enthusiastically, See, *e.g.* Ernest J. Weinrib, "Legal Formalism: On the Immanent Rationality of Law", 97 *Yale Law Journal* 949 (1988); Frederick Schauer, "Formalism", 97 *Yale Law Journal* 509 (1988); Robert S. Summers, "How Law is Formal and Why it Matters", 82 *Cornell Law Review* 1165 (1997). See also Scalia, *A Matter of Interpretation*, p. 25 ("Of all the criticisms leveled against textualism, the most mindless is that it is 'formalistic.' The answer to that is, *of course it's formalistic!* The rule of law is about form."). For a useful overview of past and current uses of "formalism", see Martin Stone, "Formalism", in *The Oxford Handbook of Jurisprudence and Philosophy of Law* (J. Coleman and S. Shapiro, eds, K. E. Himma, assoc. ed., Oxford University Press, Oxford, 2002), pp. 166–205.

[9] See Roscoe Pound, "Mechanical Jurisprudence", 8 *Columbia Law Review* 605 (1908).

[10] *United States v E.C. Knight Co.*, 156 U.S. 1 (1895).

[11] *ibid.* at 10–18; see also Holmes, *The Common Law*, p. 164 ("Bruns . . . expresses a characteristic yearning of the German mind, when he demands an internal juristic necessity drawn from the nature of possession itself, and therefore rejects empirical reasons.") (footnote omitted).

[12] In the Case Method, the subject is learned by reading a series of (appellate court) decisions in the area, analyzing closely and critically the argument offered by the courts in their decisions.

famously advocated that law was a science, whose principles and doctrines could be "discovered" in cases, much as biologists discover the principles of their science in their laboratories.[13] Langdell's approach could
be summarized as follows:

"To Langdell 'science' conjured up the ideas of order, system, simplicity, taxonomy
and original sources. The science of law involved the search for a system of general,
logically consistent principles, built up from the study of particular instances."[14]

Once the general principles have been found:

". . . it is then the task of scholars to work out, in an analytically rigorous manner,
the subordinate principles entailed by them. When these subordinate principles
have all been stated in propositional form and the relations of entailment among
them clarified, they will, Langdell believed, together constitute a well-ordered
system of rules that offers the best possible description of that particular branch
of law—the best answer to the question of what the law in that area is.[15]

　　Langdell tried to derive the law from basic axioms and logical deduction. Real-world consequences and moral evaluations just did not figure.
In one discussion of whether a proper understanding of contract law
entailed the "mailbox rule",[16] Langdell's response to the argument that
one rule "would produce not only unjust and absurd results" was: "The
true answer to this argument is, that it is irrelevant".[17]

　　As stated earlier, if one theme runs through the work of the various
American legal realists, it is opposition to legal formalism in all its mani-
festations.

REALISM AND LEGAL ANALYSIS

The attack on formalism could be divided into two separate criticisms:

(1) arguing against the idea that common law concepts and standards
　　 were "neutral" or "objective"; and

---

[13] Christopher Columbus Langdell, "Preface", in *A Selection of Cases on the Law of Contracts*
(1871), p. viii, and a speech to commemorate the 250th Anniversary of the Founding of
Harvard College (1887), both quoted in Twining, *Karl Llewellyn and the Realist Movement*,
pp. 11–12.

[14] Twining, *Karl Llewellyn and the Realist Movement*, p. 12 (footnote omitted). See also Dennis
Patterson, "Langdell's Legacy", 90 *Northwestern University Law Review* 901 (1995).

[15] Kronman, *The Lost Lawyer*, p. 171.

[16] The mailbox rule states that where a postal response to an offer is invited, the acceptance
is valid upon posting. See, *e.g. Adams v Lindsell* (1818) 106 Eng. Rep. 250 (K.B.); *Henthorn v
Fraser* [1892] 2 Ch. 27.

[17] Christopher Columbus Langdell, *A Summary of the Law of Contract* (2nd ed., Little, Brown,
and Co., Boston, 1880), pp. 20–21.

(2) arguing against the idea that general legal concepts or general legal rules could determine the results in particular cases.

As to the first, the realists argued that the premises lawyers used were open to question, and that labels and categories hid moral and policy assumptions that should be discussed openly. An example of realist analysis can be seen on the losing side of one of the most famous American tort law cases, *Palsgraf v Long Island Railroad*.[18] In that case, a railroad employee was negligent in his attempt to assist a passenger; as a result of the negligence, the passenger dropped a package, which happened to contain explosives. An explosion occurred, which led to the injury of the plaintiff, a third party who was standing some distance away. The question in the case was whether someone should be liable for all injuries "proximately caused" by that person's negligence. The majority, in an opinion written by Judge (later Justice) Benjamin Cardozo, famously decided that the plaintiff could not recover, on the basis that the railroad employee had no duty to the plaintiff, and his negligence created liability only to the passenger he was trying to help. However, for the purpose of considering American legal realism, the more interesting opinion is the dissent, written by Judge William Andrews, which included a realist attack on the solidity of the concept of "proximate cause":

"What we do mean by the word 'proximate' is, that because of convenience, of public policy, of a rough sense of justice, the law arbitrarily declines to trace a series of events beyond a certain point. This is not logic. It is practical politics."[19]

As to the second idea, which Holmes famously summarized by the comment, "General propositions do not decide concrete cases",[20] the idea is that adjudication can rarely be accurately seen as a mechanical, logical deduction from general premises. At least in difficult cases, there remains a logical gap between the general legal proposition, or the statute couched in general terms, and the result of particular cases. Holmes meant to refer to quite general legal concepts or principles. Holmes believed that specific legal rules *would* determine results in most legal

---

[18] 248 N.Y 339, 162 N.E. 99 (1928).
[19] *ibid.* at 352, 162 N.E. at 103 (Andrews J., dissenting).
[20] *Lochner v New York*, 198 U.S. 45 at 76 (1905) (Holmes J., dissenting). Apparently, Holmes was willing to back up that claim, at least in informal contest: "Holmes liked to tell his colleagues on the Supreme Court, when they were conferring about a case, that he would admit any general principle of law they proposed, and then use it to decide the case under discussion either way". Louis Menand, "Bet-tabilitariansim", *The New Republic*, November 11, 1996, pp. 47–56, at p. 48.

cases, leaving an open question for judicial legislation only at a penumbra where the application of the rule becomes unclear.[21]

Some of the later legal realists, like Jerome Frank,[22] took a more radical position: the legal phrases and concepts alone do not get us to a decision, and we are fooling ourselves and the public if we claim that they do. The final conclusion regarding, for example, whether "proximate cause" exists or not will be based on unstated premises regarding public policy (or perhaps based on unstated biases or prejudices).

One can add a third point to the attack as well. Even when one can determine what the law is *and* it is sufficient to decide the case, it may be that the law should be changed. The American legal realists were certainly not the first to subject the law to moral criticism. However, the realists' attack on the scientific pretensions of "legal science", and on the notion that law was a self-contained moral-logical system, created an opening for the moral criticism, for the possibility that legislative or judicial reform of the law might be morally (and legally) legitimate. We can see Holmes in two sentences taking much of the power out of the argument from precedent:

"It is revolting to have no better reason for a rule of law than that so it was laid down in the time of Henry IV. It is still more revolting if the grounds upon which it was laid down have vanished long since, and the rule simply persists from blind imitation of the past."[23]

For Holmes, a strong believer in judicial restraint (in judges deferring to legislative decisions and following precedent strictly[24]) this was an argument for *legislative* change of old common law rules. In the hand of other legal realists, however, the same argument was a justification for *judicial* reform of outdated rules.[25]

The realist view of legal reasoning also had implications for legal education. Given the realist analyses and criticisms given above, it is not surprising that the realists tended to be scornful of Langdell's "science of law", and all aspects of legal education that seemed to follow from it. To the extent that one can speak of "a realist view" on education, it would primarily be one of following through on the implications of other realist

---

[21] See Holmes, *The Common Law*, p. 101; *Southern Pacific v Jensen*, 244 U.S. 205 at 221 (1917) (Holmes, J., dissenting) ("I recognize without hesitation that judges do and must legislate, but they can do so only interstitially"); Grey, "Molecular Motions: The Holmesian Judge in Theory and Practice", pp. 32–36.

[22] See, *e.g.* Jerome Frank, "Are Judges Human?", 80 *University of Pennsylvania Law Review* 17 (1931).

[23] Holmes, "The Path of the Law", at 469.

[24] See Grey, "Molecular Motions: The Holmesian Judge in Theory and Practice", at 26–34.

[25] See, *e.g.* Cardozo, *The Nature of the Judicial Process*, pp. 98–141 ("The Judge as a Legislator").

views: that legal concepts should be taught in a way which demystified them; and that legal issues should be shown to be often underdetermined by legal rules alone, with policy arguments appropriate and necessary for resolution.[26]

REALISM AND THE COURTS

Judicial decision-making at the time of the realist critique was often portrayed (by judges in their opinions as well as by commentators) as being a nearly mechanical, nearly syllogistic move from basic premises to undeniable conclusion. The legal realist response was to argue that judges often have discretion, that judicial decisions were often in practice determined by factors other than the legal rules, and to move the focus from conceptual analysis to policy-based arguments and fact-finding. One can get a sense of legal realism just from the titles of some of its articles, *e.g.* "Are Judges Human?"; "What Courts Do In Fact"; "Transcendental Nonsense and the Functional Approach"; and "The Judgment Intuitive: The Function of the 'Hunch' in Judicial Decision".[27]

The classical perspective of judicial decision-making was that judges decided cases by merely discovering the appropriate legal rule, a process that required the mere application of simple logical deduction from basic principles. Legal realism offered a variety of counter-images of what they thought really went on in decision-making, a number of which are summed up in this slight caricature of realism: "judges in fact follow their instincts in deciding cases, making sham references to rules of law; generally they are themselves unaware of what they are doing, and persist foolishly in believing that they are being obedient to precedent."[28]

There were (at least) two strands to realist discussion of judicial decision-making: that decisions were strongly underdetermined by legal rules, concepts and precedent (that is, that judges in many or most cases could have, with equal warrant, come out more than one way); and that judges were (and, by some accounts, should be) highly responsive to the facts, and the way the facts were presented, in reaching their decisions.[29] One

---

[26] See Duxbury, *Patterns of American Jurisprudence*, pp. 135–149; William Fisher; Morton Horwitz and Thomas Reed eds, *American Legal Realism* (Oxford University Press, New York, 1993), pp. 270–294.

[27] Jerome Frank, "Are Judges Human?"; Jerome Frank, "What Courts Do In Fact", Parts I and II, 26 *Illinois Law Review* 645, 761 (1932); Cohen, "Transcendental Nonsense and the Functional Approach"; Joseph Hutcheson Jr., "The Judgment Intuitive: The Function of the 'Hunch' in Judicial Decision", 14 *Cornell Law Quarterly* 274 (1929).

[28] Benjamin Kaplan, "Do Intermediate Appellate Courts Have a Lawmaking Function?", 70 *Massachusetts Law Review* 10 at 10 (1985).

[29] On the last point, see, in particular, Jerome Frank, *Courts on Trial* (Princeton University Press, Princeton, 1949).

commentator has gone so far as to describe the assertion, "in deciding cases, judges respond primarily to the stimulus of the facts of the case", as the "core claim" of American legal realism.[30]

It is important to note that the claim that general principles in fact *do not* determine the results of particular cases and the claim that they *cannot* are quite distinct.[31] The first is a statement about causation in the world: why judges decide cases the way they do. The second is a statement about logical possibility, the nature of language, or the nature of rules: the point being that one cannot derive in a deductive fashion the result in (some, most, all) legal cases from general principles.

The two claims are independent; one can affirm the first without affirming the second (and probably vice versa). Both themes were present in the writings of the legal realists. Both themes have become embedded in the way modern lawyers and legal academics think about law, and in the way law is taught. If it was once subversive to think that extralegal factors influence judicial decisions, it now seems naive to doubt it. And it is commonplace to assume, at least for relatively important and difficult cases, that strong legal arguments can be found for both sides.

There are obvious ties with the first theme discussed: the indeterminacy and lack of neutrality of legal concepts, and the inability to derive unique results in particular cases from general legal rules. If that was the state of law in the abstract, then it comes as no surprise that judicial decisions cannot be based solely on these rules and concepts, and judges who claim otherwise were either fooling themselves or lying.

What was to fill the conceptual gap left when one's faith in the neutrality and determinacy of legal concepts was undermined? For many of the realists, the answer was social science, the understanding of how people actually behave, and the way in which legal rules reflect or affect behaviour. This turn to the social sciences can be seen in a number of places, including "The Brandeis Brief", a brief on legal issues that bases its legal conclusions on extensive sociological research.

The "Brandeis Brief" was named after Louis Brandeis, a legal reformer who later sat as a Justice on the United States Supreme Court. The term refers in particular to a brief Brandeis co-wrote defending the constitutionality of a state statute limiting the maximum working hours for women.[32] "Containing two pages of legal argument and ninety-five pages of sociological and economic data about the conditions of working women's lives in factories, the Brandeis brief, by highlighting social and

---

[30] Leiter, "Legal Realism", at 269.
[31] This paragraph and the next one follow part of the argument presented in Leiter, "Legal Realism", at 265–269.
[32] *Muller v Oregon*, 208 U.S 412 (1908).

economic reality, suggested that the trouble with existing law was that it was out of touch with that reality."[33]

This faith in the social sciences can also be seen indirectly through the work many realists did in the American "New Deal", creating administrative agencies and regulations meant to solve various social problems through the law.[34] The weak point of realist thinking in this area was the tendency towards technocracy, the belief that social scientific expertise by itself would be sufficient to lead to right results, missing the point that there is always a need for a moral or political structure within which to present (or to do) the empirical work; there could not be "neutral experts" on how society should be organized.[35]

AN OVERVIEW AND POSTSCRIPT

The basic misunderstanding of American legal realism by some later writers turned on a confusion regarding the purpose and point of the realists' work. For example, when the realists stated that we should see law from the perspective of a prediction of what judges will do ("the bad man's" perspective[36]), later writers misunderstand the argument when they saw that as a conceptual claim.[37]

As a conceptual claim, it would have obvious weaknesses. For example, how can a judge on the highest court see the law as a prediction of what the judges will do?; the highest court is the final word on what the law will mean and there is no other court whose decisions the judges could try to predict.[38] The predictive theory is better understood as an attempt to shake up the overly abstract and formalistic approach many judges and legal scholars used for discussing law. To put the matter another way, the realists wanted people in the legal profession to spend more time thinking about how law appears "on the ground" or (to change the metaphor) "at the sharp edge": to citizens for whom the law means only a prediction of what the trial judge will do in their case (or a prediction of how the police will treat them on the street corner).

In various ways, American legal realism can be seen as the forerunner of the perspectives on law to be discussed in the following chapters: law

---

[33] Horwitz, *The Transformation of American Law 1870–1960*, p. 209.

[34] See generally *ibid.* at pp. 213–246 ("Legal Realism, Bureaucratic State, and Law"). Neil Duxbury cautions against overstating the connection between the "New Deal" and realism in Duxbury, *Patterns of American Jurisprudence*, pp. 153–158.

[35] See Horwitz, *The Transformation of American Law 1870–1960*, pp. 217–246.

[36] See Holmes, "The Path of the Law", at 460–461.

[37] Compare Hart, *The Concept of Law*, pp. 136–141 (a conceptual reading of the view) with Leiter, "Legal Realism", at 262–264.

[38] Richard A. Posner, *The Problems of Jurisprudence* (Harvard University Press, Cambridge, Mass., 1990), p. 224.

and economics[39] (Ch. 18), critical legal studies, critical race theory and feminist legal theory (all in Ch. 19). The connection is often indirect: by undermining the confidence in the "science" of law and the ability to deduce unique correct answers from legal principles (as well as questioning the "neutrality" of those legal principles), the realists created a need for a new justification of legal rules and judicial actions. Also, the realists offered a set of arguments that could be used to support claims of pervasive bias (against the poor, against women, or against minorities) in the legal system, tools that would be used by later critical movements.

There were more short-term reactions to American legal realism within American legal thought. Some people, both within and outside academia, became uncomfortable with the skeptical, cynical and occasionally nihilistic tone of the realists. The discomfort was especially strong during the Second World War, when commentators were trying to emphasize the superiority of democratic governance over Fascism; and after the war, when the same argument was being made relative to Communism.[40] If it was good versus evil, some were not always sure that the realists were "on the right side".[41] Some writers turned to natural law theory (discussed in Ch. 5), others sought a way to concede part of the realists' criticisms, while still affirming central "rule of law" values. This path led to the legal process school, discussed briefly in Ch. 6.[42]

Suggested Further Readings

Neil Duxbury *Patterns of American Jurisprudence* (Clarendon Press, Oxford, 1995), pp. 65–159.

---

[39] One central figure in law and economics disclaims direct influence from legal realism. Richard A. Posner, *Overcoming Law* (Harvard University Press, Cambridge, Mass., 1995), p. 3. However, Posner does not consider the argument (first cogently presented by Arthur Leff, and summarized at the beginning of the next chapter) that legal realism led indirectly to law and economics, by undermining the more traditional approaches to law, with law and economics then filling the resulting moral (and academic) vacuum.

[40] See generally Edward A. Purcell, *The Crisis of Democratic Theory: Scientific Naturalism & the Problem of Value* (University Press of Kentucky, Lexington, 1973). Purcell writes:
"[The realists'] position raised two basic questions about traditional democratic theory. First, how could the idea of subjectivity of judicial decision be squared with the doctrine that free men should be subject only to known and established law, one of the hallmarks of republican as opposed to despotic government? Second, if the acts of government officials were the only real law, on what basis could anyone evaluate or criticize those acts? What, in other words, was the moral basis of the legal system in particular and of democratic government in general?" *ibid.* at p. 94.

[41] One thus comes across great article names like Ben W. Palmer, "Hobbes, Holmes, and Hitler", 31 *American Bar Association Journal* 569 (1945).

[42] For a discussion of this (traditional) view of the connection between American legal realism and legal process, see, *e.g.* Horwitz, *The Transformation of American Law* 1870–1960, pp. 247–268. For an argument that this traditional view is, at the least, too simplistic, see Duxbury, *Patterns of American Jurisprudence*, pp. 205–299.

William Fisher, Morton Horwitz and Thomas Reed eds, *American Legal Realism* (Oxford University Press, New York, 1993) (this book contains a collection of (excerpts from) many American legal realist articles, plus a thorough bibliography).

Jerome Frank, *Law and the Modern Mind* (Brentano's, New York, 1930).

Brian Leiter, "American Legal Realism", in *The Blackwell Guide to Philosophy of Law and Legal Theory* (forthcoming, M. Golding and W. A. Edmundson eds, Blackwell, Oxford, 2004)

—, "Legal Realism" in *A Companion to the Philosophy of Law and Legal Theory* (D. Patterson ed., Blackwell, Oxford, 1996), pp. 261–279.

Karl Llewellyn, "Some Realism about Realism—Responding to Dean Pound", 44 *Harvard Law Review* 1222 (1931).

Roscoe Pound, "The Call for a Realist Jurisprudence", 44 *Harvard Law Review* 697 (1931).

William Twining, *Karl Llewellyn and the Realist Movement* (University of Oklahoma Press, Norman, Oklahoma, 1985).

Chapter Eighteen

Economic Analysis of Law

In 1897, Justice Oliver Wendell Holmes, Jr. wrote, "For the rational study of the law the black-letter man may be the man of the present, but the man of the future is the man of statistics and the master of economics."[1] Holmes was prescient, though it took over 70 years for this prediction to be fully realized in legal academia.

In the United States, no approach to law in recent decades has been more influential than the economic analysis of law (also known by the shorthand "law and economics"). It dominates thinking about antitrust law, tort law, and most commercial law areas. Even areas of law which would seem uncongenial to economic analysis, like domestic relations (family law), criminal law, and constitutional law (civil liberties), have had significant contributions by law and economics analyses. There seem to be no domains free from attempts to apply this approach. Its influence is growing every year in legal academic circles in Britain and in other countries; in the United States, the influence has already been felt in judicial decisions (this last development being speeded by the appointment of prominent advocates of economic analysis, including Richard Posner and Frank Easterbrook, to positions as federal appellate court judges).

Law and economics has many origins. As will be discussed, the movement is in part grounded in utilitarianism, economic theories about interpersonal comparisons, and the works of Ronald Coase and Richard Posner. There are also other small but significant contributions along its path: for example, it was Edward H. Levi, professor and eventually president of the University of Chicago (and later Attorney General of the United States under President Gerald Ford), who came up with the idea of pairing an economist and a lawyer in the teaching of law school subjects, an action that many consider a crucial step in the development of the law and economics movement.[2]

---

[1] Holmes, "The Path of the Law", at 469. ("Black-letter law" refers to doctrinal law: the basic rules and principles of law, which were often placed in bold black letters in law treatises.)

[2] Neil A. Lewis, "Edward H. Levi, Attorney General Credited With Restoring Order After Watergate, Dies at 88", *New York Times*, March 8, 2000.

The currrent influence of law and economics can be seen in the way that even those highly critical of that approach use its terminology and respond to the issues it raises. There is a sense in which law and economics now sets the agenda, or at least offers the initial framework, for most discussions of policy and reform in American academic, legal, and political debate. Part of the power of economic analysis is that it presents a largely instrumental approach, which fits well with the analysis and evaluation of law: it forces the question, do these legal rules achieve the objectives at which they aim, and would alternative rules do any better? However critical one might be of the values and biases perhaps hidden within economics, one might still benefit from focusing, at least part of the time, on questions of consequences. For example, a reformer trying to fight racism might ask: will a proposed change in the law in fact reduce discrimination, or might there be perverse long-term effects that may work to harm the group we are trying to protect? This is the type of question that the economic approach to law has always been good at raising.

The first part of this chapter will attempt to understand law and economics by tracing its roots both in economic analysis and in American jurisprudence.

IN SEARCH OF CONSENSUS

One can start with a general question: on what basis can one argue for a court to adopt one standard rather than another, if there are no statutes or prior cases requiring a particular outcome? The novel legal issue could be whether a certain type of activity should he governed by a fault standard or by some form of strict liability; or whether an independent contractor should be treated the same way as an agent or an employee; or under what circumstances a bystander to an accident should be allowed to recover damages for nervous shock; and so on.

The traditional approach had been that a proper understanding of legal reasoning would allow one always to come to the correct answer through analogical reasoning and the subsumption of specific fact situations under general rules. However, in large part because of the criticisms of (among others) the American legal realists, the confidence that such neutral means could resolve every legal question, even the most novel or most difficult ones, dissolved.[3] When the judges said that they were "deducing" the correct answer through the simple application of logic

---

[3] See Joseph Singer, "Legal Realism Now", 76 *California Law Review* 465 at 468 (1988):
"Current debates about legal reasoning are best understood as attempts to answer the central question that the realists left unresolved: How can we engage in normative legal argument without either reverting to the formalism of the past or reducing all claims to the raw demands of political interest groups?"

and legal reasoning, the suspicion grew that the decision in fact turned on political assumptions that the judges were not revealing (and may not even have recognized).

Another basis for choosing one legal result over another is based on a moral judgment. One could argue, for example, that a correct understanding of justice requires that no one be required to pay compensation except on the basis of fault.[4] The problem is that there is no consensus in most societies about moral matters. One would hope to find a basis for legal argument and legal advocacy on which everyone, or nearly everyone, could agree.

It is in this context that the movement known as law and economics is best understood.[5] Law and economics tries to offer a basis for decision grounded on consensus. The starting point is as follows: different people have different desires, goals and values, but everyone would agree that they would rather have their desires met than not met, and they would prefer that this happen more often instead of less often.

In this way (and in a number of other ways, some of which will be discussed later), law and economics tracks the arguments of and the justification for the theory of moral philosophy known as utilitarianism. Briefly, utilitarianism holds that morality requires the doing of whatever would maximize the sum total of pleasure (while minimizing the sum total of pain).[6] The idea had been that the seeking of pleasure and the avoiding of pain are the common and universal aspects of all human life, and that since there was no basis to prefer your desires and pleasures to mine or to anyone else's, the proper basis for social choice is to choose the action which maximizes the sum total of pleasures (minus the sum total of pain) in society.[7]

Compared to other moral theories, utilitarianism has the advantage of not requiring difficult value judgments between persons or between value-systems. However, there are a number of problems with trying to use utilitarianism as a workable system for social decision-making. The

---

[4] Just such an argument is offered in Weinrib, *The Idea of Private Law.*
[5] Much of the first part of this section derives from (or at least agrees with) Arthur Leff's discussion in "Economic Analysis of Law: Some Realism About Nominalism"; 60 *Virginia Law Review* 451 (1974), which remains one of the best discussions of the strengths and weaknesses of law and economics.
[6] "Utilitarianism" has been defined as "[t]he ethical theory . . . that answers all questions of what to do, what to admire, or how to live, in terms of maximizing utility or happiness. Simon Blackburn, *The Oxford Dictionary of Philosophy* (Oxford University Press, Oxford, 1994), p. 388. (The same text defines "utility" as "[t]he basic unit of desirability".)
[7] I am not going to go into detail about the different variations of utilitarianism that have developed (for example, act utilitarianism as contrasted with rule utilitarianism), or to consider types of consequentialism which have distanced themselves from classical utilitarianism.

most important of these problems for our purposes is the difficulty (if not impossibility) of measuring and "summing" people's pleasures and pain. (There are a number of other problems with utilitarianism, problems that have been discussed at length in moral philosophy.[8])

Law and economics tries to keep the advantages of utilitarianism—avoiding making controversial value judgments—while losing its disadvantage of being unworkable for social decision-making. The transformation occurs by taking utilitarianism's discussion of "fulfilling desires", and putting it into the context of economic action. How do we determine what people want? We look at how they act: given different ways of spending their time and their money, look at the choices the people ultimately make. For example, if someone chooses to work additional (optional) hours every week, we can conclude that this person prefers the additional pay earned to the additional leisure time she could have had if she had not worked the additional hours. Economics (in general, not just in its application to law) is built on the "basic assumption" that "people are [always] rational maximizers of their satisfaction".[9]

How do we determine the relative intensity of preferences? Economics suggests: look at how much people are willing to "pay" for something—in the broadest sense of the term "pay", as we "pay" for objects in time and effort and opportunities foregone, as well as more directly with money. In the simple marketplace example, my purchasing a book indicates that I want it. If there is only one copy of a particular book on sale, and I am willing to pay four times as much as you are for the book, it is reasonable to conclude that I want the book more than you do.[10]

Thus, in two simple transformations, utilitarianism has been made into a (more or less) workable approach for analysing daily behaviour. By defining desires by actions, and by defining levels of desire by how much someone is willing to pay, the marketplace supplies both the evidence we need for determining how to maximize desires and the practical method for doing so.

If I sell you a book for $20, one would assume that I prefer the $20 to having the book, and you prefer the book to having the $20. If that were not the case, why would both of us go through with the transaction?[11]

---

[8] See, e.g. Samuel Scheffler ed., *Consequentialism and its Critics* (Oxford University Press, Oxford, 1988).

[9] Posner, *The Problems of Jurisprudence*, p. 353.

[10] At least this conclusion is warranted if the two of us have comparable wealth; how much the general approach is undermined by the fact that this assumption is often not true—that wealth inequalities are pervasive, non-trivial, and not always attributable to the subjects' prior actions—is a matter of ongoing controversy. See, e.g. Posner, *The Problems of Jurisprudence*, pp. 380–381; Leff, "Economic Analysis of Law: Some Realism About Nominalism", at 478–479.

[11] On the imperfect fit between choices, interests and consent in our lives, and the way such facts may undermine the standard law and economics analysis, see Robin West,

Since it is the case, the transaction has made us both better off (and society as a whole better off, if one defines "better off" in terms of the sum of happiness).[12]

The market transaction is thus the paradigm of a transaction that increases the sum of happiness; in a different way of phrasing, one could also say that it is the paradigm of a just transaction—in the sense that neither party to the transaction would have any right to claim that it was unjust, given that both parties consented to it. Consent and autonomy are thus the other side of, or the other justifications for, economic analysis.

When a transfer or other form of transaction leaves at least one person better off and no one worse off, the situation after the transfer or transaction is referred to in economic analysis as being "Pareto superior"[13] to the situation before. Economists also speak of situations as being "Pareto optimal" when no transfer or transaction could lead to a situation "Pareto superior" to the one in question. (Within the possible distributions of a certain set of goods, there may be—and usually is—more than one "Pareto optimal" situation. Thus "Pareto optimal" differs from the normal usage of "optimal" in that there is no implication that the situation described is "the (uniquely) best" among all possible (comparable) situations.)

It is in this sense that Pareto analysis is sometimes compared with analyses derived from Kantian moral philosophy. Kantian moral philosophy, speaking in broad terms, emphasizes autonomy and consent.[14] All participants would, by definition, consent to a transaction which left them

---

"Authority, Autonomy and Choice: The Role of Consent in the Moral and Political Visions of Franz Kafka and Richard Posner", 99 *Harvard Law Review* 384 (1985); Richard Posner, "The Ethical Significance of Free Choice: A Reply to Professor West", 99 *Harvard Law Review* 1431 (1986); Robin West, "Submission, Choice and Ethics: A Rejoinder to Judge Posner", 99 *Harvard Law Review* 1449 (1986).

[12] This assumes that our transaction does not create negative effects for third parties, an assumption which is not always warranted with market transactions.

[13] "Pareto superior" and "Pareto optimal" are named after the economist Vilfredo Pareto (1848–1923). Though the Pareto principle seems to give a self-evidently true normative principle, on closer analysis, it may in fact sometimes require or justify results contrary to other basic values, like autonomy and liberty. See Amartya K. Sen, "The Impossibility of a Paretian Liberal", 78 *Journal of Political Economy* 152 (1970), reprinted in *Choice, Welfare and Measurement* (MIT Press, Cambridge, Mass., 1982), pp. 285–290.

[14] In their haste to compare economic analysis with Kantian analysis, most law and economics theorists do not stop to note how much narrower Kant's notion of autonomy was than the one they usually employ. For example, Kant would not describe a choice or action caused by one's emotions as an autonomous action. For Kant, autonomous actions are those based on reason. See, *e.g.* Kant, *The Metaphysics of Morals* 6:408, at p. 166: "Since virtue is based on inner freedom it contains a positive command to a human being, namely to bring all his capacities and inclinations under his (reason's) control, and so to rule over himself, which goes beyond forbidding him to let himself be governed by his feelings and inclinations . . .; for unless reason holds the reins of government in its own hands, his feelings and inclinations play the master over him." See generally John Kemp, *The Philosophy of Kant* (Thoemme Press, Bristol, 1993), pp. 56–69.

either better off or as well off as before. Therefore, a moral analysis based on autonomy and consent would approve of transactions that were Pareto superior. All voluntary market transactions lead to Pareto-superior states of affairs, almost by definition (at least if there are no negative consequences for third parties).[15] The question is how the analysis would look for other (*e.g.* non-consensual, government-ordered) types of transactions.

It should be noted that if a transaction involved one person getting more of something, and everyone else having the same amount, those whose possessions had not increased might object to the transaction on the basis of equality (or its negative correlate, envy).[16] Thus, in real world terms, it is difficult to find situations where at least one person is better off and everyone else is (in every sense of the word) no worse off than they were before.

Even in a looser construction of Pareto superiority, most governmental (legislative and judicial) actions would not qualify. In most government actions—awarding contracts, assessing legal liability, setting taxes and benefits, and so on—there are winners and losers. There are groups who, by any measure, are worse off than they were before the government action or decision. If governments could only act when no one was made worse off, there would be little that could be done.

A form of analysis called "Kaldor-Hicks"[17] or "potential Pareto-superior" is sometimes offered by economists that purports to justify government actions even when some parties are left worse off.[18] This analysis is a kind of wealth-maximization claim, but with a Pareto twist. Pareto analysis, one recalls, does not speak to dollar amounts or the relative value of people's benefits: it looks only to the hard fact (a fact not requiring any further normative evaluation) of preference, that a given party prefers one state of affairs to another. For Kaldor-Hicks, the question is whether the parties made better off could, if they chose, compensate the parties who were made worse off, and still be better off. For example, if a certain government decision increases the

[15] See Richard Posner, "Utilitarianism, Economics, and Legal Theory", 8 *Journal of Legal Studies* 103 at 114 (1979).
[16] Lawrence Solum, "Constructing an Ideal of Public Reason", 30 *San Diego Law Review* 729 at 744 (1993).
[17] Named after the theorists who developed the analysis, Nicholas Kaldor (1907–1986) and J. R. Hicks (1904–1989); see Nicholas Kaldor, "Welfare Propositions of Economics and Interpersonal Comparisons of Utility", 49 *Economics Journal* 549 (1939); J.R. Hicks, "The Foundations of Welfare Economics", 49 *Economics Journal* 696 (1939). Hicks shared the 1972 Nobel Prize in Economics with Kenneth Arrow (though this text will use the conventional label, "Nobel Prize in Economics", there is, strictly speaking, no Nobel Prize in economics, and the true name of that prize is "The Bank of Sweden Prize in Economic Sciences in Memory of Alfred Nobel").
[18] See, *e.g.* George Fletcher, *The Basic Concepts of Legal Thought* (Oxford University Press, New York, 1996), pp. 158–162.

number of television sets I own, while reducing the number of books you own, I am made better off, and you worse off. Without making any value judgments about the relative worth of books and televisions (or the relative worth of desiring books and desiring televisions), one can still ask whether I would be able to compensate you (pay you money, or give you books) so that you would not feel worse off, and afterwards I would still be better off (that is, I am still happier with my situation: taking into account the extra televisions I have and the books I gave you in compensation, I would still prefer my new situation to my former situation).

The point here is not that the winning parties actually compensate the losing parties; if they did, then the combination of the government decision and the compensation would be a fully Pareto-superior move. The point is that this compensation could be paid; and thus, there is a basis for concluding, without any apparent need for controversial comparisons of value, that the post-transaction situation would be superior to the pre-transaction situation, and, therefore, that the government's action was justified.

Much of law and economics analysis involves deciding which judicial or legislative decisions are justified under a Kaldor-Hicks analysis. It does not take long analysis, however, to see that Kaldor-Hicks superiority may not be enough to persuade everyone: the losing parties in a decision may be little consoled by the fact that those better off *could have—but have not—* compensated them for their losses. How a Kaldor-Hicks approach might be justified, even with such problems, will be discussed later in the chapter. First, though, it is important to add into the mix the other central element of law and economics: the Coase theorem.

THE COASE THEOREM

If a modified, "practical" version of utilitarianism is one part of the foundation of law and economics, the other part is the discussion by Ronald Coase (1910–) (who would later win the Nobel Prize in Economics, in part for his work in this area) on the interaction of the market and the distribution of legal rights.[19]

Coase's work was an attempt to correct what he saw as two flaws in other economists' work. The first problem was specific to the discussion of law and regulation. Arthur Pigou (1877–1959) had put forward an influential view, that to keep the economy efficient businesses should be

[19] Ronald Coase, "The Problem of Social Cost", 3 *Journal of Law and Economics* 1 (1960), reprinted in Coase, *The Firm, the Market, and the Law* (University of Chicago Press, Chicago, 1988), pp. 156.

forced, by taxation, regulation or the operation of the tort system, to "internalize" the costs they impose on other activities ("externalities").[20]

Efficiency in the free market is an interaction of supply, demand, and costs, leading to an equilibrium (even if a temporary one) at a particular level of supply and price. However, if the cost of making a product is somehow subsidized (most often, by the government), then this equilibrium will be distorted and the eventual result will be that more of the product will be produced than would have been the case in a true and fair market.[21] Pigou's argument was based on the idea that the pollution an industry creates is a cost of that industry, and for that cost to be paid for by other people (whether through the extra expense of cleaning clothes dirtied by polluted air or taxes paid so that the government can clean up polluted water) is to create a subsidy for that industry. Therefore, for the market to return to being true and fair, these externalities should be internalized—the industry should have to pay the equivalent of the costs their activity has imposed on other actors.

Coase, working within the same general framework of ideas—that the efficient distribution of goods depends on a free market where activities respond to prices and costs without the distortion of subsidies—argued that Pigou's approach was badly flawed. As Coase saw it, the source of the problem was Pigou's assumption, an assumption derived from or at least shared with the common law, that where two activities are in conflict (for example, a railway causing sparks which ignite the crops on farmland near the railroad lines), one of the parties is "imposing" costs on the other. To put the same point slightly differently: the assumption is that we can tell in advance which activity is "at fault".

Coase's contrary position was that where two activities are in conflict, the "costs" or "externalities" are the product of *the combination* of the two activities. It is not merely the case that without the railway there would be no fires in the farmer's crops; it is also the case, that if the farmer did not plant crops so close to the railroad tracks, there would similarly be no fires. This is "the reciprocity of causation". Coase writes:

"In the case of cattle and the crops, it is true that there would be no crop damage without the cattle. It is equally true that there would be no crop damage without the crops. . . . If we are to discuss the problem in terms of causation, both parties cause the damage. If we are to attain an optimum allocation of resources, it is therefore desirable that both parties should take the harmful effect (the nuisance) into account in deciding on their course of action."[22]

---

[20] See A.C. Pigou, *The Economics of Welfare* (4th ed., Macmillan, London, 1932).
[21] For a more detailed discussion (including the type of graphs for which such analysis is known), see, *e.g.* Murphy and Coleman, *Philosophy of Law*, pp 182–194.
[22] Coase, "The Problem of Social Cost", in *The Firm, The Market, and the Law*, p. 112.

The extent to which Coase proved his case[23] (or persuaded his audience) regarding the reciprocity of causation remains in contention.[24] However, what Coase has shown, which cannot be easily controverted or ignored, is the extent to which the market will "solve" many problems of conflicting activities (whether or not we like the way the market "solves" these conflicts).

The second problem Coase addressed was a more general one among economists. Economic theories are built up from simplified models of the way the world works. One simplification commonly used was that there are no "transaction costs".[25] There is nothing wrong with simplifying assumptions as such. Without such assumptions, little progress might be made: the real world is so complex, with so many factors to take into account, that without simplifying assumptions it would be difficult to come to any conclusions at all. Simplified models of the world are standard, and not only in the social sciences *(e.g.* physics thought experiments often assume a world without friction). The trick is to figure out how one's conclusions may differ in the real world, where the simplified assumptions no longer hold. This was the nature of Coase's second criticism. Many economists had assumed a world without transaction costs, but had not given enough thought to how the real world might work differently, given that transaction costs are present and are pervasive.

As an initial point, Coase showed an interesting property of the world of the economists' model. In a world *without* transaction costs, contrary to

---

[23] In Richard A. Epstein, "A Theory of Tort Liability", 2 *Journal of Legal Studies* 151 at 164–165 (1973), Epstein offers the following argument against the "reciprocity of causation". Coase's position assumes the existence of a (legal or moral) system under which remedies can be imposed on infringing parties. However, if we remove the available remedies, the harm caused is in one direction only and it *does* make sense to make an initial assessment of blame (on one side) and right or priority (on the other). Epstein modifies his position somewhat in a later article: Richard A. Epstein, "Causational—In Context: An Afterword", 63 *Chicago-Kent Law Review* 653 at 664–666 (1987). In that article, Epstein continues to oppose the idea of the reciprocity of causation, but his emphasis is more on the fact that there are "well established and well understood" initial boundary lines between the interacting parties, and that these categorical property rules reduce transaction costs for resolving disputes and reaching agreements regarding future entitlements. *Ibid.* at 666.

[24] After criticizing Coase's argument about the reciprocity of causation, George Fletcher wrote: "The Pigovian theorem will continue to reign so long as the bench is staffed by lawyers rather than economists . . . Coase will never succeed in the courts, because his view of efficiency is incompatible with elementary principles of fairness." Fletcher, *The Basic Concepts of Legal Thought*, p. 167.

[25] Transaction costs are all the costs that stand in the way of a transaction that should occur ("should" occur in the sense that there is a willing buyer and a willing seller and a range of prices in which both would be willing to transact). These costs include "information costs" (how one finds out about the other party—newspaper advertisements, the costs of making inquiries among friends, and so on), negotiation costs, the costs of drawing up the contract, relevant sales taxes, and so on.

what one might think, the initial distribution of legal rights would *not* affect the final distribution of those rights, and thus would *not* affect which activities occur. Consider a simple situation, where a train going through a rural area gives off sparks which set fires on nearby crops. The initial entitlement may lie either with the railway or with the farmers: if with the farmers, then the railway will be liable to pay damages for any crops burned; if with the railway, then there will be no right of recovery.

Start with the assumption that the right lies with the farmers. If the benefit to the railway of running trains is greater than the damage done to the crops, the railway will negotiate with the farmers and pay them (presumably the cost of the damage, or slightly more) for the right to give off the sparks, and the trains will run. On the other hand, if the benefit to the railway is lower than the cost of the damage, no such arrangement will come about, for the railway will not be willing to pay what the farmers ask to give up their right, and the trains will not run. Similarly, if the right is initially with the railway, the farmers will pay the railway to prevent the giving off of sparks, if (but only if) protecting their crops is worth more to them than running the trains is to the railway.

Even though this is an intermediate step in Coase's analysis, it is probably his best-known insight. The initial distribution of entitlements (legal rights) does not matter, because they will end up with whichever party values them the most. If the right not to have train sparks is initially with the farmers, but the right to give off such sparks is worth more to the railway, the railway, after paying off the farmers, will end up with the right. Thus, if the concern is "efficiency", government regulation, at least as a question of the initial distribution of entitlements, will be irrelevant; the total value of the conflicting activities will remain the same regardless of which party initially has the entitlement to constrain the other.[26] However, recall that this is only the case in the magical world of no transaction costs.

Less well known is the second part of Coase's analysis. While the initial distribution of entitlements is in many ways irrelevant in a world without transaction costs, the initial distribution *is* significant in a world *with* substantial transaction costs, and that is just the sort of world in which we live. Because of transaction costs, an entitlement (legal right) may not end up with the party who values it most, because the extra expense of the transaction costs may make it no longer worth purchasing from its original holder. For example, you hold a right to stop me from polluting a river. The right is worth $80 to you; having the right is worth $100 to me, but effecting an exchange of the right may cost $40. It would be more efficient for the entitlement to be with me (whether initially or by voluntary bargain), because I value it more than you do, but if the right is initially given to you, it will stay with you because it is not worth it to me to pay

---

[26] See, *e.g.* Murphy and Coleman, *Philosophy of Law*, pp. 191–194.

both your asking price and the transaction costs (a total of $120, as against my valuation of the right at $100).

Coase suggests alternative responses to the problem of transaction costs: two ways to try to "raise the value of production" by reducing transaction costs—organization of the competing activities as components within a single firm, and government regulation—and a third option, leaving things as they are (on the possibility that the administrative costs of a firm or government regulation would be as great or greater than the transaction costs in the market).[27] Coase's summing up on the matter is a cautious refusal to choose dogmatically: "All solutions have costs", and "problems of welfare economics must ultimately dissolve into a study of aesthetics and morals."[28] (He goes on to suggest further empirical investigation, to determine the relative advantages of handling the problem in different ways.[29])

This final step is where Coase and the law and economics movement diverge.[30] The law and economics response to the existence of significant transaction costs (which prevent market forces from redistributing rights to those that value them the most), is to state that the government (mostly, the judiciary) should act in ways which mimic what the market would have done had there been no transaction costs. Needless to say, there are many steps in the argument between:

(1) in certain (ideal) circumstances, the market *would* redistribute rights in a certain way; and

(2) in other (non-ideal) circumstances, the government *should* mimic the effects of the market.

Unfortunately, the intermediate steps are rarely articulated by proponents of law and economics, at least usually not in a convincing way.[31]

DESCRIPTION AND ANALYSIS

The most influential figure in the law and economics movement is Richard Posner (1939–). He has written approximately 40 books and 200

[27] Coase, "The Problem of Social Cost", in *The Firm, The Market, and The Law*, pp. 114–119.
[28] *ibid.* at pp. 118, 154.
[29] *ibid.* at pp. 118–119.
[30] See generally Pierre Schlag, "An Appreciative Comment on Coase's *The Problem of Social Cost*: A View from the Left", 1986 *Wisconsin Law Review* 919 at 931–945.
[31] This is also to put aside the (epistemological) problem of whether it makes sense to speak of people, acting within a context with various transaction costs, knowing what redistributions would have occurred in a hypothetical world where none of those transaction costs existed.
  For one account of how the argument from (1) to (2) in the text necessarily misfires, see Fletcher, *The Concepts of Legal Thought*, pp. 167–168.

articles[32]—not all of them on law and economics, but that is by far his most frequent topic. In many of his earlier writings,[33] Posner argued that a theory of wealth maximization served well both as an explanation of the past actions of the common law courts and as a theory of justice, justifying how judges and other officials should act. This section will include a brief discussion of the first (descriptive or "positive") claim. The second (prescriptive or "normative") claim will he considered in greater detail in the next section.

The descriptive claim is that "the common law is best explained as if the judges were trying to maximize economic welfare."[34] The idea is that though, until recently, common law judges rarely used economic formulations,[35] and few had economic training, the doctrines they created approximate what an economist who was trying to maximize social wealth would have created.[36] A more recent formulation and defence of the view states: "It would not be surprising to find that many legal doctrines rest on inarticulate gropings toward efficiency, especially since so many legal doctrines date back to the nineteenth century when a laissez-faire ideology based on classical economics was the dominant ideology of the educated classes."[37] This is a provocative position, which has, unsurprisingly, been much contested, and has not gained general assent.[38]

A development from early law and economics of more lasting significance was the innovative way of analyzing entitlements introduced by

---

[32] And many of these publications were written after 1981, when he accepted a position as a federal appellate court judge.

[33] Posner has since pulled back from some of his more ambitious claims. See, e.g. Posner, *The Problems of Jurisprudence*, pp. 353–392; Posner, *Economic Analysis of Law* (6th ed., Aspen Publishers, New York, 2001), pp. 26–28.

[34] Posner, *The Economics of Justice*, p. 4; see also Paul H. Rubin, "Why is the Common Law Efficient?", 6 *Journal of Legal Studies* 51 (1977); George L. Priest, "The Common Law Process and the Selection of Efficient Rules", 6 *Journal of Legal Studies* 65 (1977).

[35] One well-known exception is Judge Learned Hand's "BPL" formula for determining whether an action or omission had been negligent. *United States v Carroll Towing Co.*, 159 F.2d 169 at 173 (2nd Cir. 1947); see Stephen C. Gilles, "The Invisible Hand Formula", 80 *Virginia Law Review* 1015 (1994). For an argument that the "Hand Formula" does not in fact reflect the negligence law used by the courts, either at the time of Learned Hand or currently, see Richard W. Wright, "Negligence in the Courts: Introduction and Commentary", 77 *Chicago-Kent Law Review* 425 (2002).

[36] See Posner, *The Economics of Justice*, p. 5.

[37] Posner, *Economic Analysis of Law*, p. 25.

[38] In favour of the positive claim, see, e.g. Posner, *The Problems of Jurisprudence*, pp. 353–374; William Landes and Richard Posner, *The Economic Structure of Tort Law* (Harvard University Press, Cambridge, Mass., 1987), pp. 1–24; for criticism, see, e.g. Dworkin, *A Matter of Principle*, pp. 263–266; Lewis A. Kornhauser, "A Guide to the Perplexed Claims of Efficiency in the Law", 8 *Hofstra Law Review* 591 at 610–634 (1980); Kelman, *A Guide to Critical Legal Studies*, pp. 115–116.

Guido Calabresi and A. Douglas Melamed.[39] Calabresi and Melamed noted that one's interests can be protected in either of two ways:

(1) a "property" rule, under which the interest cannot be taken or invaded without the permission of the holder; or

(2) a "liability" rule, under which the interest can be taken or invaded, but only if payment is made after the fact (the level of payment usually to be set by the courts).[40]

In American tort law, the difference is exemplified in nuisance law where a court will sometimes hold a polluter liable, but allow only monetary damages and refuse an injunction.[41] The right to obtain an injunction is a "property" remedy, as one's entitlement can be infringed only with permission; any infringement without consent would be enjoined. A damages remedy, by contrast, is merely a "liability" protection—take now, pay later.

In their article, Calabresi and Melamed consider, largely in economic terms, the relative advantages of protecting entitlements with property or liability rules[42]: for example, a liability rule might sometimes be better because it avoids obstacles to cooperation (including the costs of negotiation[43]); and a property rule would be preferred where there are fewer obstacles to cooperation, because it avoids the problem of judicial error in setting the level of compensation.

ECONOMICS AND JUSTICE

As mentioned above, in Posner's earlier work, he argued that wealth maximization was a prescriptive as well as a descriptive concept: that it is a

---

[39] Guido Calabresi and A. Douglas Melamed, "Property Rules, Liability Rules, and Inalienability: One View of the Cathedral", 85 *Harvard Law Review* 1089 (1972); see also Symposium: "Property Rules, Liability Rules, and Inalienability: A Twenty-Five Year Retrospective", 106 *Yale Law Journal* 2081–2215 (1997).

[40] The third possibility, which Calabresi and Melamed also discuss, is protecting an entitlement with an "inalienability", rule: where the state severely limits or entirely forbids the transfer of the entitlement. See Calabresi and Melamed, "Property Rules, Liability Rules, and Inalienability" at 1111–1115.

[41] The best known case is *Boomer v Atlantic Cement Co.*, 26 N.Y.2d 219, 257 N.E.2d 870, 309 N.Y.S.2d 312 (1970), where the court refused an injunction, on the basis that the cost of enjoining the nuisance (by shutting down the factory creating the pollution) was disproportionate to the amount of harm being done to the plaintiff.

[42] Calabresi and Melamed, "Property Rules, Liability Rules, and Inalienability", at 1105–1110.

[43] *e.g.* for a polluting company to negotiate with all the property-holders affected by the pollution, there will be substantial costs in just getting all the parties together, there will be costs in paying the lawyers who facilitate the settlement, and there may be additional costs created by the parties' "strategic behaviour". See Robert Cooter and Thomas Ulen, *Law and Economics* (3rd ed., Addison Wesley, Reading, Mass., 2000), pp. 87–91.

standard which should guide judges (and perhaps others) in their decisions.

Under wealth maximization, judges are to decide cases according to the principles which will maximize society's total wealth.[44] Somewhat counter-intuitively, transferring an object from one owner to another, without more, even if the transfer was involuntary, can be said to increase social wealth, because wealth is measured by what someone has paid or would be willing to pay, and the second owner may be willing to pay more for the item than the first owner was. However, Posner would say that a forced transfer would not usually be justified under "wealth maximization" principles in such circumstances, because such transfers are only appropriate where high transaction costs make a consensual (market) bargain between the parties impossible, thereby justify circumventing the market.[45]

Posner argues that wealth maximization is the best *compromise* between utility and autonomy, or that it successfully exemplifies *both* utility and autonomy.[46] As discussed earlier in this chapter, one can see law and economics' advocacy of "wealth maximization" as an attempt to construct a more practical version of utilitarianism. Welfare or happiness (two approximations of what is meant by "utility") are hard to discover or measure, so judicial and legislative decisions will not be clearly guided by an instruction to "maximize utility".[47] By contrast, maximizing wealth is something judges can do effectively within their limited role in the government, a role sufficiently constrained that the more egregious possible misuses of wealth maximization are also ruled out.[48] Posner also argued that many conventional virtues (like the work ethic, telling the truth, and keeping promises) can be more easily derived from wealth maximization than utilitarianism.[49]

As to autonomy, a moral theory that strongly emphasizes that value (Posner mentions Immanuel Kant's theory) might well require that citi-

---

[44] "The 'wealth' in 'wealth maximization' refers to the sum of all tangible and intangible goods and services, weighted by prices of two sorts: offer prices (what people are willing to pay for goods they do not already own); and asking prices (what people demand to sell what they do own)." Posner, *The Problems of Jurisprudence*, p. 356.

[45] Posner, "Utilitarianism, Economics, and Legal Theory", at 130–131; see also Posner, *The Economics of Justice*, pp. 108–109. The reason government-imposed (court-imposed) transfers should be limited to such cases is because government officials can only imperfectly mimic the market in guessing how different parties value goods; by contrast, where the market is able to operate without significant transaction costs, voluntary exchanges will naturally bring goods to the parties who value them most.

[46] See, *e.g.* Posner, *The Economics of Justice*, pp. 98, 115.

[47] *ibid*, at pp. 112–113; Posner, "Utilitarianism, Economics, and Legal Theory", at 122, 129–130.

[48] See Posner, *The Economics of Justice*, pp. 103–106; Posner, *The Problems of Jurisprudence*, pp. 372–273, 387–392.

[49] See, *e.g.* Posner, "Utilitarianism, Economics, and Legal Theory", pp. 123–126.

zens be coerced, or have their property redistributed, only where those citizens have authorized such actions by their choices, by actual consent. However, the problem with such an autonomy-based approach is that it would be unworkable if applied strictly to government decisions, for the same reason that its cognate, a Pareto-superior requirement, would be unworkable. Many government decisions affect a large number of people (not all of whom could even be identified in advance), and therefore requiring actual consent from every person affected would be clearly impossible.[50] Similarly, if one put the focus of actual consent not on individual government decisions, but on the form and institutions of government or the mode of decision-making, obtaining actual consent from every person affected—that is, from every citizen—would clearly be impractical, if not impossible.

Wealth maximization is better than utilitarianism, according to Posner, because money is easier to measure than utility. It is better than an autonomy-based approach because it allows government action even where actual consent by all those affected would not be forthcoming or would be impractical to obtain. However, because the only actions allowed would be those that maximized social wealth, everyone (or almost everyone) *would have* consented to this principle if asked, because it is a principle that leaves everyone (or almost everyone) better off in the long run.

This consent is not express consent, but a hypothetical or implied consent: what the people *would have said* had they been asked ahead of time. While someone who had been in an accident would not choose a liability system under which she would not recover, if she were choosing at an earlier time, before the accident, before she knew whether she would be a tort plaintiff, tort defendant, or neither, she would reasonably choose a system that would increase total wealth (because she would have no reason for choosing a system with lower total wealth).[51]

There are a number of basic problems with Posner's attempts to equate justice with wealth maximization[52]; there is only room in the present text to hint at some of them. Problems with Posner's discussion of consent were discussed in Ch. 11. In the paragraphs that follow, I will briefly discuss problems with Posner's comparison of wealth maximization with utility and autonomy. In a later section on the limits of law and economics, some more detailed substantive criticisms will be outlined.

---

[50] Posner, "The Ethical and Political Basis of the Efficiency Norm in Common Law Adjudication", p. 494.
[51] See Posner, *The Economics of Justice*, pp. 94–99. (I have excluded some of the details and nuances of Posner's analysis here due to limitations of space.)
[52] Posner recently has made a partial retreat on the normative claim of wealth maximization: "as a universal social norm wealth maximization is indeed unsatisfactory, but . . . it is attractive or at least defensible when confined to the common law arena." Posner, *The Problems of Jurisprudence*, p. 373.

In the attempt to create a synthesis of the best of utilitarianism and an autonomy-based approach, wealth maximization arguably loses the benefits of both. The strong point of utilitarian theories is that it is difficult to argue with the position that pleasure and happiness are good, pain and unhappiness are bad, and in nearly every circumstance it is better if the good things can he maximized and the bad things minimized. The problem for utilitarian (and related) theories is to determine when the increased pleasure or happiness or welfare of a few (or even of the vast majority) can justify suffering and sacrifice by the remainder.

By contrast, it is more contestable to say that increasing wealth is always a moral good, and it will be harder to justify the sacrifice and suffering of some on the basis of the increased wealth of others. In the terms of moral philosophy, increased wealth is usually thought of as an instrumental good: it is valuable because it can help one obtain other things which are of intrinsic moral value, like health, physical comfort, and recreation. The response may be that wealth is not offered as something good in itself, but only as a proxy for utility or other values.[53] However, while wealth maximization may be the closest *workable* approximation of utilitarianism or an autonomy-based theorem, the approximation may break down in just the kind of hard cases where we would hope that our theories could give guidance.[54]

GAME THEORY

In recent years, there have been a variety of books and articles which are descended from or related to the tradition of "law and economics" (at least in the sense that they share economics' basic assumption, mentioned at the beginning of the chapter, that "people are rational maximizers of their satisfactions"), but which take a somewhat different perspective. Among these approaches are game theory and public choice theory.[55] Game theory will be the topic of this section; public choice theory the topic of the next.

Game theory is, roughly speaking, the creation of models of "situations in which two or more players have a choice of decisions (strategies); where the outcome depends on all the strategies; and where each player has a set of preferences defined over the outcomes."[56] Game theory is the partly

---

[53] See, *e.g.* Posner, "Utilitarianism, Economics, and Legal Theory", at 121–127; Posner, *The Economics of Justice*, pp. 112–113.

[54] A similar argument is given in greater detail in Dworkin, *A Matter of Principle*, pp. 237–266; for Posner's reply, see Posner, *The Economics of Justice*, pp. 107–115.

[55] Sometimes the phrase "rational choice" theory is used to refer to the combination of game theory and public choice theory. See Daniel A. Farber and Philip P Frickey, "Public Choice Revisited" (book review), 96 *Michigan Law Review* 1715 at 1715 n.4 (1998).

[56] Blackburn, *The Oxford Dictionary of Philosophy*, p. 153.

mathematical, partly economic study of situations where each person's behaviour depends on other people's actions and choices and on expectations of what those actions and choices will be.[57] Commentators' analyses of such situations look like a discussion of games, for they consider various possible "strategies" the "players" might use to maximize their results. The contrast with traditional ("neo-classical") law and economics has been summed up as follows:

"[G]ame theory provides a superior model to traditional neo-classical economic analysis. Under traditional analysis, you have a variety of basic assumptions: people act rationally, perfect information, zero transaction costs. Under game theory, you can relax some of those assumptions. In fact, the point of game theory is to examine problems of imperfect information, strategic behavior, or transaction costs."[58]

Writers have used game theory to consider how legal rules affect people's strategic behaviour, and to try to construct arguments that current legal rules are or are not successful in meeting their proclaimed or assumed purposes (*e.g.* preventing fraud or encouraging an efficient level of accident prevention measures).[59] Law can be seen as being, sometimes by design and sometimes by accident, a key part of "the game", for it affects strongly the reasons people have for acting one way rather than another. Whether one complies with the legal standards or not can itself become an integral part of a game. For example, putting aside questions of avoiding the imposition of legal sanctions, one might want to have the reputation of being someone who always follows publicly imposed norms.

Another way of making the same point is to say that there are two parallel insights. First is the notion that bargaining between parties always happens "in the shadow of the law"—that is, that parties will take the legal rules and the likely results of potential litigation into account when negotiating.[60] The second, inverse point reflects the perspective of game theoretical approaches to the law: legal rules, in turn, should be formulated with some understanding of how people bargain, if those rules are to be effective.[61]

---

[57] The seminal works in game theory include John von Neumann, "Zur Theorie der Gesellschaftsspiele", 100 *Mathematische Annalen* 295 (1928); John von Neumann and Oskar Morgenstern, *Theory of Games and Economic Behavior* (Princeton University Press, Princeton, 1944); John Nash, "The Bargaining Problem", 18 *Econometrica* 155 (1950); and John Nash, "Equilibrium Points in N-Person Games", 36 *Proceedings of the National Academy of Sciences* 48 (1950).

[58] Kenneth Dau-Schmidt, *et al.*, "On *Game Theory and the Law*" (book review), 31 *Law and Society Review* 613, 616 (1997).

[59] See generally Douglas Baird, Robert Gertner and Randal Picker, *Game Theory and the Law* (Harvard University Press, Cambridge, Mass., 1994).

[60] See Robert H. Mnookin and Lewis Kornhauser, "Bargaining in the Shadow of the Law: The Case of Divorce", 88 *Yale Law Journal* 950 (1979).

[61] Douglas C. Baird, "Game Theory and the Law", in *The New Palgrave Dictionary of Economics and the Law*, Vol. 2 (P. Newman ed., Macmillan, London, 1998), p. 197.

One insight of game theorists (and other law and economics writers) is that legal rules meant to have one effect will often, unintentionally, have the opposite effect or no effect at all. For example, rules meant to reduce pollution by mandating expensive anti-pollution devices on new cars may have the effect of increasing pollution, as people tend to keep their older, higher-polluting cars longer, rather than pay for new cars, now much higher priced because of the required anti-pollution devices.

Among the foundational problems game theory tries to solve are:

(1) how to establish or maintain cooperation in situations where individuals seem to have incentives not to co-operate;

(2) how to co-ordinate the actions of unorganized people; and

(3) how to establish rules which deal with the inevitable asymmetries of information among parties.

The problem of co-operation is symbolized by the well-known "prisoner's dilemma". Two people who commit a crime together are arrested, but are interrogated separately. Both prisoners face the same terms of punishment:

(1) if both stay silent, they will be convicted only on a lesser charge, and will each serve a light sentence;

(2) if one party confesses and agrees to testify against the other prisoner, while the other prisoner stays silent, the testifying prisoner will get immunity from punishment, while the silent prisoner will get the maximum possible sentence; and

(3) if both parties agree to confess and testify, both will receive a large sentence, but significantly less than the maximum mentioned in the second scenario.

From the prisoners' perspective, the best outcome would be the first one, with both staying silent the same outcome that would have occurred had they been able to co-ordinate their behaviours. However, self-interest paradoxically will drive each prisoner away from that outcome, towards the outcome which *minimizes* their joint welfare.

Each prisoner thinks:

(1) if the other prisoner stays quiet, my best response would be to confess, for then I will get off without punishment; and

(2) if the other prisoner confesses, my best response would be to confess as well, for then I would avoid the maximum penalty.

Either way, confessing seems the best response; and thus both parties will confess. Though both players would benefit were they able to co-operate, self-interest takes the parties in a different direction. It is the opposite of Adam Smith's "Invisible Hand": self-interested action often drives us away from promoting the common good, not towards it.

Other variations on the prisoner's dilemma emphasize the way parties may be tempted away from a potential co-operation by the possible benefits of "defection" or by fears that the other party may "defect". Imagine an agreement in which I am to perform first, and you only later. There is the temptation for you to take the benefit of my performance, and then renege on your promise. Some of this temptation may be removed if we are players in a "repeat game": that is, when you might want to deal again with me in the future, or, at least, where you will want to maintain a reputation among our colleagues as a "reliable co-operator".

The problems of asymmetries of information are exemplified in the writings on contract default rules: regarding an issue on which contracting parties would be free to set any of a variety of possible terms,[62] what rules should be imposed by the legislature or the courts where the parties have been silent? Some commentators have argued for the use of "penalty" default rules in situations where contracts might have been left incomplete because one of the parties has more information than the other and engages in strategic behaviour. Penalty default rules are contrary to the interests of the party who has the information, creating incentives for that party to divulge the information in the course of negotiating for a different contractual term.[63]

PUBLIC CHOICE THEORY

A second later development is "public choice theory"[64]: which "applies game theory and microeconomic analysis to the production of law by legislatures, regulatory agencies, and courts."[65] (In 1986, the Nobel Prize in Economics went to James Buchanan for his work on public choice theory.)

---

[62] That is, it is not a matter where public policy allows only one possible standard.
[63] See Ian Ayres and Robert Gertner, "Filling Gaps in Incomplete Contracts: An Economic Theory of Default Rules", 99 *Yale Law Journal* 87 (1989).
[64] Even the "newest" approaches have old antecedents, and public choice theory can, by some accounts, by traced back to the work of earlier mathematicians, like the Marquis de Condorcet (1743–1794), who discovered certain paradoxes relating to voting. In a broader sense, public choice can also be traced back to the view of leaders and leadership offered by Machiavelli (1469–1527), in *The Prince* (1513).
[65] Jonathan R. Macey, "Public Choice and the Law", in *The New Palgrave Dictionary of Economics and the Law*, Vol. 3 (P. Newman ed., Macmillan, London, 1998), p. 171; see also Daniel Farber and Philip Frickey, *Law and Public Choice* (University of Chicago Press, Chicago. 1991), pp. 1–11.

ECONOMIC ANALYSIS OF LAW

In rough terms, public choice theorists try to see how much of official action can be explained, and predicted, on the basis that the officials (legislators, judges, administrators, and so on) are acting to further their individual interests. Theorists within the tradition vary in how they define self-interest: some in a narrow or cynical way as purely a matter of money or power; other theorists try to build a more subtle view of self-interest into their model, which, for example, may incorporate the officials' ideological beliefs.

If legislators and other officials are more accurately seen as acting in their narrow self-interests when they legislate, rather than acting "for the public good", then there may be reasons to change various aspects of the legal system. For example, the courts might be less deferential in considering legislation, or they might vary the way they approach interpreting ambiguous statutes[66]; also, public choice theory may offer an argument for restructuring the way legislatures or administrative agencies work, in an attempt to curb or channel the influence of interest groups on officials.[67]

Following the Coasean analysis discussed earlier in this chapter, officials and other political actors can be seen as trying to maximise their benefits while trying to get around the problem of transaction costs.[68] For example, individuals trying to influence the government reduce their transaction costs (*e.g.* the costs of getting information about issues before the legislature) by acting through organized lobbying ventures. The legislature itself can be seen as "a firm"—an organization that avoids the costs of negotiating "across markets", as well as some of the problems of ensuring compliance with agreements, by incorporating the various actors needed within a single unit.[69]

Public choice theorists are sometimes caricatured as overly cynical types who do not believe in the possibility of altruistic behaviour or action done "for the common good". To whatever extent this description of the theorists is accurate, one need not claim that action genuinely for the good of others never occurs for public choice theory to be valuable. It is sufficient that public choice theory often provides better predictions of how officials will act in certain circumstances than would other theories of official action (a standard proponents claim has been easily met).

---

[66] See, *e.g.* Farber and Frickey, *Law and Public Choice*, pp. 61–115; William N. Eskridge Jr. and John Ferejohn, "Statutory Interpretation and Rational Choice Theories", in *The New Palgrave Dictionary of Economics and the Law*, Vol. 3 (P Newman ed., Macmillan, London, 1998), pp. 535–40.

[67] See, *e.g.* Farber and Frickey, *Law and Public Choice*, pp. 12–37.

[68] See Macey, "Public Choice and the Law", pp. 171–177.

[69] *ibid.* at 174–177. On firms as means of avoiding transaction cost problems, the classic article is R. H. Coase, "The Nature of the Firm", reprinted in *The Firm, the Market and the Law*, pp. 33–55.

OTHER VARIATIONS

There is a growing literature about the proper way of understanding and explaining "social norms" and "social meanings" within the relatively individual-focused analysis of neo-classical economics.[70] The foundational work in this area was probably Robert Ellickson's *Order Without Law*,[71] which discussed the way cattle ranchers in Shasta County, California, resolved conflicts among themselves using informal rules ("social norms") that diverged significantly from the applicable legal norms. Among the other prominent figures in this field are Lawrence Lessig,[72] Cass Sunstein,[73] and Eric Posner. Posner ties his analysis of social norms to game theory, by arguing that many social norms can be understood as the direct and indirect result of people's attempts to "signal" that they would be good partners for co-operative ventures—ventures as diverse as business deals and raising a family.[74]

Some commentators have argued for a form of law and economics which incorporates a richer (and more accurate) account of human behaviour, in particular, taking into account a number of insights regarding the "bounded rationality" under which most decisions are made.[75] Herbert A. Simon (1916–2001) received the 1978 Nobel Prize in Economics in part for his work on the limits on people's abilities to analyze data and remember facts, and the (reasonable) methods we use to respond to these limitations. Daniel A. Kahneman (1934–) received the 2002 Nobel Prize in Economics (along with Vernon L. Smith) for the work he did to show, through experiments, how people tend to systematically over-estimate or under-estimate certain kinds of risks.

---

[70] See Conference: "Social Norms, Social Meaning, and the Economic Analysis of Law", 27 *Journal of Legal Studies* 537–823 (1998) (includes contributions by Robert Ellickson, Richard Posner, Lawrence Lessig, Martha Nussbaum, Erie Posner and Cass Sunstein); see also Symposium: "Law, Economics, and Norms", 144 *University of Pennsylvania Law Review* 1643–2339 (1996).

[71] Robert C. Ellickson, *Order Without Law: How Neighbors Settle Disputes* (Harvard University Press, Cambridge, Mass., 1991).

[72] See, *e.g.* Lawrence Lessig, "The Regulation of Social Meaning", 62 *University of Chicago Law Review* 943 (1995).

[73] See, *e.g.* Cass R. Sunstein, "Social Norms and Social Roles", 96 *Columbia Law Review* 903 (1996).

[74] See Eric A. Posner, *Law and Social Norms* (Harvard University Press, Cambridge, Mass., 2000).

[75] See, *e.g.* Christine Jolls; Cass R. Sunstein and Richard Thaler, "A Behavioral Approach to Law and Economics", 50 *Stanford Law Review* 1471 (1998); Cass R. Sunstein, "Behavioral Analysis of Law", 64 *University of Chicago Law Review* 1175 (1997). On bounded rationality, see, *e.g.* Daniel Kahneman, Paul Slovic and Amos Tversky eds. *Judgment Under Uncertainty: Heuristics and Biases* (Cambridge University Press, Cambridge, 1982).

THE LIMITS OF LAW AND ECONOMICS

Law and economics can be criticized in an internal way or in an external way. By an internal criticism, I mean one that accepts most of the approach's aims and assumptions; by contrast, external criticisms challenge economic analysis at those basic levels.

An example of a sharp internal criticism was offered by Jon Hanson and Melissa Hart.[76] Hanson and Hart state that the argument that certain rules will increase efficiency (in other terms, maximize social wealth) usually depends on a series of assumptions. These include assumptions regarding transactions costs, activity levels, administrative costs, risk neutrality of the parties, and the parties' legal knowledge, as well as the ability of a judge to make accurate assessments of the costs and benefits (to the parties) of alternative actions. Hanson and Hart argue that the model on which law and economics operates tends to make unrealistic assumptions or to assume fixed values on variables that will in fact vary greatly (in unpredictable and hard-to-measure ways) across parties. For example, Hanson and Hart wrote the following about "activity levels" (pointing out that accident costs are a function not only of level of care, but also of level of activity):

"To deter all accidents that could be cost-justified prevented, judges and juries would need to compare the benefits a party obtains from greater participation in the activity to the resulting increase in expected accident costs. Unfortunately, courts tend to ignore activity level considerations, and most scholars believe that, as a practical matter, courts are *unable* to conduct the necessary activity-level calculus, because of the amount of information they would need."[77]

As noted when talking about the Coase theorem, the fact that an analysis incorporates simplifying assumptions is not fatal. However, Hanson and Hart argue that when one tries to adjust the outcomes of the one's calculations and predictions by taking into account how things actually are, the prediction of efficiency is either directly undermined or left in such doubt that one has serious questions about using the model as a justification for changing (or not changing) the law.[78]

One "external" criticism of law and economics is that it is a reductive system, an approach to law and life that attempts to analyse everything in

---

[76] Jon D. Hanson and Melissa R. Hart, "Law and Economics" in *A Companion to the Philosophy of Law and Legal Theory* (D. Patterson ed., Blackwell, Oxford, 1996), pp. 318–325.

[77] *ibid.* at p. 321 (citation omitted).

[78] Arthur Leff made a similar point in more colorful language: "If a state of affairs is the product of *n* variables, and you have knowledge of or control over less than *n* variables, if you think you know what's going to happen when you vary 'your' variables, you're a booby." Leff, "Economic Analysis of Law: Some Realism About Nominalism", at 476.

terms of a single parameter (money, wealth, willingness to pay). This criticism is an analysis its terms of "commensurability". As explicated by Martha Nussbaum, commensurability regards "all the valuable things under consideration as measurable on a single scale".[79] The inevitable results of such reductions are distortions in both one's descriptions and one's prescriptions.[80]

Beyond some fairly straightforward difficulties with translating all matters into willingness to pay (first, the things we value the most we often speak of as things on which "one cannot put a price"[81]; and secondly, sometimes willingness to pay is a function merely of ability to pay, and may have little to do with how highly one values something), there remains the even more basic objection that any attempt to reduce human decisions and actions to a single variable is going to distort them beyond recognition. John Finnis[82] gave examples of the way law and economics did not (because, in Finnis' view, it cannot) draw distinctions between accidental (negligent) behaviour and intentional misdeeds (both foreseeable but unintended accidents and intentional injuries appear in one of Posner's analyses simply as costs ascribable to the party or activity),[83] distinctions which seem both basic and crucial to our moral view of the world.[84]

There are a variety of other "external" criticisms in the literature. For example:

(1) that economic analysis has inherent biases towards the rich over the poor, producers over consumers, and the status quo over reform[85];

---

[79] Martha C. Nussbaum, *Poetic Justice* (Beacon Press, Boston, 1995), p. 14. She adds that those who believe that values are commensurable must believe either that "all the valuable things are valuable because they contain some one thing that itself varies only in quantity . . . or [that] despite the plurality of values, there is an argument that shows that a single metric adequately captures what is valuable in them all."

[80] Nussbaum offers a longer list of external criticisms in Martha C. Nussbaum, "Flawed Foundations: The Philosophical Critique of (a Particular Type of) Economics", 64 *University of Chicago Law Review* 1197 (1997).

[81] Margaret Jane Radin, "Market-Inalienability", 100 *Harvard Law Review* 1849 (1987).

[82] John M. Finnis, "Allocating Risks and Suffering: Some Hidden Traps", 38 *Cleveland State Law Review* 193 at 200–205 (1990).

[83] A contrary view, defending the ability of law and economics to draw appropriate distinctions between accidental and intentional action, might be derived from the discussion of intentional wrongdoing in Landes and Posner, *The Economic Structure of Tort Law*, pp. 149–160.

[84] Arthur Leff discussed the way that the reductive analysis in law and economics eradicates psychological and sociological factors (as to the latter, race and class are obvious examples) which are crucial to a proper understanding of modern behaviour. Leff, "Economic Analysis of Law: Some Realism About Nominalism", at 469–477.

[85] See, *e.g.* Kelman, *A Guide to Critical Legal Studies*, pp. 151–185; Morton Horwitz, "Law and Economics: Science or Politics?", 8 *Hofstra Law Review* 905 (1981).

(2) that the legal way of looking at language and the world is different from the economic way of looking, and the law (and this society) would be worse off to the extent that the economic outlook is allowed to take over law[86]; and

(3) that the objectives of efficiency or wealth-maximization are irrelevant to and often incompatible with corrective justice, which is the essence of, and the only proper objective for, private law.[87]

Even if one accepts the above criticisms as valid and important (and of course, not everyone does), there still remains much that is of value to economic analysis in the law. First, there are legal questions that turn (or should turn) on purely economic matters. For example, for the purposes of competition (antitrust) law whether a particular kind of vertical or horizontal integration of companies in the long term supports, hinders or has no effect upon competition. Secondly, economic analysis has often served to sharpen the existing somewhat fuzzy legal thinking in various areas. For some, economic analysis captures in quantitative terms what had only been vaguely described by long-standing common law concepts like "reasonable care", "negligence" and "proximate cause". Also, economic analysis occasionally highlights concerns that had gotten lost when the questions were posed in traditional ways, *e.g.* in terms of "fairness" and "justice". For example, in considering the rules of bankruptcy/insolvency law, the way legal rules are developed will affect not only the creditors' rights as against the debtor (the traditional focus for analysis) but also the extent to which individual creditors have incentives to act in ways which will shrink the total amount of assets available, thus working against the interests of the creditors as a group, and perhaps against the social interest as well.[88]

Thirdly, even if one believes that efficiency/wealth maximization is at best one value among many (or an imperfect approximation of one

---

[86] See James Boyd White, "Economics and Law: Two Cultures in Tension", 54 *Tennessee Law Review* 161 (1987). For similar arguments that the economic perspective impoverishes our view of what people are like, and the possibility of individual (self-)improvement, see, *e.g.* Robin West, "The Other Utilitarians", in *Analyzing Law* (B. Bix ed., Clarendon Press, Oxford, 1998), pp. 197–222 (comparing the economists' view of individuals with that of the early utilitarians); Jonathan Lear, *Open Minded* (Harvard University Press, Cambridge, Mass., 1998), pp. 28–32 (comparing the economists' view with that of Freudian psychology).

There is also empirical evidence that exposure to economics causes more self-interested behavior (reader beware!). Robert H. Frank, Thomas Gilovich & Dennis T. Regan, "Does Studying Economics Inhibit Cooperation?", 7 *Journal of Economic Perspectives* 159 (1993).

[87] See Weinrib, *The Idea of Private Law*.

[88] See Posner, *Economic Analysis of Law*, pp. 417–423. I am indebted to Stephen Gilles for this example.

such value), one would still want to know what effects a current legal rule or practice, or a proposed change to that rule or practice, has on efficiency/wealth maximization.[89] At the least, there are occasions when an accurate (and subtle) delineation of the costs of the alternative rules or actions will influence the eventual (moral) choice between them.[90] Fourthly, the method of analysis that law and economics promotes reminds us of long-term effects we might not otherwise have considered.[91] A standard example is the landlord who wants to evict the poor, starving tenant for non-payment of rent. While our sympathies may go immediately to the tenant, we should consider the long-term consequences of a rule where the landlord could *not* evict in such circumstances. What would likely ensue is that landlords would either become reluctant to lease apartments to those who are less well off or that higher rents would be charged to everyone, to compensate for losses to non-paying tenants who cannot be evicted.[92] Therefore, while the short-term result of ruling for the tenant may be that one impoverished tenant keeps her apartment, the long-term effect may be that many other impoverished tenants cannot find (affordable) apartments to rent. Fifthly, the other analytical move that economic thinking reinforces, sometimes to a fault, is that a person's preferences can be derived from her actions, and the (relative) intensity of those preferences can often be derived by asking how much she is willing to pay (in money, or in giving up other things of value) for the matters in question. It is hardly a new discovery that a person's statements, and even her conscious beliefs, can be belied by her actions; however, it is a matter that is too often and easily forgotten. On the other hand, when one looks *only* to actions and willingness to pay to determine a person's preferences, the analysis can be equally erroneous, especially when the analysis ignores that there are some things we have not because we have chosen them (or want them), but because they are the unavoidable side-effects of things we do desire (the international traveler does not desire jet lag, but accepts it as a consequence of getting to the places she wants to see),[93] and that the unwillingness to pay a large sum may simply be a function of the inability to pay that amount.

---

[89] See, *e.g.* Posner, "Utilitarianism, Economics, and Legal Theory", at 109–110.
[90] See, *e.g. ibid.* at 109.
[91] See, *e.g.* Leff, "Economic Analysis of Law: Some Realism About Nominalism", at 459–462.
[92] See, *e.g.* Posner, "The Ethical and Political Basis of the Efficiency Norm in Common Law Adjudication", at 500; Leff, "Economic Analysis of Law: Some Realism About Nominalism", at 459–461. A third possibility is that landlords will put clauses into the leases requiring the tenants to waive their rights under the new ruling. If such clauses are later held to be unenforceable (as sometimes occurs with waiver clauses of this type), then the landlords will likely return to one of the other two strategies outlined in the text.
[93] See Finnis, "Allocating Risks and Suffering: Sonic Hidden Traps", at 201.

214 ECONOMIC ANALYSIS OF LAW

Suggested Further Readings

LAW AND ECONOMICS GENERALLY

Ronald H. Coase, "The Problem of Social Cost", 3 *Journal of Law and Economics* 1 (1960), reprinted in *The Firm, the Market, and the Law* (University of Chicago Press, Chicago, 1988), pp. 95–156.
William Landes and Richard Posner, *The Economic Structure of Tort Law* (Harvard University Press, Cambridge, Mass., 1987).
Peter Newman ed., *The New Palgrave Dictionary of Economics and the Law*, three volumes (Macmillan, London, 1998).
A. Mitchell Polinsky, *An Introduction to Law and Economics* (2nd ed., Little, Brown and Co., Boston, 1989).
Richard Posner, *Economic Analysis of Law* (6th ed., Aspen Publishing, New York, 2003).
—, *The Economics of Justice* (Harvard University Press, Cambridge, Mass., 1983).
Steven Shavell, *Foundations of Economic Analysis of Law* (forthcoming, Harvard University Press, Cambridge, Mass., 2003).

LAW AND ECONOMICS PERSPECTIVES AND CRITICISM

Jon D. Hanson and Melissa R. Hart, "Law and Economics", in *A Companion to the Philosophy of Law and Legal Theory* (D. Patterson ed., Blackwell, Oxford, 1996), pp. 311–331.
Avery Wiener Katz ed., *Foundations of the Economic Approach to Law* (Oxford University Press, New York, 1998).
Duncan Kennedy, "Law and Economics from the Perspective of Critical Legal Studies", in *The New Palgrave Dictionary of Economics and the Law*, Vol. 2 (P. Newman ed., Macmillan, London, 1998), pp. 465–474.
Lewis Kornhauser, "Economic Analysis of Law", in E. N. Zalta ed., *Stanford Encyclopedia of Philosophy*, http://plato.stanford.edu (2001).
Arthur Leff, "Economic Analysis of Law: Sonic Realism About Nominalism", 60 *Virginia Law Review* 451 (1974).
Jeffrie G. Murphy and Jules L. Coleman, *Philosophy of Law* (revised ed., Westview Press, Boulder, Colo., 1990), pp. 181–234 ("Law and Economics").
Scott Shapiro and Edward F. McClennan, "Law-and-Economics from a Philosophical Perspective", in *The New Palgrave Dictionary of Economics and the Law*, Vol. 2 (P. Newman ed., Macmillan, London, 1998), pp. 460–465.
Symposium: "Efficiency as a Legal Concern", 8 *Hofstra Law Review* 485–770 (1980) (contributors include Richard Posner, Jules Coleman, Guido Calabresi, Ronald Dworkin, Duncan Kennedy and Frank Michelman).
Symposium: "Post-Chicago Law and Economics", 65 *Chicago-Kent Law Review* 3–191 (1989) (contributors include Randy Barnett, Robert Ellickson, Richard Posner, Jonathan Macey, Daniel Farber, and Jules Coleman).
Symposium: "The Future of Law and Economics: Looking Forward", 64 *University of Chicago Law Review* 1129–1224 (1997) (includes contributions by

Ronald Coase, Richard Posner, Richard Epstein, Gary Becker, Cass Sunstein and Martha Nussbaum).

GAME THEORY

Ian Ayres, "Playing Games with the Law", 42 *Stanford Law Review* 1291 (1990).
Douglas G. Baird, "Game Theory and the Law", in *The New Palgrave Dictionary of Economics and the Law*, Vol. 1 (P. Newman ed., Macmillan, London, 1998), pp. 192–198.
Douglas G. Baird, Robert H. Gertner and Randal C. Picker, *Game Theory and the Law* (Harvard University Press, Cambridge, Mass., 1994).
Eric Rasmusen, *Games & Information: An Introduction to Game Theory* (3rd ed., Blackwell, Oxford, 2001).
Don Ross, "Game Theory", in E. N. Zalta ed., *Stanford Encyclopedia of Philosophy*, *http://plato.stanford.edu* (2002).

PUBLIC CHOICE THEORY

James M. Buchanan and Gordon Tullock, *The Calculus of Consent: Logical Foundations of Constitutional Democracy* (University of Michigan Press, Ann Arbor, 1962).
Daniel Farber and Philip Frickey, *Law and Public Choice* (University of Chicago Press, Chicago, 1991).
Jonathan R. Macey, "Public Choice and the Law", in *The New Palgrave Dictionary of Economics and the Law*, Vol. 3 (P. Newman ed., Macmillan, London, 1998), pp. 171–178.
Richard A. Posner, "Economics, Politics, and the Reading of Statutes and the Constitution", 49 *University of Chicago Law Review* 263 (1982).
Maxwell L. Stearns ed., *Public Choice and Public Law: Readings and Commentary* (Anderson Publishing Co., Cincinnati, 1997).
"Symposium on the Theory of Public Choice", 74 *Virginia Law Review* 167–518 (1988) (including contributions by Geoffrey Brennan and James Buchanan, Jonathan Macey, Daniel Farber and Philip Frickey, Mark Kelman, and William Eskridge Jr).
Gordon Tullock, "Public Choice", in *The New Palgrave Dictionary of Economics* (J. Eatwell, M. Milgate & P. Newman eds, Palgrave, New York, 1987), Vol. 3, pp. 1040–1044.

Chapter Nineteen

Modern Critical Perspectives

In the last 25 years or so, a series of loosely related critical approaches to law have developed, which have their roots in (among other places) the Civil Rights Movement, American legal realism, and European social theory.

In many cases, the advocates placed under a single label—"critical legal studies", "feminist legal theory", or "critical race theory"—share only that (the label), and a certain distance on some matters from mainstream legal theory. The point is that on almost any substantive issue or question of methodology, there will be as much variation or disagreement within those groups as there will be between those groups and other theorists. Nonetheless, these are the categories by which these theories are known and characterized by others and, to a great extent, this is how they characterize themselves as well. This chapter will offer an overview of some of the themes identified with each of the three critical approaches to the law.

CRITICAL STUDIES

The critical legal studies movement is the name given to a group of scholars who wrote about legal theory using ideas associated with Left politics or trying to use law, or legal education, or writings about the law to try to effect Left results.

Critical legal studies ("CLS"), as a self-defined group, became active in the late 1970s.[1] The vast majority of work being done under that label has been done by American scholars, but there are also followers in other countries.[2] CLS as a movement received (and often courted) a great deal of controversy and opposition, culminating in the mid-1980s with

---

[1] For a good summary of the rise and fall of CLS, see Duxbury, *Patterns of American Jurisprudence*, pp. 428–509.

[2] See, *e.g.* Peter Fitzpatrick and Alan Hunt, *Critical Legal Studies* (Blackwell, Oxford, 1987) (British CLS writers).

strongly negative articles in the major media[3] and high-profile denials of tenure to CLS adherents at the Harvard Law School and elsewhere.[4] While today there are still a number of people who identify themselves with the CLS label, much of the movement's energy has appeared to have been passed on to the affiliated, but quite distinct, schools of thought, feminist legal theory and critical race theory, about which more later.

Critical legal studies theorists saw themselves as extending and elaborating the more radical aspects of the American legal realists' programme. Among the more common themes in CLS writing were the following: the political nature of law (the ideological biases inherent in apparently neutral concepts and analyses)—"law as ideology",[5] the radical indeterminacy of the law,[6] the claim that law promotes the interests of the powerful and legitimates injustice,[7] and the argument that rights rhetoric works against the common good and against the interests of the groups the rights purport to protect.[8] Among other topics visited by adherents of CLS were the ideological implications of modern legal education,[9] criticisms of the law and economics movement,[10] and the uses

---

[3] See, e.g. Terry Eastland, "Radicals in the Law Schools", *Wall Street Journal*, January 10, 1986, p. 10; Louis Menand, "Radicalism for Yuppies", *The New Republic*, March 17, 1986, pp. 20–23; cf. Calvin Trillin, "A Reporter at Large: Harvard Law", *New Yorker*, March 26, 1984, pp. 53–83 (a somewhat more balanced report).

[4] Academics were effectively scared away from CLS, not only by the threat of denial of tenure, but by the more effective and ominous threat that schools would not hire them in the first place, if they were suspected of affiliation with CLS. The trend towards "boycotting" CLS-connected academics was strengthened by an article by Paul Carrington, then Dean of the Duke Law School, who argued that people who advocated "nihilistic" views had no place teaching in a law school. Paul D. Carrington, "Of Law and the River", 34 *Journal of Legal Education* 222 (1984). For a view from within CLS, see Jerry Frug, "McCarthyism and Critical Legal Studies" (book review), 22 *Harvard Civil Rights-Civil Liberties Law Review* 665 at 676–701 (1987).

[5] See, e.g. Lewis Kornhauser, "The Great Image of Authority", 36 *Stanford Law Review* 349 at 371–387 (1984).

[6] See, e.g. Duncan Kennedy, "Freedom and Constraint in Adjudication: A Critical Phenomenology", 36 *Journal of Legal Education* 518 (1986).

[7] See, e.g. Douglas Hay, Peter Linebaugh, John Rule, E.P. Thompson and Cal Winslow, *Albion's Fatal Tree* (Penguin, Middlesex, England, 1975); Alan David Freeman, "Legitimizing Racial Discrimination Through Antidiscrimination Law: A Critical Review of Supreme Court Doctrine", 62 *Minnesota Law Review* 1049 (1978).

[8] See, e.g. Mark Tushnet, "An Essay on Rights", 62 *Texas Law Review* 1363 (1984). The CLS critique of rights provoked a sharp response defending rights from early critical race theorists. See, e.g. Patricia J. Williams, "Alchemical Notes: Reconstructing Ideals From Deconstructed Rights", 22 *Harvard Civil Rights-Civil Liberties Law Review* 401 (1987). For a recent reply, see Duncan Kennedy, "The Critique of Rights in Critical Legal Studies", in *Left Legalism/Left Critique* (W. Brown and J. Halley eds, Duke University Press, Durham, N.C., 2003), pp. 178–228, esp. pp. 213–220.

[9] See, e.g. Duncan Kennedy, "Legal Education as Training for Hierarchy", in *The Politics of Law* (revised ed., D. Kairys ed., Pantheon, New York, 1990), pp. 38–58.

[10] See, e.g. Kelman, *A Guide to Critical Legal Studies*, pp. 11 4–185.

of radical theory in rethinking radical legal practice.[11] CLS was also known for, and to some extent known by, its attempt to apply to law the ideas of European literary theorists, social theorists and philosophers.[12] Obviously, these topics cannot be covered in detail in the short space available; I can only touch on some aspects of a few of them.

On the indeterminacy of law, CLS theorists offered a variety of views as to what they meant by "indeterminacy", what its causes allegedly are, and what consequences follow. James Boyle offered the following as a paraphrase of "the strongest version of the indeterminacy thesis ever put forward by anyone associated with CLS":

"Nothing internal to language compels a particular result. In every case the judge *could* produce a wide range of decisions which were formally correct under the canons of legal reasoning. Of course, shared meanings, community expectations, professional customs and so on may make a particular decision seem inevitable (though that happens less than many people think). But even in those cases, it is not the words of the rule that produce the decision, but, a bevy of factors whose most marked feature is that they are anything but universal, rational or objective. Legal rules are supposed not only to be determinate (after all, decisions based on race prejudice are perfectly determinate), but to produce determinacy through a particular method of interpretation. That method of interpretation alone, however, produces indeterminate results and it cannot be supplemented sufficiently to produce definite results without subverting its supposed qualities of objectivity and political and moral neutrality."[13]

On legal history, CLS theorists sometimes pointed out the way that apparently neutral rules actually work to the benefit of the powerful. However, the more common theme was the contingency of legal rules and concepts: the way that the rules could have developed other than the way they actually did. Similarly, the argument goes, the legal rules and concepts as they are now should not be treated as natural or inevitable, but as contingent and subject to change.[14]

---

[11] See, *e.g.* Peter Gabel and Paul Harris, "Building Power and Breaking Images: Critical Legal Theory and the Practice of Law", 11 *New York University Review of Law and Social Change* 369 (1982–1983).

[12] Among the thinkers most often discussed or cited are Jacques Derrida, Michel Foucault, Antonio Gramsci, Jürgen Habermas, Ludwig Wittgenstein, Karl Marx, and Jacques Lacan.

[13] James Boyle, "Introduction", in *Critical Legal Studies* (J. Boyle ed., New York University Press, New York, 1994), p. xx. This noted, there are many who attribute a more radical theory of indeterminacy to at least some of the critical legal studies theorists. For some possible variations on an indeterminacy position, and a critique of such positions, see Lawrence B. Solum, "On the Indeterminacy Crisis: Critiquing Critical Dogma", 54 *University of Chicago Law Review* 462 (1987); Kenneth J. Kress, "Legal Indeterminacy", 77 *California Law Review* 283 (1989).

[14] Among the best known CLS works on legal history are Morton Horwitz, *The Transformation of American Law 1780–1860* (Harvard University Press, Cambridge, Mass., 1977); Hay, Linebaugh, Rule, Thompson and Winslow, *Albion's Fatal Tree*; and Robert Gordon, "Critical Legal Histories", 36 *Stanford Law Review* 57 (1984).

An example of CLS's critique of the apparent neutrality of legal concepts was the attack on the public/private distinction.[15] The argument runs roughly as follows: both within and outside the legal system, a great deal is made of the difference between matters which fall within the "public" realm (and thus are properly subject to significant government control) and matters with the "private" realm (a haven from government intrusion). However, coercion and oppression also occur in the "private" realm: in the family, in domestic violence and abuse, and in private economic ordering, where the economically powerful can set oppressive terms for the economically powerless. The distinction between public and private is thus undermined; the private realm is not a haven from the coercion of the public realm. It is the government's refusal to act to protect the weak in "private matters" (domestic relations and contract) that allows and legitimates the oppression that occurs. Also, critical legal studies, like some of the legal realists, wanted to emphasize the extent to which the rules of private law were no more "natural" or "inevitable" than the rules of public law, and no less a product of official policy.[16]

Another view influential within CLS was the idea of the "fundamental contradiction". The idea, introduced by Duncan Kennedy,[17] is that "relations with others are both necessary to and incompatible with our freedom",[18] and that this contradiction—separation and connection, individual and collective—pervades both our experiences of life and the legal rules and doctrine we create. Kennedy argued that liberal (understood broadly) legal theory denies the contradiction or purports to "mediate" it, but inevitably fails in the mediation. The argument also connects the contradiction and the legitimating function of law.[19] Kennedy, and some other CLS theorists, also offered related claims about the simultaneous and contradictory commitments law makes to altruism and individualism, and to rules and standards.[20]

---

[15] See *e.g.* Frances Olsen, "The Family and the Market: A Study of Ideology and Legal Reform", 96 *Harvard Law Review* 1497 (1983); Morton Horwitz, "The History of the Public/Private Distinction", 130 *University of Pennsylvania Law Review* 1423 (1982). A good rebuttal to the realist/CLS attack on the public/private distinction can be found in Leiter, "Legal Realism", at 278–279.

[16] The legal realist articles on the subject include Robert Hale, "Coercion and Distribution in a Supposedly Non-Coercive State", 38 *Political Science Quarterly* 470 (1923); and Morris Cohen, "Property and Sovereignty", 13 *Cornell Law Quarterly* 8 (1927).

[17] Duncan Kennedy, "The Structure of Blackstone's Commentaries", 28 *Buffalo Law Review* 205 at 211–221 (1979). For brief but effective response, see Andrew Altman, *Critical Legal Studies: A Liberal Critique* (Princeton University Press, Princeton, 1990), pp. 186–189.

[18] Kennedy, "The Structure of Blackstone's Commentaries", p. 213.

[19] *ibid.* at 213–221.

[20] See Duncan Kennedy, "Form and Substance in Private Law Adjudication", 89 *Harvard Law Review* 1685 (1976); Kelman, *A Guide to Critical Legal Studies*, pp. 15–63 ("Rules and Standards"). Another comparable argument is Roberto Unger's that legal doctrine is indeterminate because it simultaneously contains antagonistic principles and counter

It is hard to be more definitive about what CLS stood for, as the theorists who considered themselves part of the movement (or were considered part of the movement by others) did not all take the same position on issues. It is not merely that different theorists emphasized different issues, but that on any given issue—*e.g.* the value of the "rule of law",[21] the value of rights rhetoric,[22] and whether law serves the interests of the powerful—different CLS theorists would be on different sides.

As there has been a large number of writers within CLS presenting a variety of views on a wide range of topics, there has been a comparably wide array of critics and topics for criticism. A brief sample of citations is offered in a footnote.[23]

FEMINIST LEGAL THEORY

Two approaches to law, feminist legal theory and critical race theory, are sometimes considered together under the label "outsider jurisprudence"[24] because they can both be seen as emanating from the same core problem: the extent to which the law reflects the perspective of and the values of white males, and the resulting effects on citizens and on members of the legal profession who are not white males.[25]

The problem about bias can be summarized by the following, from a symposium on critical race theory:

"Long ago, empowered actors and speakers enshrined their meanings, preferences, and views of the world into the common culture and language. Now their

principles (like "freedom of contract" and fairness/community in contract law). See Roberto Mangabeira Unger, *The Critical Legal Studies Movement* (Harvard University Press, Cambridge, Mass., 1986) pp. 57–75.

21 See, *e.g.* Morton Horwitz, "The Rule of Law: An Unqualified Human Good?" (book review), 86 *Yale Law Journal* 561 (1977) (arguing against E.P Thompson's view that the rule of law is always an unqualified good).

22 See, *e.g.* Tushnet, "An Essay on Rights"; Horwitz, "Rights".

23 See, *e.g.* Altman, *Critical Legal Studies: A Liberal Critique;* John Finnis, "On The Critical Legal Studies Movement", 30 *American Journal of Jurisprudence* 21 (1985), reprinted in *Oxford Essays in Jurisprudence*, Third Series (J. Eekelaar and J. Bell eds, Clarendon Press, Oxford, 1987), pp. 145–165; Neil MacCormick, "Reconstruction after Deconstruction: A Response to CLS", 10 *Oxford Journal of Legal Studies* 539 (1990).

24 See Mari Matsuda, "Public Response to Racist Speech: Considering the Victim's Story", 87 *Michigan Law Review* 2320 at 2323 and n. 15 (1989); Mary Coombs, "Outsider Scholarship: The Law Review Stories", 63 *University of Colorado Law Review* 683, at 683–684 (1992).

25 See Scott Brewer, "Introduction: Choosing Sides in the Racial Critiques Debate", 103 *Harvard Law Review* 1844 at 1850–1851 (1990) ("Moral Visions of Racial Distinctiveness"); Scott Brewer, "Pragmatism, Oppression, and the Flight to Substance", 63 *Southern California Law Review* 1753 (1990). See generally Martha Minow, *Making All the Difference* (Cornell University Press, Ithaca, N.Y., 1990).

deliberation within that language, purporting always to be neutral and fair, inexorably produces results that reflect their interests."[26]

The question of difference can be taken in steps:

(1) is the difference between the majority or powerful group and the minority or powerless group(s) simply a reflection of the years of oppression, or are the differences inherent?

(2) if there are inherent differences, how (if at all) should the law reflect or respond to these differences?

It is more common in feminist legal theory than in critical race theory to find writers who suggest that there are inherent differences between the powerful and the powerless: here, that women are different from men, and should be treated differently.

Among the problems that are common to feminist legal theory and critical race theory are those that develop from the fact that one is trying to create equality, justice, and reform in or through the legal system, against a societal background in which inequality, discrimination, and oppression are still common, if not pervasive. This leads to standard types of dilemmas in proposing reform: is it better to enforce a regime of strict facial neutrality, which might have the effect of merely reinforcing existing social inequalities; or is it better to advocate forms of special treatment, which might help in the short-term, but could have the long-term effect of reinforcing the view that the group receiving the special treatment is weak or inferior?

Finally, one might note that feminist legal theory and critical race theory, as well as critical legal studies, are all directly concerned about justice in a way that most of the other approaches to law discussed in this book are not.[27] The argument in all three approaches is basically that the law is unjust because it is systematically distorted or biased (towards men, whites, and/or the rich and powerful). However, while the arguments in these areas are often couched in terms of fairness and justice, a full theory of justice or of "the Good" is rarely articulated.

A way in which feminist legal theory and critical race theory differ from most other approaches to law (including critical legal studies) is the regular focus on proposals for reforms, ways of changing the law through legislation or judicial action, which would remove what were perceived to be injustices in the legal system or in society. One example that will be dis-

---

[26] Richard Delgado and Jean Stefancic, "Hateful Speech, Loving Communities: Why Our Notion of 'A Just Balance' Changes So Slowly", 82 *California Law Review* 851 at 861 (1994).
[27] I am grateful to Jack Balkin for pointing this out.

cussed in some detail later is a feminist proposal to change the legal treatment of sexually explicit material. This greater focus on reforming the law also indicates further connections with the American legal realists, some of whom had worked hard to reform the law in line with their ideas about how the law should operate.[28]

To turn the focus to feminist legal theory (critical race theory will be the focus of the next section): Feminist analyses have offered important critiques in a variety of contexts, from broad political analyses to cultural theories to analyses specific to particular academic disciplines. Though certain themes are common to most of what carries the label "feminist"—in particular, a belief that either theory or practice has been distorted towards the perspective or the interests of men—there is a great deal of variety, even within a single discipline, among those writers who call themselves "feminists", and here, feminist legal theory is no exception. However, to the extent that one can speak of these writers (and these texts) as a group, their impact has been significant in the United States, and is growing in other countries.[29]

As discussed earlier, part of feminist legal theory is the analysis of the extent to which the legal system reflects and reinforces a male perspective, and part is (the related) analysis of how women's differences from men should or should not he reflected in legal rules, legal institutions, and legal education.

Regarding the first aspect, Patricia Smith has argued that what feminist legal theories have in common is an opposition to the patriarchal ideas that dominate society in general, and (relevant to feminist legal theory) the legal system in particular.[30] The differences among feminist legal theorists are then seen as reflecting differences in emphasis or perspective in describing the many aspects and effects of patriarchy, differences in which problems to focus upon, and differences in strategy for overcoming the problem of patriarchy (for example, those who believe in moderate reforms as against those who believe that only radical restructuring of society will suffice).[31]

As to the second aspect, one could argue that what is common to feminist legal theories is that they are divergent responses to the inherent or socially constructed differences between men and women, responses

---

[28] See, e.g. Zipporah Wiseman, "The Limits of Vision: Karl Llewellyn and the Merchant Rules", 100 *Harvard Law Review* 465 (1987) (on the connection between realist thought and the Uniform Commercial Code).

[29] One sympathetic critic recently wrote: "To a growing extent, a jurisprudence with very little to add about the concerns and innovations of feminism will not have very much interesting to add, period." Matthew H. Kramer, *Critical Legal Theory and the Challenge of Feminism* (Rowman & Littlefield, London, 1995), p. 265.

[30] Patricia Smith, "Feminist Jurisprudence", in *A Companion to the Philosophy of Law and Legal Theory* (D. Patterson ed., Blackwell, Oxford, 1996), pp. 305–307.

[31] *ibid.* at 307–308.

regarding what these differences should mean about the way we think about law. One feminist response to difference is:

(1) *there are* intrinsic differences between men and women;

(2) society and law are organized around a male standard and a male norm, a situation which works in the short-term and the long–term against the interests of women; and (therefore)

(3) society and law should be reformed to remove that bias, and to reflect women's experiences as well as men's.

The differences between men and women which are emphasized include differences in values, ways of seeing the world, responding to other people,[32] responding to problems, ways of speaking,[33] and so on. This view has been associated generally with the work of Carol Gilligan; within legal theory, the foremost proponent is probably Robin West.[34] The argument is that alongside the traditional and conventional approach to morality (the "ethic of justice"), which emphasizes individual rights, autonomy, and distance, there is a separate type of moral thought, associated primarily (though not exclusively) with women.[35] This alternative "ethic of care" emphasizes connection, interdependence, and care-giving.

A second feminist response to difference is that there are no (significant) inherent differences between men and women, and that any aspect of the law which assumes the contrary should be changed. This position often includes the view that what differences appear among men and women are peripheral, or are the effects of contingent social or cultural forces.

A third approach, closely identified with the work of Catharine MacKinnon, argues that most of the differences there may *appear* to be between men and women are the result of the domination and exploitation of women by men.[36] Women were not allowed to work in high-status or high-paying areas, but, over time, women adapted to these restrictions by, among other things, arguing for the value of what they *were* allowed to do (*e.g.* the value of the care-giving professions, the artistic value of quilts, etc.). Women may be more likely to negotiate, to try to work things

---

[32] Carol Gilligan's work in some ways exemplifies all three. See Gilligan, *In a Different Voice*.

[33] See, *e.g.* Deborah Tannen, *You Just Don't Understand* (William Morrow, New York, 1990).

[34] See, *e.g.* Robin West, *Caring for Justice* (New York University Press, New York, 1997).

[35] See Gilligan, *In a Different Voice*. For recent work that undermines the empirical claim that the ethic of care is primarily associated with women, see Sara Jaffee and Janet Shibley Hyde, "Gender Differences in Moral Orientation: A Meta-Analysis", 126 *Psychology Bulletin* 703 (2000).

[36] See, *e.g.* Catharine A. MacKinnon, *Feminism Unmodified* (Harvard University Press, Cambridge, Mass., 1987) pp. 32–45 ("Difference and Dominance: On Sex Discrimination").

out, rather than battle in "winner take all" contests, but that is because they have learned that they would be likely to lose such contests, where society has given all the power to men, and has encouraged the oppression of women. Similarly, women may value caring and nurturing, but that is because these are the values that society (that is, men) have valued *in them*. Women are encouraged to be good mothers and nurses: they are not encouraged to be good litigators and politicians.[37]

Feminist approaches and perspectives have been applied to a wide variety of topics and issues. Among these are abortion rights,[38] rape law,[39] sexual harassment,[40] surrogate motherhood,[41] pregnancy and maternity leave,[42] and (perhaps most controversially) pornography.[43] Though the arguments necessarily vary from article to article and from author to author, the most common theme is that the current law or current approach in these areas exemplifies a male bias and/or works to the detriment of women as a group.

I will briefly discuss one of the better known topics within feminist legal theory, the MacKinnon-Dworkin proposed legislation on sexually explicit material, to give some sense of the complexity and difficulty of the issues raised. (I make no claim that this topic is representative of the issues raised by feminist theorists; I do not think any issue would be. The issues raised within feminist legal theory are so broad in range and have such different contours that any search for a "representative" issue would be doomed to failure.)

Catharine MacKinnon (1946–) and Andrea Dworkin drafted a model civil rights ordinance to combat certain kinds of sexually explicit publica-

---

[37] MacKinnon's "dominance theory" echoes the ideas of Friedrich Nietzsche (1844–1900) regarding "master morality" and "slave morality". If one is a strong person or part of a strong group, one is more likely to value strength, activity, and victory. If one is a weak person or part of a weak group, one will more likely develop a moral view that victory, strength. and wealth are all suspect, that the meek will inherit the earth, and that humility and subservience are the greatest virtues See *e.g.* Friedrich Nietzsche, *On the Genealogy of Morality*, First Essay (K. Ansell-Pearson ed., Cambridge University Press, Cambridge, 1994) (first published in 1887).

[38] See, *e.g.* MacKinnon *Feminism Unmodified*, pp. 93–102; Anita Allen, "The Proposed Equal Protection Fix for Abortion Law: Reflections on Citizenship, Gender, and the Constitution", 18 *Harvard Journal of Law and Public Policy* 419 (1995).

[39] See, *e.g.* Panel Discussion, "Men, Women and Rape", 63 *Fordham Law Review* 125 (1994); Susan Estrich, *Real Rape* (Harvard University Press, Cambridge, Mass., 1987).

[40] See, *e.g.* Catharine MacKinnon, *Sexual Harassment of Working Women* (Yale University Press, New Haven, 1979).

[41] See, *e.g.* Martha Field, "Surrogacy Contracts: Gestational and Traditional: The Argument for Nonenforcement", 31 *Washburn Law Review* 3 (1991).

[42] See, *e.g.* Minow, *Making All the Difference*, pp. 56–60; Herma Hill Kay "Equality and Difference: The Case of Pregnancy", 1 *Berkeley Women's Law Journal* 1 (1985).

[43] See, *e.g.* MacKinnon, *Feminism Unmodified*, pp. 127–213; see also Nicola Lacey, "Theory into Practice? Pornography and the Public/Private Dichotomy", 20 *Journal of Law and Society* 93 (1993).

tions.[44] Under the ordinance, anyone who had suffered directly or indirectly because of pornography[45] could sue for damages. This model ordinance was proposed (in slightly different forms) in a number of American cities, passed in two, but declared void because unconstitutional in both cases.[46]

In the words of one of the authors: "Pornography, in the feminist view, is a form of forced sex, a practice of sexual politics, an institution of gender inequality".[47] The argument is that what is at the core of (the vast majority of) pornographic material is a portrayal of women as subordinate to men, and women as enjoying their subordinate position.[48] Pornography thus has effects beyond questions about whether it should be restricted because it is "immoral" (immoral because sexually explicit). Under the MacKinnon/Dworkin view, pornography works to silence women by reinforcing the subordination of women and the perception by men that women enjoy that subordination.[49]

In the MacKinnon-Dworkin proposal, "pornography" was defined as the "graphic sexually explicit subordination of women" through pictures or words which portray women as enjoying humiliation, pain, or being the victims of rape or other violence. (The constitutional ground for invalidating the ordinance was that under the right of free expression, the government could not distinguish between material on the basis of viewpoint; thus, a statute that subjects to civil liability sexually explicit material that implies that women enjoy their subordinate position but not similar material that portrays women as not enjoying such treatment, was considered an improper government intrusion on freedom of expression.[50])

One sympathetic commentator summarized this analysis as follows,

---

[44] MacKinnon and Dworkin (no relation to Ronald Dworkin of Ch. 7) are also well-known for their views on heterosexual sex in general, though these views are often misunderstood or mis-characterized. For a sympathetic and subtle summary and analysis of MacKinnon's views on the matter, see Frances Olsen, "Feminist Theory in Grand Style" (book review), 89 *Columbia Law Review* 1147 at 1154–1160 (1989).

[45] Among the categories of injuries listed were "coercion into pornography", "forcing pornography on a person", "assault or physical attack due to pornography". and "defamation through pornography".

[46] See Mary Becker; Cynthia Grant Bowman and Morrison Torrey eds, *Feminist Jurisprudence: Taking Women Seriously* (West Publishing, St. Paul, Minn., 1994), pp. 321–322. Portions of MacKinnon and Dworkin's "Model Ordinance" are reprinted on pp. 321–324 of that text. For a sympathetic overview of the testimony and the political maneuvering when the ordinance was being considered, see Paul Brest and Ann Vandenberg, "Politics, Feminism, and the Constitution: The Anti-Pornography Movement in Minneapolis", 39 *Stanford Law Review* 607 (1987).

[47] MacKinnon, *Feminism Unmodified*, p. 148.

[48] See, e.g. *ibid.* at pp. 148, 160, 172.

[49] See, e.g. *ibid.* at pp. 146–213.

[50] *American Booksellers Assoc. Inc. v Hudnut*, 771 F.2d 323 (7th Cir. 1985), affirmed mem., 475 U.S. 1001 (1986).

placing the anti-pornography proposal into a context of a more general feminist analysis:

"MacKinnon argues that men expropriate women's sexuality, that pornography increases the sexual appeal of the subordination of women, and that the subordination of women creates what we perceive and experience as gender differences. She argues that pornography is central to women's subordination, that it makes the subordination of women sexy and constantly reinforces and eroticizes the domination-subordination dynamic. The point of regulating pornography is not to make life a little less pleasant, but it is a step toward a fundamental transformation of the relations between men and women."[51]

It is important to note that on this issue, as on many of the more controversial topics, there have been feminist theorists on both sides of the issue: in the present case, opposing the MacKinnon-Dworkin proposal, and related restrictions on sexually-explicit speech, as well as supporting such restrictions.[52] Those opposing the restrictions on pornography offer a variety of arguments, including the claims that pornography helps to undermine conventional sexual morality which oppresses or confines women; that any government regulation would inevitably affect "good" or "liberating" pornography as much if not more than "bad" or "oppressive" pornography; and that some women enjoy creating or "consuming" pornography, even types of pornography that quite expressly show women enjoying pain or subordination (such as sado-masochistic pornography).[53]

Some of the debate for and against proposals like MacKinnon/Dworkin's turned on questions about autonomy and "false consciousness".[54] To the argument by some women that they actually enjoy making or reading the type of sexually explicit material that the MacKinnon/Dworkin ordinance would restrict, a common response is that these women's perceptions of enjoyment are themselves the product of the pervasively oppressive society in which they were brought up (the argument being that women, like slaves generations earlier, find what pleasure they

---

[51] Olsen, "Feminist Theory in Grand Style", at 1160 (footnote and page references omitted). The feminism criticism of pornography, that it is not "mere speech", but helps to create or constitute a social reality which subordinates women, parallels the analysis critical race theorists offer regarding "hate speech". See Mari J. Matsuda, Charles R. Lawrence III, Richard Delgado, and Kimberlè Williams Crenshaw, *Words That Wound: Critical Race Theory, Assaultive Speech, and the First Amendment* (Westview Press, Boulder, Colo., 1993).

[52] For views opposing restrictions on sexually explicit speech, see, *e.g.* Varda Burstyn ed., *Women Against Censorship* (Douglas & McIntyre, Ltd., Vancouver, 1985); Wendy McElroy, *XXX: A Woman's Right to Pornography* (St. Martin's Press, New York, 1995).

[53] These arguments are elaborated in the texts cited in the previous footnote.

[54] "False consciousness" is "[a]n inability to see things, especially social relations and relations of exploitation, as they really are." Blackburn, *The Oxford Dictionary of Philosophy*, p. 135.

can, and what meaning they can, within their situations, and may even convince themselves that they have chosen their path voluntarily).[55] About here is where one enters troubled and troubling areas.

As to the possibility of "false consciousness", on one hand, we recognize the experience from ourselves and others we have known well, where a person seems convinced (for some reason) that something was what she wanted or was in her best interests, when it really was not. We see the effects of advertisers, politicians, religious leaders, and others trying (and sometimes succeeding) to convince us what we "should" want. (If the process of trying to create new perceptions of need and desire never succeeded, then people would have long ago stopped spending the vast amount of time and money devoted to just such projects.)

On the other hand, the picture of there being a "real me" somewhere beneath all the selves that have been imposed by societal pressures (whether commercial, religious, political or otherwise), is not entirely convincing.[56] And even if in principle one could distinguish between the "real" self and its "real" interests and desires, and the brainwashed person of day-to-day life, how is this determination to be made and (perhaps more important) who is to make it?

CRITICAL RACE THEORY

By most accounts, critical race theory developed as an offshoot of critical legal studies in the late 1980s.[57] Though here, as elsewhere, there is more than one plausible characterization of a movement's history. One could just as easily state[58] that critical race theory had its roots in the 1970s, as theorists began to consider what had and had not been accomplished by the American Civil Rights Movement.

As with all the previous topics in this part (American legal realism, law and economics, critical legal studies, and feminist legal theory), it is hard to speak about critical race theory in general, as it is a label that has been accepted by or applied to a wide variety of theorists and analyses. With

---

[55] See, *e.g.* MacKinnon, *Feminism Unmodified*, pp. 218–219; Catherine MacKinnon, *Towards a Feminist Theory of the State* (Harvard University Press, Cambridge, Mass., 1989), pp. 148–154.

[56] Questioning the unity or solidity of the "self" is a theme commonly found among "postmodernist" writers, an approach discussed in Ch. 21.

[57] Angela Harris describes the "first annual Workshop on Critical Race Theory" as having occurred in July 1989 in Madison, Wisconsin. Angela P. Harris, "Foreword: The Jurisprudence of Reconstruction", 82 *California Law Review* 741 at 741 (1994).

[58] As a number of commentators have, see, *e.g.* Richard Delgado and Jean Stefancic, "Critical Race Theory: An Annotated Bibliography", 79 *Virginia Law Review* 461 at 461 (1993); Matsuda, Lawrence, Delgado and Crenshaw, *Words That Wound*, p. 3.

that disclaimer in mind, there are some things that can be said that seem to apply to much of the area.[59] Critical race theory can be understood as having two major strands. The first strand is the theme of racism: the claim that racism is pervasive in the legal system and in society, and that it can be uncovered in many allegedly neutral concepts, procedures and analytical approaches.[60] The second strand (related to, but logically separate from, the first) is that persons from minority ethnic groups (or at least those who have suffered because of their identity as a member of one of those groups) have distinctive views, perceptions, and experiences which are not properly recognized or fully discussed in mainstream or conventional discussions of the law (whether these discussions occur in courtrooms, law school classrooms, law review articles, or newspaper reports).[61]

As regards the first strand, critical race theorists often try to show how pervasive racism affects law and legal scholarship both in areas where race is near the surface,[62] and in areas where race would not, to most observers, immediately seem relevant.[63] Commentators have also considered the extent to which racial equality is no longer a realistic goal,[64] or, at least, the extent to which minorities should focus on means other than the courts or the law to attain their objectives.[65]

One natural focus of critical race scholarship has been affirmative action (also sometimes known as "positive discrimination" or "reverse discrimination")[66], favouring candidates for positions on the basis of their

---

[59] In their annotated bibliography of critical race theory (cited in the previous footnote), Richard Delgado and Jean Stefancic list 10 "themes" as common to or distinctive of critical race theory. A somewhat different listing of six "defining elements" of critical race theory is given in Matsuda, Lawrence, Delgado and Crenshaw, *Words That Wound*, pp. 6–7. The portrait of critical race theory offered in the text will cover some of the same ground, but necessarily in a somewhat sketchier way.

[60] See, *e.g.* Harris, "Foreword: The Jurisprudence of Reconstruction", pp. 770–771. This is connected with the interesting idea of "unconscious racism". See Charles R. Lawrence III, "The Id, the Ego and Equal Protection: Reckoning with Unconscious Racism", 39 *Stanford Law Review* 317 (1987).

[61] See, *e.g.* Matsuda, Lawrence, Delgado and Crenshaw, *Words That Wound*, p. 6

[62] See, *e.g.* Kimberlé Crenshaw, "Race Reform, and Retrenchment: Transformation and Legitimation in Antidiscrimination Law", 101 *Harvard Law Review* 1331 (1988); Lani Guinier, "The Triumph of Tokenism: The Voting Rights Act and the Theory of Black Electoral Success", 89 *Michigan Law Review* 1077 (1991).

[63] See, *e.g.* Patricia J. Williams, "Fetal Fictions: An Exploration of Property Archetypes in Racial and Gendered Contexts", 42 *Florida Law Review* 81 (1990); Stephen Carter, "When Victims Happen to Be Black", 97 *Yale Law Journal* 420 (1988).

[64] See Derrick Bell, "Racial Realism", 27 *Connecticut Law Review* 363 (1992).

[65] See Girardeau A. Spann, *Race Against the Court* (New York University Press, New York, 1993); Richard Delgado, "Rodrigo's Ninth Chronicle: Race, Legal Instrumentalism, and the Rule of Law", 143 *University of Pennsylvania Law Review* 379 (1994).

[66] On affirmative action generally, see, *e.g.* Robert K. Fullinwinder, "Affirmative Action", in E. N. Zalta ed., *Stanford Encyclopedia of Philosophy*, http://plato.stanford.edu (2001).

membership in a minority ethnic group.[67] While many writers have
sought to defend and legitimate such policies within a context in which
merit-based selection is strongly preferred and discrimination based on
race usually (and rightfully) criticized, other writers have offered a more
ambivalent response.[68] The topic of affirmative action brings together
aspects of the first strand of critical race theory—the pervasiveness of
racism within society (which can serve both as a justification for such policies, and an explanation why many such policies, in their current form,
may do more harm than good)—with aspects from the second strand—
the distinctive and valuable input that minority workers, professionals,
and academics can bring to their work settings (one of the justifications
offered for affirmative action policies).

As for the second strand, part of the argument is that group identity
and experience are so central a part of who we are and so strongly affect
how we perceive the world that it is important that there be a variety of
perspectives, so that all aspects of a situation are properly seen, and the
view of the majority or dominant group is not mistaken for objectivity or
universality.[69] While this is sometimes presented as part of a grand "postmodern" theory,[70] it need not be. The claim need be no more ambitious
or controversial than that those who have experienced racial discrimination all their life may have a perspective or insights on discrimination that
those who are part of the majority would not have. One critical race theorist, Milner Ball, described the articles of his critical race theory colleagues as, among other things, "teach[ing] us about the felt effects of law
and therefore something about its nature: on being an object of property,
on being hurt by constitutionally protected speech, on being a minority
member of a white law faculty."[71]

Relative to mainstream thought, the claims of critical race theorists
vary from what would be perceived as helpful and unsurprising to what
would be perceived as radical, divisive, or improbable. The unsurprising
side of the spectrum would include what has already been mentioned, the
claim that members of oppressed minority groups experience the law

---

[67] Affirmative action policies also often favor women over men, and there is some indica-
tion that women (not members of minority groups) have been the primary beneficiary of
affirmative action in the United States.

[68] See, e.g. Derrick Bell, "Xerces and the Affirmative Action Mystique", 57 *George Washington
Law Review* 1595 (1989); Richard Delgado, "Affirmative Action as a Majoritarian Device:
Or, Do You Really Want to be a Role Model", 89 *Michigan Law Review* 1222 (1991); Mari
Matsuda, "Affirmative Action and Legal Knowledge: Planting Seeds in Plowed-Up
Ground", 11 *Harvard Women's Law Journal* 1 (1988).

[69] See, e.g. Drucilla Cornell, "Loyalty and the Limits of Kantian Impartiality" (book
review), 107 *Harvard Law Review* 2081 (1994).

[70] On postmodernism, see Ch. 21.

[71] Milner Ball, "The Legal Academy and Minority Scholars", 103 *Harvard Law Review* 1855
at 1859 (1990) (footnote omitted).

differently compared to privileged members of the majority, and on that basis have distinctive ideas and perspectives to offer. By "experience the law", I mean the dealings with aspects of the legal systems people (other than lawyers and judges) have on a day-to-day basis. For members of minority groups, this may mean bullying or distrust by police officers, or daily moments of discrimination or humiliation by members of the majority (actions which may be illegal, but for which, as a practical matter, there is no remedy within the system).[72]

Along similar, relatively uncontroversial lines, critical race theorists have argued that since members of minority groups experience life differently from members of a majority, it is valuable to have ethnic diversity in law school classrooms, law school faculties, the police force, the judiciary and so on, for that diversity will tend to bring a healthy diversity of views and ideas. One commentator summarized the argument as follows: "Just as the servant knows more than the master, those 'on the bottom' of American society see more than those at the top."[73] As noted earlier, this is part of a standard argument for affirmative action (positive discrimination).

The more controversial claims (some of which are just radical reworkings of more accepted positions) would include the view that there are certain truths that are accessible to members of minority groups which are simply not accessible to members of the majority.[74] One critical race theorist wrote:

"Minority perspectives make explicit the need for fundamental change in the ways we think and construct knowledge. . . . Distinguishing the consciousness of racial minorities requires acknowledgment of the feelings and intangible modes of perception unique to those who have historically been socially, structurally, and intellectually marginalized in the United States."[75]

An equally controversial conclusion, based on more moderate premises, is that certain subjects can only be properly or fully discussed by members

---

[72] For judicial recognition of the importance of considering the perspective of the victim, see, *e.g. Lynch v Donnelly*, 465 U.S. 668 at 688–694 (1984) (O'Connor J., concurring) (on the importance of considering the perspective of religious minorities in considering whether a government action constituted an endorsement of (the majority) religion); *Ellison v Brady*, 924 F.2d 872 at 878–879 (9th Cir. 1991) (applying "the perspective of the victim", a "reasonable woman" test, in evaluating a claim of sexual harassment).

[73] See Harris, "Foreword: The Jurisprudence of Reconstruction", p. 769 (footnote omitted).

[74] *e.g.* Mari Matsuda, "Looking to the Bottom: Critical Legal Studies and Reparations", 22 *Harvard Civil Rights-Civil Liberties Law Review* 323 at 326, 346 (1987) ("the victims of racial oppression have distinct normative insights"; "Those who are oppressed in the present world can speak most eloquently of a better one").

[75] Robin Barnes, "Race Consciousness: The Thematic Content of Racial Distinctiveness in Critical Race Scholarship", 103 *Harvard Law Review* 1864 at 1864 (1990) (footnote omitted).

of particular groups, *e.g.* only members of minority ethnic groups should or can discuss the legal and moral aspects of racism.[76]

Beyond these two main strands, one might also locate two other themes that are relatively prominent within critical race theory[77]: first, the problem of "intersectionality"—how different affiliations and different oppressions (*e.g.* race and gender) can interact[78]; and second, an emphasis on the perspective of the poor and marginalized.[79]

Along with the substantive strands to critical race theory, one can also note that the writings in this movement are often stylistically distinctive. The use of "narrative" or a "storytelling" approach in academic writings, though by no means exclusive to critical race theory,[80] is quite common within the movement's writings.[81] There are at least two alternative purposes for using storytelling in the place of more conventional normative argument.[82] First, a rich narrative can help people from the majority community begin to understand what it is like to experience the legal system as a member of a minority community[83]; secondly, stories and fables can be used to undermine oversimplified views about human motivation.[84] One might wonder about the claims a *fictional* story or fable might have on our view of the world. First, even though fictional, stories can help us learn the perspective and experiences of people whose like we might never get to know in our secluded daily lives. Secondly, a fictional story or fable will convince us to the extent that it "rings true"; thus, whether our view of the world is affected by William Golding's *Lord of the Flies* or Derrick Bell's *And We Are Not Saved* depends on whether we believe

---

[76] A position criticized in Randall Kennedy "Racial Critiques of Legal Academia", 102 *Harvard Law Review* 1745 at 1778–1787 (1989).

[77] I am grateful to Alex M. Johnson, Jr., for pointing out the importance of these themes within critical race theory.

[78] See, *e.g.* Angela P. Harris, "Race and Essentialism in Feminist Legal Theory", 42 *Stanford Law Review* 581 (1990).

[79] Mari Matsuda, "Looking to the Bottom: Critical Legal Studies and Reparations", 22 *Harvard Civil Rights-Civil Liberties Law Review* 323 (1987).

[80] See, *e.g.* William N. Eskridge Jr., "Gaylegal Narratives", 46 *Stanford Law Review* 607 (1994); Kathryn Abrams, "Hearing the Call of Stories", 79 *California Law Review* 971 (1991).

[81] See *e.g.* Delgado and Stefancic, "Critical Race Theory: An Annotated Bibliography", at 462; Richard Delgado, "Legal Storytelling: Storytelling for Oppositionists and Others: A Plea for Narrative", 87 *Michigan Law Review* 2411 (1989). Narrative has also been important in feminist legal theory for roughly the same reasons it is central to critical race theory. See, *e.g.* Martha Fineman and Nancy Thomadsen eds, *At the Boundaries of Law* (Routledge, New York, 1991), pp. 1–58 ("Perspectives from the Personal").

[82] Harris, "Foreword: The Jurisprudence of Reconstruction", at 755–757.

[83] Some of the best examples of such uses of narrative are in Patricia J. Williams, *The Alchemy of Race and Rights* (Harvard University Press, Cambridge, Mass., 1991).

[84] Among the other claims made for "narrative" are that it "serves to create and confirm identity, both individual and collective", and that it helps to "speak to" our emotions and spiritual feelings as well as our rationality. Harris, "Foreword: The Jurisprudence of Reconstruction", at 780–781 (footnote omitted).

that the characters in those "fables" are acting as real people would in the situations described.[85]

The argument against narrative as scholarship is that it can encourage or cover up a lack of rigour about facts, correlation, or causation, and that narrative, while encouraging empathy often does so in a one-sided manner (e.g. if it shows the plight of the tenant, it may fail to show the perspective of the landlord).[86]

The nature of critical race theory is such that it is unsurprising that a growing number of narrower community-based or group-based claims are developing from within critical race theory or in analogy to it: foremost among these would be "critical latino/a theory" (also known as "LatCrit theory") and "queer theory" (the latter referring to homosexuals).[87] If one's way of perceiving the world is formed in large part by the culture and community in which one grew up and the type of discrimination one has faced, it seems logical to conclude not only that minorities perceive the world differently from the majority group, but also that (e.g.) Latinos and Asian-Americans perceive the world differently from African-Americans, and one can keep pushing the point. Chicanos (Mexican-Americans) can argue (and have argued) that their experiences and culture are distinctly different from other Latinos, and similarly for Americans of West Indian descent in contrast to other "African-Americans". The argument can also be made that women within these groups experience life distinctly different from men[88], and homosexuals and bisexuals different from heterosexuals (and that homosexuals who are also members of ethnic minorities experience life different from white homosexuals[89]). The question remains, and becomes more urgent with

[85] See William Golding, *Lord of the Flies* (Perigee, New York, 1954); Derrick Bell, *And We Are Not Saved: The Elusive Quest for Racial Justice* (Basic Books, New York, 1987).
[86] See Daniel A. Farber and Suzanna Sherry, "Telling Stories Out of School: An Essay on Legal Narratives", 45 *Stanford Law Review* 807 (1993); Posner, *Overcoming Law*, pp. 368–384 (reviewing Williams, *The Alchemy of Race and Rights*).
[87] For LatCrit theory, see, e.g. Symposium: "LatCrit Theory: Latinas/os and the Law", 85 *California Law Review* 1087–1686 (1997), 10 *La Raza Law Journal* 1–600 (1997); see also Richard Delgado and Jean Stefancic ed., *The Latino Condition: A Critical Reader* (New York University Press, New York, 1998); for "queer theory", see, e.g. Francisco Valdes, "Queers, Sissies, Dykes, and Tomboys: Deconstructing the Conflation of 'Sex,' 'Gender,' and 'Sexual Orientation' in Euro-American Law and Society", 83 *California Law Review* 3 (1995); William N. Eskridge, Jr., *Gaylaw: Challenging the Apartheid of the Closet* (Harvard University Press, Cambridge, Mass., 1999). There are numerous other efforts towards group-based on community-based claims: see, e.g. Robert S. Chang, "Toward an Asian American Legal Scholarship: Critical Race Theory, Post-Structuralism, and Narrative Space", 81 *California Law Review* 1244 (1993).
[88] See, e.g. Adrien Katherine Wing ed., *Critical Race Feminism: A Reader* (New York University Press, New York, 1997); Adrien Katherine Wing ed., *Global Critical Race Feminism: An International Reader* (New York University Press, New York, 2000).
[89] See, e.g. Darren Lenard Hutchinson, "Out Yet Unseen: A Racial Critique of Gay and Lesbian Legal Theory and Political Discourse", 29 *Connecticut Law Review* 561 (1997).

each further fragmentation: are these differences "essential"—does everyone within the stated group have, and have necessarily, the same perspective and the same characteristics[90]; and is it possible, with sufficient dialogue and explanation, for persons of one group to understand the views and values of those of another group?

A related complication, both with critical race theory and with many of its related identity-based theories, is that the boundaries of these approaches often becomes blurred. Frequently there is no agreed methodology, and all that connects the members of these schools of thought is membership in an oppressed group, combined with a focus on issues affecting that group. However, that description may cover many writers who do not consider themselves part of the school in question.[91]

OTHER CRITICAL APPROACHES

There are a variety of other critical approaches to law, for example:

(1) Theories of law based on traditional Marxist teachings. Critical legal studies, discussed earlier, tended to build upon Marx's work, but to reject traditional Marxist approaches (for example, preferring the Gramscian idea that the ruling classes use law to help legitimate unjust practices, rather than the traditional Marxist idea that law consistently works for the direct benefit of the powerful). However, one can still find traditional Marxist critiques of law.[92]

(2) The application of sociology to law, known variously as "socio-legal studies" and "law and society" has a long history of offering empirically grounded critiques of current laws and legal practices, and suggestions for change. While sociology aims to be descriptive and morally neutral, many of those who identify with "socio-legal studies" or "law and society" have "progressive" or radical views, and so these movements have often been thought of as more "critical" than scientific.[93]

---

[90] For an important and influential criticism from critical race theory on the apparent essentialism of some feminist writing, see Angela P. Harris, "Race and Essentialism in Feminist Legal Theory", 42 *Stanford Law Review* 581 (1990).

[91] For example, Frank Wu, who wrote an excellent book on issues regarding racism against Asian-Americans, *Yellow: Race in America Beyond Black and White* (Basic Books, New York, 2002), is frequently described as being (or "accused" of being) a critical race theorist, but he does not describe himself as part of that school.

[92] See, *e.g.* Evgeny B. Pashukanis, *The General Theory of Law and Marxism* (3rd ed., Transaction Publishers, Piscataway, N.J., 2001) (3rd ed. originally published, 1927); Jeffrey Reiman, "The Marxian Critique of Criminal Justice", 6 *Criminal Justice Ethics* 30 (1987).

[93] See, *e.g.* Roger Cotterrell, "Subverting Orthodoxy, Making Law Central: A View of Sociolegal Studies", 29 *Journal of Law and Society* 632 (2002).

(3) Theories grounded on the work of Jürgen Habermas, and his work on generating moral and political values from the objective or the norm of an "ideal speech situation."[94]

(4) Postmodern legal theory, which is discussed in greater detail in Ch. 21.

Suggested Further Readings

CRITICAL LEGAL STUDIES

James Boyle ed., *Critical Legal Studies* (New York University Press, New York, 1994).

Critical Legal Studies Symposium, 36 *Stanford Law Review* 1–674 (1984) (a wide-ranging collection, which includes articles on the history of CLS and articles critical of CLS, as well as pieces explaining or applying CLS ideas).

Douglas Hay, Peter Linebaugh, John G. Rule, E.P. Thompson and Cal Winslow, *Albion's Fatal Tree* (Penguin, Middlesex, 1975).

Alan Hunt, "The Theory of Critical Legal Studies", 6 *Oxford Journal of Legal Studies* 1 (1986).

David Kairys, ed., *The Politics of Law* (3rd ed., Pantheon, New York, 1998) (contributors include Duncan Kennedy, Robert Gordon, Morton Horwitz, Mark Kelman, Peter Gabel, and Frances Olsen).

Mark Kelman, *A Guide to Critical Legal Studies* (Harvard University Press, Cambridge, Mass., 1987).

Duncan Kennedy, *A Critique of Adjudication (fin de siècle)* (Harvard University Press, Cambridge, Mass., 1997).

Roberto Mangabeira Unger, *The Critical Legal Studies Movement* (Harvard University Press, Cambridge, Mass., 1986).

FEMINIST LEGAL THEORY

Katharine T. Bartlett and Rosanne Kennedy ed., *Feminist Legal Theory: Readings in Law and Gender* (Westview Press, Boulder, Colo., 1991).

Nancy E. Dowd and Michelle S. Jacobs ed., *Feminist Legal Theory: An Anti-Essentialist Reader* (New York University Press, New York, 2003).

Martha Fineman and Nancy Thomadsen ed., *At the Boundaries of Law: Feminism and Legal Theory* (Routledge, New York, 1991).

Carol Gilligan, *In a Different Voice: Psychological Theory and Women's Development* (Harvard University Press, Cambridge, Mass., 1982, rev. ed., 1993)

---

[94] See, *e.g.* Jürgen Habermas, *Between Facts and Norms: Contributions to a Discourse Theory of Law and Democracy* (W. Rehg, trans., MIT Press, Cambridge, Mass., 1996); Michel Rosenfeld and Andrew Arato eds, *Habermas on Law and Democracy: Critical Exchanges* (University of California Press, Berkeley, 1998).

Christine Littleton, "Feminist Jurisprudence: The Difference Method Makes", 41 *Stanford Law Review* 751 (1989).

Catharine MacKinnon, *Feminism Unmodified* (Harvard University Press, Cambridge, Mass., 1987).

Patricia Smith, "Feminist Jurisprudence and the Nature of Law", in *A Companion to the Philosophy of Law and Legal Theory* (D. Patterson ed., Blackwell, Oxford, 1996), pp. 302–310.

Patricia Smith ed., *Feminist Jurisprudence* (Oxford University Press, Oxford, 1993).

D. Kelly Weisberg ed., *Feminist Legal Theory: Foundations* (Temple University Press, Philadelphia, 1993).

CRITICAL RACE THEORY

Derrick Bell, *And We Are Not Saved* (Basic Books, New York, 1987).

Kimberlé Crenshaw, Neil Gotanda, Gary Peller, and Kendall Thomas eds, *Critical Race Theory: The Key Writings That Formed the Movement* (The New Press, New York, 1995).

Richard Delgado, "The Imperial Scholar: Reflections on a Review of Civil Rights Literature", 132 *University of Pennsylvania Law Review* 561 (1984).

Richard Delgado ed., *Critical Race Theory: The Cutting Edge* (Temple University Press, Philadelphia, 1995) (containing 50 articles on a wide range of topics from many different authors).

Richard Delgado and Jean Stefancic, *Critical Race Theory: An Introduction* (New York University Press, New York, 2001).

Richard Delgado and Jean Stefancic eds, *The Latino/a Condition: A Critical Reader* (New York University Press, New York, 1998).

Daniel A. Farber and Suzanna Sherry, *Beyond All Reason: The Radical Assault on Truth in American Law* (Oxford University Press, New York, 1997).

Randall Kennedy, "Racial Critiques of Legal Academia", 102 *Harvard Law Review* 1745 (1989).

Girardeau A. Spann, *Race Against the Court: The Supreme Court and Minorities in Contemporary America* (New York University Press, New York, 1993).

Symposium: Critical Race Theory, 82 *California Law Review* 741–1125 (1994).

Francisco Valdes, Jerome McCristal Culp and Angela P. Harris eds, *Crossroads, Directions, and a New Critical Race Theory* (Philadelphia: Temple University Press, 2002).

Patricia J. Williams, *The Alchemy of Race and Rights* (Harvard University Press, Cambridge, Mass., 1991).

OTHER CRITICAL APPROACHES

Richard L. Abel ed., *The Law & Society Reader* (New York University Press, New York, 1995).

Roger Cotterrell, *The Sociology of Law: An Introduction* (2nd ed., Butterworths, London, 1992).

Evgeny B. Pashukanis, *The General Theory of Law and Marxism* (3rd ed., Transaction Publishers, Piscataway, N.J., 2001) (3rd ed. originally published, 1927)

Chapter Twenty

Law and Literature

It was perhaps inevitable, during times when legal academics more and more frequently sought answers in other disciplines, that many of them would focus on literature and literary theory Speaking constructively, much of literary studies, like much of legal studies, involves the interpretation of texts and the problems that come with interpretation; thus it would not be surprising if one field had something to teach the other. Speaking cynically, reading and writing about Charles Dickens or Franz Kafka will almost always be more interesting than reading and writing about the Rule Against Perpetuities or Bills of Exchange.

It is not only recently that legal commentators and other academics have noticed the connections between law and literature. Benjamin Cardozo, a major figure from the "New Deal"/American legal realist period wrote an article decades ago on the literary styles of judicial opinions[1]; and in the early 1970s, William R. Bishin and Christopher D. Stone mixed literary and philosophical materials in an influential casebook that ranged from jurisprudence to legal ethics.[2] At roughly the same time, James Boyd White published what many consider the first book of the law and literature movement, *The Legal Imagination.*[3] However, it was only from the early 1980s on that the supply of articles and books in the area went from occasional to plentiful.[4]

INTERPRETATION AND CONSTRAINT

One thing which seems to connect literature and law is the process of interpretation: finding meaning in or from texts. The question then

---

[1] Benjamin N. Cardozo, "Law and Literature", 14 *Yale Review* 699 (1925).
[2] William R. Bishin and Christopher D. Stone, *Law, Language and Ethics: An Introduction to Law and Legal Method* (Foundation Press, Mineola, N.Y., 1972).
[3] James Boyd White, *The Legal Imagination: Studies in the Nature of Legal Thought and Expression* (Little, Brown, and Co., Boston, 1973).
[4] See, *e.g.* Symposium: "Law and Literature", 60 *Texas Law Review* 373–586 (1982).

becomes: is the interpretation which readers of novels do, or which literary theorists practice, the same interpretation that is done by judges and others trying to understand the law?[5]

One of the strongest advocates for the two kinds of interpretation being the same is Ronald Dworkin. Dworkin has argued that "constructive interpretation"—an interpretation that works to make the object being interpreted the best it can be of the genre it is—is the correct approach both to all forms of artistic interpretation and to understanding social practices, including law.[6]

Dworkin, prior to fully developing the concept of "constructive interpretation, offered another connection between law and literature, and between legal and literary interpretation. He asserted that a judge acting within a common law system was like one author in a chain of authors collectively writing a novel, with each person adding a "chapter" to what came before.[7] The subsequent authors are constrained by what has been written before, but still retain a significant level of freedom. However, within that freedom the authors have an obligation to make the text the best it can be. Similarly for judges who are constrained—to a point—by precedent, and who are to make the law the best it can be.

Arguing the contrary position, Richard Posner claims that while there might he surface similarities between law and literature, as both centre on the interpretation of texts, there are institutional differences and differences of purpose that mean that law has little to learn from literary theory.[8] A text can be good literature in part *because it is* subject to many possible interpretations; by contrast, a statute or judicial decision which was subject to many equally tenable interpretations would be "bad law". Posner also offers a second contrast: one need not know anything about the author's intentions to appreciate good literature, and some schools of literary interpretation *(e.g.* "New Criticism") argue strongly against reference to authorial intentions. By contrast, it is an important aspect of the governmental structure that judges applying laws try to determine the intentions of the lawmakers. The lawmakers in such circumstances are

---

[5] For an early discussion on the subject, see Kenneth S. Abraham. "Statutory Interpretation and Literary Theory: Some Common Concerns of an Unlikely Pair", 32 *Rutgers Law Review* 676 (1979).

[6] See Dworkin, *Law's Empire*, pp. 45–68. Dworkin's general approach to law and legal theory is discussed in Ch. 7.

[7] See Dworkin, *A Matter of Principle*, pp. 158–162. In the world of literature, actual chain novels are rare, but they do exist. See, *e.g.* Carl Hiaasen, *et al.*, *Naked Came the Manatee* (Putnam, New York, 1996); Roddy Doyle, *et al.*, *Yeats is Dead* (Joseph O'Connor ed., Alfred A. Knopf, New York, 2001); William Bernhardt, *et al.*, *Natural Suspect* (Ballantine Books, New York, 2001).

[8] See Richard A. Posner, *Law and Literature* (Harvard University Press, Cambridge, Mass. 1988), pp. 209–268. (A revised edition of this book appeared in 1998, in which some of the relevant discussion has been excised or modified.)

trying to send a message, and judges are acting merely as an agent of the legislature, and it would be illegitimate for them to interpret those laws contrary to its intentions (even if doing so would make the laws morally better).[9] Posner summarizes the differences, as he sees them:

"The judge is trying to decode a communication from his superiors in the constitutional hierarchy and must use all available information, including whatever can be learned of the conscious intentions of those who wrote the provision that is being interpreted. The test of a literary interpretation, in contrast, can be purely pragmatic and utilitarian—does it make the work of literature richer, more instructive, more beautiful?"[10]

Another debate falling within the broad scope of law, literary theory, and interpretation involves the extent to which interpreters (be they legal officials or readers interpreting novels) are constrained in their interpretations by the texts being interpreted. Against what might seem the conventional view, that texts strongly constrain interpretation, Owen Fiss offered a fairly radical view of the matter. His argument was that the text only constrains (and then only in part, allowing some discretion) when one takes into account the "disciplining rules" of the institutional setting in which the interpreter is acting.[11] Thus, an American or English judge interpreting the text is constrained by the words of the text *combined with* the rules accepted within the relevant legal system regarding the relative weight to be given various elements of the text (and the context)—for example, that system's conventions regarding statutory interpretation.

However, for Stanley Fish, replying to Fiss, this position was still not radical enough.[12] For Fish, "disciplining rules" or other codified guidelines could hardly serve as the means for constraining the interpretation of primary texts, for they are themselves texts. If texts are not self-interpreting for novels or statutes, why would they be for the codified rules for reading statutes or novels? Fish's alternative is that "being situated within a field of practice"—having been trained within a particular practice and discipline—one internalizes particular ways of perceiving, conceptualizing, and discussing the objects of the practice (whether they be

---

[9] In the original edition of his text, Posner stops short of endorsing an "original intent" approach to interpreting legal texts:
"I admit the relevance of intention about intention and hence the propriety of treating broadly worded statutory and constitutional phrases . . . as delegations to the judiciary to create and not merely determine meaning."
Richard A. Posner, *Law and Literature* (Harvard University Press, Cambridge, Mass., 1988), p. 245.
[10] *ibid.*
[11] See Owen Fiss, "Objectivity and Interpretation", 34 *Stanford Law Review* 739 (1982).
[12] See Stanley Fish, "Fish v Fiss", 36 *Stanford Law Review* 1325 (1984), reprinted in *Doing What Comes Naturally* (Clarendon Press, Oxford, 1989), pp. 120–140.

novels, statutes, or constitutions).[13] These internalized standards, values, and ways of perceiving are, Fish asserts, both necessary and sufficient to explain interpretive constraints.

Some commentators treat interpretation as largely or entirely unconstrained. Sanford Levinson, heeding the lessons of some philosophers and literary critics, once somewhat reluctantly concluded that there were no effective constraints on interpretation and no bases for labelling one interpretation correct and another incorrect.[14] It hardly needs remarking that a view that judges are largely or entirely unconstrained in their interpretations of constitutions, statutes, and precedents creates significant problems of legitimacy. The problems would come both from the anti-democratic nature of the decisions (a problem which would not arise if the judges were merely applying the clear meaning or clear intentions of democratically elected lawmakers), and from "Rule of Law" issues (if interpretation is unconstrained, it is likely also unpredictable—and decisions affecting people's liberty and property would be made without any sort of due notice).

CRITICS

There have been a number of criticisms of law and literature as a movement, and of the values implicit in the movement. The following is a sample of those criticisms.

Robert Cover worried that an excessive emphasis on the subtle points of literary theory and its possible applications to legal interpretation might cause us to stop seeing the way that legal interpretation in practice is not a genteel academic discussion of theory, but rather a practice which has drastic consequences every day. He famously began his article, "Violence and the Word": "Legal interpretation takes place in a field of pain and death."[15] Legal interpretation is, as a practical matter, about the signalling and the justification of violence; for such purposes, good institutional design and an effective use of ritual and symbol are likely at least as important as the persuasiveness of one's "interpretations".[16] As a connected point, Cover states that it is probably no accident that the American legal system (and many others) require a certain level of con-

---

[13] See Fish, "Fish v Fiss", at 1330–1332, 1339–1347, see also Stanley Fish, "Dennis Martinez and the Uses of Theory", 96 *Yale Law Journal* 1773 (1987), reprinted in *Doing What Comes Naturally* (Clarendon Press, Oxford, 1989), pp. 372–398.

[14] Sanford Levinson, "Law as Literature", 60 *Texas Law Review* 373 (1982).

[15] Robert M. Cover, "Violence and the Word", 95 *Yale Law Journal* 1601 (1986) (footnote omitted).

[16] See *ibid.* at 1618–1625. For a response to Cover, see James Boyd White, "What Can a Lawyer Learn from Literature" (book review), 102 *Harvard Law Review* 2014 at 2045–2046 (1989).

sensus before significant punishments are imposed—the trial court's decision must be affirmed on appeal, and/or at least two members of a multijudge appellate panel must agree. The Dworkinian image of a single judge with his or her grand vision of the legal system[17] does not fit the practice; because the agreement of multiple judges is required, the decision rendered, and the justifications offered, are likely to reflect the compromise of a variety of views.[18]

Robin West, like Cover, emphasizes the fact that adjudication is not, or not only, interpretation, but is (also) an act of power.[19] In a related point, she argues that interpretations, both literary and legal, but especially legal, tend to express or incorporate the perspective of a particular group. Those who do not share that perspective are excluded and silenced by the interpretation.[20] Holding one view of a constitution, a statute, or a society's traditions as correct, while rejecting contending views, both reflects and strengthens the power of the winning side.

MISCELLANEOUS CONNECTIONS

(1) An important connection between law and literature is the move towards the use of narrative within (or "as") legal scholarship, a move discussed in Ch. 19.[21] This has taken a number of forms: *e.g.* biography or autobiography as a means of making a point with implications for law or legal theory[22]; the use of fable to make comparable points[23]; and the use of fictional or factual stories to illustrate conundrums within doctrine.[24]

---

[17] See the discussion of Dworkin's legal theory in Ch. 7.
[18] See Cover, "Violence and the Word", at 1624–1628; Bix, *Law, Language and Legal Determinacy*, pp. 111–118; see also Cass R. Sunstein, "Incompletely Theorized Agreements", 108 *Harvard Law Review* 1733 (1995) (discussing how the need to secure agreement on a result and on low-level principles works to discourage judges from putting forward grand theories).
[19] See Robin West, "Adjudication is Not Interpretation: Some Reservations about the Law-as-Literature Movement", 54 *Tennessee Law Review* 203 (1987), reprinted in *Narrative, Authority, and Law* (University of Michigan Press, Ann Arbor, 1993). pp. 89–176. For a response from within the law and literature movement, see, *e.g.* James Boyd White, "Law and Literature: 'No Manifesto'", 39 *Mercer Law Review* 739 at 746–749 (1988).
[20] See West, *Caring for Justice*, pp. 180–188.
[21] See also Symposium: "Legal Storytelling", 87 *Michigan Law Review* 2073–2494 (1989) (which includes contributions by Patricia Williams, David Luban, Mari Matsuda, Derrick Bell, and Richard Delgado); Anthony G. Amsterdam and Jerome S. Bruner, *Minding the Law* (Harvard University Press, Cambridge, Mass., 2000).
[22] See, e.g. Williams, *The Alchemy of Race and Rights*.
[23] See, e.g. Bell, *And We Are Not Saved*.
[24] See, *e.g.* Norval Morris, *The Brothel Boy and Other Parables of the Law* (Oxford University Press, Oxford, 1992).

(2) The inverse point comes from commentators who emphasize the extent to which narrative, storytelling, and "translation" are already prevalent and important parts of legal practice: *e.g.* the way effective advocates mold and colour facts to "tell a story" to persuade a judge or jury; and the way that we must "translate" law when applying it to circumstances that were not foreseen when the law was formulated.[25]

(3) There has been interesting work done on a literary-type analysis of judicial writing: *e.g.* on the rhetorical tricks used by judges to make their opinions more persuasive.[26]

(4) A somewhat different take on the connection between law and literature comes from those who believe that fiction, at least well-written fiction, is useful to moral education, and is particularly recommended for those who judge others. The argument is that literature is valuable for gaining empathy, and empathy valuable for effective judging and moral analysis.[27]

(5) Finally, sometimes included in "law and literature" are analyses of the way lawyers or the legal system are portrayed in literature or in popular culture,[28] or the way that legal questions may serve as important plot elements in works of literature.[29]

Suggested Further Readings

Peter Brooks and Paul Gewirtz eds, *Law's Stories: Narrative and Rhetoric in the Law* (Yale University Press, New Haven, 1996).

---

[25] See, *e.g.* Robert Weisberg, "Proclaiming Trials as Narratives: Premises and Pretenses", in *Law's Stories: Narrative and Rhetoric in Law* (P. Brooks and P. Gewirtz eds, Yale University Press, New Haven, 1996), pp. 61–83; James Boyd White, *Justice as Translation* (University of Chicago Press, Chicago, 1990).

[26] See, *e.g.* Posner, *Law and Literature: A Misunderstood Relation*, pp. 281–299; Richard H. Weisberg, "How Judges Speak: Some Lessons on Adjudication in *Billy Budd, Sailor* with an Application to Justice Rehnquist", 57 *New York University Law Review* 1 (1982); Sanford Levinson, "The Rhetoric of the Judicial Opinion", in *Law's Stories: Narrative and Rhetoric in Law* (P. Brooks and P. Gewirtz eds, Yale University Press, New Haven, 1996), pp. 187–205.

[27] See Nussbaum, *Poetic Justice*; see also Robin West, "Law and Fancy" (book review), 95 *Michigan Law Review* 1851 (1997); and Thomas Morawetz, "Empathy and Judgment" (book review), 8 *Yale Journal of Law & the Humanities* 517 (1996). Both West and Morawetz review *Poetic Justice*, and argue against some of its central points.

[28] See, *e.g.* Richard H. Weisberg, "The Quest for Silence: Faulkner's Lawyer in a Comparative Setting", 4 *Mississippi College Law Journal* 193 (1984); David Ray Papke, "The Advocate's Malaise: Contemporary American Lawyer Novels", 38 *Journal of Legal Education* 413 (1988).

[29] See, *e.g.* G. H. Treitel, "Jane Austen and the Law", 100 *Law Quarterly Review* 549 at 557–584 (1984).

Stanley Fish, *Doing What Comes Naturally: Change, Rhetoric, and the Practice of Theory in Literary and Legal Studies* (Clarendon Press, Oxford, 1989).

Sanford Levinson and Steven Mailloux eds, *Interpreting Law and Literature* (Northwestern University Press, Evanston, Ill., 1988).

Richard A. Posner, *Law and Literature: A Misunderstood Relation* (Harvard University Press, Cambridge, Mass., rev. ed., 1998).

Symposium: "Law and Literature", 60 *Texas Law Review* 373–586 (1982).

James Boyd White, *Heracles' Bow: Essays on the Rhetoric and Poetics of Law* (University of Wisconsin Press, Madison, 1985), especially Chs 2, 5 and 6.

—, *Justice as Translation: An Essay in Cultural and Legal Criticism* (University of Chicago Press, Chicago, 1990).

Chapter Twenty One

Pragmatism and Postmodernism

Pragmatism and postmodernism are joined in their rejection of traditional or conventional ideas about truth and justification. The critical (and sometimes dismissive) attitude towards traditional forms of analysis is shared, as are some of the arguments used in the criticism. However, the two approaches quickly diverge, both in tone and in conclusion.[1]

Pragmatism focuses on success and achievement, on "what works", while postmodernism, in most of its incarnations, celebrates, or at least emphasizes, the fragmentary, the incoherent, the irrational, and the paradoxical.[2]

PRAGMATISM

One must distinguish philosophical pragmatism, a movement primarily of the early decades of the twentieth century, from pragmatism in law, though there is some overlap. Philosophical pragmatism was primarily an American movement, whose important figures included Charles Sanders Peirce (1839–1914), John Dewey (1859–1952), and William James (1842–1910), brother of author Henry James.[3] Philosophical pragmatism

---

[1] For one discussion of the overlap and differences between pragmatism and postmodernism (what the authors in the piece call "post-structuralism"—for some, "post-structuralism" is a distinct movement, one focused particularly on criticizing "structuralism", but that is not the way the term is used in this article), see Margaret Jane Radin and Frank Michelman, "Pragmatist and Poststructuralist Critical Legal Practice", 139 *University of Pennsylvania Law Review* 1019 (1991).

[2] For an analysis that combines deconstruction and paradox-centered thinking on one side, and political, legal and moral philosophy on the other, see Kramer, *Critical Legal Theory and the Challenge of Feminism.*

[3] Though some commentators trace the origins of pragmatism to the English moral and political philosopher, Jeremy Bentham (1748–1832), with his view that actions should be evaluated (solely) in terms of the good or evil consequences that they produce.

There are prominent *modern* philosophers who have labeled themselves as "pragmatists", in particular, Richard Rorty (1931–). See, *e.g.* Richard Rorty, *Philosophy and the Mirror of Nature* (Princeton University Press, Princeton, 1979).

principally offered an unconventional approach to meaning and truth. This approach might be summarized: (a) that the meaning of a doctrine is equivalent to the practical effects or experimental results of adhering to it; and (b) that something is true to the extent that it succeeds (in a broad sense) over the long term.[4] Science and the scientific method were often presented as the best examples of (and best arguments for) pragmatism: theories which "worked"—which yielded useful predictions or beneficial innovations were considered "true", while those which did not were discarded.

There was a substantial overlap between philosophical pragmatism and legal pragmatism in the early years of the twentieth century:

(a) Oliver Wendell Holmes Jr was friends with many of the prominent philosophical pragmatists, and his work on law expresses similar ideas;

(b) the philosophical pragmatist John Dewey "crossed over" to write two important law review articles[5]; and

(c) some of the important writers in American legal realism (see Ch. 17), as well as their immediate predecessors, used language and arguments borrowed from the philosophical pragmatists (even if the connection was sometimes not acknowledged).

On the last point, consider the following from Roscoe Pound:

"[Legal] rules are not prescribed and administered for their own sake, but rather to further social ends. An exposition of how they are prescribed and administered is inadequate. The problem is not merely how law-making and law-administering functions are exercised, but also how they may be exercised so as best to achieve their purpose, and what conception of these functions by those who perform them will conduce best thereto. Here, certainly, the pragmatic criterion is sound. The true juristic theory, the true juristic method, is one that brings forth good works.[6]

[L]egal precepts should be worked out and should be tested by their results, by their practical application, and not solely by logical deduction from principles derived by historical study of Roman and Germanic law."[7]

---

[4] See, e.g. Ted Honderich ed., *The Oxford Companion to Philosophy* (Oxford University Press, Oxford, 1995), pp. 710–713 (entry on 'pragmatism").

[5] John Dewey, "Logical Method and the Law", 10 *Cornell Law Quarterly* 17 (1924); John Dewey, "The Historical Background of Corporate Legal Personality", 35 *Yale Law Journal* 655 (1926).

[6] Pound, "The Scope and Purpose of Sociological Jurisprudence" Pt I, at 598; see also Cardozo, *The Nature of the Judicial Process*, p. 98 ("Few rules in our time are so well established that they may not be called upon to justify their existence as means adapted to an end.").

[7] Pound, "The Scope and Purpose of Sociological jurisprudence" Pt II, at 142.

Consider also the following from Oliver Wendell Holmes, Jr.:

"You can give any conclusion a logical form. You always can imply a condition in a contract. But why do you imply it? It is because of some belief as to the practice of the community or of a class, or because of some opinion as to policy, or, in short, because of some attitude of yours upon a matter not capable of exact quantitative measurement, and therefore not capable of founding exact logical conclusions. Such matters really are battle grounds where the means do not exist for determinations that shall be good for all time, and where the decision can do no more than embody the preference of a given body in a given time and place. We do not realize how large a part of our law is open to reconsideration upon a slight change in the habit of the public mind. No concrete proposition is self-evident, no matter how ready we may be to accept it . . ."[8]

In both quotations, the echoes of philosophical pragmatism are clear. Modern legal pragmatism is related to the philosophical pragmatism of decades ago, though the connection sometimes seems loose, and at times no more than a family resemblance. Many of the legal scholars who called themselves "pragmatists" seem to be referring more to the colloquial term than to the philosophical school—in the sense that most modern business people like to consider themselves "pragmatic": worried about "what works", worried about "the bottom line", not caught up in senseless philosophical hair-splitting, and so on. At the same time, other legal pragmatists take quite seriously the connections between their work and the works of the philosophical pragmatists[9] (either with the original philosophical pragmatists Dewey, Peirce, and James, or with the modern philosophical pragmatists, e.g. Richard Rorty and Hilary Putnam[10]).

One of the theorists at the forefront of the self-proclaimed "pragmatists" in legal theory has been, somewhat surprisingly, Richard Posner.[11]

---

[8] Holmes, "The Path of the Law", at 466. Earlier in the passage, Holmes wrote: "The language of judicial decision is mainly the language of logic. And the logical method and form flatter that longing for certainty and for repose which is in every human mind. But certainty generally is an illusion, and repose is not the destiny of man." *Ibid.* at 465–466.

[9] For an insightful critique of the view that legal theory can learn much from pragmatism, see Brian Z. Tamanaha, *Realistic Socio-Legal Theory: Pragmatism and A Social Theory of Law* (Clarendon Press, Oxford, 1997), pp. 35–57.

[10] See, *e.g.* Hilary Putnam, *Words & Life* (J. Conant ed., Harvard University Press, Cambridge, Mass., 1994), pp. 151–241.

[11] See Posner, *The Problems of Jurisprudence*, pp. 454–469 ("A Pragmatist Manifesto"); Posner, *Overcoming Law*, pp. 4–21. For considerations of Posner's credentials as a pragmatist, see Eric Rakowski, "Posner's Pragmatism" (book review), 104 *Harvard Law Review* 1681 (1991); Stanley Fish, "Almost Pragmatism: Richard Posner's Jurisprudence" (book review), 57 *University of Chicago Law Review* 1447 (1990).

Another legal theorist, of a quite different school, who has recently taken up the "pragmatist" label is Jules Coleman. See Jules Coleman, *The Practice of Principle: In Defence of a Pragmatist Approach to Legal Theory* (Oxford University Press, Oxford, 2001), esp. pp. 3–12.

A person of consistently high and diverse productivity, Posner tries to maintain a delicate and difficult balance between being "pragmatic"— and thus, by his own view of pragmatism, "empirical . . . skeptical . . . [and] antidogmatic"[12]—and being one of the foremost advocates of the economic approach to descriptive and normative legal theory.[13] He does this in part by lowering somewhat his claims for economic analysis,[14] and in part by trying to equate economics and pragmatism.[15] The equation has some tenability, though one would imagine that a devoted pragmatist might be more willing to look to sources and resources other than economics more frequently than Posner seems to do.[16]

A good example of Posner's form of pragmatism is his approach to precedent.[17] The argument is that we should not adhere to old rules and old categories simply for their own sake, or out of reverence for tradition. Adherence to precedent has a purpose and a value: to reduce the cost of decision-making, to increase predictability and thus to encourage planning (reliance on past decisions, through the assumption that future decisions will come out the same way). Thus, when one comes to a situation where those values are only weakly evoked, other values might justify ignoring the call of precedent. For example, when one deals with new technologies, or new forms of property, little by way of efficiency or predictability is likely served by forcing new problems into old categories. It is better, Posner would argue, to try to find the rules of law which are best on the merits (*i.e.* those that will help the development of the industry, or will ensure fair compensation for investment, and so on).

One line of criticism regularly directed at pragmatists (both philosophical and legal) is that if truth and correctness are to be determined according to the usual practices of the community, there is a risk that one's theory will be basically conservative—that it will be difficult to argue that a community's social practices are systematically unjust, for there is no foundational standard of truth from which one can criticize the conventional or the commonplace.[18]

---

[12] Posner, *Overcoming Law*, pp. 5, 6.

[13] The sixth edition of Posner's casebook, *Economic Analysis of Law*, the leading casebook in the area, was published in 2003.

[14] See, *e.g.* Posner, *Economic Analysis of Law*, p. 28 ("there is more to justice than economics, a point the reader should keep in mind in evaluating normative statements in this book").

[15] Posner writes: law and economics "epitomizes the operation in law of the ethic of scientific inquiry, pragmatically understood. Far from being reductionist, as its detractors believe, economics is the instrumental science par excellence." Posner, *Overcoming Law*, p. 15.

[16] Posner attempts to respond to criticisms similar to that implied in the text in *ibid.* at pp. 15–21.

[17] See Posner, *Economic Analysis of Law*, pp. 560–561; Posner, *Overcoming Law*, 399.

[18] An example of an article which considers this objection seriously and tries to overcome it is Margaret Jane Radin, "The Pragmatist and the Feminist", 63 *Southern California Law Review* 1699 (1990). For an example from the side of modern philosophical pragmatism,

POSTMODERNISM

If legal pragmatism has its roots in the philosophical pragmatist movement of earlier decades, legal postmodernism could be seen to develop out of the cluster of "postmodern" movements in a variety of other areas: perhaps most distinctly in architecture and literary theory, but also philosophy, painting, and music.

While I have frequently noted in this part of the book that the theorists grouped together under a movement label (whether by others or by self identification) often diverge in their attitudes, beliefs, themes, and methodology, the divergence may be especially broad with "postmodernism".[19] Perhaps the best one can do is to point to some ideas and positions that seem to appear in a large number (though far from all) of the writers who identify themselves, or are identified by others, as legal postmodernists.

The postmodernists writing in law tend to draw strongly on a variety of thinkers from literary theory and social theory: e.g. Jacques Derrida, Michel Foucault, Paul de Man, Jean-François Lyotard, and Richard Rorty. They also tend to take ideas from other theorists whose work, if considered in its entirety, arguably would not fit comfortably with the postmodernist project: e.g. Friedrich Nietzsche, Ludwig Wittgenstein, and Martin Heidegger.

Among the themes identified with postmodernism are:

(1) rejecting the idea of a foundational or transcendent source for truth or justification[20];

(2) rejecting the notion of determinate unique meanings for statements, texts, or events;

(3) the claim that truth and identity are socially constructed or culturally constructed;

(4) the rejection of all grand narratives (e.g. seeing history as a movement towards ever greater rationality or ever greater liberty, or seeing law as a movement "from status to contract"[21]); and

---

see Hilary Putnam, "Pragmatism and Moral Objectivity", in *Women, Culture, and Development* (M.C. Nussbaum and J. Glover eds, Clarendon Press, Oxford, 1995), pp. 199–224.

[19] See, e.g. Jennifer Wicke, "Postmodern Identity and the Legal Subject", 62 *University of Colorado Law Review* 455 at 456 (1991): "There are more than thirty-one flavors of postmodern . . . Postmodernism names a debate us theory, a set of discourses and disciplines, a criterion of style in aesthetics, a historical period, and a way of life."

[20] In philosophical terms, postmodernists tend to reject foundationalism, essentialism, metaphysical realism, and the correspondence theory of truth.

[21] See Sir Henry Sumner Maine, *Ancient Law* (University of Arizona Press, Tucson, 1986), p. 165 (first published in 1861).

(5) a strong emphasis on the irrational or unconscious influences on action and belief.[22]

Postmodernism thus seems to converge with pragmatism in its treatment of truth and justification,[23] though in other ways it is a far more radical view.

The postmodernist challenge to there being a single correct (and stable) meaning or interpretation to a statement, a text, or an event is often discussed under the label "deconstruction", though there are radically different understandings of what "deconstruction" entails and what its consequences for literature and life might be.[24]

A number of theorists within the critical traditions discussed in Ch. 19 have drawn upon postmodernist ideas. Critical legal scholars arguing for the indeterminacy of law have drawn upon deconstruction,[25] and the postmodernist emphasis on the social or cultural construction of identity fits well with those attacking conventional ideas about race and gender.[26]

There are other ways in which postmodernism does not seem to fit well with the critical project. While postmodernism may show that the establishment views and traditional social rules have no foundation and no (unique) claim to truth or correctness, the acid of the postmodernist critique would seem to work equally well on the views and rules the reformers would put in their place. Postmodernism is a useful tool of the Left only when it is used selectively.[27] Postmodernism, when taken seriously, can have a distinctively conservative effect, as the notion that truth, meaning, and justice may be entirely subjective or context-bound works to undermine the strength of any argument for radical social change. Postmodernists (and those working under similar labels, like "post-

---

[22] See, *e.g.* Pierre Schlag, "Normativity and the Politics of Form", 139 *University of Pennsylvania Law Review* 801 (1991).

[23] Which is why and how a neo-pragmatist like Richard Rorty is often identified with postmodernism.

[24] The seminal work in the area is Jacques Derrida, *Of Grammatology* (G.C. Spivak, trans., Johns Hopkins University Press, Baltimore, 1974); For an overview of the uses of deconstruction, see Christopher Norris, "Jurisprudence, Deconstruction and Literary Theory: A Brief Survey and Critical Review", 1 *Res Publica* 57 (1995); for two quite different views of what deconstruction is and what its implications are for theory, see Matthew H. Kramer, *Hobbes and the Paradoxes of Political Origins* (St. Martin's Press, New York, 1997), pp. 1–53; Jack Balkin, "Deconstructive Practice and Legal Theory", 96 *Yale Law Journal* 743 (1987).

[25] See, *e.g.* Kennedy, *A Critique of Adjudication*, pp. 348–350.

[26] See, *e.g.* Crenshaw, Gotanda, Peller and Thomas eds, *Critical Race Theory*, pp. 440–494 ("Race and Postmodernism"); Becker, Bowman and Torrey eds, *Feminist Jurisprudence*, pp. 110–118 ("Postmodernist Feminism").

[27] See, *e.g.* Jack Balkin, "Tradition, Betrayal, and the Politics of Deconstruction", 11 *Cardozo Law Review* 1613 (1990).

structuralism" and "deconstruction") are regularly accused of being unable to ground claims of ("objective") injustice or evil, a charge such theorists seem to have some trouble refuting.[28]

Suggested Further Readings

PRAGMATISM

Michael Brint and William Weaver eds, *Pragmatism in Law & Society* (Westview Press, Boulder, Colo., 1991) (includes pieces by Richard Posner, Stanley Fish, Richard Rorty, Margaret Jane Radin, Hilary Putnam, and Ronald Dworkin; the book is based on "Symposium on the Renaissance of Pragmatism in American Legal Thought", 63 *Southern California Law Review* 1569–1853 (1990)).

Thomas C. Grey, "Holmes and Legal Pragmatism", 41 *Stanford Law Review* 787 (1989).

Louis Menand ed., *Pragmatism: A Reader* (Vintage Books, New York, 1997) (includes selections by Charles Sanders Peirce, William James, Oliver Wendell Holmes Jr, John Dewey, and some selections from contemporary writers).

Richard Warner, "Legal Pragmatism", in *A Companion to Philosophy of Law and Legal Theory* (D. Patterson ed., Blackwell, Oxford, 1996), pp. 385–393.

POSTMODERNISM

Jack Balkin, "What is Postmodern Constitutionalism?", 90 *Michigan Law Review* 1966 (1992).

Costas Douzinas; Ronnie Warrington and Shaun McVeigh, *Postmodern Jurisprudence* (Routledge, London, 1991).

M.D.A. Freeman, *Lloyd's Introduction to Jurisprudence* (7th ed., Sweet & Maxwell, London, 2001), pp. 1253–1334 ("Postmodern Jurisprudence").

Fredric Jameson, *Postmodernism, or, The Cultural Logic of Late Capitalism* (Duke University Press, Durham, N.C., 1991).

Christopher Norris, *Deconstruction: Theory & Practice* (Methuen, London, 1982).

Dennis Patterson, "Postmodernism", in *A Companion to Philosophy of Law and Legal Theory* (D. Patterson ed., Blackwell, Oxford, 1996), pp. 375–384.

---

[28] See, *e.g.* Werner Hamacher, Neil Hertz and Thomas Keenan eds, *Responses: On Paul de Man's Wartime Journalism* (University of Nebraska Press, Lincoln, Neb., 1989) (arguing about the links, if any, between de Man's deconstructionist theory and his anti-Semitic articles for a collaborationist newspaper during World War II); Edward Rothstein, "Moral Relativity Is a Hot Topic? True. Absolutely.", *New York Times*, July 13, 2002; Peter Berkowitz, "Fish Story", *New Republic Online*, http://www.thenewrepublic.com, posted June 28, 2002 (both discussing Stanley Fish's defence of postmodernism's ability to make moral judgments about the terrorist attack of September 11, 2001).

"Postmodernism and Law: A Symposium", 62 *University of Colorado Law Review* 439–636 (1991) (includes contributions by Pierre Schlag, David Kennedy, Mary Joe Frug, and Dale Jamieson).

Symposium: "Deconstruction and the Possibility of Justice", 11 *Cardozo Law Review* 919–1726 (1990) (includes contributions by Jacques Derrida, J. Hillis Miller, Jonathan Culler, Drucilla Cornell, and Pierre Schlag).

Bibliography

Abel, Richard L. ed., *The Law & Society Reader* (New York University Press, New York, 1995)

Abraham, Kenneth S., "Statutory Interpretation and Literary Theory: Some Common Concerns of an Unlikely Pair", 32 *Rutgers Law Review* 676 (1979)

Abrams, Kathryn, "Hearing the Call of Stories", 79 *California Law Review* 971 (1991)

Alexander, Larry, "All or Nothing at All? The Intentions of Authorities and the Authority of Intentions", in *Law and Interpretation* (A. Marmor, ed., Clarendon Press, Oxford, 1995), pp. 357–404

—, "Harm, Offense, and Morality", 7 *Canadian Journal of Law and Jurisprudence* 199 (1994)

—, "Precedent", in *A Companion to Philosophy of Law and Legal Theory* (D. Patterson ed., Blackwell, Oxford, 1996), pp. 503–513

Alexander, Larry and Schauer, Frederick, "On Extrajudicial Constitutional Interpretation", 110 *Harvard Law Review* 1359 (1997)

Allen, Anita, "The Proposed Equal Protection Fix for Abortion Law: Reflections on Citizenship, Gender, and the Constitution", 18 *Harvard Journal of Law and Public Policy* 419 (1995)

Altman, Andrew, *Critical Legal Studies: A Liberal Critique* (Princeton University Press, Princeton, 1990)

Amsterdam, Anthony G. and Bruner, Jerome S., *Minding the Law* (Harvard University Press, Cambridge, Mass., 2000)

Aquinas, Thomas, *The Treatise on Law* (R. J. Henle, trans. & ed., University of Notre Dame Press, Notre Dame, Indiana, 1993)

Archard, David, "Political and Social Philosophy", in *The Blackwell Companion to Philosophy* (N. Bunnin and E. P. Tsui-James eds, Blackwell, Oxford, 1996), pp. 257–289

Aristotle, *The Complete Works of Aristotle* (J. Barnes ed., Princeton University Press, Princeton, 1984), two vols

Aron, Raymond, *Main Currents in Sociological Thought* (R. Howard and H. Weaver, trans., Anchor Books, New York, 1970), Vols I and II

Ashworth, Andrew, *Sentencing and Criminal Justice* (Weidenfeld & Nicolson, London, 1992)

Audi, Robert, ed., *The Cambridge Dictionary of Philosophy* (Cambridge University Press, Cambridge, 1995)

Augustine, *The City of God* (M. Dods, trans., Hafner Publishing, New York, 1948), two vols

Austin, J. L., *How to Do Things With Words* (J. O. Urmson and M. Sbisa eds, Harvard University Press, Cambridge, Mass., 1975)

Austin, John, *Lectures on Jurisprudence, or The Philosophy of the Positive Law*, two vols (4th ed., R. Campbell ed., John Murray, London, 1879) (Thoemme Press reprint, Bristol, 2002)

—, *The Province of Jurisprudence Determined* (W.E. Rumble ed. Cambridge University Press, Cambridge, 1995)

Avineri, Shlomo and de-Shalit, Avner eds, *Communitarianism and Individualism* (Oxford University Press, Oxford,1992)

Ayres, Ian, "Playing Games with the Law", 42 *Stanford Law Review* 1291 (1990)

Ayres, Ian and Gertner, Robert, "Filling Gaps in Incomplete Contracts: An Economic Theory of Default Rules", 99 *Yale Law Journal* 87 (1989)

Baird, Douglas G., "Game Theory and the Law", in *The New Palgrave Dictionary of Economics and the Law* (P. Newman ed., Macmillan, London, 1998), Vol. 2, pp. 192–198

Baird, Douglas G., Gertner, Robert H. and Picker, Randal C., *Game Theory and the Law* (Harvard University Press, Cambridge, Mass., 1994)

Balkin, Jack, "Deconstructive Practice and Legal Theory", 96 *Yale Law Journal 743* (1987)

—, "Tradition, Betrayal, and the Politics of Deconstruction", 11 *Cardozo Law Review* 1613 (1990)

—, "What is Postmodern Constitutionalism?", 90 *Michigan Law Review* 1966 (1992)

Ball, Milner, "The Legal Academy and Minority Scholars", 103 *Harvard Law Review* 1855 (1990)

Barnes, Robin, "Race Consciousness: The Thematic Content of Racial Distinctiveness in Critical Race Scholarship", 103 *Harvard Law Review* 1864 (1990)

Barnett, Randy E., *The Structure of Liberty* (Clarendon Press, Oxford, 1998)

Bartlett, Katharine and Kennedy, Rosanne eds, *Feminist Legal Theory: Readings in Law and Gender* (Westview Press, Boulder, Colo., 1991)

Bayles, Michael, *Hart's Legal Philosophy: An Examination* (Kluwer Academic Publishers, Dordrecht, 1992)

Becker, Mary; Bowman, Cynthia Grant and Torrey, Morrison ed., *Feminist Jurisprudence: Taking Women Seriously* (West Publishing, St Paul, 1994)

Bell, Daniel, "Communitarianism", in E. N. Zalta ed., *Stanford Encyclopedia of Philosophy, http://plato.stanford.edu* (2001)

Bell, Derrick, *And We Are Not Saved* (Basic Books, New York, 1987)

—, *Faces at the Bottom of the Well* (Basic Books, New York, 1992)

—, "Racial Realism", 27 *Connecticut Law Review* 363 (1992)

—, "Xerces and the Affirmative Action Mystique", 57 *George Washington Law Review* 1595 (1989)

Bentham, Jeremy, "Anarchical Fallacies", reprinted in *Nonsense upon Stilts: Bentham, Burke and Marx on the Rights of Man* (J. Waldron ed., Methuen, London, 1987), pp. 46–69

—, "Truth versus Ashhurst", in *The Works of Jeremy Bentham* (W. Tait, Edinburgh, 1843), Vol. V, pp. 233–237

Berkowitz, Peter, "Fish Story", *New Republic Online, http://www.thenewrepublic.com*, posted June 28, 2002

Berlin, Isaiah, "The Purpose of Philosophy", in *Concepts and Categories* (Penguin, New York, 1981), pp. 1–11

Bernhardt, William, *et al.*, *Natural Suspect* (Ballantine Books, New York, 2001)
Beyleveld, Deryck and Brownsword, Roger, *Law as a Moral Judgment* (Sweet & Maxwell, London, 1986)
Bishin, William R. and Stone, Christopher D. eds, *Law, Language and Ethics: An Introduction to Law and Legal Method* (Foundation Press, Mineola, N.Y., 1972)
Bix, Brian, "A. D. Woozley and the Concept of Right Answers in Law", 5 *Ratio Juris* 58 (1992), reprinted in modified form in *Law, Language and Legal Determinacy* (Clarendon Press, Oxford, 1993), pp. 79–88
——, "Conceptual Questions and Jurisprudence", 1 *Legal Theory* 415 (1995)
——, "Consent, Sado-Masochism and the English Common Law", 17 *Quinnipiac Law Review* 157 (1997)
——, "H.L.A. Hart and the Hermeneutic Turn in Legal Theory", 52 *SMU Law Review* 167 (1999)
——, "John Austin", in E. N. Zalta ed., *Stanford Encyclopedia of Philosophy*, *http://plato.stanford.edu* (2001)
——, *Law, Language, and Legal Determinacy* (Clarendon Press, Oxford, 1993)
——, "Law as an Autonomous Discipline", in *The Oxford Handbook of Legal Studies* (forthcoming, P. Cane and M. Tushnet eds, Oxford University Press, Oxford, 2003)
——, "Legal Positivism", in *Blackwell Guide to Philosophy of Law and Legal Theory* (forthcoming, W. A. Edmundson and M. P. Golding eds, Blackwell, Oxford, 2004)
——, "Natural Law Theory", in *A Companion to the Philosophy of Law and Legal Theory* (D. Patterson ed., Blackwell, Oxford, 1996), pp. 223–240
——, "Natural Law Theory: The Modern Tradition", in *The Oxford Handbook of Jurisprudence and Philosophy of Law* (J. Coleman and S. Shapiro, eds, K. E. Himma, assoc. ed., Oxford University Press, Oxford, 2002), pp. 61–103
——, "On Description and Legal Reasoning", in *Rules and Reasoning* (L.R. Meyer ed., Hart Publishing, Oxford, 1999), pp. 7–28
——, "On the Dividing Line Between Natural Law Theory and Legal Positivism," 75 *Notre Dame Law Review* 1613 (2000)
——, "Patrolling the Boundaries: Inclusive Legal Positivism and the Nature of Jurisprudential Debate", 12 *Canadian Journal of Law & Jurisprudence* 17 (1999)
——, "Questions in Legal Interpretation", in *Law and Interpretation* (A. Marmor ed., Clarendon Press, Oxford, 1995), pp. 137–154
——, "Questions in Legal Interpretation", 18 *Tel Aviv Law Review* 463 (1994)
——, "Will versus Reason: Truth in Natural Law, Positive Law, and Legal Theory", in *Truth* (forthcoming, K. Pritzl ed., Catholic University of America Press, Washington, D.C., 2004)
Blackburn, Simon, *The Oxford Dictionary of Philosophy* (Oxford University Press, Oxford, 1994)
Blackstone, William, *Commentaries on the Law of England* (Clarendon Press, Oxford, 1765–1769), four volumes
Bourke, Vernon J., *Will in Western Thought: An Historico-Critical Survey* (Sheed and Ward, New York, 1964)
Boyle, James, "Introduction", in *Critical Legal Studies* (J. Boyle ed., New York University Press, New York, 1994), pp. xiii—liii
Boyle, James ed., *Critical Legal Studies* (New York University Press, New York, 1994)
Brest, Paul, "The Misconceived Quest for the Original Understanding", 60 *Boston University Law Review* 204 (1980)

Brest, Paul and Vandenberg, Ann, "Politics, Feminism, and the Constitution: The Anti-Pornography Movement in Minneapolis", 39 *Stanford Law Review* 607 (1987)

Brewer, Scott, "Introduction: Choosing Sides in the Racial Critiques Debate", 103 *Harvard Law Review* 1844 (1990)

—, "Pragmatism, Oppression, and the Flight to Substance", 63 *Southern California Law Review* 1753 *(1990)*

Brint, Michael and Weaver William eds, *Pragmatism in Law & Society* (Westview Press, Boulder, Colo., 1991)

Brooks, Peter and Gewirtz, Paul eds, *Law's Stories: Narrative and Rhetoric in the Law* (Yale University Press, New Haven, 1996)

Buchanan, James M. and Tullock, Gordon, *The Calculus of Consent: Logical Foundations of Constitutional Democracy* (University of Michigan Press, Ann Arbor, 1962)

Burstyn, Varda ed., *Women Against Censorship* (Douglas & McIntyre, Ltd., Vancouver, 1985)

Calabresi, Guido and Melamed, A. Douglas, "Property Rules, Liability Rules, and Inalienability: One View of the Cathedral", 85 *Harvard Law Review* 1089 (1972)

Campbell, Kenneth, "Legal Rights", in E. N. Zalta ed., *Stanford Encyclopedia of Philosophy*, *http://plato.stanford.edu* (2001)

Campbell, Tom D., *The Legal Theory of Ethical Positivism* (Dartmouth, Aldershot, 1996)

Cardozo, Benjamin N., "Law and Literature", 14 *Yale Review* 699 (1925)

—, *The Nature of the Judicial Process* (Yale University Press, New Haven, 1921)

Carrington, Paul D., "Of Law and the River", 34 *Journal of Legal Education* 222 (1984)

Carter, Stephen, "When Victims Happen to Be Black", 97 *Yale Law Journal* 420 (1988)

Chang, Robert S., Toward an Asian American Legal Scholarship: Critical Race Theory, Post-Structuralism, and Narrative Space", 81 *California Law Review* 1244 (1993)

Chang, Ruth ed., *Incommensurability, Incomparability, and Practical Reason* (Harvard University Press, Cambridge, Mass., 1997)

Christie, George and Martin, Patrick eds, *Jurisprudence: Text and Readings on the Philosophy of Law* (2nd ed., West Publishing, St. Paul, Minn., 1995)

Cicero, Marcus Tullius, *De Re Publica: De Legibus* (C.W. Keyes, trans., Harvard University Press, Cambridge, Mass., 1928)

Coase, Ronald H., "The Nature of the Firm", reprinted in *The Firm, the Market and the Law* (University of Chicago Press, Chicago, 1988), pp. 33–55

—, "The Problem of Social Cost", 3 *Journal of Law and Economics* 1 (1960), reprinted in *The Firm, the Market and the Law* (University of Chicago Press, Chicago, 1988), pp. 95–156

Cohen, Felix, "Transcendental Nonsense and the Functional Approach", 35 *Columbia Law Review* 809 (1935)

Cohen, L. Jonathan, *The Dialogue of Reason* (Clarendon Press, Oxford, 1986)

Cohen, Morris, *Law and the Social Order* (Archon Books, New York, 1967)

—, "Property and Sovereignty", 13 *Cornell Law Quarterly* 8 (1927)

Coleman, Jules L., "Authority and Reason", in *The Autonomy of Law* (R. George ed., Oxford University Press, Oxford, 1996), pp. 287–319

—, "Incorporationism, Conventionality and the Practical Difference Thesis", 4 *Legal Theory* 381 (1998)

—, *Markets, Morals and the Law* (Cambridge University Press, Cambridge, 1988)

—, "Methodology", in *The Oxford Handbook of Jurisprudence and Philosophy of Law* (J. L. Coleman and S. Shapiro eds, K. E. Himma assoc. ed., Oxford University Press, Oxford, 2002), pp. 311–351

—, "Negative and Positive Positivism", 11 *Journal of Legal Studies* 139 (1982), reprinted in *Market, Morals and the Law* (Cambridge University Press, Cambridge, 1988), pp. 3–27

—, "The Normative Basis of Economic Analysis: A Critical Review of Richard Posner's *The Economics of Justice*", 34 *Stanford Law Review* 1105 (1982)

—, *The Practice of Principle: In Defence of a Pragmatist Approach to Legal Theory* (Oxford University Press, Oxford, 2001)

—, "Second Thoughts and Other First Impressions", in *Analyzing Law: New Essays in Legal Theory* (B. Bix ed., Clarendon Press, Oxford, 1998), pp. 257–322

—, "Truth and Objectivity in Law", 1 *Legal Theory* 33 (1995)

Coleman, Jules L., ed., *Hart's Postscript: Essays on the Postscript to the Concept of Law* (Oxford University Press, Oxford, 2001)

Coleman, Jules L. and Leiter, Brian, "Legal Positivism", in *A Companion to the Philosophy of Law and Legal Theory* (D. Patterson ed., Blackwell, Oxford, 1996), pp. 241–260

Conference: "Social Norms, Social Meaning, and the Economic Analysis of Law", 27 *Journal of Legal Studies* 537–823 (1998)

Coombs, Mary, "Outsider Jurisprudence: The Law Review Stories", 63 *University of Colorado Law Review* 683 (1992)

Cooter, Robert and Ulen, Thomas, *Law and Economics* (3rd ed., Addison Wesley, Reading, Mass., 2000)

Cornell, Drucilla, "Loyalty and the Limits of Kantian Impartiality" (book review), 107 *Harvard Law Review* 2081 (1994)

Cotterrell, Roger, *The Politics of Jurisprudence* (Buttcrworths, London, 1989)

—, *The Sociology of Law: An Introduction* (2nd ed., Butterworths, London, 1992)

—, "Subverting Orthodoxy, Making Law Central: A View of Sociolegal Studies", 29 *Journal of Law and Society* 632 (2002).

Cover, Robert M., "Violence and the Word", 95 *Yale Law Journal* 1601 (1986)

Coyle, Sean, "Are There Necessary Truths About Rights?", 15 *Canadian Journal of Law and Jurisprudence* 21 (2002)

Crenshaw, Kimberlé, "Race, Reform, and Retrenchment: Transformation and Legitimation in Antidiscrimination Law", 101 *Harvard Law Review* 1331 (1988)

Crenshaw, Kimberlé; Gotanda, Neil; Peller, Gary and Thomas, Kendall eds, *Critical Race Theory: The Key Writings That Formed the Movement* (The New Press, New York, 1995)

Critical Legal Studies Symposium, 36 *Stanford Law Review* 1674 (1984)

Cross, Rupert, *Statutory Interpretation* (Butterworths, London, 1976)

Cross, Rupert; Bell, John and Engle, George, *Statutory Interpretation* (3rd ed., Butterworths, London, 1995)

Cross, Rupert and Harris, J. W, *Precedent in English Law* (4th ed., Clarendon Press, Oxford, 1991)

Daniels, Norman ed., *Reading Rawls: Critical Studies of A Theory of Justice* (Basic Books, New York, 1990)

Dau-Schmidt, Kenneth, *et al.*, "On *Game Theory and the Law*", 31 *Law and Society Review* 613 (1997)

Davidson, Donald, *Inquiries into Truth and Interpretation* (Clarendon Press, Oxford, 1984)

Davies, Howard and Holdcroft, David eds, *Jurisprudence: Texts and Commentary* (Butterworths, London, 1991)

Delgado, Richard, "Affirmative Action as a Majoritarian Device: Or, Do You Really Want to be a Role Model", 89 *Michigan Law Review* 1222 (1991)

—, "The Imperial Scholar: Reflections on a Review of Civil Rights Literature", 132 *University of Pennsylvania Law Review* 561 (1984)

—, "Rodrigo's Ninth Chronicle: Race, Legal Instrumentalism, and the Rule of Law", 143 *University of Pennsylvania Law Review* 379 (1994)

—, "Storytelling for Oppositionists and Others: A Plea for Narrative", 87 *Michigan Law Review* 2411 (1989)

Delgado, Richard ed., *Critical Race Theory: The Cutting Edge* (Temple University Press, Philadelphia, 1995)

Delgado, Richard and Stefancic, Jean, "Critical Race Theory: An Annotated Bibliography", 79 *Virginia Law Review* 461 (1993)

—, *Critical Race Theory: An Introduction* (New York University Press, New York, 2001).

—, "Hateful Speech, Loving Communities: Why Our Notion of 'A Just Balance' Changes So Slowly", 82 *California Law Review* 851 (1994)

Delgado, Richard and Stefancic, Jean eds, *The Latino/a Condition: A Critical Reader* (New York University Press, New York, 1998)

Derrida, Jacques, *Of Grammatology* (G. C. Spivak, trans., Johns Hopkins University Press, Baltimore, 1974)

Devlin, Patrick, *The Enforcement of Morals* (Oxford University Press, Oxford, 1965)

Dewey, John, "The Historical Background of Corporate Legal Personality", 35 *Yale Law Journal* 655 (1926)

—, "Logical Method and the Law", 10 *Cornell Law Quarterly* 17 (1924)

Dickson, Julie, *Evaluation and Legal Theory* (Hart Publishing, Oxford, 2001)

Douzinas, Costas; Warrington, Ronnie and McVeigh, Shaun, *Postmodern Jurisprudence* (Routledge, London, 1991)

Dowd, Nancy E. and Jacobs, Michelle S. eds, *Feminist Legal Theory: An Anti-Essentialist Reader* (New York University Press, New York, 2003)

Doyle, Roddy, *et al.*, *Yeats is Dead* (Joseph O'Connor ed., Alfred A. Knopf, New York, 2001)

Duff, Anthony and Garland, David eds, *A Reader on Punishment* (Oxford University Press, Oxford, 1994)

Dupré, John, "Natural Kinds and Biological Taxa", 90 *Philosophical Review* 66 (1981)

Duxbury, Neil, *Patterns of American Jurisprudence* (Clarendon Press, Oxford, 1995)

—, "Post-Realism and Legal Process", in *A Companion to the Philosophy of Law and Legal Theory* (D. Patterson ed., Blackwell, Oxford, 1996), pp. 291–301

Dworkin, Gerald, "Paternalism", in E. N. Zalta ed., *Stanford Encyclopedia of Philosophy, http://plato.stanford.edu* (2002)

Dworkin, Gerald ed., *Morality, Harm and the Law* (Westview Press, Boulder, Colo., 1994)

Dworkin, Ronald, *Law's Empire* (Harvard University Press, Cambridge, Mass., 1986)

—, "Legal Theory and the Problem of Sense", in *Issues in Contemporary Legal Philosophy* (R. Gavison ed., Clarendon Press, Oxford, 1987), pp. 9–20

—, "Liberal Community", 77 *California Law Review* 479 (1989)

—, *A Matter of Principle* (Harvard University Press, Cambridge, Mass., 1985)

—, "My Reply to Stanley Fish (and Walter Benn Michaels): Please don't Talk about Objectivity Any More", in *The Politics of Interpretation* (W.J.T. Mitchell ed., University of Chicago Press, London, 1983), pp. 287–313

—, "On Gaps in the Law", in *Controversies about Law's Ontology* (P. Amselek and N. MacCormick eds, Edinburgh: Edinburgh University Press, 1991), pp. 84–90

—, "Pragmatism, Right Answers and True Banality", in *Pragmatism in Law and Society* M. Brint and W. Weaver eds, (Westview Press, Boulder, Colo., 1991), pp. 359–388

—, "A Reply by Ronald Dworkin", in *Ronald Dworkin and Contemporary Jurisprudence* (M. Cohen ed., Duckworth, London, 1984), pp. 247–300

—, *Taking Rights Seriously* (Duckworth, London, 1977)

—, "Thirty Years On", 115 *Harvard Law Review* 1655 (2002)

Eastland, Terry, "Radicals in the Law Schools", *Wall Street Journal*, January 10, 1986, p. 10

Eekelaar, J.M., "Principles of Revolutionary Legality", in *Oxford Essays in Jurisprudence, Second Series* A. W. B. Simpson ed., (Clarendon Press, Oxford, 1973), pp. 22–43

Eisenberg, Melvin Aron, *The Nature of the Common Law* (Harvard University Press, Cambridge, Mass., 1988)

Ellickson, Robert C., *Order Without Law: How Neighbors Settle Disputes* (Harvard University Press, Cambridge, Mass., 1991)

Epstein, Richard A., "Causation — In Context: An Afterword", 63 *Chicago-Kent Law Review* 653 (1987)

—, "The Harm Principle—and How it Grew", 45 *University of Toronto Law Journal* 369 (1995)

—, "A Theory of Strict Liability", 2 *Journal of Legal Studies* 151 (1973)

Eskridge, William N., Jr., *Gaylaw: Challenging the Apartheid of the Closet* (Harvard University Press, Cambridge, Mass., 1999)

—, "Gaylegal Narratives", 46 *Stanford Law Review* 607 (1994)

—, "Textualism, The Unknown Ideal?", 96 *Michigan Law Review* 1509 (1998)

Eskridge, William N. Jr and Ferejohn, John, "Statutory Interpretation and Rational Choice Theories", in *The New Palgrave Dictionary of Economics and the Law* (P. Newman ed., Macmillan, London, 1998), Vol. 3, pp. 535–540

Eskridge, William N. Jr. and Frickey, Philip P., "An Historical and Critical Introduction to *The Legal Process*", in Henry M. Hart, Jr and Albert M. Sacks, *The Legal Process: Basic Problems in the Making and Application of Law* (W. Eskridge and P. Frickey eds, Foundation Press, Westbury, NY, 1994), pp. li–cxxxvi

Eskridge, William N., Jr.; Frickey, Philip P. and Garrett, Elizabeth eds, *Cases and Materials on Legislation: Statutes and the Creation of Public Policy* (3rd ed., West Group, St. Paul, 2001)

Estrich, Susan, *Real Rape* (Harvard University Press, Cambridge, Mass., 1987)

Etzioni, Amitai, *The Spirit of Community: Rights, Responsibilities, and the Communitarian Agenda* (Crown Publishers, New York, 1993)

Farber, Daniel A. and Frickey, Philip P, *Law and Public Choice* (University of Chicago Press, Chicago, 1991)

—, "Public Choice Revisited", 96 *Michigan Law Review* 1715 (1998)

Farber, Daniel A. and Sherry, Suzanna, *Beyond All Reason: The Radical Assault on Truth in American Law* (Oxford University Press, New York, 1997)

—, "Telling Stories Out of School: An Essay on Legal Narratives", 45 *Stanford Law Review* 807 (1993)

Farrell, Daniel M., "The Justification of General Deterrence", 94 *Philosophical Review* 367 (1985)

Feinberg, Joel, "The Expressive Function of Punishment", in *Doing and Deserving: Essays in the Theory of Responsibility* (Princeton University Press, Princeton, 1970), pp. 95–118

—, *The Moral Limits of the Criminal Law* (Oxford University Press, Oxford, 1984–1988), four vols

—, "The Nature and Value of Rights", 4 *Journal of Value Inquiry* 19 (1970)

Field, Martha, "Surrogacy Contracts: Gestational and Traditional: The Argument for Nonenforcement", 31 *Washburn Law Review* 3 (1991)

Fineman, Martha A., "Contract, Marriage and Background Rules", in *Analyzing Law: New Essays in Legal Theory* (B. Bix ed., Clarendon Press, Oxford, 1998), pp. 183–195

—, *The Neutered Mother, the Sexual Family, and Other Twentieth Century Tragedies* (Routledge, New York, 1995)

Fineman, Martha and Thomadsen Nancy, eds, *At the Boundaries of Law: Feminism and Legal Theory* (Routledge, New York, 1991)

Finnis, John M., "Allocating Risks and Suffering: Some Hidden Traps", 38 *Cleveland State Law Review* 193 (1990)

—, *Aquinas: Moral, Political, and Legal Theory* (Oxford University Press, Oxford, 1998)

—, "The Authority of Law in the Predicament of Contemporary Social Theory", 1 *Notre Dame Journal of Law, Ethics and Public Policy* 115 (1984)

—, "Concluding Reflections", 38 *Cleveland State Law Review* 231 (1990)

—, *Fundamentals of Ethics* (Georgetown University Press, Washington, D.C., 1983)

—, "Is Natural Law Theory Compatible with Limited Government?", in *Natural Law, Liberalism and Morality: Contemporary Essays* (R. George ed., Clarendon Press, Oxford, 1996), pp. 1–26

—, "Law as Co-ordination", 2 *Ratio Juris* 97 (1989)

—, "Liberalism and Natural Law Theory", 45 *Mercer Law Review* 687 (1994)

—, *Moral Absolutes: Tradition, Revision, and Truth* (Catholic University of America Press, Washington, D.C., 1991)

—, "Natural Law and Legal Reasoning", 38 *Cleveland State Law Review* 1 (1990), reprinted in modified form in *Natural Law Theory* (R. George ed., Clarendon Press, Oxford, 1992), pp. 134–157

—, *Natural Law and Natural Rights* (Oxford: Clarendon Press, 1980)

—, "Natural Law: The Classical Tradition", in *The Oxford Handbook of Jurisprudence and Philosophy of Law* (J. Coleman & S. Shapiro, eds, K. E. Himma, assoc. ed., Oxford University Press, Oxford, 2002), pp. 1–60

—, "On Reason and Authority in *Law's Empire*" (book review), 6 *Law and Philosophy* 357 (1987)

—, "On 'The Critical Studies Movement'", 30 *American Journal of Jurisprudence* 21 (1985), reprinted in *Oxford Essays in Jurisprudence, Third Series* (J. Eekelaar and J. Bell eds, Clarendon Press, Oxford, 1987), pp. 145–165

—, "On the Incoherence of Legal Positivism," 75 *Notre Dame Law Review* 1597 (2000)

—, "Revolutions and Continuity of Law", in *Oxford Essays in Jurisprudence, Second Series* A. W. B. Simpson ed., (Clarendon Press, Oxford, 1973), pp. 44–76

—, "The Truth in Legal Positivism", in *The Autonomy of law* (R. George ed., Clarendon Press, Oxford, 1996), pp. 195–214

Finnis, John M. ed., *Natural Law* (Dartmouth Pub. Co., London; New York University Press, New York, 1991), two vols

Fish, Stanley, "Almost Pragmatism: Richard Posner's Jurisprudence", 57 *University of Chicago Law Review* 1447 (1990)

—, "Dennis Martinez and the Uses of Theory", 96 *Yale Law Journal* 773 (1987), reprinted in *Doing What Comes Naturally* (Clarendon Press, Oxford, 1989), pp. 372–398

—, *Doing What Comes Naturally: Change, Rhetoric, and the Practice of Theory in Literary and Legal Studies* (Clarendon Press, Oxford, 1989)

—, "Fish vs. Fiss", 36 *Stanford Law Review* 1325 (1984), reprinted in *Doing What Comes Naturally* (Clarendon Press, Oxford, 1989), pp. 120–140

Fisher, William; Horwitz, Morton and Reed, Thomas eds, *American Legal Realism* (Oxford University Press, New York, 1993)

Fiss, Owen, "Objectivity and Interpretation", 34 *Stanford Law Review* 739 (1982)

Fitzpatrick, Peter and Hunt, Alan, eds, *Critical Legal Studies* (Blackwell, Oxford, 1987)

Fletcher, George, *Basic Concepts of Legal Thought* (Oxford University Press, New York, 1996)

Foot, Philippa, "Moral Arguments", 67 *Mind* 502 (1958)

Frank, Jerome, "Are Judges Human?", Parts I & II, 80 *University of Pennsylvania Law Review* 17, 233 (1931)

—, *Courts on Trial* (Princeton University Press, Princeton, 1949)

—, *Law and the Modern Mind* (Brentano's, New York, 1930)

—, What Courts Do In Fact", Pts I and II, 26 *Illinois Law Review* 645, 761 (1932)

Frank, Robert H.; Gilovich, Thomas; and Regan, Dennis T., "Does Studying Economics Inhibit Cooperation?", 7 *Journal of Economic Perspectives* 159 (1993)

Freeman, Alan David, "Legitimizing Racial Discrimination Through Antidiscrimination Law: A Critical Review of Supreme Court Doctrine", 62 *Minnesota Law Review* 1049 (1978)

Freeman, M. D. A., *Lloyd's Introduction to Jurisprudence* (7th ed, Sweet & Maxwell, London, 2001)

Frug, Jerry, "McCarthyism and Critical Legal Studies", 22 *Harvard Civil Rights-Civil Liberties Law Review* 665 (1987)

Fuller, Lon L., "Human Purpose and Natural Law", 53 *Journal of Philosophy* 697 (1956), reprinted at 3 *Natural Law Forum* 68 (1958)

—, *The Morality of Law* (revised ed., Yale University Press, New Haven, 1969)

—, "Positivism and Fidelity to Law—A Reply to Professor Hart", 71 *Harvard Law Review* 630 (1958)

—, *The Principles of Moral Order* (K.I. Winston ed., Duke University Press, Durham, 1981)

—, "Reason and Fiat in Case Law", 59 *Harvard Law Review* 376 (1946)

—, "A Rejoinder to Professor Nagel", 3 *Natural Law Forum* 83 (1958)

Fullinwinder, Robert K., "Affirmative Action", in E. N. Zalta ed., *Stanford Encyclopedia of Philosophy, http://plato.stanford.edu* (2001)

Gabel, Peter, Book Review, 91 *Harvard Law Review* 302 (1977)

Gabel, Peter and Harris, Paul, "Building Power and Breaking Images: Critical Legal Theory and the Practice of Law", 11 *New York University Review of Law and Social Change* 369 (1982–1983)

Garvey, Stephen P., "Can Shaming Punishments Educate?", 65 *University of Chicago Law Review* 733 (1998)

Gavison, Ruth, ed., *Issues in Contemporary Legal Philosophy: The Influence of H.L.A. Hart* (Clarendon Press, Oxford, 1987)

George, Robert P., *In Defense of Natural Law* (Clarendon Press, Oxford, 1999)

—, *Making Men Moral* (Clarendon Press, Oxford, 1993)

—, "Natural Law and Positive Law", in *The Autonomy of Law: Essays on Legal Positivism* (Robert P. George ed., Clarendon Press, Oxford, 1996), pp. 321–334

—, "Natural Law Ethics", in *A Companion to Philosophy of Religion* (P. L. Quinn and C. Taliaferro eds, Blackwell,Oxford, 1997), pp. 460–465

—, "Recent Criticism of Natural Law Theory", 55 *University of Chicago Law Review* 1271 (1988)

George, Robert P. ed., *The Autonomy of Law: Essays on Legal Positivism* (Clarendon Press, Oxford, 1996)

—, *Natural Law Theory: Contemporary Essays* (Clarendon Press, Oxford, 1992)

—, *Natural Law, Liberalism, and Morality: Contemporary Essays* (Clarendon Press, Oxford, 1996)

Gewirth, Alan, *Reason and Morality* (University of Chicago Press, Chicago, 1978)

Gilles, Stephen G., "The Invisible Hand Formula", 80 *Virginia Law Review* 1015 (1994)

Gilligan, Carol, *In a Different Voice: Psychological Theory and Women's Development* (Harvard University Press, Cambridge, Mass., 1982, rev. ed., 1993)

Golding, Martin P, *Legal Reasoning* (Broadview Press, Ontario, 2001)

—, *Philosophy of Law* (Prentice-Hall, Englewood Cliffs, N.J., 1975)

Golding, William, *Lord of the Flies* (New York: Perigee, 1954)

Goldstein, Laurence ed., *Precedent in Law* (Clarendon Press, Oxford, 1987)

Gordon, Robert, "Critical Legal Histories", 36 *Stanford Law Review* 57 (1984)

Gray, John Chipman, *The Nature and Sources of the Law* (Columbia University Press, New York, 1909)

Green, Leslie, "Legal Positivism", in E. N. Zalta ed., *Stanford Encyclopedia of Philosophy, http://plato.stanford.edu* (2003).

Greenawalt, Kent, "Legal Enforcement of Morality", in *A Companion to the Philosophy of Law and legal Theory* (D. Patterson ed., Blackwell, Oxford, 1996), pp. 475–487

Grey Thomas C. "Holmes and Legal Pragmatism", 41 *Stanford Law Review* 787 (1989)

—, "Molecular Motions: The Holmesian Judge in Theory and Practice", 37 *William & Mary Law Review* 19 (1995)

Griffith, John, *The Politics of the Judiciary* (Fontana, London, 1985)

Grisez, Germain C., "The First Principle of Practical Reason: A Commentary on the *Summa Theologiae*, 1–2, Question 94, Art. 2", 10 *Natural Law Forum* 168 (1965)

Guest, Stephen, *Ronald Dworkin* (2nd ed., Edinburgh University Press, Edinburgh, 1997)

Guinier, Lani, "The Triumph of Tokenism: The Voting Rights Act and the Theory of Black Electoral Success", 89 *Michigan Law Review* 1077 (1991)

Habermas, Jürgen, *Between Facts and Norms: Contributions to a Discourse Theory of Law and Democracy* (W. Rehg, trans., MIT Press, Cambridge, Mass., 1996)

Hacker, P. M. S. and Raz, Joseph eds, *Law, Morality and Society: Essays in Honour of H.L.A. Hart* (Clarendon Press, Oxford, 1977)

Hale, Sir Matthew, *The History of the Common Law of England* (6th ed., Henry Butterworth, London, 1820)

Hale, Robert, "Bargaining, Duress, and Economic Liberty", 43 *Columbia Law Review* 603 (1943)

—, "Coercion and Distribution in a Supposedly Non-Coercive State", 38 *Political Science Quarterly* 470 (1923)

Halpin, Andrew, "Concepts, Terms, and Fields of Inquiry", 4 *Legal Theory* 187 (1998)

—, *Reasoning with Law* (Hart Publishing, Oxford, 2001)

Hamacher, Werner; Hertz, Neil and Keenan, Thomas, eds, *Responses: On Paul de Man's Wartime Journalism* (University of Nebraska Press, Lincoln, Neb., 1989)

Hanson, Jon D. and Hart, Melissa R., "Law and Economics", in *A Companion to the Philosophy of Law and Legal Theory* (D. Patterson ed., Blackwell, Oxford, 1996), pp. 311–331

Harel, Alon, "What Demands are Rights? An Investigation into the Relation between Rights and Reasons", 17 *Oxford Journal of Legal Studies* 101 (1997)

Harman, Gilbert, "Doubts About Conceptual Analysis", in *Philosophy in Mind: The Place of Philosophy in the Study of Mind* (M. Michael and J. O'Leary-Hawthorne eds, Kluwer, Dordrecht, 1994), pp. 43–48

Harris, Angela P., "Foreword: The Jurisprudence of Reconstruction", 82 *California Law Review* 741 (1994)

—, "Race and Essentialism in Feminist Legal Theory", 42 *Stanford Law Review* 581 (1990)

Harris, J. W., *Law and Legal Science* (Clarendon Press, Oxford, 1979)

—, *Legal Philosophies* (2nd ed., Butterworths, London, 1997)

—, "Rights and Resources – Libertarians and the Right to Life", 15 *Ratio Juris* 109 (2002)

Hart, H.L.A., "Are There Any Natural Rights?", 64 *Philosophical Review* 175 (1955)

—, "Comment", in *Issues in Contemporary Legal Philosophy* (R. Gavison ed., Clarendon Press, Oxford, 1987), pp. 35–42

—, *The Concept of Law* (Clarendon Press, Oxford, 1961; 2nd ed., 1994)

—, "Definition and Theory in Jurisprudence", 70 *Law Quarterly Review* 37 (1954), reprinted in *Essays in Jurisprudence and Philosophy* (Clarendon Press, Oxford, 1983), pp. 21–48

—, *Essays in Jurisprudence and Philosophy* (Clarendon Press, Oxford, 1983)

—, *Essays on Bentham: Jurisprudence and Political Theory* (Clarendon Press, Oxford, 1982)

—, *Law, Liberty and Morality* (Oxford University Press, Oxford, 1963)

—, "Positivism and the Separation of Law and Morals", 71 *Harvard Law Review* 593 (1958), reprinted in *Essays in Jurisprudence and Philosophy* (Clarendon Press, Oxford, 1983), pp. 49–87

—, "Postscript", in *The Concept of Law* (P A. Bulloch and J. Raz eds, 2nd ed., Clarendon Press, Oxford, 1994), pp. 238–276

—, *Punishment and Responsibility: Essays in the Philosophy of Law* (Oxford University Press, Oxford, 1968)

Hart, Henry M., Jr and Sacks, Albert M., *The Legal Process: Basic Problems in the Making and Application of Law* (W. Eskridge, Jr. and P. Frickey eds, Foundation Press, Westbury, N.Y., 1994)

Hartney, Michael, "Introduction" and "Appendix: Bibliography of Kelsen's Publications in English", in Hans Kelsen, *General Theory of Norms* (M. Hartney, trans. and ed., Clarendon Press, Oxford, 1991), pp. ix-liii, 440–454

Hay, Douglas; Linebaugh, Peter; Rule, John; Thompson, E.P and Winslow, Cal, *Albion's Fatal Tree* (Penguin, Middlesex, England, 1975)

Herget, James E. and Wallace, Stephen, "The German Free Law Movement as the Source of American Legal Realism", 73 *Virginia Law Review* 399 (1987)

Hiassen, Carl, *et al.*, *Naked Came the Manatee* (Putnam, New York, 1996)

Hicks, J. R., "The Foundations of Welfare Economics", 49 *Economics Journal* 696 (1939)

Higgins, Ruth C. A., "Obedience, Respect, and the Law" (forthcoming, Oxford University Press, Oxford, 2004)

Hill, H. Hamner, "H.L.A. Hart's Hermeneutic Positivism: On Some Methodological Difficulties in *The Concept of Law*", 3 *Canadian Journal of Law and Jurisprudence* 113 (January 1990)

Hill, Thomas E., Jr., *Respect, Pluralism and Justice: Kantian Perspectives* (Oxford University Press, Oxford, 2000)

Himma, Kenneth Einar, "Inclusive Legal Positivism", in *The Oxford Handbook of Jurisprudence and Philosophy of Law* (J. Coleman and S. Shapiro eds, K. E. Himma. assoc. ed., Oxford University Press, Oxford, 2002), pp. 125–165

Hittinger, Russell, *A Critique of the New Natural Law Theory* (University of Notre Dame Press, Notre Dame, 1987)

Hobbes, Thomas, *Leviathan* (R. Tuck ed., Cambridge University Press, Cambridge, 1996)

Hohfeld, Wesley, "Some Fundamental Conceptions as Applied in Judicial Reasoning", 23 *Yale Law Journal* 16 (1913)

—, "Fundamental Legal Conceptions as Applied in Judicial Reasoning", 26 *Yale Law Journal* 710 (1917)

Holmes, Oliver Wendell, Jr., *The Common Law* (M. D. Howe ed., Little, Brown, and Co., Boston, 1963)

—, "The Path of the Law", 10 *Harvard Law Review* 457 (1897), reprinted in 110 *Harvard Law Review* 991 (1997)

—, "Privilege, Malice and Intent", 8 *Harvard Law Review* 1 (1894)

Homer, *The Iliad* (W.H.D. Rouse, trans., Thomas Nelson and Sons, Edinburgh, 1938)

Honderich, Ted ed., *The Oxford Companion to Philosophy* (Oxford University Press, Oxford, 1995)

Honoré, A.M., *Making Law Bind* (Clarendon Press, Oxford, 1987)

—, "The Necessary Connection Between Law and Morality", 22 *Oxford Journal of Legal Studies* 489 (2002)

Horwitz, Morton J., "The History of the Public/Private Distinction", 130 *University of Pennsylvania Law Review* 1423 (1982)

—, "Law and Economics: Science or Politics?", 8 *Hofstra Law Review* 905 (1981)

—, "Rights", 23 *Harvard Civil Rights-Civil Liberties Law Review* 393 (1988)

—, "The Rule of Law: An Unqualified Human Good?", 86 *Yale Law Journal* 561 (1977)

—, *The Transformation of American Law 1780–1860* (Harvard University Press, Cambridge, Mass., 1977)

—, *The Transformation of American Law 1870–1960: The Crisis in Legal Orthodoxy* (Oxford University Press, Oxford, 1992)

Hunt, Alan, "The Theory of Critical Legal Studies", 6 *Oxford Journal of Legal Studies* 1 (1986)

Hurley, Susan, *Natural Reasons* (Oxford University Press, Oxford, 1989)

Hutcheson, Joseph C., Jr., "The Judgment Intuitive: The Function of the 'Hunch' in Judicial Decision", 14 *Cornell Law Review* 274 (1929)

Hutchinson, Darren Lenard, "Out Yet Unseen: A Racial Critique of Gay and Lesbian Legal Theory and Political Discourse", 29 *Connecticut Law Review* 561 (1997)

Jaffee, Sara and Hyde, Janet Shibley, "Gender Differences in Moral Orientation: A Meta-Analysis", 126 *Psychology Bulletin* 703 (2000)

Jameson, Fredric, *Postmodernism, or, The Cultural Logic of Late Capitalism* (Duke University Press, Durham, N.C., 1991)

Jolls, Christine; Sunstein, Cass R. and Thaler, Richard, "A Behavioural Approach to Law and Economics", 50 *Stanford Law Review* 1471 (1998)

Jolowicz, H. F., *Roman Foundations of Modern Law* (Oxford University Press, Oxford, 1957)

Jurisprudence Symposium, 11 *Georgia Law Review* 969–1424 (1977)

Kadish, Sanford H. and Schulhofer, Stephen J. eds, *Criminal Law and Its Processes* (7th ed., Aspen Publishing, New York, 2001)

Kahneman, Daniel; Slovic, Paul and Tversky, Amos eds, *Judgment Under Uncertainty: Heuristics and Biases* (Cambridge University Press, Cambridge, 1982)

Kairys, David ed., *The Politics of Law* (3rd ed., Pantheon, New York, 1998)

Kaldor, Nicholas, "Welfare Propositions of Economics and Interpersonal Comparisons of Utility", 49 *Economics Journal* 549 (1939)

Kamm, F. M., "Rights", in *The Oxford Handbook of Jurisprudence and Philosophy of Law* (J. L. Coleman & S. Shapiro eds, K. E. Himma, assoc. ed., Oxford University Press, Oxford, 2002), pp. 476–513

Kant, Immanuel, *The Metaphysics of Morals* (M. Gregor ed., Cambridge University Press, Cambridge, 1996)

Kaplan, Benjamin, "Do Intermediate Appellate Courts Have a Lawmaking Function?", 70 *Massachusetts Law Review* 10 (1985)

Katz, Avery Wiener ed., *Foundations of the Economic Approach to Law* (Oxford University Press, New York, 1998)

Kay, Herma Hill, "Equality and Difference: The Case of Pregnancy", 1 *Berkeley Women's Law Journal* 1 (1985)

Kay, Richard, "Adherence to the Original Intentions in Constitutional Adjudication: Three Objections and Responses", 82 *Northwestern University Law Review* 226 (1988)

Kelly, J. M., *A Short History of Western Legal Theory* (Clarendon Press, Oxford, 1992)

Kelman, Mark, *A Guide to Critical Legal Studies* (Harvard University Press, Cambridge, Mass., 1987)

Kelsen, Hans, *General Theory of Law and State* (Russell & Russell, New York, 1945)

General Theory of Norms (M. Hartney, trans. and ed., Clarendon Press, Oxford, 1991)

—, *Introduction to the Problems of Legal Theory* (B.L. Paulson and S. L. Paulson, trans., Clarendon Press, Oxford, 1992)

—, "On the Basis of Legal Validity", 26 *American Journal of Jurisprudence* 178 (1981) (trans. S. L. Paulson)

—, *The Pure Theory of Law* (M. Knight, trans., University of California Press, Berkeley, Calif., 1967)

Kemp, John, *The Philosophy of Kant* (Thoemme Press, Bristol, 1993)

Kennedy, Duncan, *A Critique of Adjudication (fin de siècle)* (Harvard University Press, Cambridge, Mass., 1997)

—, "The Critique of Rights in Critical Legal Studies", in *Left Legalism/Left Critique* (W. Brown and J. Halley eds, Duke University Press, Durham, N.C., 2003), pp. 178–228

—, "Form and Substance in Private Law Adjudication", 89 *Harvard Law Review* 1685 (1976)

—, "Freedom and Constraint in Adjudication: A Critical Phenomenology", 36 *Journal of Legal Education* 518 (1986)

—, "Law-and-Economics from the Perspective of Critical Legal Studies", in *The New Palgrave Dictionary of Economics and the Law* (P Newman ed., Macmillan, London, 1998), Vol. 2, pp. 465–474

—, "Legal Education as Training for Hierarchy", in *The Politics of Law* (revised ed., D. Kairys ed., Pantheon, New York, 1990), pp. 38–58

—, "The Structure of Blackstone's Commentaries", 28 *Buffalo Law Review* 205 (1979)

Kennedy, Randall, "Racial Critiques of Legal Academia", 102 *Harvard Law Review* 1745 (1989)

Kornblith, Hilary, *Naturalizing Epistemology* (2nd ed., MIT Press, Cambridge, Mass, 1994)

Kornhauser, Lewis A., "The Great Image of Authority", 36 *Stanford Law Review* 349 (1984)

—, "A Guide to the Perplexed Claims of Efficiency in the Law", 8 *Hofstra Law Review* 591 (1980)

—, "Economic Analysis of Law", in E. N. Zalta ed., *Stanford Encyclopedia of Philosophy*, http://plato.stanford.edu (2001)

Kramer, Matthew H., *Critical Legal Theory and the Challenge of Feminism* (Rowman & Littlefield, London, 1995)

—, *Hobbes and the Paradoxes of Political Origins* (St. Martin's Press, New York, 1997)

—, *In Defense of Legal Positivism: Law Without Trimmings* (Oxford University Press, Oxford, 1999)

—, "Rights Without Trimmings", in Matthew H. Kramer; N.E. Simmonds and Hillel Steiner, *A Debate Over Rights: Philosophical Enquiries* (Clarendon Press, Oxford, 1998), pp. 7–111

—, "Scrupulousness Without Scruples: A Critique of Lon Fuller and His Defenders", 18 *Oxford Journal of Legal Studies* 235 (1998), reprinted in modified form in *In Defense of Legal Positivism: Law Without Trimmings* (Oxford University Press, Oxford, 1999), pp. 37–77

Kress, Kenneth J., "Legal Indeterminacy", 77 *California Law Review* 283 (1989)

Kretzmann, Norman, "*Lex Iniusta Non Est Lex*: Laws on Trial in Aquinas' Court of Conscience", 33 *American Journal of Jurisprudence* 99 (1988)

Kripke, Saul, *Wittgenstein on Rules and Private Language* (Harvard University Press, Cambridge, Mass., 1982)

Kronman, Anthony T., *The Lost Lawyer* (Harvard University Press, Cambridge, Mass., 1993)

Lacey, Nicola, "Theory into Practice? Pornography and the Public/Private Dichotomy", 20 *Journal of Law and Society* 93 (1993)

Landes, William and Posner, Richard, *The Economic Structure of Tort Law* (Harvard University Press, Cambridge, Mass., 1987)

Langdell, Christopher Columbus, *A Summary of the Law of Contract* (2nd ed., Little, Brown, and Co., Boston, 1880)

Lawrence, Charles R., III, "The Id, the Ego and Equal Protection: Reckoning with Unconscious Racism", 39 *Stanford Law Review* 317 (1987)

Lear, Jonathan, *Open Minded* (Harvard University Press, Cambridge, Mass., 1998)

Leff, Arthur, "Economic Analysis of Law: Some Realism About Nominalism", 60 *Virginia Law Review* 451 (1974)

Leiter, Brian, "American Legal Realism", in *The Blackwell Guide to Philosophy of Law and Legal Theory* (forthcoming, M. Golding and W. A. Edmundson eds, Blackwell, Oxford, 2004)

——, "Legal Realism", in *A Companion to the Philosophy of Law and Legal Theory* (D. Patterson ed., Blackwell, Oxford, 1986), pp. 261–279

——, "Naturalism and Naturalized Jurisprudence", in *Analyzing Law: New Essays in Legal Theory* (B. Bix ed., Clarendon Press, Oxford, 1998), pp. 79–104

——, "Naturalism in Legal Philosophy", in E. N. Zalta ed., *Stanford Encyclopedia of Philosophy*, http://plato.stanford.edu (2002)

——, "Realism, Hard Positivism, and Conceptual Analysis", 4 *Legal Theory* 533 (1998)

——, "Rethinking Legal Realism: Toward a Naturalized Jurisprudence", 76 *Texas Law Review* 267 (1997)

Lessig, Lawrence, "The Regulation of Social Meaning," 62 *University of Chicago Law Review* 943 (1995)

Lessnoff, Michael ed., *Social Contract Theory* (New York University Press, New York, 1990)

Levi, Edward H., *An Introduction to Legal Reasoning* (University of Chicago Press, Chicago, 1949)

Levinson, Sanford, "Law as Literature", 60 *Texas Law Review* 373 (1982)

——, "The Rhetoric of the judicial Opinion", in *Law's Stories: Narrative and Rhetoric in Law* (P Brooks and P. Gewirtz eds, Yale University Press, New Haven, 1996), pp. 187– 205

Levinson, Sanford and Mailbox, Steven eds, *Interpreting Law and Literature* (Northwestern University Press, Evanston, Ill., 1988)

Lewis, Neil A., "Edward H. Levi, Attorney General Credited With Restoring Order After Watergate, Dies at 88", *New York Times*, March 8, 2000

Limerick, Patricia Nelson, "More Than Just Beads and Feathers", *New York Times Book Review*, January 8, 1995

Littleton, Christine, " Feminist Jurisprudence: The Difference Method Makes", 41 *Stanford Law Review* 751 (1989)

Llewellyn, Karl N., *The Bramble Bush* (Oceana, New York, 1930)

—, *The Common Law Tradition: Deciding Appeals* (Little, Brown, & Co., Boston, 1960)
—, "A Realistic Jurisprudence — The Next Step", 30 *Columbia Law Review* 431 (1930)
—, "Some Realism about Realism—Responding to Dean Pound", 44 *Harvard Law Review* 1222 (1931)
Locke, John, *Essays on the Law of Nature* (W. von Leyden ed., Clarendon Press, Oxford, 1954)
—, *Two Treatises on Government* (P. Laslett ed., 2nd ed., Cambridge University Press, Cambridge, 1967)
Lucy, William, *Understanding and Explaining Adjudication* (Oxford University Press, Oxford, 1999)
Lukes, Stephen, "Perspectives on Authority", in *Authority* (J. Raz ed., New York University Press, New York, 1990), pp. 203–217
Lundstedt, A. Vilhelm, *Legal Thinking Revised: My Views on Law* (Almqvist & Wiksell, Stockholm, 1956)
Lyons, David, *Ethics and the Rule of Law* (Cambridge University Press, Cambridge, 1984)
—, *Moral Aspects of Legal Theory* (Cambridge University Press, Cambridge, 1993)
—, *Rights* (Wadsworth, Belmont, Calif., 1979)
MacCormick, Neil, *H.L.A. Hart* (Stanford University Press, Stanford, Calif., 1981)
—, *Legal Reasoning and Legal Theory* (Clarendon Press, Oxford, 1978)
—, "Reconstruction after Deconstruction: A Response to CLS", 10 *Oxford Journal of Legal Studies* 539 (1990)
—, "Rights in Legislation", in *Law, Morality and Society* (P. M. S. Hacker and J. Raz eds, Clarendon Press, Oxford, 1977), pp. 189–209
—, "Why Cases Have Rationes and What These Are", in *Precedent in Law* (L. Goldstein ed., Clarendon Press, Oxford, 1987), pp. 155–182
Macey, Jonathan R., "Public Choice and the Law", in *The New Palgrave Dictionary of Economics and the Law* (P Newman ed., Macmillan, London, 1998), Vol. 3, pp. 171–178
Machiavelli, Niccolò, *The Prince* (P. Bondanella and M. Musa, trans., Oxford: Oxford University Press, 1984)
MacKinnon, Catharine A., *Feminism Unmodified* (Harvard University Press, Cambridge, Mass., 1987)
—, *Sexual Harassment of Working Women* (Yale University Press, New Haven, 1979)
—, *Towards a Feminist Theory of the State* (Harvard University Press, Cambridge, Mass., 1989)
Maier, Pauline, *American Scripture: Making the Declaration of Independence* (Knopf, New York, 1997)
Maine, Henry Sumner, *Ancient Law* (University of Arizona Press, Tucson, 1986)
Marmor, Andrei, "Exclusive Legal Positivism," in *The Oxford Handbook of Jurisprudence and Philosophy of Law* (J. Coleman and S. Shapiro eds, K. E. Himma. assoc. ed., Oxford University Press, Oxford, 2002), pp. 104–124
—, *Interpretation and Legal Theory* (Clarendon Press, Oxford, 1992)
—, *Positive Law and Objective Values* (Clarendon Press, Oxford, 2001)
—, "The Pure Theory of Law", in E. N. Zalta ed., *Stanford Encyclopedia of Philosophy*, http://plato.stanford.edu (2002)
Marmor, Andrei ed., *Law and Interpretation* (Clarendon Press, Oxford, 1995)

Massaro, Toni M., "The Meanings of Shame: Implications for Legal Reform", 3 *Psychology, Public Policy and Law* 645 (1997)

—, "Shame, Culture, and American Criminal Law", 89 *Michigan Law Review* 1880 (1991)

Matsuda, Mari, "Affirmative Action and Legal Knowledge: Planting Seeds in Plowed-Up Ground", 11 *Harvard Women's Law Journal* 1 (1988)

—, "Looking to the Bottom: Critical Legal Studies and Reparations", 22 *Harvard Civil Rights-Civil Liberties Law Review* 323 (1987)

—, "Public Response to Racist Speech: Considering the Victim's Story", 87 *Michigan Law Review* 2320 (1989)

Matsuda, Mari; Lawrence, Charles; Delgado, Richard and Crenshaw, Kimberlé Williams, *Words that Wound: Critical Race Theory, Assaultive Speech and the First Amendment* (Westview Press, Boulder, Colo., 1993)

McElroy, Wendy, *XXX: A Woman's Right to Pornography* (St. Martin's Press, New York, 1995)

McGinn, Colin, *Wittgenstein on Meaning* (Basil Blackwell, Oxford, 1984)

Meese, Edwin, III, "The Law of the Constitution", 61 *Tulane Law Review* 979 (1987)

Menand, Louis, "Bet-tabilitarianism", *The New Republic*, November 11, 1996, pp. 47–56

—, "Radicalism for Yuppies", *The New Republic*, March 17, 1986, pp. 20–23

Menand, Louis ed., *Pragmatism: A Reader* (Vintage Books, New York, 1997)

Michelman, Frank I., "The Supreme Court 1985 Term—Foreword: Traces of Self-Government", 100 *Harvard Law Review* 4 (1986)

Mill, John Stuart, *On Liberty and Utilitarianism* (Bantam, New York, 1993)

Minow, Martha, *Making All the Difference* (Cornell University Press, Ithaca, 1990)

Mnookin, Robert H. and Kornhauser, Lewis A., "Bargaining in the Shadow of the Law: The Case of Divorce", 88 *Yale Law Journal* 950 (1979)

Moore, Michael S., *Educating Oneself in Public: Critical Essays in Jurisprudence* (Oxford University Press, Oxford, 2000)

—, "The Interpretive Turn in Modern Theory: A Turn for the Worse?", 41 *Stanford Law Review* 871 (1989)

—, "Law as a Functional Kind", in *Natural Law Theories* (R. George ed., Clarendon Press, Oxford, 1992), pp. 188–242

—, "Metaphysics, Epistemology and Legal Theory" (book review), 60 *Southern California Law Review* 453 (1987)

—, "The Moral Worth of Retribution", in *Responsibility, Character and the Emotions* (F. Schoeman ed., Cambridge University Press, Cambridge, 1987), pp. 179–219

—, "A Natural Law Theory of Interpretation", 58 *Southern California Law Review* 277 (1985)

—, "Moral Reality Revisited", 90 *Michigan Law Review* 2424 (1992)

Morawetz, Thomas, "Empathy and Judgment", 8 *Yale Journal of Law & the Humanities* 517 (1996)

—, "Law as Experience: Theory and the Internal Aspect of Law", 52 *SMU Law Review* 27 (1999)

—, *The Philosophy of Law: An Introduction* (Macmillan, New York, 1980)

Morison, W. L., *John Austin* (Edward Arnold, London, 1982)

Morris, Herbert, "Persons and Punishment", 52 *Monist* 475 (1968)

Morris, Norval, *The Brothel Boy and Other Parables of the Law* (Oxford University Press, Oxford, 1992)

Müller, Ingo, *Hitler's Justice: The Courts of the Third Reich* (D.L. Schneider, trans., Harvard University Press, Cambridge, Mass., 1991)

Murphy, Jeffrie G. and Coleman, Jules L., *Philosophy of Law: An Introduction to Jurisprudence* (revised ed., Westview Press, Boulder, Colo., 1990)

Murphy, Mark C., "The Natural Law Tradition in Ethics", in E. N. Zalta ed., *Stanford Encyclopedia of Philosophy*, http://plato.stanford.edu (2002)

Nader, Laura, "The Anthropological Study of Law", 67 *American Anthropologist* 3 (1965)

Nash, John, Jr., "The Bargaining Problem", 18 *Econometrica* 155 (1950)

—, "Equilibrium Points in N-Person Games", 36 *Proceedings of the National Academy of Sciences* 48 (1950)

The New English Bible (Oxford University Press, New York, 1971)

Neumann, John von, "Zur Theorie der Gesellschaftsspiele", 100 *Mathematische Annalen* 295 (1928)

Neumann, John von and Morgenstern, Oskar, *Theory of Games and Economic Behavior* (Princeton University Press, Princeton, 1944)

Newman, Peter ed., *The New Palgrave Dictionary of Economics and the Law* (Macmillan, London, 1998), three vols

Nietzsche, Friedrich, *Beyond Good and Evil* (W. Kaufmann, trans., Vintage Books, New York, 1966)

—, *On the Genealogy of Morality* (K. Ansell-Pearson ed., Cambridge University Press, Cambridge, 1994)

Nino, Carlos, ed., *Rights* (New York University Press, New York, 1992)

Norris, Christopher, *Deconstruction: Theory & Practice* (Methuen, London, 1982)

—, "Jurisprudence, Deconstruction and Literary Theory: A Brief Survey and Critical Review", 1 *Res Publica* 57 (1995)

Nozick, Robert, *Anarchy, State, and Utopia* (Basic Books, New York, 1974)

—, *Philosophical Explanations* (Harvard University Press, Cambridge, Mass., 1981)

Nussbaum, Martha C., "Flawed Foundations: The Philosophical Critique of (a Particular Type of) Economics", 64 *University of Chicago Law Review* 1197 (1997)

—, *Poetic Justice: The Literary imagination and Public Life* (Beacon Press, Boston, 1995)

Oakley, Francis, "Medieval Theories of Natural Law: William of Ockham and the Significance of the Voluntarist Tradition", 6 *Natural Law Forum* 65 (1961)

Okin, Susan Moller, *Justice, Gender, and the Family* (Basic Books, New York, 1989)

Olivecrona, Karl, *Law as Fact* (Stevens & Sons, London, 1971)

Olsen, Frances, "The Family and the Market: A Study in Ideology and Legal Reform", 96 *Harvard Law Review* 1497 (1983)

—, "Feminist Theory in Grand Style", 89 *Columbia Law Review* 1147 (1989)

Palmer, Ben W., "Hobbes, Holmes, and Hitler", 31 *American Bar Association Journal* 569 (1945)

Panel Discussion, "Men, Women and Rape", 63 *Fordham Law Review* 125 (1994)

Papineau, David, *Philosophical, Naturalism* (Basil Blackwell, Oxford, 1993)

Papke, David Ray, "The Advocate's Malaise: Contemporary American Lawyer Novels", 38 *Journal of Legal Education* 413 (1988)

Pashukanis, Evgeny B., *The General Theory of Law and Marxism* (3rd ed., Transaction Publishers, Piscataway, N.J., 2001)

Patterson, Dennis, "Langdell's Legacy", 90 *Northwestern University Law Review* 901 (1995)

—, "Postmodernism", in *A Companion to Philosophy of Law and Legal Theory* (D. Patterson ed., Blackwell, Oxford,1996), pp. 375–384

Paul, Jeffrey, ed., *Reading Nozick: Essays on Anarchy, State, and Utopia* (Rowman and Littlefield, Totowa, N.J., 1981)

Paulsen, Michael Stokes, "The Most Dangerous Branch: Executive Power to Say What the Law Is", 83 *Georgetown Law Journal* 217 (1994)

Paulson, Stanley L., "Continental Normativism and Its British Counterpart: How Different Are They?", 6 *Ratio Juris* 227 (1993)

—, Kelsen's Legal Theory: The Final Round", 12 *Oxford Journal of Legal Studies* 265 (1992)

—, "Lon L. Fuller, Gustav Radbruch, and the 'Positivist' Theses", 13 *Law and Philosophy* 313 (1994)

—, "Material and Formal Authorisation in Kelsen's Pure Theory", 39 *Cambridge Law Journal* 1 72 (1980)

—, "The Neo-Kantian Dimension of Kelsen's Pure Theory of Law", 12 *Oxford Journal of Legal Studies* 311 (1992)

—, "Towards a Periodization of the Pure Theory of Law", in *Hans Kelsen's Legal Theory* (L. Gianformaggio ed., G. Giappichelli, Torino, 1990), pp. 11–47

Paulson, Stanley L. and Paulson, Bonnie Litschewski eds, *Normativity and Norms: Critical Perspectives on Kelsenian Themes (Clarendon* Press, Oxford, 1998)

Penner, J. E., *The Idea of Property in Law* (Clarendon Press, Oxford, 1997)

Perry, Stephen R., "The Distributive Turn: Mischief, Misfortune and Tort Law", in *Analyzing Law: New Essays in Legal Theory* (B. Bix ed., Clarendon Press, Oxford, 1998), pp. 141–162

—, "Interpretation and Methodology in Legal Theory", in *Law and Interpretation* (A. Marmor ed., Clarendon Press, Oxford, 1995), pp. 97–135

—, "Judicial Obligation, Precedent, and the Common Law", 7 *Oxford Journal of Legal Studies* 215 (1987)

Pettit, Philip, "Republicanism", in E. N. Zalta, ed., *Stanford Encyclopedia of Philosophy*, http://plato.stanford.edu/ (2003).

Pigou, A C., *The Economics of Welfare* (4th ed., Macmillan and Co., London, 1932)

Plato, *The Complete Dialogues of Plato* (E. Hamilton and H. Cairns ed., Princeton University Press, Princeton, 1961)

Pocock, J. G. A., *The Machiavellian Moment: Florentine Political Thought and the Atlantic Republican Tradition* (Princeton University Press, Princeton, 1975).

Polinsky, A. M., *An Introduction to Law and Economics* (2nd ed., Little, Brown, and Co., Boston, 1989)

Posner, Eric A., *Law and Social Norms* (Harvard University Press, Cambridge, Mass., 2000)

Posner, Richard A., *Economic Analysis of Law* (6th ed., Aspen, New York, 2003)

—, *The Economics of Justice* (Harvard University Press, Cambridge, Mass., 1983)

—, "Economics, Politics, and the Reading of Statutes and the Constitution", 49 *University of Chicago Law Review* 263 (1982)

—, "The Ethical and Political Basis of the Efficiency Norm in Common Law Adjudication", 8 *Hofstra Law Review* 487 (1980), reprinted in modified form in *The Economics of Justice* (Harvard University Press, Cambridge, Mass., 1983), pp. 88–115

—, "The Ethical Significance of Free Choice: A Reply to Professor West", 99 *Harvard Law Review* (1986)

—, *Law and Literature: A Misunderstood Relation* (Harvard University Press, Cambridge, Mass., 1988, rev. ed., 1998)

—, *Overcoming Law* (Harvard University Press, Cambridge, Mass., 1995)

—, *The Problems of Jurisprudence* (Harvard University Press, Cambridge, Mass., 1990)

—, "Utilitarianism, Economics, and Legal Theory", 8 *Journal of Legal Studies* 103 (1979)

Postema, Gerald J., "Philosophy of the Common Law", in *The Oxford Handbook of Jurisprudence and Philosophy of Law* (J. L. Coleman & S. Shapiro eds, K. E. Himma., assoc. ed., Oxford University Press, Oxford, 2002), pp. 588–622

—, "'Protestant' Interpretation and Social Practices", 6 *Law and Philosophy* 283 (1987)

"Postmodernism and Law: A Symposium", 62 *University of Colorado Law Review* 439–636 (1991)

Pound, Roscoe, "The Call for a Realistic Jurisprudence", 44 *Harvard Law Review* 697 (1931)

—, "Mechanical Jurisprudence", 8 *Columbia Law Review* 605 (1908)

—, "The Scope and Purpose of Sociological Jurisprudence" (Pt I), 24 *Harvard Law Review* 591 (1911); (Pt II), 25 *Harvard Law Review* 140 (1912)

Priest, George L., "The Common Law Process and the Selection of Efficient Rules", 6 *Journal of Legal Studies* 65 (1977)

"Propter Honoris Respectum: John Finnis", 75 *Notre Dame Law Review* 1597–1892 (2000)

Purcell, Edward A., *The Crisis of Democratic Theory: Scientific Naturalism & the Problem of Value* (University Press of Kentucky, Lexington, 1973)

Putnam, Hilary, "The Meaning of 'Meaning'", in *Mind, Language and Reality* (Cambridge University Press, New York, 1975), pp. 215–271

—, "Pragmatism and Moral Objectivity", in *Women, Culture, and Development* (M. C. Nussbaum & J. Glover eds, Clarendon Press, Oxford, 1995), pp. 199–224

—, *Words & Life* (J. Conant ed., Harvard University Press, Cambridge, Mass., 1994)

Putnam, Ruth Anna, "Why Not a Feminist Theory of Justice?", in *Women, Culture, and Development: A Study of Human Capabilities* (M. C.. Nussbaum & J. Glover eds, Clarendon Press, Oxford, 1995), pp. 298–331

Radin, Margaret Jane, "Market Inalienability", 100 *Harvard Law Review* 1 89 (1987)

—, "The Pragmatist and the Feminist", 63 *Southern California Law Review* 1699 (1990)

—, "Reconsidering the Rule of Law", 69 *Boston University Law Review* 781 (1989)

Radin, Margaret Jane and Michelman, Frank, "Pragmatist and Poststructuralist Critical Legal Practice", 139 *University of Pennsylvania Law Review* 1019 (1991)

Rasmusen, Eric, *Games & Information: An Introduction to Game Theory* (3rd ed., Blackwell, Oxford, 2001)

Rawls, John, "The Basic Liberties and Their Priority", in *The Tanner Lectures on Human Values* (University of Utah Press, Salt Lake City, 1982), Vol. 3, pp. 1–87

—, "The Idea of an Overlapping Consensus", 7 *Oxford Journal of Legal Studies* 1 (1987)

—, "Justice as Fairness", 54 *Journal of Philosophy* 653 (1957); in expanded form, 67 *Philosophical Review* 164 (1958)

—, *Justice as Fairness: A Restatement* (E. Kelly ed., Harvard University Press, Cambridge, Mass., 2001)

—, "Justice as Fairness: Political not Metaphysical", 14 *Philosophy & Public Affairs* 223 (1985)

—, "Kantian Constructivism in Moral Theory", 77 *Journal of Philosophy* 515 (1980)

—, "Legal Obligation and the Duty of Fair Play", in *Law and Philosophy* (S. Hook ed., New York University Press, New York, 1964), pp. 3–18

—, *Political Liberalism* (Columbia University Press, New York, 1993)

—, "The Priority of Right and Ideas of the Good", 17 *Philosophy & Public Affairs* 251 (1988)

—, *A Theory of Justice* (Harvard University Press, Cambridge, Mass., 1971, rev. ed., 1999)

Raz, Joseph, "Authority, Law and Morality", in *Ethics in the Public Domain* (Clarendon Press, Oxford, 1994), pp. 194–221.

—, *The Authority of Law* (Clarendon Press, Oxford, 1979)

—, "Autonomy, Toleration, and the Harm Principle", in *Issues in Contemporary Legal Philosophy* (R. Gavison ed., Clarendon Press, Oxford, 1987), pp. 313–333

—, *The Concept of a Legal System* (2nd ed., Clarendon Press, Oxford, 1980)

—, *Ethics in the Public Domain* (Clarendon Press, Oxford, 1994)

—, "Facing Up", 62 *Southern California Review* 1153 (1989)

—, "Intention in Interpretation", in *The Autonomy of Law* (R. George ed., Clarendon Press, Oxford, 1996), pp. 249–286

—, "Legal Rights", 4 *Oxford Journal of Legal Studies* 1 (1984), reprinted in *Ethics in the Public Domain* (Clarendon Press, Oxford, 1995), pp. 238–260

—, "Legal Principles and the Limits of Law", in *Ronald Dworkin and Contemporary Jurisprudence* (M. Cohen ed., Duckworth, London, 1984), pp. 73–87

—, "Legal Theory", in *Blackwell Guide to Philosophy of Law and Legal Theory* (forthcoming, M. P. Golding and W. A. Edmundson eds, Blackwell, Oxford, 2004)

—, "Liberty and Trust", in *Natural Law, Liberalism and Morality: Contemporary Essays* (R. George ed., Clarendon Press, Oxford, 1996), pp. 113–129

—, *The Morality of Freedom* (Clarendon Press, Oxford, 1986)

—, "The Obligation to Obey: Revision and Tradition", 1 *Notre Dame Journal of Law, Ethics & Public Policy* 139 (1984)

—, "On the Nature of Law" (Kobe Lectures of 1994), 82 *Archiv für Rechts- und Sozialphilosophie* 1 (1996)

—, "Postema on Law's Autonomy and Public Practical Reasons: A Critical Comment", 4 *Legal Theory* 1 (1998)

—, *Practical Reason and Norms* (2nd ed., Princeton University Press, Princeton, 1990)

—, "Two Views on the Nature of the Theory of Law: A Partial Comparison", 4 *Legal Theory* 249 (1998)

Reiman, Jeffrey, "The Marxian Critique of Criminal Justice", 6 *Criminal Justice Ethics* 30 (1987)

Roberts, Simon, *Order and Dispute* (Penguin, Middlesex, England, 1979)

Rorty, Richard, *Philosophy and the Mirror of Nature* (Princeton University Press, Princeton, 1979)

Rosenberg, Jay, *The Practice of Philosophy* (2nd ed., Prentice-Hall, Englewood Cliffs, N.J., 1984)

Rosenfeld, Michel and Arato, Andrew eds, *Habermas on Law and Democracy: Critical Exchanges* (University of California Press, Berkeley, 1998)

Ross, Alf, "Tu-Tu", 70 *Harvard Law Review* 812 (1957)

Ross, Don, "Game Theory", in E. N. Zalta ed., *Stanford Encyclopedia of Philosophy*, http://plato.stanford.edu (2002)

Rothstein, Edward, "Moral Relativity Is a Hot Topic? True. Absolutely.", *New York Times*, July 13, 2002

Rubin, Paul H., "Why is the Common Law Efficient?", 6 *Journal of Legal Studies* 51 (1977)

Russell, Bertrand, "Vagueness", in *Collected Papers of Bertrand Russell* (J. Slated ed., Unwin Hyman, London, 1988), Vol. 9, pp. 147–154

Ryan, Alan ed., *Justice* (Oxford University Press, Oxford, 1993)

Sandel, Michael J., *Liberalism and the Limits of Justice* (2nd ed., Cambridge University Press, Cambridge, 1998)

—, "Morality and the Liberal Ideal", *The New Republic*, May 7, 1984, pp. 15–17

Scalia, Antonio, *A Matter of Interpretation* (A. Gutmann ed., Princeton University Press, Princeton, 1997)

Schauer, Frederick, Critical Notice, 24 *Canadian Journal of Philosophy* 495 (1994)

—, "Formalism", 97 *Yale Law Journal 509* (1988)

—, "Fuller's Internal Point of View", 13 *Law and Philosophy* 285 (1994)

—, *Playing by the Rules* (Clarendon Press, Oxford, 1991)

—, "Positivism Through Thick and Thin", in *Analyzing Law* (B. Bix ed., Clarendon Press, Oxford, 1998), pp. 65–78

Scheffler, Samuel ed., *Consequentialism and its Critics* (Oxford University Press, Oxford, 1988)

Schlag, Pierre, "An Appreciative Comment on Coase's *The Problem of Social Cost: A View from the Left*", 1986 *Wisconsin Law Review* 919

—, "Normativity and the Politics of Form", 139 *University of Pennsylvania Law Review* 801 (1991)

Sebok, Anthony J., "Finding Wittgenstein at the Core of the Rule of Recognition", 52 *SMU Law Review* 75 (1999)

Sen, Amartya K., "The Impossibility of a Paretian Liberal," 78 *Journal of Political Economy* 152 (1970), reprinted in *Choice, Welfare and Measurement* (MIT Press, Cambridge, Mass., 1982), pp. 285–290

Shapiro, Scott J., "The Difference That Rules Make", in *Analyzing Law* (B. Bix ed., Clarendon Press, Oxford, 1998), pp. 33–62

—, "On Hart's Way Out," 4 *Legal Theory* 469 (1998)

Shapiro, Scott J. and McClennan, Edward F, "Law-and-Economics from a Philosophical Perspective", in *The New Palgrave Dictionary of Economics and the Law* (P. Newman ed., Macmillan, London, 1998), Vol. 2, pp. 460–465

Shavell, Steven, *Foundations of Economic Analysis of Law* (forthcoming, Harvard University Press, Cambridge, Mass., 2003)

Shiner, Roger, *Norm and Nature: The Movements of Legal Thought* (Clarendon Press, Oxford, 1992)

Simmonds, N. E., *Central Issues in Jurisprudence: Justice, Law and Rights*, (Sweet & Maxwell, London, 1986, 2nd ed., 2002)

—, "Rights at the Cutting Edge", in Matthew H. Kramer; N.E. Simmonds and Hillel Steiner, *A Debate Over Rights: Philosophical Enquiries* (Clarendon Press, Oxford, 1998), pp. 113–232

Simmons, A. John, *Moral Principles and Political Obligations* (Princeton University Press, Princeton, 1979)

Simpson, A.W.B., "English Common Law", in *The New Palgrave Dictionary of Economics and the Law* (P. Newman ed., Macmillan, London, 1998), Vol. 2, pp. 57–70

—, "The Ratio Decidendi of a Case and the Doctrine of Binding Precedent", in *Oxford Essays in Jurisprudence* (A. G. Guest ed., Oxford University Press, Oxford, 1961), pp. 148–175

Singer, Joseph, "Legal Realism Now", 76 *California Law Review* 465 (1988)

Smith, M.B.E., "Is There a Prima Facie Obligation to Obey the Law?", 82 *Yale Law Journal* 950 (1973)

—, "The Duty to Obey the Law", in *A Companion to the Philosophy of Law and Legal Theory* (D. Patterson ed., Blackwell, Oxford, 1996), pp. 465–474

Smith, Patricia, "Feminist Jurisprudence", in *A Companion to the Philosophy of Law and Legal Theory* (D. Patterson ed., Blackwell, Oxford, 1996), pp. 302–310

Smith, Patricia ed., *Feminist Jurisprudence* (Oxford University Press, Oxford, 1993)

Solomon, Robert C. and Murphy, Mark C. eds, *What Is Justice? Classic and Contemporary Readings* (Oxford University Press, New York, 1990)

Solum, Lawrence, "Constructing an Ideal of Public Reason", 30 *San Diego Law Review* 729 (1993)

—, "On the Indeterminacy Crisis: Critiquing Critical Dogma", 54 *University of Chicago Law Review* 462 (1987)

Soper, Philip, "Choosing a Legal Theory on Moral Grounds", in *Philosophy and Law* (J. Coleman and E. F. Paul eds, Blackwell, Oxford, 1987), pp. 31–48

—, "Legal Theory and the Problem of Definition" (book review), 50 *University of Chicago Law Review* 1170 (1983)

Sophocles, "Antigone", in *The Oedipus Plays of Sophocles* 187–252 (P. Roche, trans., Mentor, New York, 1958)

Spann, Girardeau A., *Race Against the Court* (New York University Press, New York, 1993)

Stavropoulos, Nicos, *Objectivity in Law* (Clarendon Press, Oxford, 1996)

Stearns, Maxwell L. ed., *Public Choice and Public Law: Readings and Commentary* (Anderson Publishing Co., Cincinnati, 1997)

Steiner, Hillel, "Working Rights", in Matthew H. Kramer; N.E. Simmonds and Hillel Steiner, *A Debate Over Rights: Philosophical Enquiries* (Clarendon Press, Oxford, 1998), pp. 233–301

Stephen, James Fitzjames, *Liberty, Equality, Fraternity* (Liberty Fund, Indianapolis, 1993)

Stone, Martin, "Formalism", in *The Oxford Handbook of Jurisprudence and Philosophy of Law* (J. Coleman and S. Shapiro, eds, K. E. Himma, assoc. ed., Oxford University Press, Oxford, 2002), pp. 166–205

Summers, Robert S., "How Law is Formal and Why it Matters", 82 *Cornell Law Review* 1165 (1997)

—, *Lon L. Fuller* (Stanford University Press, Stanford, 1984)

Sunstein, Cass R., "Behavioural Analysis of Law", 64 *University of Chicago Law Review* 1175 (1997)

—, "Beyond the Republican Revival", 97 *Yale Law Journal* 1539 (1988)

—, "Incompletely Theorized Agreements", 108 *Harvard Law Review* 1733 (1995)

—, "Social Norms and Social Roles", 96 *Columbia Law Review* 903 (1996)

Symposium: "Critical Race Theory", 82 *California Law Review* 741–1125 (1994)
Symposium: "Deconstruction and the Possibility of Justice", 11 *Cardozo Law Review* 919–1726 (1990)
Symposium: "LatCrit 'Theory: Latinas/os and the Law", 85 *California Law Review* 1087–1686 (1997), 10 *La Raza Law Journal* 1–600 (1997)
Symposium: "Law, Economics, and Norms", 144 *University of Pennsylvania Law Review* 1643–2339 (1996)
Symposium: "Law and Incommensurability", 146 *University of Pennsylvania Law Review* 1169–1731 (1998)
Symposium: "Law and Literature", 60 *Texas Law Review* 373–586 (1982)
Symposium: "Legal Storytelling", 87 *Michigan Law Review* 2073–2494 (1989)
Symposium on Efficiency as a Legal Concern, 8 *Hofstra Law Review* 485–770 (1980)
Symposium on *Law's Empire*, 6 *Law and Philosophy* 281–438 (1987)
Symposium on Lou Fuller, 13 *Law and Philosophy* 253–418 (1994)
Symposium on Post-Chicago Law and Economics, 65 *Chicago-Kent Law Review* 3–191 (1989)
"Symposium on the Renaissance of Pragmatism in American Legal Thought", 63 *Southern California Law Review* 1569–1853 (1990)
"Symposium on the Theory of Public Choice", 74 *Virginia Law Review* 167–518 (1988)
Symposium: "*Postscript* to H.L.A. Hart's *The Concept of Law*", 4 *Legal Theory* 249–547 (1998)
Symposium: "Property Rules, Liability Rules, and Inalienability: A Twenty-Five Year Retrospective", 106 *Yale Law Journal* 2081–2215 (1997)
Symposium: "The Future of Law and Economics: Looking Forward", 64 *University of Chicago Law Review* 1129–1224 (1997)
Tamanaha, Brian, *Realistic Socio-Legal Theory: Pragmatism and a Social Theory of Law* (Clarendon Press, Oxford, 1997)
Tannen, Deborah, *You Just Don't Understand* (William Morrow, New York, 1990)
Taylor, Charles, *Philosophy and the Human Sciences* (Cambridge University Press, Cambridge, 1985)
Thomas, W. John, "Social Solidarity and the Enforcement of Morality Revisited: Some Thoughts on H.L.A. Hart's Critique of Durkheim", 32 *American Criminal Law Review* 49 (1994)
Tierney, Brian, *The Idea of Natural Rights: Studies on Natural Rights, Natural Law and Church Law 1150–1625* (Scholars Press, Atlanta, 1997)
Treitel, G. H., "Jane Austen and the Law", 100 *Law Quarterly Review* 549 (1984)
Trillin, Calvin, "A Reporter at Large: Harvard Law", *New Yorker*, March 26, 1984, pp. 53–83
Tullock, Gordon, "Public Choice", in *The New Palgrave Dictionary of Economics* (J. Eatwell, M. Milgate & P. Newman eds, Palgrave, New York, 1987), Vol. 3, pp. 1040–1044
Tur, Richard and Twining, William, eds, *Essays on Kelsen* (Clarendon Press, Oxford, 1986)
Tushnet, Mark, "An Essay on Rights", 62 *Texas Law Review* 1363 (1984)
Twining, William, "Academic Law and Legal Philosophy: The Significance of Herbert Hart", 95 *Law Quarterly Review* 557 (1979)
—, "The Bad Man Revisited", 58 *Cornell Law Review* 275 (1973)

—, *Karl Llewellyn and the Realist Movement* (University of Oklahoma Press, Norman, Oklahoma, 1985)

Unger, Roberto Mangabeira, *The Critical Legal Studies Movement* (Harvard University Press, Cambridge, Mass., 1986)

Valdes, Francisco, "Queers, Sissies, Dykes, and Tomboys: Deconstructing the Conflation of 'Sex,' 'Gender,' and 'Sexual Orientation' in Euro-American Law and Society", 83 *California Law Review* 3 (1995)

Valdes, Francisco; Culp, Jerome McCristal and Harris, Angela P. eds, *Crossroads, Directions, and a New Critical Race Theory* (Temple University Press, Philadelphia, 2002)

Waldron, Jeremy, "Legislators' Intentions and Unintentional Legislation", in *Law and Interpretation* (A. Marmor ed., Clarendon Press, Oxford, 1995), pp. 329–356

—, *"Lex Talionis"*, 34 *Arizona Law Review* 25 (1992)

—, *Liberal Rights: Collected Papers 1981–1991* (Cambridge University Press, Cambridge, 1993)

—, "The Plight of the Poor in the Midst of Plenty," *London Review of Books*, 15 July 1999

—, "Why Law—Efficacy, Freedom, or Fidelity?", 13 *Law and Philosophy* 259 (1994)

Waldron, Jeremy, ed., *Nonsense upon Stilts: Bentham, Burke and Marx on the Rights of Man* (Methuen, London, 1987)

Walker, David M., *The Oxford Companion to Law* (Clarendon Press, Oxford, 1980)

Waluchow, W. J., *Inclusive Legal Positivism* (Clarendon Press, Oxford, 1994)

Walzer, Michael, *Interpretation and Social Criticism* (Harvard University Press, Cambridge, Mass., 1987)

—, *Spheres of Justice* (Basic Books, New York, 1983)

—, *Thick and Thin: Moral Argument at Home and Abroad* (University of Notre Dame Press, Notre Dame, 1994)

Warner, Richard, "Legal Pragmatism", in *A Companion to Philosophy of Law and Legal Theory* (D. Patterson ed., Blackwell, Oxford, 1996), pp. 385–393

Waugh, Patricia ed., *Postmodernism: A Reader* (Edward Arnold, London, 1992)

Weber, Max, *Economy and Society* (G. Roth & C. Wittich eds, Bedminster Press, New York, 1968), two vols

—, *The Methodology of the Social Sciences* (E. Shils and H. Finch eds, Free Press, New York, 1949)

—, *The Protestant Ethic and the Spirit of Capitalism* (T. Parsons, trans., Scribner, New York, 1976)

Wechsler, Herbert, "Howard Neutral Principles in Constitutional Law", 73 *Harvard Law Review* 15 (1959)

Weinreb, Lloyd L., *Natural Law and Justice* (Harvard University Press, Cambridge, Mass., 1987)

—, *Oedipus at Fenway Park: What Rights Are and Why There Are Any* (Harvard University Press, Cambridge, Mass., 1994).

Weinrib, Ernest J., "The Case for a Duty to Rescue", 90 *Yale Law Journal* 247 (1980)

—, *The Idea of Private Law* (Harvard University Press, Cambridge, Mass., 1995)

—, "Legal Formalism: On the Immanent Rationality of Law", 97 *Yale Law Journal* 949 (1988)

Weisberg, D. Kelly ed., *Feminist Legal Theory: Foundations* (Temple University Press, Philadelphia, 1993)

278

BIBLIOGRAPHY

Weisberg, Richard H., "How Judges Speak: Some Lessons on Adjudication in *Billy Budd, Sailor* with an Application to Justice Rehnquist", 57 New York *University Law Review* 1 (1982)

—, "The Quest for Silence: Faulkner's Lawyer in a Comparative Setting," 4 *Mississippi College Law Journal* 193 (1984)

Weisberg, Robert, "Proclaiming Trials as Narratives: Premises and Pretenses", in *Law's Stories: Narrative and Rhetoric in Law* (P Brooks and P Gewirtz eds, Yale University Press, New Haven, 1996), pp. 61–83

West, Robin, "Adjudication is Not Interpretation: Some Reservations about the Law-as-Literature Movement", 54 *Tennessee Law Review* 203 (1987), reprinted in *Narrative, Authority, and Law* (University of Michigan Press, Ann Arbor, 1993), pp. 89–176

—, "Authority, Autonomy and Choice: 'The Role of Consent in the Moral and Political Visions of Franz Kafka and Richard Posner", 99 *Harvard Law Review* 384 (1985)

—, *Caring for Justice* (New York University Press, New York, 1997)

—, "Jurisprudence and Gender", 55 *University of Chicago Law Review* 1 (1988)

—, "Law and Fancy", 95 *Michigan Law Review* 1851 (1997)

—, "The Other Utilitarians", in *Analyzing Law: New Essays in Legal Theory* (B. Bix ed., Clarendon Press, Oxford, 1998), pp. 197–222

—, "Submission, Choice, and Ethics: A Rejoinder to Judge Posner", 99 *Harvard Law Review* 1449 (1986)

White, Alan R., "Conceptual Analysis", in *The Owl of Minerva: Philosophers in Philosophy* (C. J. Bontmepo and S. J. Odell eds. McGraw-Hill, New York, 1975), pp. 103–117

White, James Boyd, "Economics and Law: Two Cultures in Tension", 54 *Tennessee Law Review* 161 (1987)

—, *Heracles' Bow: Essays on the Rhetoric and Poetics of Law* (University of Wisconsin Press, Madison, 1985)

—, *Justice as Translation* (University of Chicago Press, Chicago, 1990)

—, "Law and Literature: 'No Manifesto'", 39 *Mercer Law Review* 739 (1988)

—, *The Legal Imagination: Studies in the Nature of Legal Thought and Expression* (Little, Brown, and Co., Boston, 1973)

—, "What Can a Lawyer Learn from Literature" (book review), 102 *Harvard Law Review* 2014 (1989).

Whitman, James Q, "What is Wrong with Inflicting Shame Sanctions?", 107 *Yale Law Journal* 1055 (1998).

Wicke, Jennifer, "Postmodern Identity and the Legal Subject", 62 *University of Colorado Law Review* 455 (1991)

Wieacker, Franz, *A History of Private Law in Europe* (T. Weir, trans., Clarendon Press, Oxford, 1995).

Williams, Bernard, *Ethics and the Limit of Philosophy* (Harvard University Press, Cambridge, Mass., 1985)

Williams, Patricia J., "Alchemical Notes: Reconstructing Ideals From Deconstructed Rights", 22 *Harvard Civil Rights-Civil Liberties Law Review* 401 (1987)

—, *The Alchemy of Race and Rights* (Harvard University Press, Cambridge, Mass., 1991)

—, "Fetal Fictions: An Exploration of Property Archetypes in Racial and Gendered Contexts", 42 *Florida Law Review* 81 (1990)

Winch, Peter, *The Idea of a Social Science* (Routledge, London, 1958)

Winfield, Richard Dien, *Law in Civil Society* (University of Kansas Press, Lawrence, Kansas, 1995)

Wing, Adrien Katherine ed., *Critical Race Feminism: A Reader* (New York University Press, New York, 1997)

—, *Global Critical Race Feminism: An International Reader* (New York University Press, New York, 2000)

Winston, Kenneth, "The Ideal Element in a Definition of Law", 5 *Law and Philosophy* 89 (1986)

—, "Introduction", in Lon Fuller, *The Principles of Social Order* (K. Winston ed., Duke University Press, Durham, N.C., 1981), pp. 11–44

Wiseman, Zipporah, "The Limits of Vision: Karl Llewellyn and the Merchant Rules", 100 *Harvard Law Review* 465 (1987)

Wittgenstein, Ludwig, *Philosophical Investigations* (3rd ed., G. E. M. Anscombe, trans., Macmillan, New York, 1968)

Wolff, Robert Paul, *Understanding Rawls: A Reconstruction and Critique of A Theory of Justice* (Princeton University Press, Princeton, 1977)

Wright, Georg Henrik von, *Norm and Action* (Routledge & Kegan Paul, London, 1963)

Wright, Richard W., "Negligence in the Courts: Introduction and Commentary", 77 *Chicago-Kent Law Review* 425 (2002)

Wu, Frank, *Yellow: Race in America Beyond Black and White* (Basic Books, New York, 2002)

List of Cases

Index